D1404912

Essential
Check Point
FireWall-1™

An Installation, Configuration, and Troubleshooting Guide

Dameon D. Welch-Abernathy

✦✦ Addison-Wesley

Boston • San Francisco • New York • Toronto • Montreal
London • Munich • Paris • Madrid
Capetown • Sydney • Tokyo • Singapore • Mexico City

©2000 Check Point Software Technologies Ltd. All rights reserved. Check Point, the Check Point logo, FireWall-1, FireWall-1 SecureServer, FloodGate-1, INSPECT, IQ Engine, Meta IP, MultiGate, Open Security Extension, OPSEC, Provider-1, SVN, User-to-Address Mapping, VPN-1, VPN-1 Accelerator Card, VPN-1 Appliance, VPN-1 Certificate Manager, VPN-1 Gateway, VPN-1 SecuRemote, VPN-1 SecureServer, and ConnectControl are trademarks or registered trademarks of Check Point Software Technologies Ltd. or its affiliates.

Many of the designations used by manufacturers and sellers to distinguish their products are claimed as trademarks. Where those designations appear in this book, and Addison-Wesley was aware of a trademark claim, the designations have been printed in initial capital letters or in all capitals.

Although we have made every effort to ensure the correctness and completeness of the material contained in this book, we cannot provide any warranties. The information provided is on an "as is" basis. The author and the publisher shall have neither liability nor responsibility if a person or an entity suffers a loss or damage from correctly or incorrectly applying the information contained in this book.

The publisher offers discounts on this book when ordered in quantity for special sales. For more information, please contact:

Pearson Education Corporate Sales Division
One Lake Street
Upper Saddle River, NJ 07458
(800) 382-3419
corpsales@pearsontechgroup.com

Visit AW on the Web: www.aw.com/cseng/

Library of Congress Cataloging-in-Publication Data

Welch-Abernathy, Dameon D.
    Essential Check Point FireWall-1 : an installation, configuration, and troubleshooting guide / Dameon D. Welch-Abernathy.
        p. cm.
    Includes bibliographical references and index.
    ISBN 0-201-69950-8 (alk. paper)
        1. Computer networks—Security measures—Computer programs. 2. Computer security—Computer programs. 3. Fire Wall-1. I. Title.

  TK 5105.59.W45 2001
  005.8—dc21   2001041246

Copyright © 2002 by Pearson Education, Inc.

All rights reserved. No part of this publication may be reproduced, stored in a retrieval system, or transmitted, in any form, or by any means, electronic, mechanical, photocopying, recording, or otherwise, without the prior consent of the publisher. Printed in the United States of America. Published simultaneously in Canada.

ISBN 0-201-69950-8
Text printed on recycled paper
1 2 3 4 5 6 7 8 9 10—CRS—0504030201
First printing, October 2001

Contents

Chapter 11   **SecuRemote and Secure Client**   **365**

Foreword

The Internet has given rise to an enormous exchange of data, of which some may be considered information. It is a forum where everyone can express their opinion. Many users participate in public forums where discussions take place. Questions are asked in hopes of getting answers that will solve problems and remove confusion. This is where I first encountered Dameon Welch-Abernathy in 1996, on the fw-1-mailinglist@us.checkpoint.com. In the beginning, there were a few of us who understood Check Point FireWall-1 as compared to the multitude who were asking questions. Unselfishly, Mr. Welch-Abernathy served the public by offering free support. And when that was not enough, he archived the knowledge he obtained on a Web site, famously known as www.phoneboy.com. And now, we have his book.

When Mr. Welch joined Nokia in 1999, I was ecstatic in that I now had a peer who would assist us in building a reputation for Check Point FireWall-1 support within the Nokia Technical Assistance Center. As reflected in the content of this book, his understanding of the nuances of FireWall-1 is outstanding. We have worked together on many issues worldwide, and I continue to depend on his "Welch-of-knowledge" on a regular basis.

This book represents a collection of experiences that go back many years, which both the experienced and new user will ultimately find invaluable.

Jerald Josephs
District SE Manager
Nokia Internet Communications

Preface

Every book has to have a chapter that explains it. This book is no exception. By the end of the preface, you should know:

- How this book came to be

- What this book is and is not

- Why you should buy (or sell) this book

- What typographical conventions are used in this book

- Some of the people who made this book possible

How This Book Came to Be

In 1996, I began to support Check Point FireWall-1. Things were quite different back then. FireWall-1 was a much simpler product, Check Point did not have much of a support department, and there were really no public resources on FireWall-1 aside from a mailing list. My employer at the time had a little known Web site that had many frequently asked questions (FAQ) on FireWall-1. This Web site was the impetus that helped to create PhoneBoy's FireWall-1 FAQ, which I started in April 1998.

Because of my Web site and my participation on the FireWall-1 mailing list, I became well known and respected in the FireWall-1 community. My FAQ page was and still is considered one of the definitive resources on FireWall-1. Even people within Check Point use my page, and they also send me corrections from time to time.

Several people had approached me about the idea of writing a book on the topic of FireWall-1. Such a project seemed rather large, and I was unsure of my ability to tackle it alone. It was little more than an idea until Lance Spitzner approached me to be a coauthor on a book on FireWall-1. Sensing the scope of such a project, I brought in Jerald Josephs, who was also well known in the FireWall-1 community, and in June 1999, we began to write.

Somewhere in the middle of this project, it came to pass that I was the only person left working on this book. The details why are not important, but it was not part of the original plan. My life had changed dramatically with the birth of my son, Jaden, especially the amount of time I could spend on this project. However, I felt I had come too far not to finish; so with a little more determination, I set about the task of finishing this book.

What This Book Is and Is Not

What you are holding in your hands now is a book about Check Point FireWall-1. It covers the essentials of the product. Each chapter discusses a major feature of the product or a specific topic that will help you plan for your FireWall-1 installation. You get step-by-step configuration instructions for many features in FireWall-1 complete with screen shots and several sample configurations that you can try. The book also includes lots of information from my FireWall-1 FAQ.

Although I do cover most features in FireWall-1, not every feature of FireWall-1 is covered in this text. Those features I have chosen to cover are based on my experience as someone who has supported this product since 1996. Other peripheral topics, like encryption and network security, are covered briefly as they relate to FireWall-1, but are not covered in great detail. I feel that other authors do a better job of covering these topics.

A summary of the chapters in this book follows. Note that where sample configurations are said to exist in a chapter, it means there are step-by-step examples that you can follow to set up your own equipment, provided you have it.

Chapter 1: Introduction to Firewalls briefly discusses firewalls in general, the different technologies used in today's firewalls, and how they are used in FireWall-1.

Chapter 2: Planning Your Firewall Installation talks about the issues that should be considered prior to installing a firewall, such as understanding your current network topology, establishing a formalized security policy, and reviewing the various types of licenses that exist in FireWall-1.

Chapter 3: Installing FireWall-1 walks you through the initial configuration of FireWall-1 when it is loaded for the first time. This chapter also covers the basics of preparing your system for a firewall installation.

Chapter 4: Building Your Rulebase explains the basics of creating a security policy within FireWall-1 and includes how to use the Policy Editor application.

Chapter 5: Logging and Alerts explains how logging and alerting works in Fire-Wall-1. Details about how to use the Log Viewer and System Status Viewer applications are also provided.

Chapter 6: Remote Management explains how to manage multiple firewall modules from a single management console. Sample configurations are provided in this chapter.

Chapter 7: Authentication explains how you can provide access control for services based on individual users. Sample configurations are provided in this chapter.

Chapter 8: Content Security explains how you can restrict the kind of content that enters or leaves your network via HTTP, FTP, and SMTP. Sample configurations are provided in this chapter.

Chapter 9: Network Address Translation explains what NAT is, why it is a necessary evil, and how to configure NAT within FireWall-1. Sample configurations are provided in this chapter.

Chapter 10: Site-to-Site VPNs explains what a Virtual Private Network (VPN) is and how to configure FireWall-1 to support this feature. Sample configurations are provided in this chapter.

Chapter 11: SecuRemote and Secure Client builds on Chapter 10. It explains how to establish client-to-site VPNs using Check Point's Windows-based VPN client called *Secure Client,* which is also known as *SecuRemote.* Sample configurations are provided in this chapter.

Chapter 12: High Availability explains state synchronization and how it plays a role in High Availability firewalls. Also covered are the problems that arise when implementing multiple firewalls in parallel along with some ideas on how to overcome these problems.

Chapter 13: INSPECT is an overview of the language that is the heart of Check Point's FireWall-1. Several examples of working INSPECT code are provided in the chapter as well as in the appendices.

The Appendices cover topics such as hardening an operating system, sample INSPECT code, performance tuning, recommended books, and Web sites on the Internet to obtain software and more information.

Conventions

FireWall-1 runs on multiple operating systems, but there are two basic kinds of platforms: UNIX and Windows NT. My personal bias is UNIX; therefore, all pathnames and the like, unless otherwise specified, are always given in their UNIX form. For those of you who use Windows NT and are not familiar with UNIX conventions, the following paragraph describes how to convert the paths from a UNIX form to a Windows NT form.

Almost all paths given include `FWDIR`, which is an environment variable that should be defined and points to the directory that FireWall-1 is installed under. To reference this variable on a UNIX platform, it is preceded by a dollar sign (e.g., `$FWDIR`). On a Windows platform, the variable is surrounded by percent signs (e.g., `%FWDIR%`). Path components on a UNIX platform are separated by forward slashes (e.g., /), whereas on Windows NT, they are separated by back slashes (e.g.,\).

To convert the path `$FWDIR/bin` to its Windows NT equivalent, replace `$FWDIR` with %FWDIR% and replace the forward slash with a back slash. On Windows NT, the path should look like this: %FWDIR%\bin.

Unless otherwise specified, all commands mentioned throughout the text should work on both UNIX and Windows NT. Examples of commands that you type in (and their output) will appear in courier font. I also use this font for filenames. The commands you type in will appear in a **bold courier** font. If what you type in will not echo back on the screen (usually because it is a password), this will be reflected in a ***bold italic courier*** font.

To put it all together, the following sample output results from running the UNIX passwd command to change my password:

```
# passwd dwelch
Enter login password: abc123
New password: def456
Re-enter new password: def456
passwd (SYSTEM): passwd successfully changed for dwelch
#
```

The pound/hash sign is the UNIX prompt and is typically used for the Super-User account. I type in the command **passwd dwelch** (which echoes to the screen). I am then prompted to enter my old password, ***abc123***, which does not echo to the screen. Next, I am prompted to enter a new password, ***def456***, which also does not echo to the screen. I am then asked to confirm my new password as my password choice, which means I type it again. Finally, I am told my password has been changed successfully.

Thanks To . . .

- My wife, Alisa, and my son, Jaden, who put up with me spending far more time working on this book than any of us planned. If it were not for their patience, I would have never finished this book.

- Lance Spitzner and Jerald Josephs, who played a big role in this book taking shape. If it were not for you two, I would not have even started this book in the first place.

- Matthew Gast, for allowing me to commiserate with him as a fellow author, for motivation, and for reviewing the book.

- Derin Mellor for providing me with several ideas that I used in Chapter 12.

- Atul Sharma and Michael Williams for their help in fleshing out Chapter 13. Atul also provided a sample INSPECT script included in Appendix F.

- My editors: Stephane Thomas, Marcy Barnes, and Anne Marie Walker.

- My reviewers: Joe Balsama, Paul Keser, and Bob Bruen. Your reviews were invaluable to this process.

- Folks at Nokia: Paul Esch, Matthew Gulbranson, John Spiller, Qian Zhao, John Kobara, Bo Chen, Ed Ingber, Claudio Basegra, Scott McComas, "Uncle" Kelly Robertson, and all the guys in TAC.

- Folks at Check Point: Bob Bent, Luanne Lemmer, Oren Green, Patrick Plawner, Reut Sorek, Gilad Yadin, Gil Carman, Erica Ziemer, and Tiffany Shockley.

- A bunch of people who I'm sure I've forgotten.

- And finally, to the rest of you who have visited my Web site, contributed to the process, and kept me employable. ☺

Dameon D. Welch-Abernathy
a.k.a. PhoneBoy
dwelch@phoneboy.com
PGP Fingerprint: 72A2 8D9D BDC0 98D2 1E5D 3A2D 09D0 A5C1 597F 5D2A
July 2001

1

Introduction to Firewalls

This chapter provides a brief overview of firewalls—what they can and cannot do. It is not meant to comprehensively cover the topic of firewalls or network security in general. These topics are better covered by more-general texts. In this chapter, you will explore some of the technologies used in firewalls, investigate which technologies are used by FireWall-1, and establish why FireWall-1 is the right firewall for you. Examples of how a given technology handles a specific service are also provided.

By the end of this chapter, you should be able to:

- Understand what technologies firewalls typically employ
- Understand what a firewall is and is not capable of
- Discuss the pros and cons of different firewall technologies
- Understand why FireWall-1 is the right firewall for the job

What Is a Firewall?

A firewall is a device that allows multiple networks to communicate with one another according to a defined security policy. They are used when there is a need for networks of varying levels of trust to communicate with one another. For example, a firewall typically exists between a corporate network and a public network like the Internet. It can also be used inside a private network to limit access to different parts of the network. Wherever there are different levels of trust among the different parts of a network, a firewall can and should be used.

Firewalls are similar to routers in that they connect networks together. Firewall software runs on a host, which is connected to multiple networks that have varying degrees of trust (e.g., your internal network and the Internet). The host operating system (OS) is responsible for performing routing functions, which many operating systems are capable of doing. The host operating system should be as secure as possible long before firewall software is ever installed on it. This not only means knowing how the operating system was installed but also making sure that all of the security patches are applied and that unnecessary services and features are disabled or removed. More details about these security issues are provided in Chapter 3.

Firewalls are different from routers in that they are able to provide security mechanisms for permitting and denying traffic, such as authentication, encryption, content security, and address translation. Although many routers provide similar capabilities (such as high-end devices from Cisco), their primary function is to route packets between networks. Security was not part of their initial design, but rather an afterthought. A firewall's primary function is to enforce a security policy and is designed with this in mind.

What a Firewall Cannot Do

It is important to realize that a firewall is a tool for enforcing a security policy and is only as effective as the security policy it is enforcing. It cannot protect you from the following dangers:

- *Malicious use of authorized services:* A firewall cannot, for instance, prevent someone from using an authenticated Telnet session to compromise your internal machines.
- *Users not going through the firewall:* A firewall can only restrict connections that go through it. It cannot protect you from people who can go around the firewall, for example, through a dial-up server behind the firewall.
- *Social engineering:* If intruders can somehow obtain passwords they are not authorized to have or otherwise compromise authentication mechanisms through social engineering mechanisms, the firewall won't stop them. For example, a hacker could call your users pretending to be a system administrator and ask them for their passwords to "fix some problem."
- *Flaws in the host OS:* A firewall is only as secure as the operating system on which it is installed. There are many flaws present in operating systems that a firewall cannot protect against. This is why it is important that you properly secure the OS and apply the necessary security patches before you install the firewall and on a periodic basis thereafter.
- *All threats that may occur:* Firewall designers often react to problems discovered by hackers, who are usually a step ahead of the firewall manufacturers.

Overview of Firewall Security Technologies

Many companies engage in marketing hype to try to prove that their technology is better. Despite the hype, all firewall security technology can be broken down into three basic types: packet filtering, application layer gateways, and Stateful Inspection (also called stateful packet filtering).

Packet Filters

Packet filters screen all network traffic at the network and transport layer of the TCP/IP packet. This means they look at source and destination IP addresses, protocol number, and, in the case of TCP and UDP, source and destination port numbers. Packet filtering is built into routers as well as some UNIX kernels. Usually, when site administrators start thinking about network security, they start with packet filtering because it is inexpensive. Most routers on the market today, even consumer-grade models, support some form of packet filtering. Because routers are needed to connect different networks together (especially when connecting to the Internet), the additional cost for using this technology is minimal. Packet filtering requires very little extra memory and processing power, so even a low-end router can handle a fairly moderate load. Packet filtering is also fairly transparent to legitimate users.

The biggest downside to packet filters is that they are difficult to maintain. Although this point is certainly arguable, even an expert can have trouble configuring a moderately complex set of access lists or Linux ipchains rules. Many consumer-grade routers that have packet filtering do not have an adequate interface or are very limited in what they can filter.

Packet filters also do not screen above the network and transport layers. This means they cannot do things like:

- Provide content security (e.g., virus scanning or filtering based on specific sites and Web pages accessed).
- Authenticate services (i.e., make sure only authorized users use a service).
- Dynamically open and close ports for applications as they require them. This is necessary for applications like RealAudio, FTP, and H.323 applications.
- Validate a particular port that is only used for a specific service (e.g., making sure that only valid HTTP traffic traverses port 80).

Application Proxies

Proxies take requests from clients and make them connect to servers on the client's behalf. In some cases, the client will explicitly connect to the proxy server. In other cases, the proxy will intercept the connection with help from the underlying OS or network architecture. Because an application proxy is usually specific to the network service, it can be fully aware of the session. This means the proxy can do content screening, provide authentication, and ensure that only the particular service is used (e.g., an HTTP proxy can make sure that only HTTP traffic is allowed through), or it can provide other application-specific services such as caching. It also provides a well-formed connection to servers on the other side of the firewall, because it opens up connections on behalf of the clients.

This extra capability comes at a price, though. Application proxies require memory and CPU cycles just like any other application. Generally speaking, application proxies use more memory and CPU cycles than packet filtering, although how much they use depends on the specific circumstances. If you want to use application proxies to provide services to the Internet, each application you want to run through your firewall must have a proxy written for it or the application must be compatible with a "generic" proxy that will work with simple TCP or UDP connections. Because many applications are not being developed to work with an application proxy, some applications simply cannot be proxied. The client/server model is somewhat broken by application proxies because the application proxy will always originate the connection from the server's point of view.[1] In large environments, the throughput of application proxies is another drawback.

Stateful Inspection

Stateful Inspection combines the best features of packet filters and application layer gateways. Check Point's Stateful Inspection engine rests between the data link and network layers (e.g., between the network interface card and the TCP/IP driver). TCP/IP packets from the network layer on up are scanned according to your security policy and will either be allowed through or stopped. The TCP/IP stack will not see dropped or rejected packets, which can provide an extra layer of protection. Stateful Inspection can look at the entire packet and make security policy decisions based on the contents and *context* of the packet. It also keeps track of any active connection in a state table. For some services (like FTP), it can dynamically open ports between two hosts so that the communication will succeed, and then close it when it is done.

Stateful Inspection requires slightly more memory and CPU cycles than packet filtering because it has to do more, but it takes substantially less memory and CPU usage than does an application proxy. Stateful Inspection is best when the engine is made aware of how a protocol functions, although Check Point does not make use of Stateful Inspection for every protocol. Because Stateful Inspection does track connection state regardless of the service, it is better than a packet filter, but you are limited to opening specific ports and allowing the traffic through without further checking.

---

1. Some would argue that this is actually not a problem. Whether or not this is a problem depends on the specific application and what you are trying to track down.

Technology Comparison: Passive FTP

It might be useful to compare how the different technologies handle complex connection types. One such connection type is Passive FTP, which is used by Web browsers when they initiate an FTP connection.

Passive FTP requires:

- a TCP connection from a client to port 21 on the FTP server.
- a TCP connection from a client to some random high port on the FTP server for data communication. The ports used for this communication are communicated to the client when it requests passive mode via the PASV command.

For this comparison, let's assume the FTP server is behind your firewall, and you need to allow people on the Internet to FTP to this machine.

Packet Filtering

Packet filtering can handle standard FTP quite nicely because it uses fixed TCP ports (20 and 21). However, in order to allow Passive FTP, the packet filter has to open all TCP ports above 1024 to allow Passive FTP to work with the FTP server. This is a gaping hole that can be used by programs other than FTP to compromise your systems.

Application Proxies

An application proxy is aware of the FTP connection and opens all the necessary ports and connections to complete the FTP connection. However, each TCP or UDP connection through an application proxy requires twice the normal number of connections on the proxy server (one for each side of the connection). A normal Passive FTP connection requires two open connections on a client machine. On the application level gateway, this translates to four open TCP connections.

Most operating systems have a limit to the number of simultaneous connections they can handle. If enough connections are going through the machine at the same time, this limit will be reached and no further connections will be allowed through. In high-performance, high-capacity networks, using a proxy for FTP connections is simply asking for trouble.

Stateful Inspection

Stateful Inspection understands connection context. When the PASV command is sent from the client to the server, Stateful Inspection reads the server's response and opens the ports necessary to complete the connection. It also restricts the IP addresses that can use these ports to the client and server. The connection then goes through the firewall normally. Because Stateful Inspection allows the native OS to route, no connections are established on the firewall itself. Once the connection is properly terminated, the ports opened by the PASV command are closed.

Technology Comparison: Traceroute

Traceroute is used to show the particular path a connection will take through the various routers and gateways within the network and gives you a basic idea of the latency between any two hosts on a network. It is a common troubleshooting tool used by network administrators. There are two varieties of traceroute: UDP and ICMP. UDP traceroute is used by most every UNIX implementation. ICMP traceroute is typically used by Microsoft operating systems, though some UNIX implementations also allow you to perform an ICMP traceroute. How traceroute functions can be used to show the strengths of Stateful Inspection and the weaknesses of packet filtering and application proxies.

UDP traceroute involves sending out packets to a port above 31000—the actual ports used will vary based on implementation. ICMP traceroute uses ICMP Echo Requests instead. In both cases, the client generates a number of packets (usually three) over a period of time (usually one second) to the server using a Time To Live (TTL) value of 1. Each subsequent set of packets will have an increasingly higher TTL value. As the packets "hop" to each router or gateway between the client and the server, the TTL is decremented. As the TTL value is increased, the packets are able to get closer and closer to the server.

During a traceroute session, any of the following can occur:

- The server responds with an ICMP Echo Reply message or an ICMP Port Unreachable packet (i.e., the traceroute has finally reached the server).
- An intermediate router or gateway gets a packet with a TTL value of 1; it decrements the TTL to zero and sends back an ICMP Time Exceeded message. A router or gateway cannot route a packet with a TTL of zero.
- An intermediate router or gateway determines it has no route to the server and sends back an ICMP Destination Unreachable message.
- An intermediate router or gateway fails to respond either because it is configured to not respond to or pass traceroute traffic or because it is down.
- The client decides it has sent too many sets of traceroute packets (the default is 30) and stops.

For any firewall solution to securely allow traceroute through,[2] it must take all of these situations into account. Let's explore how each of the firewall technologies can address passing traceroute.

---

2. Most firewall administrators do not want to allow traceroute into their network from the outside, but do wish to allow internal hosts to initiate it outbound and only appropriate reply traffic back in.

Packet Filtering

With packet filtering, you would have to allow the following types of traffic to pass through your packet filter:

- All UDP Ports above 31000
- ICMP Echo Request

Conversely, you would also have to allow the following types of packets to enter your network from any host:

- ICMP Echo Reply
- ICMP Time Exceeded
- ICMP Destination Unreachable
- ICMP Port Unreachable

Although these rules would allow legitimate traceroute traffic, they can also allow packets that were not in response to a valid traceroute request. As these kinds of unsolicited packets are often used in Denial of Service (DoS) attacks, it is important that you only allow in packets that are in response to a traceroute or ping query. Packet filtering alone is not an adequate tool to allow traceroute to function yet protect you from DoS attacks. It is important to note that the UDP ports allowed could also be used for something other than traceroute.

Application Proxies

UDP can be proxied to some degree, but due to its nature, ICMP cannot easily be proxied. As a result, a specialized proxy and traceroute client is necessary. In a relatively small, controlled, homogeneous environment, this may be feasible. In a large, heterogeneous environment protected by application proxies, it may not be possible to allow all clients traceroute through the firewall.

Stateful Inspection

With Stateful Inspection, you can watch for either a UDP packet with a low TTL value or an ICMP Echo Request packet coming from a particular client. Once this happens, you can temporarily permit the necessary ICMP packets to return to the client initiating the outgoing traceroute request. After you have received the appropriate response (i.e., an ICMP Echo Reply, Port Unreachable, or Destination Unreachable) and/or after a specific period of time (say 60 seconds), you can stop allowing the necessary ICMP packets to the client.

FireWall-1 4.0 and later support Stateful Inspection of ICMP in this manner, although many people have had problems getting it to work correctly. If you are using an earlier version of FireWall-1 or are having issues with Check Point's built-in ICMP filtering, look at the INSPECT code written by Bill Burns at Netscape, which filters ping and traceroute correctly. This code is included with permission in Appendix E.

What Kind of Firewall Is FireWall-1?

Check Point advertises FireWall-1 as primarily a Stateful Inspection firewall. Although this is certainly FireWall-1's biggest strength, FireWall-1 uses both Stateful Inspection and application proxies. Application proxies are used when content security or user authentication is necessary for HTTP, Telnet, rlogin, FTP, and SMTP. Stateful Inspection is used for all other security functions. To be fair, most commercial and even homegrown firewalls employ some combination of these two technologies as none of the technologies can provide all the necessary functionality.

FireWall-1 also offers some other interesting capabilities, many of which are covered in future chapters:

- Site-to-site VPNs
- Client-to-site VPNs
- Content filtering (with the help of third-party products)
- Address translation
- Authentication (integrated with third-party authentication servers)
- Enterprise-wide policy management
- High availability (with the help of third-party products)
- INSPECT, a language with which you can modify Check Point's Stateful Inspection engine

Do You Really Need FireWall-1?

Whether or not you really need FireWall-1 might seem like a strange question to ask in a book about FireWall-1. Chances are your company has already come to the conclusion that you do need FireWall-1 somewhere in your network, or else your company would not have purchased it, and you would likely not be reading this book. One of the important points this book makes is that FireWall-1 is simply a tool used to enforce a security policy. In some cases, using this tool may be overkill. In others cases, this tool is just one of many that are used.

Let's look at a one- or two-person site. In this case, whether or not to use a firewall depends on what the network connection is and what needs to be protected. If the connection is an analog dial-up connection to the Internet that does not stay up a majority of the time, a firewall may not be entirely necessary. If the connection is something more permanent, like a leased line, Digital Subscriber Line (DSL), cable modem, or if what goes on at this site is highly sensitive or valuable, a firewall may be necessary. If the people who occupy this site are technically savvy, perhaps they will set up their external router with an access list or set up a multi-homed host with FreeBSD or Linux. Or, they may even use one of the many consumer-grade firewall devices on the market. Depending on what the site's needs are, these solutions may be sufficient.

Now let's look at a slightly larger site, say one that employs 25 to 50 people. This type of site is likely to have some sort of permanent Internet connection. It may even have an externally accessible server or two like a mail server and a Web server. Again, as mentioned previously, this type of site could probably get away with setting up a multi-homed host with FreeBSD or Linux, or an access list on a router. Perhaps the site also needs to allow one or two people access to the internal network from home. At this point, a few "holes" would be added to the firewall. At a later time, a few other people might want to do some sort of specialized application through the firewall and a few more holes would get added. Pretty soon the firewall starts looking like Swiss cheese.

Now let's talk about a large corporate site with thousands of people. A site like this could use a firewall or two. One obvious place to put a firewall would be at the external connection to the world, but firewalls could also be used internally to protect certain sensitive departments like Human Resources, R&D, or Accounting. And perhaps this corporate site is also responsible for some smaller remote offices. These remote offices would likely need secure access into the internal network at the corporate site. Also, the corporate site might like to be able to manage the security policy for the remote sites. And, of course, there are those who want to work from home or who need secure access to the corporate network from the Internet.

People tend to think of security needs in terms of the size of the network involved. The preceding examples are typical of what I have experienced in the real world. What type of firewall you require, if any at all, really comes down to your specific needs or the needs of an organization. A one- or two-person site might be developing source code that could potentially be worth millions of dollars, thus network security becomes important. Another example might be a university network with thousands of students where an open environment is far more important than a secure environment—although you can bet that certain parts of the network, like admissions and finance, require very tight security. The main question you have to ask when considering a firewall is, what is at stake if an unauthorized person gains access to my network?

FireWall-1 is an appropriate solution for networks of all shapes and sizes. This is because FireWall-1 is one of the few firewalls that can grow with your needs. In a network with few needs, it can start out as a simple Internet firewall. As your needs change, you can easily add firewalls and still be able to easily keep track of and manage your corporate-wide security policy. As your network grows, you can readily upgrade or change the platform on which FireWall-1 is installed and add functionality, such as a VPN, quite easily. Because FireWall-1 works the same on all supported platforms, you will not have to spend a significant amount of time reconfiguring or relearning the product. Adding new functionality is usually as simple as adding a new license string and modifying your configuration to support the new feature. With the added functionality of INSPECT, you can program FireWall-1 to securely support just about any service.

With the help of this book, you will be able to effectively use FireWall-1 in just about any network environment you are working in.

More Information

There are many other network security topics that could have been covered in this chapter. And even the topics covered could have been covered in greater depth. However, the focus of this book is not on general security topics, but rather FireWall-1. Many of these topics are covered in-depth in other books by other authors. Appendix J includes a list of Web sites with more information on interesting software. Appendix K includes a list of recommended books.

Chapter

2

Planning Your Firewall Installation

Careful planning should precede the installation of any firewall. In this chapter, I first discuss determining the current state of your network by developing a network topology. Next, I discuss setting down some basic security policies in writing. I then cover discovering "zones of trust" and figuring out where to put your firewalls. And finally, one of the trickiest parts of a FireWall-1 installation is discussed: licensing.

By the end of this chapter, you should be able to:

- Explain what a security policy is and how it applies to your organization
- Be able to break down a security policy into three critical components: what, who, and how
- Develop an overall firewall architecture and rulebase design using your organization's security policy as a guide
- Understand what license types are available, how they are enforced, and how to get them

Network Topology

Before you begin to think about installing a firewall, or any other security device for that matter, you should document what your network looks like. This means generating a map of the network, which illustrates all of the major points of interest, and diagramming how they all logically connect together. Although it is not necessary to document individual workstations, you should document:

- Wide Area Network (WAN) connections
- Dial-up connections
- Internet connections

- Routers
- Firewalls
- Important servers (either individually or as a group)

Because a firewall is a perimeter-based security device, it is most effective when the number of entry and exit points is limited. The process of documenting these entry points into the network may prompt you to reorganize your network in such a way as to limit the number of entry or exit points. This is not entirely a bad thing.

In a multisite company (i.e., a company that occupies more than one physical location), getting a complete network topology may be difficult or impossible. Someone at each physical location should be responsible for maintaining a local network map. A cloud, or a similar symbol, can represent a remote network. This is what is typically used to represent the Internet.

Once you have a clear understanding of the components in your network, you can begin to determine where the different zones of trust are. Many people tend to only think of two zones: everything outside the firewall and everything inside the firewall. Although this is certainly a start, it is a bit more complicated than that. If you have servers that are externally accessible from the Internet, you could consider creating a demilitarized zone (DMZ), or Service Network. Servers in the DMZ are accessible from any network. The purpose of a DMZ is to isolate all servers that are accessible from untrusted sources, like the Internet, so that if someone compromises one of those servers, the intruder will only have limited access to externally accessible servers. Servers in the DMZ should be fortified and secured as much as possible and should not be allowed to initiate connections to internal systems.

In many networks, there are several levels of trust. For instance, sensitive Human Resources or Accounting functions may take place in a separate part of the network that should be inaccessible to all but authorized users. There may be parts of the network that contain users who cannot be trusted, or they may contain machines of unknown danger. For example, there may be experimental sections of the network where it is important to set up servers and machines quickly as well as training labs.

Each network and each situation are different. You may need to interview managers and even individual users to determine where these zones of trust should be. Once you have determined what the zones of trust are, the most effective locations of firewalls will become self-evident.

A Word about Subnetting

Keep in mind that a firewall is a device similar to a router in that traffic is passed from one interface to another. Like any router, each interface must be connected to a logically different network. This means that if you are to insert a firewall into an existing network, you must make sure that each physical interface of the firewall is on a unique subnet.[1] Depending on your existing network, this may mean subnetting existing network space, adding address space, or employing Network Address Translation (NAT). (See Chapter 9 for more information.) For network segments that are only accessible inside the firewall, RFC-1918 address space can be easily added. NAT is only necessary if those segments access a public network like the Internet.

Each zone of trust should also be on a separate physical network. This can be accomplished with Virtual LANs[2] (VLANs) on a switch, although physically different and unconnected switches or hubs are preferred because it may be possible to compromise the switch in some way.

Developing a Sitewide Security Policy

A security policy is the critical first step toward securing your organization's network. It lays the overall foundation of how your organization approaches security issues. It explains what resources are important, who is responsible for those resources, and the general guidelines on how your organization will protect those resources. It does not go into detail about *how* this policy is enforced. That is often decided by the security administrators.

Firewalls are a technical tool used to enforce the security policy. A firewall is not the only tool that can be used to enforce a security policy, but it plays a major role in many organizations. With a clearly defined policy, you will know precisely who will maintain your firewalls and what kinds of changes will be allowed. Without a policy, it is not clear what the purpose of the firewall is, nor is it clear what kinds of changes to the policy are allowed. As a result, different people will enforce different rules, which may often conflict with one another. What was enforced one day may be changed the next. Rules might be randomly added and dropped with no real coherent plan. The outcome would be an effective tool configured ineffectively.

In FireWall-1, users tend to think of the conglomeration of rules that are created in a rulebase as a security policy. The sort of security policy discussed in this section has nothing to do with FireWall-1, at least not yet. A security policy is a written document that should be simple to read and states what resources should be secured and under what conditions access will be provided or denied. It does not provide details on what needs to be done to secure the organization.

The first challenge you will have is creating a simple document that can be used by everyone. Too often extensive security policies are created, which cover every conceivable

---

1. A notable exception to this statement is the Nokia IP51 and IP55. They support a bridging mode that allows the same subnet to be on the WAN and LAN interfaces. However, these are designed for use in small offices (50 hosts maximum) where there is limited address space.

2. VLANs essentially provide a way to treat a single switch as multiple physical LAN segments. This is done via the software that controls the switch.

situation. These documents become so large and cumbersome that no one has time to either read or understand the document. By keeping the document short and simple, you will have a usable document that is able to be understood by all. As stated earlier, there are three general areas you want to include in your security policy: what is important, who is responsible for it, and guidelines on how to protect it.

The What, Who, and How

You should first identify the assets you need to protect, the value of which will often determine what steps are reasonable and prudent to protect them. For most companies, specific types of information have to be protected from unauthorized access. Oftentimes, people protect servers, systems, or users. Although this is often necessary in the course of protecting the data, keep in mind that the primary goal is to protect the information. When the information moves from one system to another, you may have to update your security policy on the firewall or other devices to ensure that data remains protected.

The second area of security policies is ownership, namely who is responsible for what. Ownership and responsibility should begin at the upper management levels of your organization and work its way down. It is critical that all parts of your organization have someone who is held accountable for that area. For example, most organizations have someone in charge of financial affairs, marketing, sales, and customer service. This is just as true for network security. The security policy needs to define someone responsible for both the administration of the firewall and the approval of the policy the firewall is to enforce. The individual rules that are configured into your firewall can have a major impact on your organization. Someone in your organization should be responsible for approving all requests for the rulebase to be changed. In organizations where this administrator is not defined, one person may add a rule, whereas another person might remove the same rule. If there is only one person (or group of persons) responsible for approving rulebase changes, you can avoid these problems.

The security policy should not name specific individuals, but instead name positions. Individuals come and go. If John Doe is responsible for the firewalls, as defined by the security policy, then what happens when John Doe leaves the company or moves to a new position? All positions should be defined by a title, such as Chief Security Officer (CSO) or Firewall Administrator. The positions themselves should be clearly defined in this policy as well.

In addition, the security policy should cover basic guidelines on how to secure its assets. The security policy should not explain in technical detail how rules are enforced, only basic guidelines. The technical detail should be determined by the people in charge of implementing the policy (i.e., the security team). Technology changes too rapidly to be detailed in a security policy. The security policy should only provide guidelines or basic standards as to what will be implemented.

For example, the policy should provide guidelines for employees' user authentication. Your organization's security policy could state that all Internet access to the company's intranet Web server must be securely authenticated using some type of token-based or one-time password scheme. This is *what* is required. *How* this is enforced should be left to the security team. For this book, the *how* could be enforced by Check Point FireWall-1. The firewall would intercept any HTTP requests to the intranet Web server and require authentication first. This could be done through the use of the HTTP Security Server tied into a SecurID-based authentication system. Mentioning either FireWall-1 or SecurID by name in the security policy document would be inappropriate.

It is your security policy that guides your firewall implementation and maintenance. A firewall is just a technical implementation of the security policy. If you and your organization do not understand your security policy, you will not be able to properly implement and maintain your firewall.

Implementing Firewalls without a Written Security Policy

For many of you, your organization may not have a security policy or, if a security policy does exist, it is poorly documented or understood. The problem then is that the firewall must be implemented and maintained, but without much guidance on what it is supposed to enforce. Normally in these situations, a firewall is quickly constructed, and rules are added as needed. No prior planning is done. If you find yourself or your organization in this situation, there are steps you can take to prevent problems from occurring. The best solution is to create a security policy as soon as possible. If this cannot be done, short-term measures can be taken. First, be careful. If you are responsible for maintaining the firewall, including implementing the firewall rules, you could be held responsible if something happens. Even if you were told by someone from a different department to create a new rule (such as the marketing department requesting access to its internal Web server from the Internet), you could be liable for a security breach.

In order for network security to be properly implemented, you must educate management and get them to buy into the process. This may mean spending some time with upper management explaining to them the importance of network security. Without support from upper management, all attempts to implement proper network security are doomed to fail. It is highly recommended that someone in upper management (perhaps your boss) be responsible for security. Ask him or her to identify someone to approve the firewall rules and make sure that person has adequate authority with which to do this. Organizations that already have a clearly defined security policy will have these policies and procedures already defined. Unfortunately, if your organization does not have a security policy, or the security policy does not cover firewalls, you will have to do much of this yourself.

Once you have identified areas of responsibility and procedures for approving and maintaining the firewall, your life will become a lot less stressful, with less liability lying on your shoulders.

An Example of a Security Policy

Instead of reviewing an entire security policy, a portion of a security policy follows. It is designed to give you an idea of what a security policy document might look like. Keep in mind that no two security policies are alike. Every organization's policy document has its own unique format and issues. This example not only gives you a better idea of what a security policy can look like but also provides specific examples of what to look for in relation to firewalls. As covered earlier, a security policy should be general in nature, covering who is responsible for what. This particular section describes the management and procedures for implementing and maintaining Company X's firewalls. A sample Internet Usage Policy can be found in Appendix H.

Company X Information Security Policy

Section 010: Firewall Implementation and Management

SUMMARY
Firewalls are a critical security asset used to protect Company X's information resources. It is critical that all firewalls be configured, implemented, and maintained in a standardized and secure fashion. In response to the risks, this document describes Company X's official policy regarding firewall implementation and management.

I. CONFIGURATION AND IMPLEMENTATION

A. *Operating System:* Before a firewall can be installed on an operating system, that operating system must be fully secured and tested in accordance with the Chief Security Officer. See Appendix A for more information on operating-system standards.

B. *Responsibility:* Before implementation, an administrator must be identified as responsible for the firewall. This administrator is fully responsible for both maintaining the firewall software and the underlying operating system. The administrator may select up to two other individuals to assist in maintaining the firewall. However, these individuals must be approved by the Chief Security Officer.

C. *Access:* Only the administrator and approved assistant(s) may access the firewall or operating system. Thus, there can be no more than three accounts for the firewall and operating system. Only the firewall administrator may have administrative access to the operating system and firewall software.

D. *Default Rule:*   All of Company X's firewalls are based on the premise: That which is not expressly permitted is denied.

II. MAINTAINING

A. *Logs:*   The firewall administrator is responsible for ensuring the daily review and archiving of firewall logs.

B. *Rules:*   Only the firewall administrator is authorized to make any changes in the firewall rulebase. All requests must be forwarded to the firewall administrator and be approved by the Chief Security Officer prior to the enactment of any changes.

The preceding section covers the policies and procedures of maintaining the organization's firewalls. It is highly recommended as it helps define who is responsible for what. Notice that specific names are not used, only positions. This ensures that as people change positions, the security policy does not have to be continually updated. In addition, this section states the overall policy for firewall rulebases, specifically: That which is not expressly permitted is denied. The firewall can enforce this policy by denying all traffic. The rulebase is then modified to allow only that which is expressly permitted.

Fun with Check Point Licensing

Perhaps one of the more challenging aspects of FireWall-1 is licensing the product. Even those who have been selling and supporting FireWall-1 for a number of years tend to get tripped up by Check Point's licensing from time to time. Throughout the book, I will mention where specific licenses are needed to perform certain functions. In this section, I specifically discuss where license considerations come into play during the initial installation.

The major components that require licensing are:

- Firewall module
- Management console
- Management Graphical User Interface (GUI) applications

A firewall module enforces your security policy and sends log information to a management console. This is typically referred to as *the firewall.* The management console is responsible for storing, compiling, and pushing the security policies out to the firewall modules. It also receives logging information from the firewall modules and processes alerts. The Management GUI applications allow you to view, edit, and install security policies, view logs, and see the status of all installed firewall modules. The Management GUIs communicate to the management console, which does all of the actual work.

With some exceptions, which I will note in the following sections, each of these components may exist on separate systems. You can even mix and match the platforms on which each of these components exist.[3] For example, you can have the firewall on a Nokia platform, the management console on Solaris, and the Management GUIs on Windows.

Node-Limited Firewall Licenses

Node-limited firewall licenses are restricted in terms of the number of IP addresses that can be behind the firewall. FireWall-1 listens for any IP-based traffic on all interfaces except the one deemed external. This is decided by the user and listed in `$FWDIR/conf/external.if`. Anytime it hears hosts talking to each other with an address on a nonexternal interface, it notes the IP addresses. Once FireWall-1 has heard *n* IPs (plus a 10-percent fudge factor), connections from the *n+1* hosts generate e-mails to root and messages to syslog or the event viewer. When the license is exceeded by a large number of hosts on a busy network, FireWall-1 consumes itself with logging and mailing out messages about exceeding your license. In many cases, this causes the firewall to process traffic very slowly, if at all.

So what are the implications of how FireWall-1 enforces a node-limited license? *Anything* behind your firewall with an IP address will eventually be found out. This includes noncomputer components like printers, coffee makers, and so on. Anything with an IP address that talks on your LAN will be heard, eventually. Also, machines with multiple IP addresses will most likely be counted more than once. Peripherals that do not use TCP/IP should not be counted. Machines that only use AppleTalk, IPX, NetBEUI, and so on should also not be counted. Because FireWall-1 only looks for IP traffic, it should safely ignore these machines.

There are plenty of ways to deliberately mislead or fool the license. For example, machines can be hidden behind a choke router, a switch, a proxy server, or another FireWall-1 box. However, Section 2.5 of the January 2000 End User License Agreement for Check Point FireWall-1 clearly states that this is not permitted:

> The Product is licensed to You based on the applicable Licensed Configuration purchased. The License permits the use of the Product in accordance with the designated number of IP addresses[. . .]. It is a violation of this End User License Agreement to create, set-up, or design any hardware, software, or system which alters the number of readable IP addresses presented to the Product with the intent, or resulting effect, of circumventing the Licensed Configuration.

In any case, these sorts of licenses are only appropriate for use where you can guarantee the number of hosts behind a single gateway. More importantly, these licenses should only be used where an external network can only be reached through a single

---

3.   In a High Availability configuration, each firewall in the cluster must be on the same platform.

interface. If it can be reached through more than one interface or you have no way to control the number of hosts behind the firewall, this type of license should not be used.

Single-Gateway Product

A single-gateway product (also referred to as a firewall Internet gateway) is a node-limited firewall module bundled with a management console. This management console is only capable of managing a single-firewall module, and the firewall module must be installed on the same host as the management console. Because a single-gateway product includes a node-limited firewall license, it has the same restrictions as those stated in the previous section.

Inspection Module

An inspection module is a firewall module that lacks the functionality of the Security Servers, such as content security and authentication, which will be discussed in Chapters 7 and 8. It is not a commonly used license but is sold in certain instances where only packet filtering and encryption will be used.

FireWall-1 Host

In FireWall-1 4.1, there is a new license type that is designed to protect a single host. It has all the functionality of a standard firewall module except for the fact it is not allowed to forward packets.

Management Console

If your single-gateway product does not include a management console, you need to obtain a separate license for the management console. You can install the management console on the same platform as the firewall. If you plan on managing multiple firewalls or use High Availability, having your management console on a different platform is recommended. For more information on remote management, see Chapter 6.

Motif GUI Licenses

A separate license is needed if you want to use the Management GUIs on any other platform other than a Windows platform. This is because Check Point must pay a licensing fee to the company that provides Check Point with the toolkit used to make the GUI for these platforms. These licenses were free in FireWall-1 4.0, but they require additional purchase in FireWall-1 4.1 and later. The license is tied to the IP address or hostid of your management console and will be installed on your management console.

Small-Office Products

Small-office products are similar to inspection modules in that they are missing the functionality of a full firewall module. However, they are slightly better than inspection modules because they can manage content security. They provide protection for anywhere from 5 to 50 IP addresses and run on specialized hardware. Depending on the small-office product in question, encryption is also an available feature. The licenses are tied to the system's externally accessible IP address, but the licenses themselves are installed on the management console.

Getting Licenses

Each product you purchase will be given a certificate key. This certificate key, once registered at http://license.checkpoint.com, can be used to obtain your permanent license key for your product. The actual process, if everything goes well, is very straightforward. Not only will you be given the license information on a Web page, you will also be sent an e-mail with the same information. Save this e-mail and print the license page. You will need this information when installing the product. You will also need the certificate key when you upgrade at a later date, as the same certificate key will be used for the updated product as well (provided you purchase a software subscription, which should be activated at the same time the product is licensed).

There are two ways to license a FireWall-1 installation: on a hostid or an IP address. The hostid is an ID number based on information burned onto the motherboard. Hostid-based licensing can only occur on Sparc Solaris or HP/UX, as these hardware types actually support this type of license. On AIX, you can use a hostid-based license, but the hostid of an AIX box is actually based on an IP address, so there is no point. Windows NT and Nokia do not allow hostid-based licenses and can only be licensed by IP addresses.

IP-address-based licenses require that the IP address noted in the license be associated with an interface that is active when FireWall-1's kernel-loadable module loads at boot time. On a Solaris platform, the licensed IP address must be associated with the physical interface (i.e., it cannot be an interface alias).

It is relatively easy to get evaluation licenses to do the testing and even the initial deployment of your firewall. Your Check Point reseller can obtain an evaluation license for you. Also, with each "eval pack" (which contains a CD and some documentation), you get a certificate key that can be used to generate two 30-day evaluation licenses.

In some cases, it has taken many months to get the correct permanent licenses, especially when upgrading from one version of FireWall-1 to the next, so do not be surprised if this happens to you. Unfortunately, there is no magic to this process. Making sure you have copies of your certificate keys and software subscription IDs helps tremendously but does not guarantee success in obtaining a permanent license quickly. If you find you must run a production firewall on an evaluation license, make sure that you request new evaluation licenses at least a week before you actually need them. It may take at least that long to hunt down another license that you can use. The same is true with an upgrade of permanent licenses: Request the upgrade at least a week (or more) before you actually need them.

There are actually two kinds of evaluation licenses: those that are tied to an IP address/hostid and those that are not (which are sometimes called *floating evals*). Licenses of the latter type will display the word *eval* where an IP address or hostid would be. Check Point no longer offers floating evaluation licenses. However, these licenses are still used within Check Point and occasionally make their way into the outside world. These licenses are only good for a limited period of time. They usually have a start date of some sort where if the system is dated before this time, the license will be invalid. As such, you cannot backdate your system to use one of these licenses indefinitely.

During the FireWall-1 3.0 time frame, Check Point changed over to a system where evaluation licenses were tied to a specific IP or hostid, which is still in use today. The dirty little secret about these licenses was that they are actually *permanent* licenses that have an expiration date. It appeared that you can backdate the system to use these licenses. However, I am quite certain that this is against Check Point's Licensing Agreement.

Summary

Although it is impossible to describe every situation you might encounter during the planning phase of installation, this chapter covered the basic elements you need to know to ensure that your installation process is successful. Making sure you understand your existing network structure, establishing a written security policy, and understanding how Check Point licenses work are key to the success of your initial installation.

Chapter

3

Installing FireWall-1

In this chapter, the installation of FireWall-1, from building the system to loading the software, is discussed. The actual configuration of FireWall-1 is covered in later chapters.

By the end of the chapter, you should be able to:

- Select the operating system that is best for your environment
- Properly harden an operating system
- Install the firewall software and any related service packs

Selecting an Operating System

The first step in building your firewall is selecting the operating system that the application will run on. With FireWall-1, you have several options:

- Windows NT/2000 Workstation or Server
- Solaris (Sparc or x86)
- HPUX
- AIX
- Nokia IPSO
- Linux

Each operating system has its advantages and disadvantages. Some of the advantages and disadvantages are listed in the sections that follow where each operating system is discussed. However, no one OS is best for every environment. The single most important criteria for choosing an OS should be in the skill set of your administrators. Whichever OS you select, make sure your security staff is knowledgeable in that particular OS. Even if you select the best operating system in the world, you will have problems if you lack the skilled personnel to build and maintain the operating system. Your firewall will not be as secure or as stable as it should be without a properly configured OS.

The following sections discuss the various operating systems on which FireWall-1 will run.

Windows NT/2000

The assumption in this section is that Windows NT 4.0 Server or Windows 2000 Server/Advanced Server will be used. Check Point only supports FireWall-1 on Windows NT Server or Windows 2000 Server/Advanced Server. Windows NT Workstation and Windows 2000 Professional can be used in test environments, but they are not recommended in a production environment because Microsoft has limited each product to ten concurrent connections. Windows NT Server and Windows 2000 Server/Advanced Server also include additional capabilities not present in Windows NT Workstation, such as mirrored drives. In this text, comments regarding Windows NT will also apply to Windows 2000 unless otherwise specified.

Advantages

Some of the advantages of using Windows NT Server and Windows 2000 Server/Advanced Server include:

- *Ease of use:* Windows NT has a GUI interface that many people are familiar with. This makes installation and maintenance of the operating system and firewall more user-friendly.
- *Widely used:* Windows NT is widely deployed. Windows 2000 is less popular, only because it is newer, although the new Windows NT is a popular choice for FireWall-1 installations. There is plenty of documentation on both Windows NT and FireWall-1 on Windows NT.
- *First-tier OS:* Windows NT is a first-tier OS, meaning that new Check Point features will appear on Windows NT (and other first-tier operating systems) first.
- *Lots of third-party software:* If FireWall-1 does not provide a particular function, there is likely to be a third-party application that will.

Disadvantages

Some of the disadvantages of using Windows NT Server and Windows 2000 Server/Advanced Server include:

- *Remote administration:* Compared to UNIX, Windows NT is more difficult to remotely administer, because most administration tasks can only be performed with a graphical user interface.
- *Command-line access:* Windows NT lacks a powerful command-line interface. This makes advance troubleshooting more difficult for both the OS and the

firewall software. Many of the advanced troubleshooting methods covered in this book are more difficult to perform on Windows NT.

Sparc Solaris

The original versions of FireWall-1 ran on SunOS and Solaris. Needless to say, Solaris is well supported both in terms of FireWall-1 and in terms of third-party applications.

Advantages

The advantages of using Sparc Solaris include:

- *Widely used:* Solaris is widely used and is a popular choice for FireWall-1 installations. There is plenty of documentation on both Solaris and FireWall-1 on Solaris.
- *First-tier OS:* Solaris is a first-tier OS, meaning new Check Point features will appear on Solaris (and other first-tier operating systems) first.
- *Command-line access:* UNIX systems have a strong command-line interface. This makes troubleshooting both the operating system and the firewall application easier, especially by remote.
- *High-end hardware support:* Solaris tends to support high-end hardware including lots of memory and large disk drives. This means Solaris is a very scalable platform.
- *Third-party software:* Although not as big of an advantage as on Windows NT, many applications you may need to use in conjunction with FireWall-1 will also run on Solaris.

Disadvantages

The disadvantages of using Sparc Solaris include:

- *Training:* Solaris, like most flavors of UNIX, requires more skill and training. It takes an experienced administrator to optimize the operating system. Not only can good Solaris administrators be difficult to find, but they may also cost more.
- *Policy Editor costs:* Policy Editor requires extra costs to deploy on Solaris. You are better off running Policy Editor from a Windows platform and connecting to a management console, which can run on any platform.

x86 Solaris

x86 Solaris is relatively easy for Check Point to support, because it is so similar to Sparc Solaris. However, it is not quite the same.

Advantages

The advantages of using x86 Solaris include:

- *Similarities to Sparc Solaris:* Despite the fact that Solaris x86 is not widely used, it is nearly identical to Sparc Solaris, which is widely used and is a popular choice for FireWall-1 installations. There is plenty of documentation on both Solaris and FireWall-1 on Solaris, which can be utilized for x86 Solaris.
- *Cheaper than Sparc Solaris:* PC hardware has been historically cheaper than Sparc hardware. However, Sparc hardware is getting cheaper.
- *Command-line access:* UNIX systems have a strong command-line interface. This makes troubleshooting both the operating system and the firewall application easier, especially by remote.

Disadvantages

The disadvantages of using x86 Solaris include:

- *Not a first-tier OS:* This means that Check Point does not add new features to x86 Solaris right away, if at all.
- *Training:* Solaris, like most flavors of UNIX, requires more skill and training. It takes an experienced administrator to optimize the operating system. Not only can good Solaris administrators be difficult to find, but they may also cost more.
- *Hardware:* Not all hardware is supported by x86 Solaris, and it can be challenging to get x86 Solaris to recognize supported hardware. (I once did a FireWall-1 installation on x86 Solaris. I spent one day of a two-day installation just getting Solaris x86 to work correctly.)
- *Policy Editor does not run on x86 Solaris:* You must run the Policy Editor from a Windows platform.

AIX and HP/UX

Both IBM and Hewlett Packard make versions of UNIX on which FireWall-1 can run. Both are similar in that they share the same advantages and disadvantages.

Advantages

Some of the advantages of using AIX and HP/UX include:

- *Command-line access:* UNIX systems have a strong command-line interface. This makes troubleshooting both the operating system and the firewall application easier, especially by remote.

- *High-end hardware support:* Both AIX and HP/UX tend to support high-end hardware including lots of memory and large disk drives. This means both AIX and HP/UX are scalable.

Disadvantages

Some of the disadvantages of using AIX and HP/UX include:

- *Deployment and resources:* Compared to Solaris, AIX and HP/UX are not as widely deployed. As such, good information on HP/UX and AIX is harder to come by, not to mention the lack of information on using either of these operating systems with FireWall-1.
- *Not a first-tier OS:* New FireWall-1 features do not appear on AIX or HP/UX right away. In fact, they often appear on AIX and HP/UX last because the vast majority of users choose other platforms.
- *Training:* Similar to Solaris, both HP/UX and AIX require more training to administer. Not only can good HP/UX or AIX administrators be difficult to find, but they may also cost more.
- *Third-party software:* Due to the small installed base of FireWall-1 on these platforms, vendors may not release versions of their software for either operating system. If they do, it is almost always after Windows NT and Solaris versions are released.

Nokia Security Platform (IPSO)

The Nokia Security Platform includes the VPN-1 Appliance and Nokia IPxxx boxes.[1] They are specifically designed to run particular applications, like FireWall-1. The OS is a modified version of FreeBSD called IPSO. The terms *Nokia platform* and *IPSO* are used interchangeably throughout this text. Much of the OS is controlled with a Web-based interface called Voyager.

Advantages

Some advantages of using IPSO include:

- *Ease of use:* Configuration of the OS is performed with a standard Web browser.
- *Command-line access:* Although much of the configuration is done with a standard Web browser, a standard UNIX command line is available to perform troubleshooting and monitoring (which is where I feel the use of the command line is most important).

---

1.   The Nokia IP51 and IP55 platforms are based on VxWorks, not IPSO. The IP71 is based on LINUX.

- *Pre-secured:* Most of what is considered insecure has been removed from the OS or is relatively easy to disable in Voyager. The OS itself has also been hardened.

- *Widely used:* Recent figures indicate that at least 35 percent of new Check Point sales are on IPSO.

- *Higher-quality product:* Both Nokia and Check Point quality assurance (QA) test the OS and FireWall-1 together.

- *First-tier OS:* IPSO is a first-tier OS, meaning that new Check Point features generally appear on IPSO (and other first-tier operating systems) first.

- *Upgrades:* Upgrades tend to be far easier on IPSO than they are on other platforms. With some limitations, you can easily switch between versions of FireWall-1 and IPSO.

- *Rack-mountable:* Most Nokia application platforms are rack-mountable and are suitable for use in a secured machine room.

- *Support:* A single vendor provides support for both FireWall-1 and IPSO.

Disadvantages

Some disadvantages of using IPSO include:

- *Customization:* What you gain in terms of a good user experience, you lose in terms of the ability to customize the box. It is not possible to develop your own applications to run on the box without getting a software development kit from Nokia—something Nokia does not give out freely. You can certainly write your own shell scripts, but Perl and many other GNU and open-source UNIX utilities are not included as part of the OS. Some open-source applications are available from Nokia Customer Support but are not provided with any support.

- *Command-line access:* The downside to Voyager is that the ability to configure certain options via the command line have been removed or at least significantly changed. Nokia recommends that Voyager be used to make all configuration changes and is the only company-supported way to make most changes.

- *Third-party applications:* There are few third-party applications that run on IPSO. Nokia is increasing the number of vendors that run applications on the platform, but certainly not at the rate that applications are being made available on other UNIX platforms.

Linux

Linux is a UNIX-like operating system made available under the GNU Public License, meaning that you have free access to the source code and can make any modifications you like.[2] Many Linux distributions, such as Red Hat, are similar to Solaris in administration. Most UNIX administrators can easily convert to a Linux environment.

Advantages

The advantages of using Linux include:

- *UNIX features:* Linux shares the same advantages of most versions of UNIX— strong remote management and a command-line interface.
- *Open Source:* Not only can you get the operating system free of charge but also the source code. You can also modify the kernel to suit your security requirements.

Disadvantages

The disadvantages of using Linux include:

- *New operating system:* Linux is relatively new to the business world, especially for FireWall-1.
- *Distribution specific:* FireWall-1 is only supported on Red Hat Linux 6.x, although a few folks have made it work on other versions of Red Hat and even other distributions like Mandrake, SuSE, and Debian.
- *Limited to Ethernet interfaces:* As of FireWall-1 4.1 service pack 2 (SP2), only Ethernet interfaces are supported.
- *Support for FireWall-1 4.1 and later:* Only FireWall-1 4.1 and later are supported on Linux: This means that if you use a Linux platform as a management console, you cannot manage FireWall-1 4.0 and earlier firewall modules with it.

Installing the Operating System

Once you have chosen an OS, you should make sure you have the necessary hardware, software, and configuration information to install it. You can then install it, taking extra care to make sure you only install and configure what you need, and disable what you don't.

Preparing for the OS Installation

After selecting your operating system, you can begin to plan your build. Before the actual build process begins, there is some preliminary information and resources you

---

2. The Linux kernel itself is under the GPL; various other programs included with most Linux distributions are either GPL or other similar open-source licenses.

need to confirm. The following checklist covers most of the important considerations. Complete this checklist before you begin the installation process, as it will simplify the build process and identify any configuration issues before you begin building the box(es).

- Do you have the required hardware?
  - Ensure that you have enough network interface cards. It never hurts to have extra network ports handy in case your network grows.
  - Ensure that you have the disk space for logs on your management console.
- Do you have the operating system installation media?
  - Ensure that you also have a proper license for your operating system (if necessary).
  - Determine which version of the OS you are going to install.
  - Obtain the latest system patches or service packs.
- Do you have the FireWall-1 installation media or on an accessible FTP server?
  - Obtain the proper licenses.
  - Obtain the latest service packs for FireWall-1.
  - If installing via FTP, determine the IP address of the FTP server.
  - If installing via FTP, determine the username and password necessary to access this software.
  - If installing via FTP, ensure that it is accessible from where you plan on installing the platform.
- How will you configure the operating system? Establish the system configuration by determining the following information:
  - System name
  - Names, IPs, and net mask of all interface cards
  - IP address of DNS server
  - Default router and additional network routes
  - Disk partitions
  - User accounts and passwords
- How will you configure the firewall? Determine the following information for the firewall configuration:
  - IP addresses of GUI client
  - IP addresses of remote modules or management module (if required)
  - Accounts for firewall administration

Guidelines for the OS Installation

Once you have identified the required information, you can begin the build process. The first step in building your operating system is to start with a new installation. Never trust previous installations of an operating system. By installing and configuring the operating system from scratch, you know exactly how it has been configured and can better trust it. Each operating system has its own unique installation process. You will want to build an install checklist for your respective operating system.

When you receive a Nokia Security Platform from the factory, it comes preinstalled with IPSO and a fresh configuration you must configure via a console cable. These installations can generally be trusted, but you should verify that the latest versions of the OS and FireWall-1 are present on the box. It is possible that an earlier version of either FireWall-1 or IPSO is loaded on the platform. You can either upgrade the existing software or simply reinstall the system from scratch from an FTP server where you have loaded all of the necessary software bits.

It is critical to install the minimal installation components required for the firewall. The OS hardening process begins with the installation. Most UNIX systems allow the user to select the applications or packages that will be installed during the installation process. By selecting the minimal installation, you can limit the vulnerabilities present in the new operating system. With other operating systems, such as Windows NT, unnecessary components are installed by default and no choice is given as to whether they are to be installed or not. Once the installation is complete, additional services, such as Workstation and Server, need to be removed. For examples on minimal installation and hardening the operating system, see Appendix A. General hints on hardening the operating system are covered in greater detail in the "Securing the Operating System" section in this chapter.

During the installation and build procedure, ensure that the system is never attached to a live network. Attaching an unsecured operating system to a network exposes it to a variety of risks. It is quite possible to have a system probed, attacked, and compromised within 15 minutes of being connected to the Internet! If you need to add software to your system, such as operating system patches or additional software, use an intermediate system to download the required software. You can then either burn the software to a CD or directly connect the two systems over a private, secured network.

Once the operating system has been installed, the next step is to configure it for your environment. This usually consists of adding system accounts (in a secure manner discussed in the "Securing the Operating System" section in this chapter) and configuring all networking including DNS. This is where the preceding checklist comes in handy. Remember, the operating system is responsible for all networking and routing, not FireWall-1. The firewall only determines what can and cannot happen. Once a session has been approved or authenticated by the firewall, it is up to the operating system to send the packets in the correct direction. You must ensure that you set up networking properly, or traffic will not reach its destination. Each operating system has its own specific ways of setting up interfaces and routing. If you are employing address translation, refer to Chapter 9 for additional notes about changes to routing that might need to be made.

Once the system has been fully secured and configured, build a lab network that replicates the network point that your firewall will be protecting. Have lab equipment replicate the routers and networks the firewall will be routing from and to. This way your network configurations can be tested before being implemented. Unfortunately, many organizations do not have the luxury of a lab to test their configurations. A second technique is to verify the system configuration during the implementation phase. Once the system is ready and the firewall has been installed and configured, the box is deployed on the network. Once plugged into the network, turn off both the firewall and routing on the box (only do this with a fully armored system). Then, from the box, attempt to ping every network that should be accessible from the firewall, including the Internet. The key point in doing so is to confirm that the operating system is properly configured before turning on the firewall. If the system can ping every network it is supposed to, more than likely, the system is properly configured. If you cannot ping a network that should be accessible, fix the problem before the firewall is turned on. Once again, use this method only with a fully armored system and IP routing turned off.

Securing the Operating System

The entire purpose of a firewall is to secure your resources. However, a firewall is only as secure as the operating system it resides on. If the operating system is compromised, so is the firewall, defeating your organization's security. Therefore, you need to build the operating system as securely as possible. Each operating system has unique and specific issues. For detailed examples on how to properly build a secure system for a firewall, see Appendix A. However, there are standard concepts that apply to every operating system; these are described as follows.

Securing an operating system requires several basic steps. The first step is to remove any unnecessary applications and software. If the firewall does not require it, remove it. The new system should be a dedicated firewall. Do not run other applications on it, such as DNS, Web server, mail server, and so on. The more applications you have on your system, the greater the risk for compromise. If an application is not installed, it cannot be compromised. As discussed earlier, this armoring process begins during installation, where only the bare minimum required software is installed. Once the installation is complete, ensure that all other unnecessary services are turned off. You can verify that services are not running by running `netstat -na` and making sure that you can account for all the ports shown as listening. You can also run a port scanner against the system to validate what `netstat -na` shows you. Even if a service is not running, binaries remaining on the operating system can be locally exploited; these need to be removed. For examples on how to verify your systems, see Appendix A.

The next step is to patch the operating system. New exploits and vulnerabilities are constantly being identified for all operating systems. Patches help protect against these known vulnerabilities. Make sure the new system is fully patched after the initial installation. For Windows NT, this requires the latest service packs and hot fixes. For Solaris, the latest recommended patch cluster from Sun is recommended. Patching an operating system is not a one-time event; due diligence must be exercised to ensure that all the latest security patches are applied. Security Focus, at www.securityfocus.com, is an excellent source for this information. As these new vulnerabilities are discovered, vendors release new patches to update their operating systems.

After you have applied all the latest patches and hot fixes, you should update and secure whatever services and applications you are running on the box just as you would your operating system. Most services can be secured to some extent. If the service cannot be secured, you may want to replace it with an alternative or eliminate it all together. For example, those of you who are running Telnet or FTP daemons on UNIX systems will want to install TCP Wrappers to limit who can access these services. Replacing these services with more-secure applications is an even better solution. Secure Shell (SSH) can be used like Telnet and FTP to log on to a system and transfer files to a system. It also provides stronger authentication and encryption than Telnet or FTP alone. Regardless, ensure that whichever additional applications you are running on the operating system are current and secured.

Logging is another critical feature. Just like the firewall, most operating systems log user and kernel activity on the system. Ensure that your operating system is logging important events. This helps you to better troubleshoot because logs can often warn you if something is going wrong. They can also let you know if someone is trying to break in, because login failures are usually logged. Logs also leave an audit trail, telling you who did what, which is especially important when something goes wrong. Many organizations use a dedicated log server to store system logs. The firewall operating system can be configured not only to log all system information locally but also to send the logs over the network to the dedicated log server. This ensures two sources of logging information in case one source becomes corrupted or inaccessible. Regardless of which options you choose, ensure that your operating system is logging all system and user activity. However, also note that too much logging can slow the system down, so although logging is a good thing overall, judicious use of logging is best.

In addition, you should secure user access to the operating system. More than one person should have access to the system, but not too many. Limit the access to a small group of people who are trusted—three is a good number. The more people who have access to the operating system, the greater the chance that something can go wrong. These accounts should have hard-to-guess passwords or even require a one-time password scheme. You should also have these accounts established on the local system only. Do not use any network login scheme like Network Information Service (NIS) or a Windows NT Domain Logon.

Never use a generic account for the initial login. Often, part of breaking into a system is choosing the right username to try. Common usernames like admin, root, fwadmin, guest, and so on are tried because they are highly likely to exist on a system. Disable these logins, if possible, and require a login that identifies a specific user. This same rule applies to the Firewall Administrator account used to access the FireWall-1 Management GUIs (more about these in Chapter 4).

Always require users to first authenticate themselves; then allow them to gain the necessary access. This procedure builds in at least two layers of authentication (which is more secure) and leaves an audit trail of who is doing what. For Windows NT systems, there are third-party versions of the switch user (su) binary, which allows users to log in with a nonprivileged account and then "switch user" to a more privileged user to run those commands that require additional privileges. Make sure users only have the access they absolutely require. Do not give them root or administrator access if they do not require it to administer or maintain the system. The same is true for the FireWall-1 Management GUIs.

As far as routing goes, it is recommended that you only use static routes on a firewall. If you must use a dynamic routing, ensure that you have enabled authentication to limit the possibility of importing spoofed routes and log any authentication failures. Additionally, you can use FireWall-1 to restrict who is allowed to send routing updates.

Installing FireWall-1

Once you have properly installed, configured, and secured your operating system, you are ready to install the firewall software. The installation instructions included with your FireWall-1 CD explain the specific steps necessary to load the software from the CD. The software included on your CD is often a base release. Frequently, a FireWall-1 service pack needs to be installed to bring the software up-to-date. You should install this service pack after completing the initial configuration.

On UNIX platforms, the GUI, FireWall-1, and the Backward Compatibility Module (to manage FireWall-1 4.0 and earlier firewalls from a 4.1 management console) need to be installed as separate packages. On IPSO, FireWall-1, Floodgate-1 (on 4.1 versions), and the Backward Compatibility Module are all included in the base package, so there is no need to install a separate package for them. On Windows NT, the Backward Compatibility Module is installed as part of the base installation. Make sure you install the packages you need.

 NOTE!   All IPSO-based releases of FireWall-1 are complete, meaning previous versions are not required when doing an installation of the latest service pack. You can simply load the latest service pack with the `newpkg` command before beginning the installation process. See the release notes for the specific service pack for more information about upgrading from previous service packs.

You should always load your management console first, and then load individual firewall modules.

UNIX-Based Systems

Once the software is loaded, you should define the FWDIR variable to where the software was installed. You need to add this information to your administrator's .cshrc or .profile. You should also add `$FWDIR/bin` to your path variable. On Linux and IPSO, this occurs automatically. In fact, attempting to do so on IPSO can have unpredictable results, especially when you upgrade.

Before beginning the installation process, ensure that your hostname is properly defined in your `/etc/hosts` file. Take the output of the `hostname` command and make sure there is an entry for that host in `/etc/hosts`. On an IPSO platform, you do this from the Host Address Assignment page in Voyager. In both cases, the IP address should be the external, routable address of your system. If you use DNS, these entries should also match the host file entry.

When you are ready to configure the software, run the command `cpconfig`. On FireWall-1 4.0 and earlier releases, run `fwconfig`. The following command output shows a FireWall-1 4.1 installation on a Linux platform. For simplicity, everything (management console and firewall module) is installed on a single box. In reality, the software installed on the platform will not change regardless of which installation option you choose, but the questions you are asked during the installation will be somewhat different, and different options will be written to `$FWDIR/conf/product.conf`. Note that if you are asked to specify a management console or firewall module to manage, skip those questions at this time, and configure them as specified in Chapter 6.

```
# cpconfig
Welcome to Check Point Configuration Program
=====================================================
Checking available options. Please wait........

Choosing Installation
_____

(1) VPN-1 & FireWall-1 Stand Alone Installation
(2) VPN-1 & FireWall-1 Distributed Installation
```

```
Option (1) will install VPN-1 & FireWall-1
Internet GateWay (Management Server and Enforcement Module)
on a single machine.

Option (2) will allow you to install specific
components of the VPN-1 & FireWall-1 Enterprise Products
on different machines.

Enter your selection (1-2/a): 1
```

The next option allows you to choose which module you would like to install. Again, this does not change the software installed on the platform; it simply changes the questions you will be asked during installation.

```
Installing VPN-1 & FireWall-1 Stand Alone Installation.

Which module would you like to install?
_____ -

(1) VPN-1 & FireWall-1 - Limited hosts (25, 50, 100 or 250)
(2) VPN-1 & FireWall-1 - Unlimited hosts
(3) VPN-1 & FireWall-1 - SecureServer

Enter your selection (1-3/a) [2]: 2
```

If you choose the Limited Hosts option, you will be asked to select the external interface. Use the name as specified in ifconfig when asked. The next question asks if you want to start FireWall-1 automatically on boot. The location it will modify (or add) will vary depending on the OS. On IPSO, you will not be asked this question. Instead, whether or not FireWall-1 starts at boot time is controlled in Voyager. Generally speaking, you want FireWall-1 to start at boot time, so answer yes to this question.

```
Do you wish to start VPN-1 & FireWall-1 automatically from
/etc/rc.d/rc.local (y/n) [y] ? y
```

The next question asks if you would like to add a license. You can either add the license here or use the fw putkey command later. In this example, a license key is entered. This license is stored in $FWDIR/conf/cp.license ($FWDIR/conf/fw.license in FireWall-1 4.0 and earlier).

```
Configuring Licenses...
========================
The following licenses are installed on this host:
Do you want to add licenses (y/n) [n] ? y
Host:10.0.0.10
Date:28Nov2000
String:abcdefG1h-iJKLMn2OP-Q34rStuvw-xY5zaBCDe
Features:cpsuite-eval-3des-v41 cprs:4.1:rs5 cpsuite-eval-3des-v41
cprs:4.1:rs5 CK-123456789ABC
```

```
This is Check Point VPN-1(TM) & FireWall-1(R) Version 4.1 (29Oct2000
12:53:47)

Host              Expiration Features
10.0.0.10         29Nov2000  cpsuite-eval-3des-v41 cprs:4.1:rs5 cpsuite
eval-3des-v41 cprs:4.1:rs5 CK-123456789ABC
```

The next question asks if you want to add firewall administrators. These are accounts specific to the FireWall-1 Management GUIs. They do not correspond to OS accounts or users that relate to authentication for any other service. You should create at least one account here. In this example, an administrator with write permissions for all GUIs is created. The possible permissions you can choose are discussed in more detail in Chapter 4. These administrators are stored in $FWDIR/conf/fwmusers.

```
Configuring Administrators...
==============================
No VPN-1 & FireWall-1 Administrators are currently
defined for this Management Station.
Do you want to add users (y/n) [y] ? y
Administrator name: dwelch
Password: abc123
Verify Password: abc123
Permissions for all Management Clients (Read/[W]rite All, [R]ead Only
All, [C]ustomized) w

Administrator dwelch was added successfully and has
Read/Write permissions to all management clients
Read/Write permissions for Reporting Module
Read/Write permissions for Log Consolidator

Add another one (y/n) [n] ? n
```

Next, choose the IP addresses that will be allowed to connect with the FireWall-1 Management GUIs. You can specify either DNS-resolvable names or IP addresses. Localhost (127.0.0.1) will always be permitted.

```
Configuring GUI clients...
===========================
GUI clients are trusted hosts from which
Administrators are allowed to log on to this Management Station
using Windows/X-Motif GUI.
Do you want to add GUI clients (y/n) [y] ? y
Please enter the list hosts that will be GUI clients.
Enter hostname or IP address, one per line, terminating with CTRL-D or
your EOF
```

```
character.
10.0.0.1
10.0.0.2
^D
Is this correct (y/n) [y] ? y
```

The next question is in regard to the configuration of the SMTP Security Server. For now, let's accept the defaults. More information about the various options can be found in Chapter 8.

```
Configuring SMTP Server...
===========================
Following are the current values of the SMTP Server configuration:
timeout: 900
scan_period: 2
resend_period: 600
abandon_time: 432000
maxrecipients: 50
rundir:
postmaster: postmaster
default_server:
error_server:
Would you like to modify the above configuration (y/n) [y] ? n
```

FireWall-1 can export information about itself to its own SNMP daemon, which can be queried by an SNMP management console. IPSO has its own SNMP daemon process, and it will return FireWall-1-specific information, namely data that you can view in the System Status Viewer. On an IPSO box or in any other situation where the ability to query a firewall via SNMP is not needed, you should say no to the following question.

```
Configuring SNMP Extension...
=============================
The SNMP daemon enables VPN-1 & FireWall-1 module
to export its status to external network management tools.
Would you like to activate VPN-1 & FireWall-1 SNMP daemon ? (y/n) [n] ? n
```

If you want to allow FireWall-1 binaries and files to be executable by a non-root user of a specific group, you can specify that when configuring groups. Note that Super-User privileges will still be needed for many commands. Generally, most people specify no group, meaning only the Super-User can access and execute FireWall-1 binaries and files.

```
Configuring Groups...
=====================
VPN-1 & FireWall-1 access and execution permissions
```

```
Usually, a VPN-1 & FireWall-1 module is given group permission
for access and execution.
You may now name such a group or instruct the installation
procedure to give no group permissions to the VPN-1 & FireWall-1 module.
In the latter case, only the Super-User will
be able to access and execute the VPN-1 & FireWall-1 module.
Please specify group name [<RET> for no group permissions]:
No group permissions will be granted. Is this ok (y/n) [y] ? y
Setting Group Permissions... Done.
```

IP forwarding allows a system to forward packets between interfaces (i.e., route). Most systems start up with IP forwarding enabled. However, it is not wise to have this enabled until FireWall-1 loads a security policy. In the vast majority of cases, you will want to disable IP forwarding. On IPSO, IP Forwarding is always disabled at boot time when FireWall-1 is installed, despite your answer to this question.

```
Configuring IP forwarding...
==============================
Do you wish to disable IP forwarding at boot time (y/n) [y] ? y
IP forwarding disabled
```

The default filter is a security policy that is loaded prior to FireWall-1's attempts to download a security policy from the management console or load the last policy that was installed on the firewall. If FireWall-1 cannot do either of these tasks at startup, the default filter will be the policy that the firewall will enforce until a new policy is manually loaded or fetched.

There are two default policies: boot and drop. The boot policy does the following:

- Drops all packets with IP Options
- Accepts packets to and from the same IP address (allows the firewall to talk to itself)
- Accepts all outbound TCP, UDP, and ICMP packets
- Accepts all inbound ICMP, broadcast packets, or established TCP/UDP connections
- Drops all other packets

The drop filter drops all packets except for packets to and from the same IP address, dropping everything else.

On IPSO, the drop filter is always chosen on systems prior to version 4.1 SP3 (you are not given a choice), although it is possible to switch between them or even generate your own default filter on any platform. See Chapter 13 for more details.

```
Configuring Default Filter...
==============================
Do you wish to modify your /etc/rc.d/rc3.d boot scripts to allow a
default filter to be automatically installed during boot (y/n) [y] ? y
Please note that when you change your default runlevel you will need to
link FW-1 startup scripts to that runlevel's directory
Which default filter do you wish to use?
_____

(1) Allow only traffic necessary for boot
(2) Drop all traffic
NOTE: If you are installing the VPN-1 & FireWall-1 module, and not
      reconfiguring, it is recommended you choose option (1) in order
      to allow communications with the VPN-1 & FireWall-1 management.
      After installing a policy on the module from the management, you
      can reconfigure the default filter to option (2)
Enter your selection (1-2) [1]: 2
Generating default filter
```

If you are installing a management console, you will be asked to establish a random pool used to generate a certificate authority key as well as other encryption keys the management console will generate in the future. Encryption keys are explained in Chapter 10. The random pool is generated by measuring time between keystrokes. Use many different characters at different paces to establish a good random pool.

```
Configuring Random Pool...
===========================
You are now asked to perform a short random keystroke session.
The random data collected in this session will be used for generating
Certificate Authority RSA keys.
Please enter random text containing at least six different characters.
You will see the '*' symbol after keystrokes that are too fast or too
similar to preceding keystrokes. These keystrokes will be ignored.
Please keep typing until you hear the beep and the bar is full.
     [....................]
Thank you.
```

The following warning lets you know that when upgrading from a previous version of FireWall-1 to a later version (say from 4.0 to 4.1), you need to reload the policy from the management console, as the compiled policies are incompatible between major versions of FireWall-1.

```
NOTE:
After an upgrade installation the VPN-1 & FireWall-1 module cannot fetch
the old security policy from the management until the policy is reloaded
from the VPN-1 & FireWall-1 management station. This means the module
will have no security policy installed until you load the policy from
the management station.
```

On non-IPSO platforms, you are reminded to add a definition for the `FWDIR` variable to .cshrc or .profile as well as add $FWDIR/bin to the path variable. If you do not do this, you will not be able to easily execute FireWall-1 commands. On IPSO, you do not need to define `FWDIR` or add $FWDIR/bin to your path, because IPSO does this automatically.

```
* * * * * * * * * * * * * * * * * * * * * * * * * * * * * * * * * * * * * * * * * * * * * * * * * * * * * * * * * * * * *
                          DON'T FORGET TO:
1. add the line:     setenv FWDIR /etc/fw      to .cshrc
              or   FWDIR=/etc/fw; export FWDIR     to .profile
2. add  $FWDIR/bin  to path
* * * * * * * * * * * * * * * * * * * * * * * * * * * * * * * * * * * * * * * * * * * * * * * * * * * * * * * * * * * * *
```

The installation is now complete. On some platforms where a firewall module is loaded (with or without a management console), a reboot is required before FireWall-1 can be started. On systems where a reboot is not required (or you are just loading a management console), you can start FireWall-1 immediately. If you are going to install a service pack, you should not start FireWall-1 right away.

```
***************** Installation completed successfully *****************

Do you wish to start VPN-1 & FireWall-1 now? (y/n) [y] ? y
```

At this point, on non-IPSO platforms, you should install any service packs that need to be added to the base release that came on your CD. You do not need to install all the service packs in order, just the latest one, although you should double-check the release notes for your particular service pack just to be certain. The release notes for the service pack not only explain exactly how to install it but also provide procedures for backing it out at a later time.

Windows NT/2000

On Windows NT, the installation process is started when setup.exe loads the software to the system. As in the previous example, everything (firewall and management console) is installed on the same platform (see Figure 3-1). As with UNIX, all software is loaded, but different options will be enabled in the following Registry entry: \\HKEY_LOCAL_MACHINE\SOFTWARE\CheckPoint\FW1\4.1 (or 4.0 if a 4.0 installation).

Click Next, and select the appropriate module (see Figure 3-2). In this case, Gateway Module-Unlimited hosts is selected.

If you select the Limited Hosts option, you need to specify the external interface after you click Next. Specify the name of the external interface as shown in `ipconfig`. Click Next, and then select whether or not you want to install the Backward Compatibility Module to manage FireWall-1 4.0 and earlier modules (see Figure 3-3).

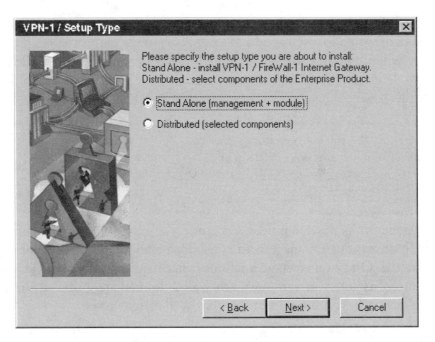

Figure 3-1   Select Stand Alone or Distributed installation

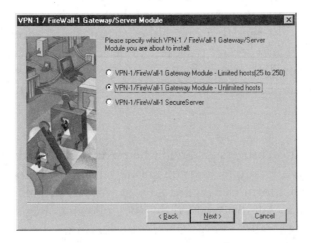

Figure 3-2   Module to be installed

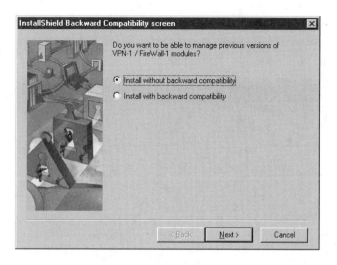

Figure 3-3   Installing backward compatibility

Click Next, and choose the installation directory (see Figure 3-4). It is strongly recommended that you use the default location. Many people have had problems installing FireWall-1 on Windows NT/2000 in a non-default location. Whichever directory you choose, ensure that the name of the directory does not have any spaces in it, or you will definitely have problems.

Click Next, and the license page appears (see Figure 3-5).

Click Add, and fill in the license details (see Figure 3-6).

Click OK, and then click Next. On this screen, you define your FireWall-1 Management GUI users (see Figure 3-7). These users only manage FireWall-1 via the Management GUIs and do not correspond to OS accounts or accounts used for authentication of other services via FireWall-1.

Click Add, and fill in the details for the user (see Figure 3-8).

Click OK, and then click Next. On this screen, you need to specify an IP address that will be used to create an entry in the Windows NT hosts file for your local system (see Figure 3-9). Click Change IP, and choose the external, routable address (if there is one). Click OK.

Click Next, and then specify the IP address(es) or DNS-resolvable hostnames of hosts that will be allowed to connect to this management console (see Figure 3-10).

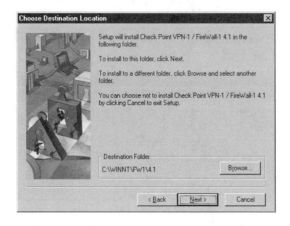

Figure 3-4 Choosing the installation directory

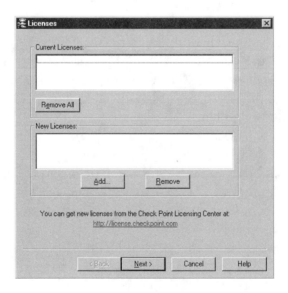

Figure 3-5 Installed licenses

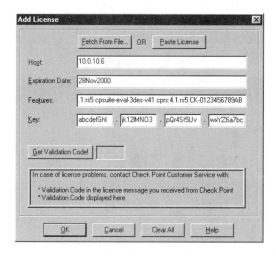

Figure 3-6   Adding a license

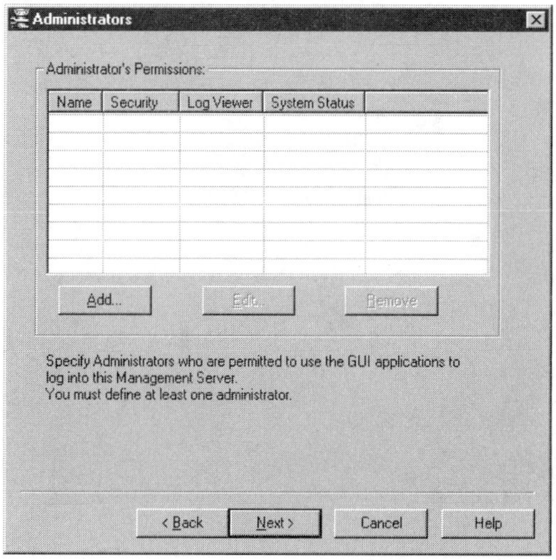

Figure 3-7   Management GUI users

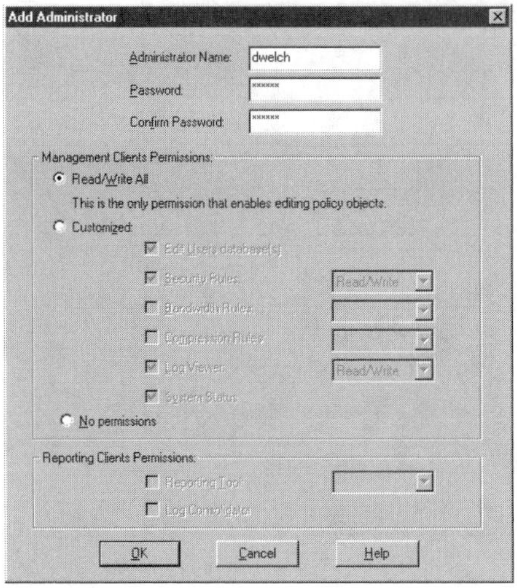

Figure 3-8   Adding Management GUI administrators

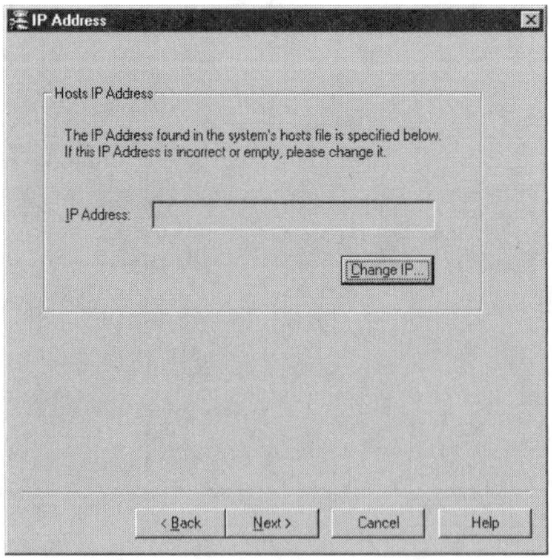

Figure 3-9   Adding an entry in the hosts file

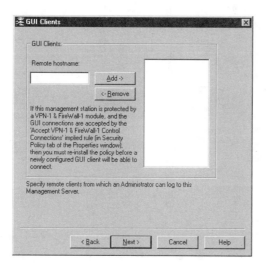

Figure 3-10   Adding authorized IP addresses for Management GUIs

Click Next. On this screen, you specify Remote Modules to manage and/or management consoles that will manage this station (see Figure 3-11). However, this is not the best place to do this. See Chapter 6 for instructions on how to set up Remote Modules. Skip this screen, and perform the steps in Chapter 6.

Click Next, and then choose whether or not to control IP Forwarding in FireWall-1 (see Figure 3-12).

Click Next. On this screen, you set up the SMTP Security Server preferences (see Figure 3-13). These preferences are configured in Chapter 8.

Click Next. You then need to establish a random seed for generating encryption keys (see Figure 3-14). More information about encryption keys is found in Chapter 10.

Click Next. You are asked if you want to restart your computer (see Figure 3-15). Do not reboot just yet.

Once the install is complete, you should define FWDIR and also add %FWDIR%\bin to the path. In Windows NT, go to the Control Panel, choose System Applet (see Figure 3-16), and then select the Environment tab. Add FWDIR as a system variable and C:\winnt\fw1\4.1\bin (or wherever you installed FireWall-1) to the path variable. The preceding step is not necessary, but it will make your life easier in the long run.

If you are going to install a FireWall-1 service pack, do it at this point. After the installation, reboot your computer.

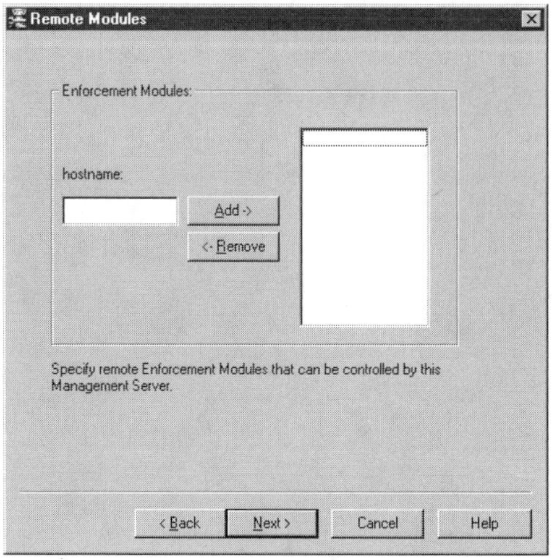

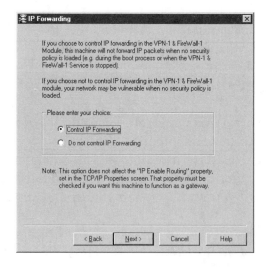

Figure 3-11   Adding Remote Modules to manage

Figure 3-12   Controlling IP forwarding

Figure 3-13   Configuring SMTP Security Server settings

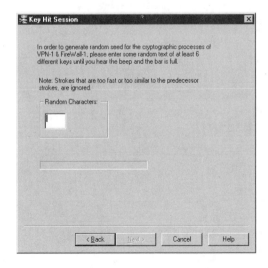

Figure 3-14   Establishing a random pool

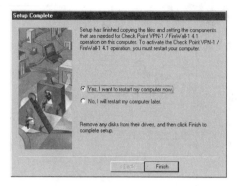

Figure 3-15 Rebooting after installation

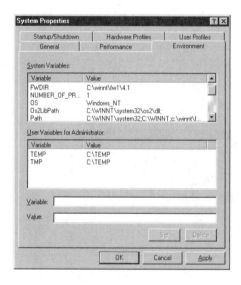

Figure 3-16 Configuring FWDIR as an environment variable

Summary

Although this chapter did not cover every contingency or situation you may encounter in your installation, it provided you with a guided procedure for completing the initial installation of FireWall-1. Configuration of the rulebase and other options in FireWall-1 are covered in later chapters.

4

Building
Your Rulebase

This chapter covers how to build a basic rulebase. I'll start by discussing how to set up access to the FireWall-1 Management GUIs. I'll then discuss the different kinds of objects you can create. Next, the various components that make up your rulebase, including the rulebase properties and anti-spoofing, are explained. Finally, making a rulebase, including certain rules that should appear in every rulebase, is covered.

By the end of this chapter, you should be able to:

- Understand what the Management GUIs do
- Control access to the Management GUIs
- Understand the order in which anti-spoofing, rulebase properties, and the rules themselves will actually be applied
- Determine which rules should be in every rulebase
- Create a rulebase

The Management GUIs

The Management GUIs allow you to create and edit your security policy as well as view policy logs and system status. There are three distinct applications that make up the Management GUIs:

- *Policy Editor (fwpolicy):* Allows you to view and modify your security policy. This application is covered in this chapter.
- *Log Viewer (fwlog):* Allows you to view your firewall logs. This application is covered in Chapter 5.
- *Status Viewer (fwstatus):* Allows you to view basic system status and display alerts from your firewalls. This application is also covered in Chapter 5.

These GUIs view data stored on the management console via a TCP connection on port 258. They do not store any information locally except for preferences for the application itself. The most common (and recommended) platform on which to run the GUIs is Windows (95, 98, NT, or 2000). A Motif version exists for most UNIX platforms. It uses the same code as the Windows platform and is nearly identical in appearance, but it runs on an emulation layer that, at least in the past, is slow and has been known to be buggy and leak memory. To add insult to injury, Check Point has decided to charge extra for the use of this GUI as of FireWall-1 4.1. The reported reason for this is that Check Point has to pay a licensing fee to the company that provides the emulation layer.

For those who have used FireWall-1 for a long time, the old Open-Look-based GUI tools (`fwui`, `fwlv`, `fwss`) are available on Sparc Solaris and HP/UX. However, these tools can only be run from the management console and are deprecated. Their use is no longer recommended, and Check Point no longer supports the use of these GUIs. Therefore, they are not covered in this book.

Whichever platform you choose to run the GUIs on, you must configure your management console to allow the GUIs to be run from particular workstations. This means establishing users and IP address(es) that are permitted to use them.

Configuring a Management User

It is important to note that the users mentioned in this section can only authenticate to the Management GUIs. They do not in any way correspond to specific user accounts on the operating system or to users who authenticate for other services through the firewall. The latter type of users is discussed in Chapter 7.

In order to configure users for the Management GUIs, you can:

- Add users via `cpconfig` (FireWall-1 4.1 and later) or use the `fwconfig` utility (version 4.0 and earlier)
- Run `fwm -a` on a UNIX platform
- Run `fw m -a` on all platforms including Windows NT

The permissions you will be able to enter will depend on which version of FireWall-1 you are using. FireWall-1 4.1 and later offer more control over permissions than earlier versions. Both FireWall versions also integrate with other Check Point products like MetaIP, Floodgate, the Compression Module, and the Check Point Log Reporting Tool, so you have to set permissions for all of these products in addition to the permissions that just relate to FireWall-1. If you add a user via `cpconfig` on Windows NT, a screen that looks like Figure 4-1 appears.

If you add a user via the command line, you will be prompted for the same permissions.

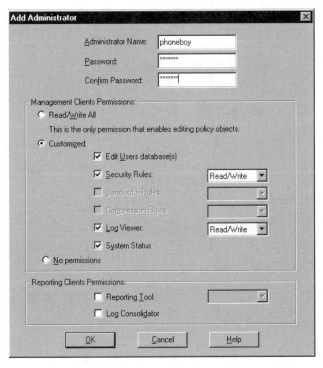

Figure 4-1   cpconfig on Windows NT

```
# fw m -a
User: phoneboy
Permissions for the Enterprise product (read/[W]rite,[N]one,
[C]ustomise): w
Permissions for Reporting Tool ([N]one,[R]ead Only,read/[W]rite): w
Permissions for Log Consolidator([N]one,read/[W]rite): w
Password: test123
Verify Password: test123
User fwadmin added successfully
```

The preceding example creates a user who can do anything. The user being created in the following example can do everything except edit network objects.

```
# fw m -a
User: jerald
Permissions for the Enterprise product (read/[W]rite,[N]one,
[C]ustomise): c
        Do you want to allow user edit (y/n) [n] ? y
        Do you want to allow rules edit (y/n) [n] ? y
                Permissions for Security Policy ([N]one,[R]ead
Only,rules [E]dit): e
                Permissions for Bandwidth Policy ([N]one,[R]ead
```

```
Only,rules [E]dit): e
                Permissions for Compression Policy ([N]one,[R]ead Only,
rules [E]dit): e
        Permissions for System Status ([N]one, read/[W]rite): w
        Permissions for Log Viewer ([N]one,[R]ead Only,read/[W]rite): w
Permissions for Reporting Tool ([N]one,[R]ead Only,read/[W]rite): w
Permissions for Log Consolidator([N]one,read/[W]rite): w
Password: test123
Verify Password: test123
User fwadmin-lite added successfully
```

A password must be no more than eight characters in length. If you want to change the password of an existing user, run `fwm -a` again or use `cpconfig/ fwconfig` to make the change. Table 4-1 lists some of the other command-line options for the `fwm` (or `fw m` in Windows NT) command.

Table 4-1 Command-line options for fwm

Flag	Description
`-a foo`	Adds or updates the user name 'foo'
`-wX`	Sets permissions for this user. X can be: w: Read/Write (all permissions) u: User Edit (read-only for all others) r: Read-Only (can view rulebases and objects) m: Monitor Only (cannot use Policy Editor, but can use the other apps) lxxxxxxxx: Specific permissions. This is described in Table 4-2.
`-s abc123`	Sets the user's password to "abc123" (requires –a)
`-r foo`	Removes the user 'foo'
`-p`	Prints a list of administrative (GUI) users
`-p -i`	Prints a list of administrative (GUI) users with each user's specific permissions
`-g rulebase.W`	Imports the file `rulebase.W` into the `rulebases.fws` file, which contains all the rulebases on your management console

You can set specific permissions by using "-wlxxxxxxxx", where xxxxxxxx is an 8-digit hexadecimal number (32-bit number) that indicates the assigned permissions. The bits are numbered from right to left (the first bit on the right is bit 0) and are defined as shown in Table 4-2.[1]

---

1. Check Point provided this information with the caveat that it may change at some point in the future.

Table 4-2   Specific permission bits for the fwm command

Bit	Description
0	Log Viewer Read
1	Log Viewer Read/Write
2	System Status
4	Edit User Database
6	Security Policy Rules Read
7	Security Policy Rules Read/Write
9	Bandwidth Rules Read
10	Bandwidth Rules Read/Write
12	Compression Rules Read
13	Compression Rules Read/Write
15	Redundant Policy Read
16	Redundant Policy Read/Write
18	Objects Write
20	CE (Log Consolidator)
22	Reporting Tool Read
23	Reporting Tool Read/Write

Configuring Which Hosts Can Use Management GUIs

Once you know how to create a specific user for the Management GUIs, you need to tell your management console which IP addresses are allowed to use them. The IPs that are allowed to connect are configured in the file $FWDIR/conf/gui-clients. The file contains a simple list, one IP address, or DNS hostname per line. You cannot specify a range of IPs. Note that the localhost (i.e., the management console) is always allowed to connect regardless of the contents of this file, although a proper username and password must still be entered. With FireWall-1 4.1, if you use the "Enable Fire-Wall-1 Control Connections" property to allow access to your management console, you need to reload your security policy before the new GUI can connect.

Being able to manage your security policy from *any* machine on your internal network may be desirable. Listing all possible IPs your clients may come from may not be. A highly recommended way to get around the limitation that you cannot use the GUI applications from any host is to install an SSH server on the management console and use port forwarding on the SSH client. Port forwarding works by forwarding data from a local port to the remote host or port. On your SSH client, you would configure the port forwarding as follows:

- Local port 258
- Remote hostname is management-console
- Report port is 258

In your GUI, you would connect to localhost (127.0.0.1) instead of the management console's hostname or IP. Your SSH client will forward the communication over the SSH connection (which is, of course, encrypted) to the management console. The SSH daemon on the management console will then send the connection to port 258 on itself. The management console will see the connection coming from localhost, which of course is always allowed.[2]

Now you can effectively manage your FireWall-1 security policy from anywhere with strong encryption, stronger authentication (using an RSA or DSA key), and compression (which SSH provides). This is highly recommended if you must use a slow link to manage your security policy.

An alternative to SSH for people using Windows NT/2000 for a management console is ZeBeDee, which is similar to SSH in that it provides many of the same functions, but the client and the server run under both Windows and UNIX platforms.

Files Modified by the GUIs

The Management GUI directly reads from and writes to the following files on the management console. If any of these files require manual editing, make sure that no one is connected via the GUI. You can do this by killing the fwm process via the command `fw kill fwm`.

- *$FWDIR/conf/objects.C: Your network objects and services*
- *$FWDIR/conf/rulebases.fws*: Your rulebases
- *$FWDIR/conf/fwauth.NDB**: Your user database and encryption keys[3]

The Management GUI also reads from, but does not directly write to:

- *$FWDIR/log/fw.log: Security policy log*
- *$FWDIR/log/fw.alog: Accounting log*

---

2. If you are using an SSH client on UNIX, the command necessary to do this requires you to be logged in as root or to run the SSH binary SUID. UNIX systems do not allow unprivileged users to bind to ports below 1024 (i.e., a privileged port). Windows systems do not have a problem with binding.

3. On UNIX/IPSO platforms, fwauth.NDB is simply one file. On Windows NT, fwauth.NDB contains a number that points to a file named fwauth.NDBx.

- *$FWDIR/log/fw.vlog: Active log*
- *$FWDIR/log/fw.*ptr: Log pointer files*

Security Policy Editor Restrictions

Only one user can be logged in to the Security Policy Editor in a read-write mode at any given time. This is to prevent multiple managers from overwriting each other's changes. This also means that a user with only Users-Edit privileges can prevent an administrator with Read-Write from logging in using read-write mode. When this occurs, you will get the error message shown in Figure 4-2.

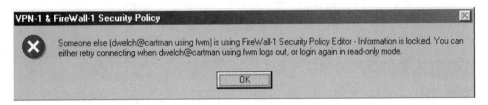

Figure 4-2   Error message from Policy Editor

GUI Demonstration Mode

For those of you who have to demonstrate FireWall-1 and do not have easy access to a management console, there is a demonstration mode built into the Security Policy Editor and the Log Viewer. You can log in with any username and password. The host you log in to is *local. Figure 4-3 shows an example.

This demonstration mode allows you to work with the files installed in the same directory as your GUI. They are demo versions of `objects.C`, `rulebases.fws` and other files. Although not all parts of the GUI will be available in *local mode, it is

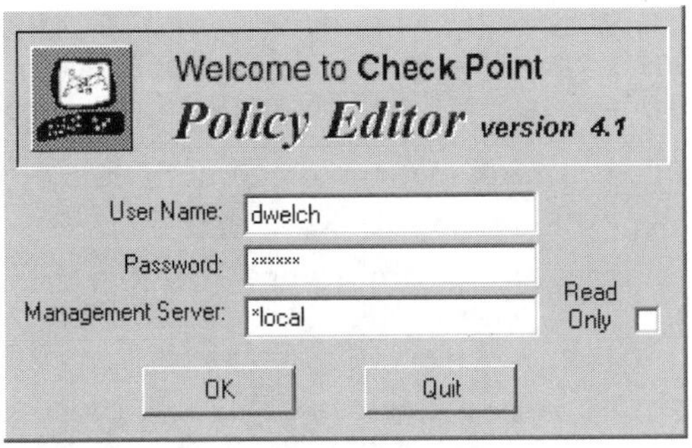

Figure 4-3   Sample logon in *local mode

perfect for demonstrating the GUI to others without having to use it on a live system.[4] It is also possible to edit objects via the GUI or replace the included demo files with your own. The files you need to modify include, but may not be limited to:

- `rules.fws`: Contains all defined rulebases. It is exactly the same format as `$FWDIR/conf/rulebases.fws` on the management console.
- `objects.fws`: Contains all users and services. It is exactly the same format as `$FWDIR/conf/objects.C` on the management console.
- `users.fws`: Contains users and groups for the demo rulebases. Note that this file is of a different format than `$FWDIR/conf/fwauth.NDB`. To get a feel for the format, create some users in *local mode and view the file.
- `lv_recs.fws`: Contains demonstration log entries.

Rulebase Components

A rulebase is a representation of a policy that determines who can do what and when. In the Policy Editor, there are several elements that make up this policy: objects, rules, anti-spoofing, and the policy properties. This section covers the creation and composition of these components.

Objects

You can create several types of objects in FireWall-1. However, I will only focus on three types of objects in this section: network objects, services, and time.

Network Objects

There are several types of network objects. They are designed to represent various parts of your network and objects that you manage with your FireWall-1 management console. You create these objects by selecting Network Objects from the Manage menu or by clicking on this icon:

Workstation

Let's first look at the *workstation* object. This object is meant to define a single workstation on your network. You also use this kind of network object to define the firewall(s) that you will manage, and/or your management console. Figure 4-4 shows the main components of a workstation object. Note that there are other components that make up a workstation object. These components are covered in other sections of the book as they are needed.

---

4.   Many of the screen shots for this book were generated in *local mode.

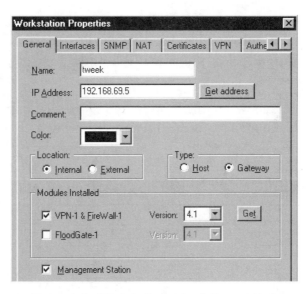

Figure 4-4   Workstation object, General tab

Settings on the General tab include:

Name: Indicates the name you give the object. It should be a name that is different from any other object. Avoid the names "fw" or "fw1" because they have been known to cause problems.

IP Address: Indicates the object's primary IP address. If you are defining a firewall, this IP address should be the external, routable IP address. The Get button allows you to get an IP address if the object name is resolvable via DNS.

Comment: Describes the object in more detail. This is optional.

Color: Specifies the object's color.

Location: Specifies an object as internal if it is within your realm of control (i.e., you can install a policy on it), external if it is not. Internal versus external is somewhat of a misnomer. Generally speaking, this setting is only relevant for objects representing gateways. In FireWall-1 4.1 SP4 and later, this setting is only set-able on objects where the UPN-1 and FireWall-1 Installed box is checked.

Type: Indicates that an object is a gateway if the object has more than one IP address and can route packets. An object is a host if it only has a single IP address and does not route packets.

VPN-1 & FireWall-1: Select this box if the object has FireWall-1 installed on it (i.e., the object will be used to enforce a security policy). Make sure you specify the correct version of FireWall-1.

FloodGate-1: Select this box if the object has FloodGate installed on it (i.e., the object will be used to enforce a bandwidth policy).

Management Station: Select this box if the workstation object is a FireWall-1 management console.

Another important tab within the Workstation Properties, particularly for objects representing firewalls you manage, is the Interfaces tab, which is shown in Figure 4-5.

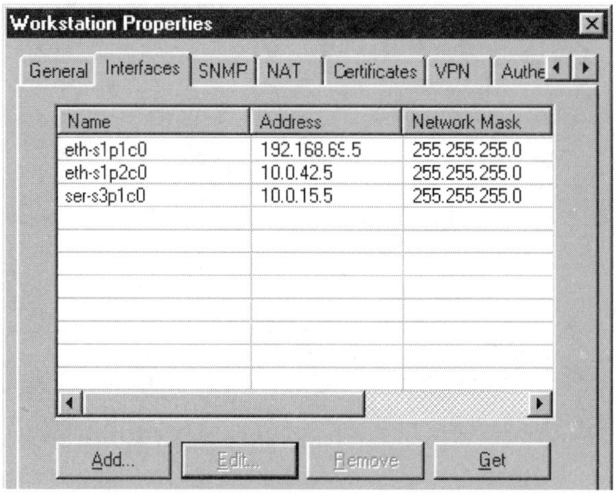

Figure 4-5   Workstation object, Interfaces tab

For an object that is defined with FireWall-1 4.1 installed, the Get button will get the interface information using an authenticated control connection (see Chapter 6). In all other versions of FireWall-1 and for objects that do not have FireWall-1 installed, SNMP is used to get this information. In situations where these methods will not work, you can add the interfaces manually, as shown in Figure 4-6.

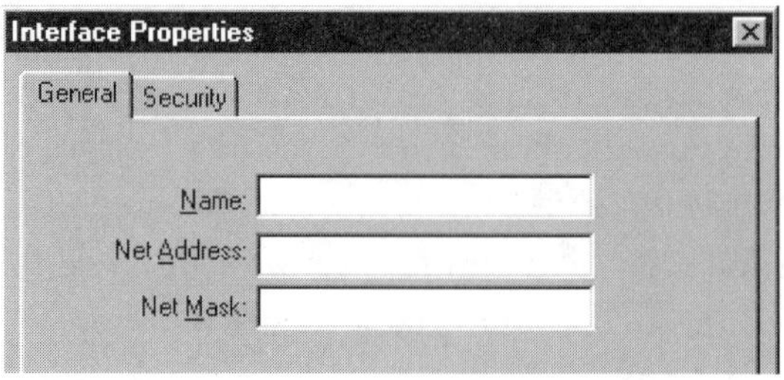

Figure 4-6   Manually adding interfaces

Settings on the Interfaces tab include:

Name: Indicates the physical name of the interface. It should match the name as given in `ifconfig -a` (in UNIX or IPSO) or `ipconfig` (in Windows NT).

Net Address: Indicates the interface's IP address. You must specify the interface's physical IP address. You cannot specify an interface alias.

Net Mask: Indicates the net mask for the interface's IP address.

For internal objects with FireWall-1 installed, the Security tab of this window is used to define anti-spoofing for an interface. I discuss Security tab settings in the "Policy Properties" section later in this chapter.

Network

The network object is used to specify a network or a subnet thereof. The IP address and net mask defines the network as shown in Figure 4-7.

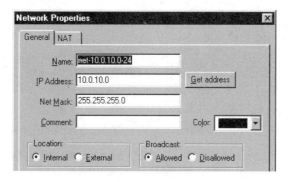

Figure 4-7   Network object

The General tab settings for Network Properties include:

Name: Indicates the name you give the network.

IP Address: Indicates the network's IP address. You should use the first IP address of the network.

Net Mask: Indicates the network's net mask.

Comment: Describes the network in more detail.

Location: Specifies an object as internal if it is within your realm of control (i.e., you can install a policy on it), external if it is not. This setting is purely for your own reference.

Broadcast: Determines whether or not to include the broadcast address of the network in the network definition.

The NAT tab is discussed in Chapter 9.

> NOTE! As of FireWall-1 4.1 SP3, you are not allowed to create an object with a net mask of 255.255.255.255. You must create these kinds of objects as workstation objects.

Domain

The domain object is used to specify a particular DNS domain. FireWall-1 determines if an IP address fits within this domain by performing a reverse DNS lookup on the appropriate IP address (i.e., performs an IP to name translation). This means that the host that enforces the security policy must be able to perform DNS queries. If it cannot do so for whatever reason, that IP address is not considered part of this domain. To specify a particular domain, provide a domain name beginning with a dot. For example, to specify phoneboy.com as a domain name use ".phoneboy.com".

Domain objects are not recommended, because DNS is typically not considered a reliable source of information (i.e., it can easily be spoofed), although I suppose once the Secure DNS extensions are widely deployed, this will be less of an issue. However, domain objects also cause a performance hit for all connections because their IP addresses must be looked up.

Router/Switch

Router/switch types of objects are only used when you want to manage an access control list on a router or use the Check Point FireWall-1 features that can be embedded into certain vendors switches. These features are not widely in use and therefore will not be covered in this book. Unless you plan on using these features, you will not need to create these types of objects.

Integrated Firewall

Until recently, integrated firewall types of objects were also used infrequently. However, with the recent introduction of the SmallOffice products (with hardware manufactured by Nokia[5] and Intrusion.com), these types of objects will likely be used much

---

5. Nokia acquired Ramp Networks, which was making three products that ran Check Point SmallOffice: the Ramp 610i, the SecureRamp 1700, and the SecureRamp 2700. These products are still being developed by Nokia, but they have been renamed the Nokia IP55, IP51, and IP71, respectively.

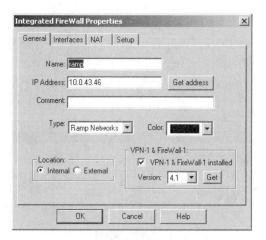

Figure 4-8   Integrated firewall object

more. Not all SmallOffice products will be represented as integrated firewall objects. Figure 4-8 shows what these objects look like.

The General tab settings for Integrated FireWall Properties include:

Name: Indicates the name you give the object. It should be a unique name from any other object. Avoid the names "fw" or "fw1" because they have been known to cause problems.

IP Address: Indicates the object's primary IP address. This IP address should be the external, routable IP address. The Get button allows you to get an IP address if the object name is resolvable via DNS.

Comment: Describes the object in more detail. This is optional.

Type: Indicates the type of integrated firewall this object is. In the preceding example, "Ramp Networks" is what you would use for the Nokia IP51 and IP55 (which were sold under different names before Ramp Networks was acquired by Nokia).

Color: Specifies the object's color.

Location: Specifies an object as internal if it is within your realm of control (i.e., you can install a policy on it), external if it is not.

VPN-1 & FireWall-1 Installed: Select this box if the object has FireWall-1 installed on it (i.e., the object will be used to enforce a security policy). Make sure you specify the correct version of FireWall-1.

Note that the Interfaces tab functions exactly like it does in a workstation object. Other tabs will vary depending on the type of integrated firewall you choose.

Group

Group objects combine multiple objects so you can refer to them as a single entity. For example, if the network objects net-10.0.10.0-24 and net-10.0.11.0-24 represent your internal network, you can group them together and call them internal-net, as shown in Figure 4-9.

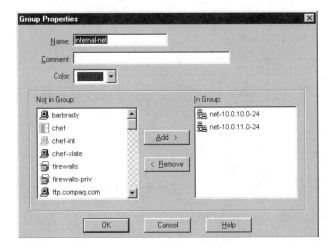

Figure 4-9 Sample group object

Address Range

Address range objects are used to define a range of addresses for the purposes of address translation. They cannot be used for any purposes other than address translation rules. These objects are discussed in Chapter 9.

Services

You can create four types of services: TCP, UDP, RPC, or Other (ICMP is basically a form of Other). Similar to network objects, you can also group these services together. Most services you will need are already predefined in FireWall-1, but there are times when you will need to define your own. Figure 4-10 shows such a definition for SSH.

The General tab settings for TCP Service Properties include:

Name: Indicates the name you give the service. The port number can automatically be filled in with the Get button if the name matches the service's file entry on the management console.

Comment: Describes the service in more detail.

Color: Specifies the object's color.

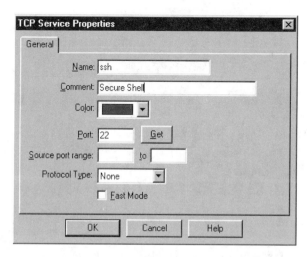

Figure 4-10 Sample TCP service definition

Port: Indicates the port number that corresponds to the service. In this case, it is 22. You can also specify a port range (x-y) as well as ports above or below a certain number (e.g., >1024, <1024).

Source Port Range: Specifies the source's port range. Normally, any source port is allowed. However, if you want to restrict the source port (the port the client uses to connect to the service) to a specific range, you can do that by using this setting.

Protocol Type: Specifies the protocol type. For most services, this is left as None. However, if you are using this service in conjunction with content security, set the protocol type accordingly (see Chapter 8).

Fast Mode: Select this box if you want FireWall-1 to only check the initial SYN packets for this service. ACK packets with this port number are not checked against the state tables. Although this has historically increased the speed at which these packets are passed, not checking against state tables will cause the service to no longer work with certain features of FireWall-1, namely: authentication, NAT, and encryption. It also creates a huge security hole because people can send TCP ACK packets for a specific service through your firewall without the packets being checked, which is actually the subject of at least one denial-of-service attack. In FireWall-1 4.1, Fast Mode only provides a minimal performance gain and will be removed in the next major release of FireWall-1.

For UDP connections, the options on the General tab are the same. Figure 4-11 shows an example of the General tab in UDP Service Properties. The Get button resolves the service port based on the name provided in the Name column.

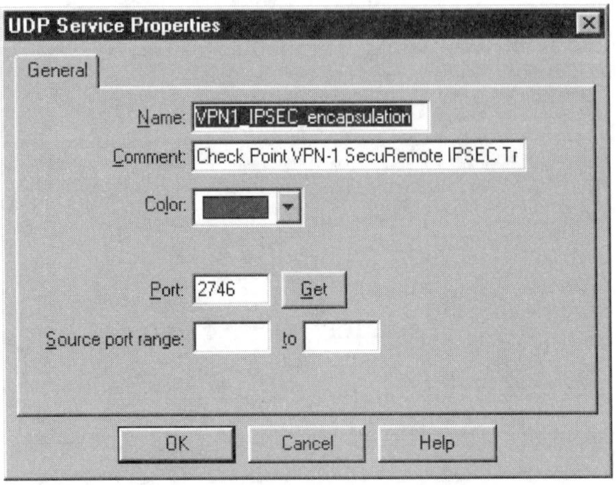

Figure 4-11 Sample UDP service definition

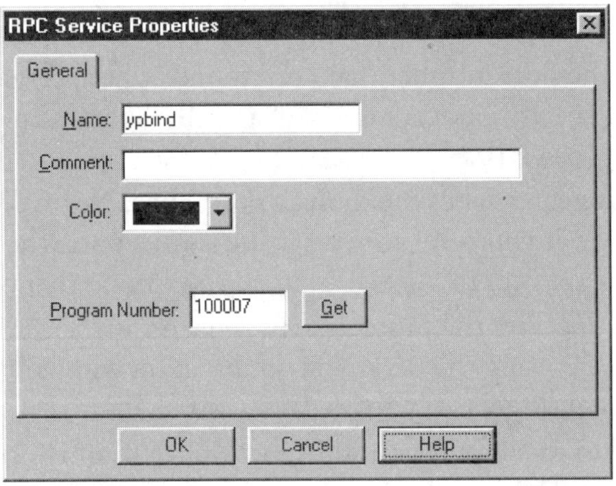

Figure 4-12 Sample RPC service definition

For RPC, you simply define a name and an RPC program number, as shown in Figure 4-12. The Get button acquires the needed information from the RPC file on a UNIX platform.

For services of type Other (or ICMP), you need to write INSPECT code. These kinds of services are discussed in Chapter 13.

Time

Time objects are created to define different time periods of the day. These objects allow certain activities to take place at certain times of the day and/or on certain days, but not others. You create these objects by selecting Time from the Manage menu. Figure 4-13 shows an example.

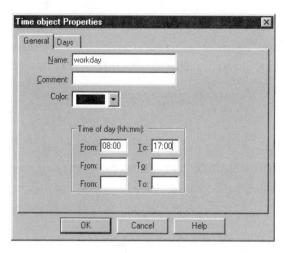

Figure 4-13   Sample time object definition, General tab

The General tab settings for Time Object Properties include:

Name: Indicates the name you give the time period.

Comment: Describes the time period in more detail.

Color: Specifies the object's color.

Time of Day: Specifies up to three different time periods in a 24-hour format. Note that this only controls when the connection can *start*; if the connection continues past these time frames, it will still be allowed.

The Days component can be defined as shown in Figure 4-14.

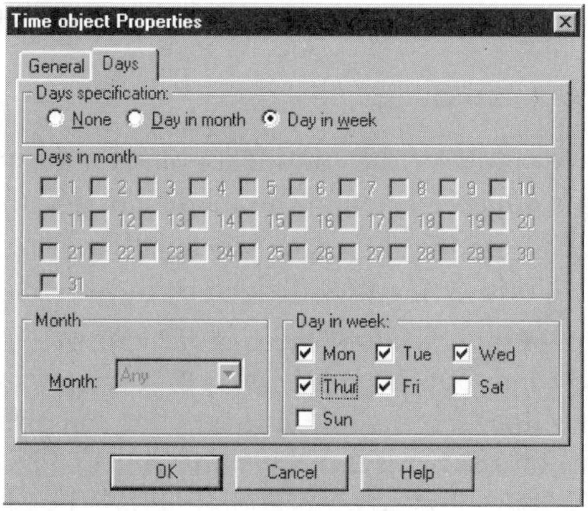

Figure 4-14   Sample time object definition, Days tab

The Days tab settings include:

Days specification: "None" means every day. "Day in month" allows you to specify a specific date or dates in a particular month. "Day in week" allows you to specify particular days of the week.

Days in month: If you selected "Day in month," you can specify particular days in a month.

Month: If you selected "Day in month," you can specify a specific month.

Day in week: If you selected "Day in week," you can specify certain days in a week.

Anti-Spoofing

Anti-spoofing is defined in the workstation object representing your firewall on the Interfaces tab, specifically with the Valid Addresses setting. When you define anti-spoofing, you are making the following assertions:

- Only packets with source IP in Valid Addresses can come into this interface.
- Only packets with destination IP in Valid Addresses can be routed out of this interface.

For example, if valid address is 192.168.182.0/24 and interface is le0:

- Packet with source IP address 192.168.182.4 can come into le0.
- Packet with source IP address 192.168.1.8 cannot come into le0.
- Packet with destination IP address 192.168.182.4 can come into le0.
- Packet with destination IP address 10.0.0.4 cannot come into le0.

Figure 4-15 shows the different options you can choose for the Valid Addresses setting.

The Valid Addresses options include:

Any (the default): All addresses are considered valid on this interface. Note that IP Options checking is still performed in this mode, but no other checking is done.

This Net: This option specifically means "the logical network this interface is on." There is no magic to this setting. It is defined by the interface's IP address and net mask per the configuration screen. All other networks are not considered valid.

No Security Policy: This option means "do not enforce *any* security policy on this interface." Not only does this include anti-spoofing but also your security policy. In the vast majority of cases, this is not recommended. The only place where this setting makes sense is in the synchronization interface in a High Availability configuration (see Chapter 12). Because the only thing that should occur on this

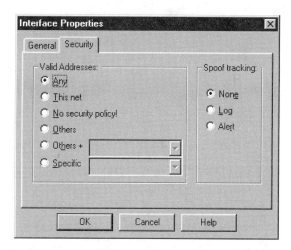

Figure 4-15   Valid Addresses setting

interface is state synchronization traffic, it should be relatively safe to disable the security policy on this interface.

Others: This option is typically used on your interface facing your Internet connection. All IP addresses *not* specified on other interfaces' Valid Addresses settings are valid on this interface.

Others +: This option allows you to specify IP addresses that appear on both your internal and external interfaces. Usually the all-ones or all-zeros broadcast addresses fall into this category, but sometimes this is also needed with Network Address Translation (NAT).

Specific: This option refers to a defined group of network objects (networks, hosts) that make up the Valid Addresses for this interface. This is typically used where there are multiple networks reachable from this interface and/or when NAT is used. If a host reachable from this interface has a "translated" IP address, you need to include the translated IP address in this interface's Valid Addresses setting.

Spoof tracking can be set to None (no logging), Log, or Alert. If you enable antispoofing, it is *highly* recommended that you enable logging of this property. All antispoofing drops will log as Rule 0 (see Chapter 5). If you want to log IP Options drops, go to the Log and Alert tab of the Rulebase Properties and enable IP Options Drop logging (see the next section).

Policy Properties

The Properties screens control various parts of the rulebase. It is important to understand what these properties are and how they affect your rulebase. All implied rules are enforced eitherbound (both inbound and outbound) and can be applied in the following ways:

- *First:* The property is applied before any rules listed in the rulebase.
- *Before-Last:* The property is applied before the last rule listed in the rulebase.
- *Last:* The property is applied *after* the last rule listed in the rulebase.

Let's look at two tabs under Properties that affect the rulebase: Security Policy and Services. Figure 4-16 shows the Log and Alert tab, so you can enable IP Options Drop logging.

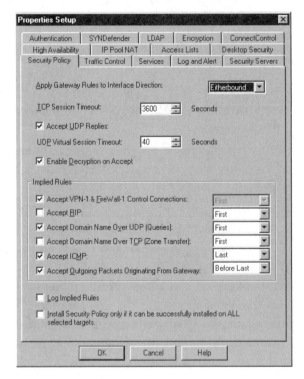

Figure 4-16   Policy Properties, Security Policy tab

The options on the Security Policy tab include:

Apply Gateway Rules to Interface Direction: Rules can be applied to a specific firewall (which assumes eitherbound inspection), "gateways" (i.e., all workstation objects defined as an internal gateway with FireWall-1 installed), or "integrated firewalls." When "gateways" or "integrated firewalls" are specified, this property controls how these rules are enforced. Eitherbound (the default in FireWall-1 4.1) enforces the rule as the packet enters the firewall and as the packets leave the firewall. Inbound enforces the rule only as the packet enters the gateway, which for most practical purposes will be just as secure as eitherbound and slightly faster. Outbound enforces the rule as the packet leaves the gateway. This last setting is generally not recommended.

Accept UDP Replies: When a UDP packet with source port X and destination port Y is accepted by the security policy, and this property is selected (it is by default), it is placed into the state tables. Reply packets (i.e., those with source port Y and destination port X) are then permitted. FireWall-1 assumes a UDP connection is over when there is no traffic between the two hosts on these ports after a period of time (default 40 seconds). This is how Check Point adds virtual state to UDP, as UDP itself implies no such state.

Enable Decryption on Accept: This option decrypts encrypted packets that are received by FireWall-1 that would be accepted by an accept rule (versus an encrypt rule). This property will cause problems if a firewall that is not an endpoint to a site-to-site or client-to-site VPN sees encrypted packets. This property should be disabled.

Accept VPN-1 & FireWall-1 Control Connections: This option allows various FireWall-1 modules to communicate via FireWall-1 communication ports. Prior to version 4.1, it allowed any host to access FireWall-1 on TCP ports 256, 257, and 258. In version 4.1, it only allows these connections from hosts defined in $FWDIR/conf/masters and $FWDIR/conf/gui-clients as appropriate. This also allows your firewall to be accessible on TCP port 256 and/or TCP port 264 from anywhere.

Accept RIP: If you are running Routing Information Protocol (RIP) on your firewall and you require the ability to communicate with other routers via RIP, this property can be selected to permit the necessary traffic, although you can also create explicit rules. Most people who run dynamic routing protocols run Open Shortest Path First (OSPF), so this property can generally be safely disabled in the vast majority of cases.

Accept Domain Name Over UDP (Queries): This option permits all UDP port 53 traffic from anywhere to anywhere. This is actually a very dangerous setting and should be disabled because non-DNS traffic (such as Back Orifice) could easily use UDP port 53. See FAQ 4.7 later in this chapter for information on how to enable DNS verification, which makes this property far less dangerous.

Accept Domain Name Over TCP (Zone Transfer): This option is only necessary if your primary and secondary DNS servers are separated by your firewalls. As with the preceding option, this is a dangerous default that should be disabled unless DNS verification is enabled.

Accept ICMP: Generally, this property can be disabled, although you need to leave it enabled to take advantage of Check Point's Stateful Inspection for ICMP in FireWall-1 4.0 and later. Many people have reported problems with how this property works. Chapter 13 talks about how accepting ICMP can be done better with custom INSPECT code.

Accept Outgoing Packets Originating from Gateway: This property refers to packets leaving the gateway, whether they originate from the firewall or they are routed by the firewall. This property is required when Apply Gateway Rules to Interface Direction is Inbound, or packets will never leave the gateway. If Apply Gateway Rules to Interface Direction is set to Eitherbound or Outbound, this property can be disabled.

Log Implied Rules: A long-overdue addition to FireWall-1 4.1 is the ability to log everything accepted by this property's screen. Selecting this checkbox allows for logging of implied rules. Anything that gets logged will show up as Rule 0.

Install Security Policy only if it can be successfully installed on ALL selected targets: When a policy is installed, you are able to choose which targets will have the policy installed on it. This property, when enabled, only allows the policy to actually be installed if all selected targets are accessible and FireWall-1 is able to upload the policy to all these targets.

The other Properties screen that affects the policy is the Services tab, which is shown in Figure 4-17.

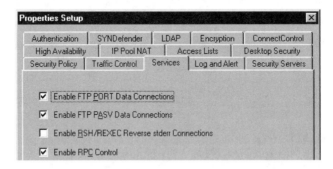

Figure 4-17   Policy Properties, Services tab

The options on the Services tab include:

Enable FTP PORT Data Connections: In order for FTP to work correctly from most command-line clients, FTP PORT commands must be seen by FireWall-1 so it knows which ports to use. Generally, this option needs to be enabled, but can be disabled if you want to force all clients to use PASV mode.

Enable FTP PASV Data Connections: In order for FTP to work from most proxy servers, Web browsers, or graphical FTP clients, PASV mode must be supported by the firewall. FireWall-1 must know to look for PASV commands to allow the connection. This option is generally enabled by default.

Enable RSH/REXEC Reverse stderr Connections: To use RSH or REXEC through the firewall, this property must be enabled for the connection to work correctly. Generally, RSH is considered insecure, so this property is disabled by default.

Enable RPC Control: If you are going to allow UNIX RPC-based services through the firewall, this property must be enabled so that FireWall-1 can intercept the portmapper connection to open the correct ports. Note that Windows NT-based RPC services are handled by a different service enabled in the rulebase.

To enable IP Options Drop logging (recommended), go to the Log and Alert tab, which is shown in Figure 4-18.

Set the IP Options Drop to Log (or Alert) if you want IP Options logging to occur. Other options on this screen are discussed in Chapter 5.

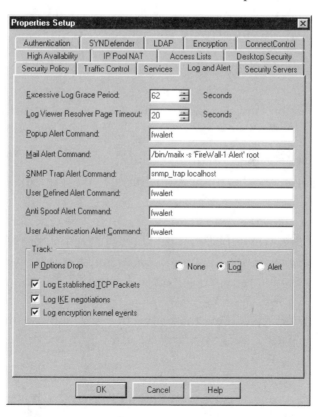

Figure 4-18   Policy Properties, Log and Alert tab

Rules

In order to determine who can do what, you must create rules. The rules should be created and listed in the order you want them enforced. In the following sections, I discuss the actual order that rules are applied in, but for the sake of discussion at this point, let's assume they will be enforced in the order shown in the rulebase.

Each rule has several elements. In many cases in this book, I will not show all the elements, as they are not always relevant. However, in this section, I will discuss all of them.

Source and Destination

In the source and destination part of the rule, you input the hosts that will be allowed to originate a connection or be an allowed destination for a connection. Multiple objects can be listed in this part of the rule. If there are multiple sources or destinations listed in a rule, they are treated as an *or*, meaning that any host that matches will be matched.

Service

In the service part of the rule, you input the services that are allowed between the source(s) and destination(s) listed in the rule. If there are multiple services listed, they are treated as an *or*, meaning that any service listed in the rule will match.

Action

If the source, destination, and services match, an action is applied. The actions are as follows:

- *Accept:* Allow the connection through the firewall.
- *Drop:* Do not allow the connection through the firewall, no notification to sender.
- *Reject:* Do not allow the connection through the firewall; notify the sender with a TCP RST or an ICMP Destination Unreachable as appropriate.
- *User/Client/Session Auth:* Allow the connection through the firewall provided the user successfully authenticates. See Chapter 7 for more details on these actions.
- *Encrypt/Client Encrypt:* Allow the connection through the firewall and encrypt or decrypt the packet. See Chapters 10 and 11 for more details on these actions.

Track

After an action is taken on the packet, you need to determine how to log it. There are several options you can choose; more details about these options appear in Chapter 5.

- *None (blank):* Do not log.
- *Short:* Limited information about the packet is written to the log.
- *Long:* All available information about the packet is written to the log.
- *Account:* Usually used with an `accept`. The number of bytes and length of the connection are logged to the accounting log file as well as a normal long log entry, which is written to the normal log. Do not use this option lightly, because it increases the amount of CPU time FireWall-1 uses to log the information.
- *Alert/Mail Alert/SNMP Trap/User Defined:* Long log and execute an action to notify the administrator.

Install On

In the install-on part of the rule, you indicate which gateway(s) will be responsible for enforcing this rule. These can be gateways (the default), integrated firewalls, a specific target (which implies eitherbound), or Src or Dst. Src means install the rule on all gateways and enforce only in the outbound direction. Dst means install the rule on all gateways and enforce only in the inbound direction.

Time

In the time part of the rule, you select a time object that represents when this rule will apply. If the time/date does not match, the rule does not apply.

Comment

The comment part of the rule contains a description of the rule. In some versions of FireWall-1, a carriage return in the comment can cause problems, so try to avoid using carriage returns. Also, it is unwise to use characters in comments that are not typically ASCII characters (like umlauts) because they can sometimes cause a policy installation to fail.

Sample Rules

Figure 4-19 shows you a sample rule that is fairly common in most installations.

Source	Destination	Service	Action	Track	Install On	Time	Comment
internal-net	internal-net	http ssh https	accept		Gateways	Any	Allow internal users access to the Internet.

Figure 4-19   Sample Rule #1

This rule permits the internal network to use HTTP, HTTPS, and SSH to any host not on the internal network.[6] You might see a rule like the one in Figure 4-20 on a Nokia Security Platform.

Source	Destination	Service	Action	Track	Install On	Time	Comment
firewalls net-10.0.10.0-24 chief	vrrp.mcast.net ospf.mcast.net ospf-dr.mcast.net firewalls	ospf vrrp	accept		Gateways	Any	Used to permit OSPF and VRRP between the firewalls.

Figure 4-20   Sample Rule #2

This rule permits OSPF and VRRP packets from the hosts in the firewalls group, all hosts described in net-10.0.10.0-24 and the gateway chief to the firewalls group, and the special addresses vrrp.mcast.net, ospf.mcast.net, and ospf-dr. mcast.net. This rule will be enforced on all gateways, and packets that match this rule will not be logged. It is a common rule found on a pair of Nokia firewalls running VRRP and OSPF.

Another rule you will commonly see is shown in Figure 4-21.

Source	Destination	Service	Action	Track	Install On	Time	Comment
Any	Any	Any	drop	Long	Gateways	Any	Drop all other traffic

Figure 4-21   Sample Rule #3

This rule drops all packets and logs the packets. It shows up as the last rule in your rulebase.

Order of Operations

Established connections are allowed provided they are listed in the state tables and are accepted and address translated as necessary. For new connections, the order of operation for FireWall-1 (and surrounding pieces) is:

1. Inbound anti-spoof check (verifies that the source IP is included in the interface's Valid Addresses setting)
2. Inbound check against the rulebase (includes properties)
3. Routing by the OS

---

6. You might wonder why I did not choose *any* in the destination field. Typically, you do not need the firewall to reach the internal network. *Any*, although a setting even I use in a rulebase from time to time, is considered insecure. For more details about this setting, consult the Black Hat 2000 Security briefing on FireWall-1, which can be found at www.dataprotect.com/bh2000/. There is also a mirror of this document at www.phoneboy.com/docs/bh2000/.

4. Outbound anti-spoof check (verifies that the destination IP is included in the interface's Valid Addresses setting)

5. Outbound check against the rulebase (includes properties)

6. NAT

The rulebase is applied in the directions specified by the Apply Gateway Rules to Interface Direction property, or specified rules may be installed on Src (outbound), Dst (inbound), or on a specific target (eitherbound). Once a packet matches a rule, it performs the action listed in the Action field and no further rulebase processing occurs on that packet. For authenticated connections not going through Security Servers, the rules and properties are processed in this order:

1. Rulebase Properties listed as *First*. Matches are accepted and not logged.

2. Rules 1 through n-1 (assuming n rules) are processed and logged according to their individual settings.

3. Rulebase Properties listed as *Before Last*. Matches are accepted and not logged.

4. Rule n is processed and logged according to its setting.

5. Rulebase Properties listed as *Last*. Matches are accepted and not logged.

6. Implicit Drop rule is matched (no logging occurs).

Figure 4-22 shows a diagram of the preceding sequence, which helps demonstrate what happens during this process.

Various versions of the FireWall-1 documentation state that the rules are examined in the sequence they are presented in the rulebase. This is generally correct, but you must also take into consideration what is permitted by the Properties screens. The Properties rules will be enforced appropriately with respect to your rulebase. This means the Properties rules marked *First* will be applied before your rulebase, *Before Last* will be applied between rules n-1 and n, and *Last* will be applied after your last rule.

There is one case where FireWall-1 does not process the rules in order but instead uses the rule that is most permissive: when authentication for HTTP, FTP, Telnet, and rlogin is used and such a rule is matched in the rulebase. If a user authentication rule matches the packet (i.e., the source, destination, and service match), then before authentication occurs, all rules in the rulebase are evaluated. The least restrictive rule will be used. An example of this is shown in Chapter 7.

So what is a good rule of thumb when ordering the rules in your rulebases? The following list shows how I typically order my rulebase based on action types:

1. Client Encrypt Rules

2. FireWall to FireWall Encryption rules

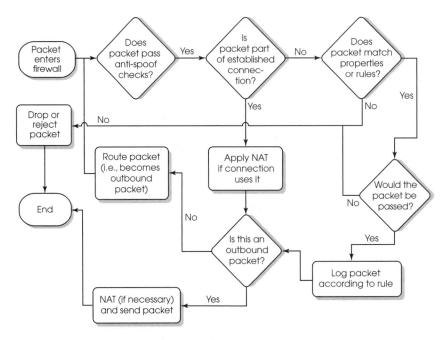

Figure 4-22   Flowchart of packet evaluation

3. Incoming (from Internet) Accept rules
4. Outgoing (to Internet) Accept rules
5. Client Authentication rules
6. Session Authentication rules
7. User Authentication rules
8. Clean-up rule (drop all)

Note that any rules that will be used heavily should be moved as close to the top of the rulebase as possible because it will improve performance, particularly if there are more than 30 rules or so.

Making Your First Rulebase

Now that the various components have been discussed, I will talk about making a rulebase. The rulebase is what determines who can do what, where, and when. In order to make a rulebase, you need to create and configure the various components that make up the rulebase. The order of business should be:

1. Get a map of the network(s) the firewall is designed to protect. It does not need to be a totally detailed map, but it needs to cover the major points of interest: physical and logical network segments being protected, any special hosts (exter-

nally accessible hosts or any hosts that require special access or restrictions), and all routers one hop away from the firewall.

2. Create network objects for each network segment and special hosts. Do not create the firewall at this step.

3. Create groups that make up all the networks on each leg of the firewall. This is for anti-spoofing.

4. Create the firewall workstation object(s) and configure anti-spoofing.

5. Adjust rulebase properties as appropriate.

6. Install the security policy.

You might think you should create the firewall workstation object first. However, the reason you create it *last* is so you can define anti-spoofing at the same time you create the firewall workstation object.

Knowing Your Network

Knowing what you are protecting is half the battle. If you do not have a network map, the process of generating one should give you an idea of how the various parts of your network talk to one another. You need to find out what network segments (physical and logical) are present, how they talk to one another, what routers are present, and so on. Although there are programs that claim to be able to automatically "map" a network for you, the best approach is to sit down and just figure it out. In some situations, this is actually fairly easy because there are only a couple of network segments. However, in large networks, figuring out the entire network may be too large a task for a single person to do. In this case, delegate responsibility to people who are in the best position to know how their part of the network is configured.

Regardless of how you collect all the information, generate a network map of some kind. Although it is not required, having a visual representation of your network is extremely helpful in crafting policy. To guide you through the rest of the steps, the network pictured in Figure 4-23 will be used. This network has two segments: an internal segment with PCs and workstations, and a DMZ with an e-mail and www server.

 NOTE! In the sample network diagrams throughout this book, I will be using the RFC-1918 address space. I am tracking the 192.168.0.0/16 address space as routable, though it normally is not.

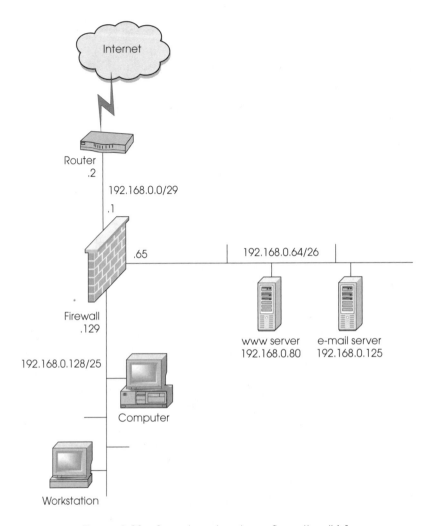

Figure 4-23   Sample network configuration #4-1

Defining Objects

There are seven network objects that need to be created:

- An object of type network for 192.168.0.128/25, called net-192.168.0.128-25
- An object of type network for 192.168.0.64/26, called net-192.168.0.64-26
- A group object called net-internal, which contains net-192.168.0.128-25
- A group object called net-dmz, which contains net-192.168.0.64-26
- A workstation object for the www server, called www-server
- A workstation object for the e-mail server, called email-server
- A workstation object for the firewall/management console itself, called tweek

Unless you are allowing access to or from hosts outside of the dmz or the internal segment, it is not necessary to define anything in addition to these objects. Figures 4-24 through 4-27 show how the net-192.168.0.64-26, the net-dmz, the email-server, and the firewall are defined.

The last object is the most important to discuss, especially with regard to how it is created. The other objects are fairly self-explanatory and will not be explained in detail.

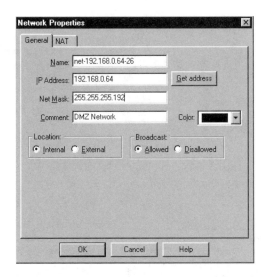

Figure 4-24   Definition for net-192.168.0.64-26

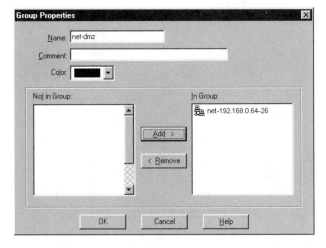

Figure 4-25   Definition for net-dmz

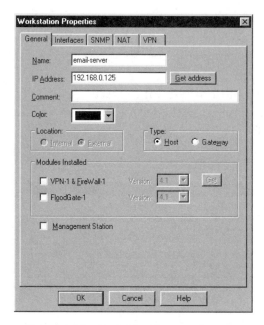

Figure 4-26 Definition for email-server

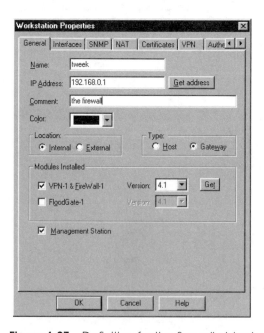

Figure 4-27 Definition for the firewall object

The name should match the hostname of the box. The name should not be a reserved word, a defined service name, or contain an illegal character. See the "Frequently Asked Questions" section later in this chapter for more details. The IP address listed should be the external, routable IP address of the firewall. The name of the object should be resolvable to this IP address via the local hosts file. The licensed IP address of the firewall should also be the same as the IP address. The location of the object should be "Internal," the type of object should be "Gateway," and the "VPN-1 & FireWall-1" check box should be selected. A workstation object defined in the described manner is referred to as an "Internal Gateway with FireWall-1 installed." There *always* needs to be at least one workstation object defined in this manner. If the management module is also on the same platform, select the Management Station check box.

Defining the Rules

In Chapter 2, I discussed defining a sitewide security policy. If you have a policy document, generating the rules for your security policy in FireWall-1 should be relatively straightforward. If you do not have such a document, it might not be a bad time to generate one. One way to create this document is to sit down with some department heads in a conference room with the network drawn on the whiteboard and define some rules. When I used to install FireWall-1 at customer sites, part of my installation process would be to do exactly that: sketch the network on a whiteboard and make a list of requirements of who needs to do what, where, and when. The result of this process should be a list of simple-to-understand statements that can easily be turned into rules in FireWall-1.

Using the sample network shown in Figure 4-23 and some arbitrary business rules, the following set of statements can be generated. The business rules will obviously be different for each network.

1. Everyone can access the e-mail server via SMTP. Access to this service will not be logged on the firewall.
2. Everyone can access the www server via HTTP. Access to this service will not be logged on the firewall.
3. Hosts on the internal network (192.168.0.128/25) can access the SMTP server via POP3. Access to this service will be logged short.
4. Hosts on the internal network can access the HTTP server via SSH. Access to this service will be logged short.
5. Hosts on the internal network can access the Internet via HTTP, HTTPS, and FTP. Access to these services will be logged long.
6. Except for the preceding rules, all other traffic should be dropped. All dropped packets will be logged long.

These business rules translate to the rules in the rulebase pictured in Figure 4-28.

No.	Source	Destination	Service	Action	Track	Install On
1	Any	email-server	smtp	accept		Gateways
2	Any	www-server	http	accept		Gateways
3	net-internal	email-server	pop-3	accept	Short	Gateways
4	net-internal	www-server	ssh	accept	Short	Gateways
5	net-internal	net-dmz	http https ftp	accept	Long	Gateways
6	Any	Any	Any	drop	Long	Gateways

Figure 4-28   Sample rulebase

Tweaking the Policy Properties

The following list contains some guidelines for setting the various Properties settings as well as rules to use in place of these Policy Property settings. In FireWall-1 4.1, you can log these properties by selecting the "Log Implied Rules" check box, which in some cases eliminates the need to add explicit rules.

Apply Gateway Rules to Interface Direction: Eitherbound or Inbound are generally reasonable choices.

Accept UDP Replies: Unless you do not want to allow UDP through the firewall, it is recommended you leave this setting enabled. You can accomplish this task with special services or INSPECT script, but it is generally more secure (and easier) to let the property handle it.

Enable Decryption on Accept: This property should be disabled in most cases.

Accept FireWall-1 Control Connections: Until you have successfully installed a security policy, it is recommended that this setting be enabled. In FireWall-1 4.1, leaving this enabled is relatively safe. In earlier versions of FireWall-1, it is generally not safe to leave this property enabled, and specific rules would need to be applied. Figure 4-29 shows the rules that you would need to create.

The last service, fw1_rdp, needs to be created as shown in Figure 4-30 (the standard predefined RDP service will not work).

Accept RIP: Unless you are running RIP on your firewall, this property can be safely disabled. To allow this via a rule, you must create the rule shown in Figure 4-31.

Source	Destination	Service	Action	Track	Install On	Time	Comment
checkpoint-modules	checkpoint-modules	FW1 FW1_log	accept		firewalls	Any	Allow firewalls and management consoles to communicate with one another.
gui-clients	management-console	FW1_mgmt	accept		Gateways	Any	Allows GUI Clients to connect to the management console.
Any	management-console	FW1	accept		Gateways	Any	Allows SecuRemote clients to download topology from a FireWall-1 4.0 Management Module.
Any	management-console firewalls	FW1_topo	accept		Gateways	Any	Allows Secure Client 4.1 clients to download topology from a FireWall-1 4.1 Management or FireWall Module.
Any	firewalls	FW1_rdp	accept		Gateways	Any	This is necessary to permit FWZ encryption to work.

Figure 4-29   Rule to accept FireWall-1 control connections

User Defined Service Properties

General

Name: FW1_rdp

Comment:

Color: ▉ ▼

Match: udp, dport=259

Pre-Match:

Prologue: accept_fw1_rdp;

OK   Cancel   Help

Figure 4-30   Service definition for fw1_rdp

Source	Destination	Service	Action	Track	Install On	Time	Comment
firewalls	rip-devices rip-broadcast-addresses	rip rip-response	accept		firewalls	Any	Permits RIP traffic between all firewalls, modules, routers, and broadcast addresses which RIP packets will appear.
rip-devices	firewalls rip-broadcast-addresses	rip rip-response	accept		Gateways	Any	Permits RIP traffic from routers to firewalls and broadcast addresses.

Figure 4-31   Rule to accept RIP

Accept Domain Name Over UDP (Queries): In FireWall-1 4.1 SP2 and later, you can enable verification of DNS queries as shown in FAQ 4.7 later in this chapter. On previous versions of FireWall-1 or if you do not want to enable the DNS verification feature, you should instead use the rule shown in Figure 4-32.

Accept Domain Name Over TCP (Zone Transfer): This property is only necessary if your primary and secondary DNS servers are separated by your firewalls. If you cannot or do not want to enable DNS verification as in the previous property, use the rule shown in Figure 4-33.

Source	Destination	Service	Action	Track	Install On	Time	Comment
🖥 dns-clients	🖥 dns-servers	📶 domain-udp	🔨 accept		GW Gateways	⊕ Any	Permits DNS queries from specified clients to specified servers.

Figure 4-32 Rule to allow DNS over UDP

Source	Destination	Service	Action	Track	Install On	Time	Comment
🖥 dns-servers	🖥 dns-servers	📶 domain-tcp	🔨 accept		GW Gateways	⊕ Any	Permits zone transfers between the various DNS servers.

Figure 4-33 Rule to allow DNS over TCP

Accept ICMP: To take advantage of Stateful Inspection for ICMP built into Fire-Wall-1 4.1 and later, enable this property and set it to Before Last. If you enable this property, be sure to add rules in your rulebase to drop ICMP from undesirable sources before your last rule. If you want to use the Stateful Inspection for ICMP documented in Chapter 13, you need to disable this property. To allow pings and traceroute through the firewall, you need the rules shown in Figure 4-34.

Source	Destination	Service	Action	Track	Install On	Time	Comment
🖥 net-internal	⊕ Any	📶 echo-request 📶 traceroute	🔨 accept		GW Gateways	⊕ Any	Allow outbound ping and traceroute requests.
⊕ Any	🖥 net-internal	📶 echo-reply 📶 dest-unreach 📶 time-exceeded	🔨 accept		GW Gateways	⊕ Any	Allow replies to ping and traceroute requests. Without stateful inspection, this rule will allow unsolicited echo-reply, et. al. as well.

Figure 4-34 Rule to allow ICMP

Accept Outgoing Packets: This property is required when Apply Gateway Rules to Interface Direction is Inbound or else packets will never leave the gateway. If you set Apply Gateway Rules to Interface Direction to Eitherbound, you can disable this property.

Rules That Should Be in Every Rulebase

There are some rules that are just a good idea to include in your rulebase regardless of what your security policy states. These rules are common in many installations, and there are good reasons for them.

The first rule that should be part of your rulebase is the last rule in your rulebase: the "any any any drop" rule (see Figure 4-21). Even if this rule is not specified, it is always *implied*. However, you should add a rule explicitly with logging so you know about all unauthorized traffic. Another good rule is a rule denying all traffic to the firewalls, what many refer to as a stealth rule, which is shown in Figure 4-35.

Source	Destination	Service	Action	Track	Install On	Time	Comment
Any	firewalls	Any	drop	Long	Gateways	Any	Drop traffic destined for the firewall

Figure 4-35   Stealth rule

It may seem strange to explicitly drop traffic to your firewall if your last rule is "deny all" anyway. However, this separates that traffic so you can more easily see what traffic is being directed at your firewall. You can also perform a different tracking option, such as an alert. Normally, this rule goes at or near the top of your rulebase. However, it should appear *after* any rule that permits traffic directly to the firewall. An example of such a rule is shown in Figure 4-36. This rule allows VRRP to the firewall, which is relevant only to Nokia platforms.

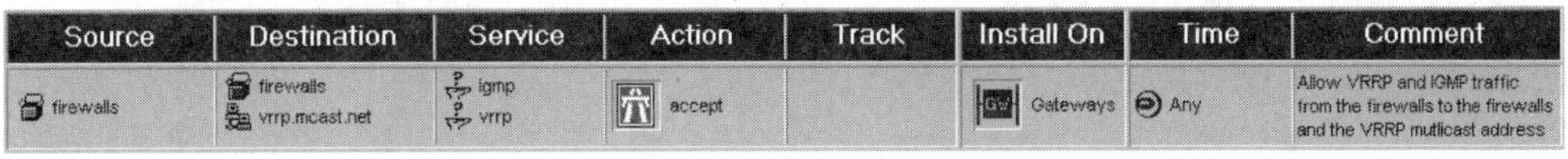

Source	Destination	Service	Action	Track	Install On	Time	Comment
firewalls	firewalls vrrp.mcast.net	igmp vrrp	accept		Gateways	Any	Allow VRRP and IGMP traffic from the firewalls to the firewalls and the VRRP multicast address

Figure 4-36   Rule to allow VRRP to the firewall

The VRRP and IGMP services are defined as services of type Other as shown in Figures 4-37 and 4-38.

One rule I typically like to add to rulebases is a rule that rejects ident packets, as shown in Figure 4-39. Ident is used by some services to identify the remote end of the connection, although it is relatively easy to spoof. Internet Relay Chat (IRC) and SMTP are the most-common services that use ident. Most SMTP servers can live without ident information, whereas most IRC servers cannot. If you simply drop

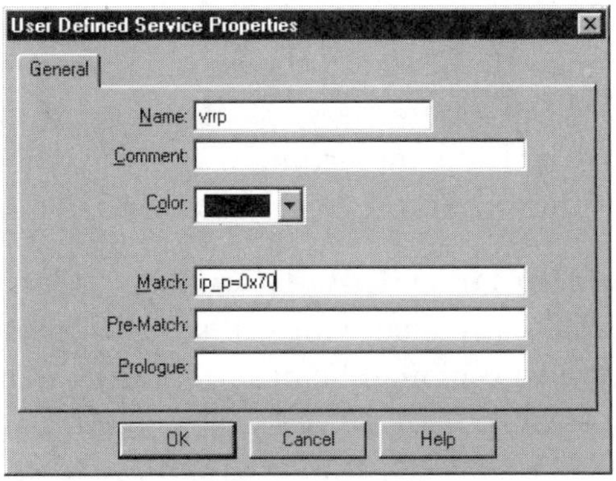

Figure 4-37   VRRP Service definition

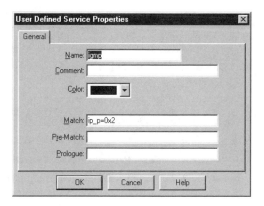

Figure 4-38   IGMP Service definition

Figure 4-39   Rule to reject ident service

incoming ident packets, these services will appear to hang until the attempted ident connection times out. By rejecting the packets instead of dropping them, you can avoid this delay.

Installing the Policy

Once you have created a good policy, you need to install it. You do this by selecting Install from the Policy menu or by clicking this button in the GUI: ![button]. A series of dialog boxes are then displayed informing you about various aspects of your security policy that might need correcting. In addition, you will see a screen where you can select which gateways to install the policy on. If the installation is done correctly, you should see something similar to the screen shown in Figure 4-40.

If an error or problem is encountered, you might receive one of the following error messages. Note that this list does not contain every possible problem you might encounter, but it does contain the most common errors.

No machines eligible for Policy Installation!: If you forgot to define an Internal Gateway with FireWall-1 installed, you will see this message. Make sure at least one object is defined in this manner before attempting to install a policy.

Rule x hides/conflicts with Rule y for Services z: This message means that Rule x is constructed in such a way that Rule y would *never* apply. Consider the example shown in Figure 4-41.

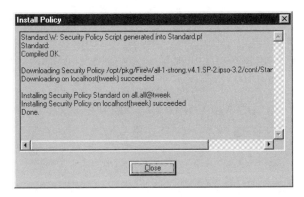

Figure 4-40   Result of policy installation

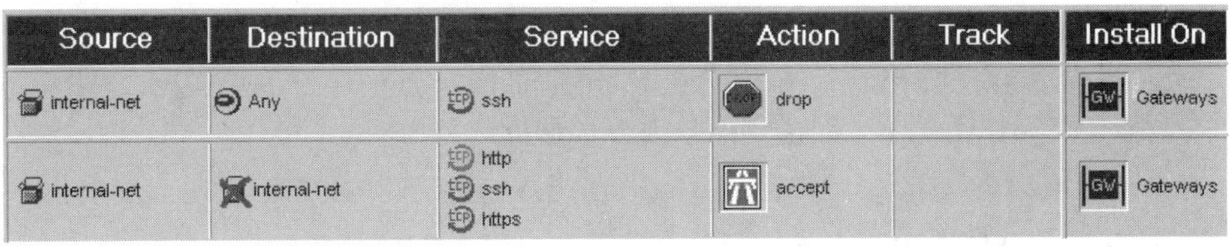

Source	Destination	Service	Action	Track	Install On
internal-net	Any	ssh	drop		Gateways
internal-net	internal-net	http ssh https	accept		Gateways

Figure 4-41   Rulebase with conflicts

The first rule would deny the internal network access via HTTP before the second rule could allow it. Therefore, the second rule could never allow HTTP from the internal network.

Authentication for command load failed: This error message displays when your management module and firewall module are on separate platforms, and you have not established an authenticated control connection between them. See Chapter 6 for more details.

External interface not set by this loading: This error occurs on node-limited licenses when you have not defined your external interface in $FWDIR/conf/external.if. Use ifconfig (UNIX/IPSO) or ipconfig /all (Windows NT) to determine the name of your *physical* external interface and add it to this file.

Connection timed out or refused: A "connection timed out" message occurs if the remote firewall module is disconnected from the network or has a policy loaded on it that prevents the management module from communicating with it. Connection refused may occur for a similar reason, but also occurs when the "fwd" process is no longer active. On a UNIX/IPSO platform, type **fw kill fwd; fwd**. On a Windows NT platform, restart the FireWall-1 service in the Windows NT Services Manager.

Frequently Asked Questions

This section contains some questions that are frequently asked in terms of general policy configuration. Specific features have their own section. The FAQ are numbered so they can be referred to in the text.

4.1: Which Files Make up My Security Policy?

The user-defined part of the security policy lives in $FWDIR/conf. Specifically, these files include:

- *objects.C:* All network objects, services, and rulebase properties are stored in this file.
- *fwauth.NDB*:* This is the user database file, which also stores the encryption keys used for the VPN features of FireWall-1.
- *rulebases.fws:* This file contains all policies that are generated.
- **.W:* This file contains individual policy files that get converted to .pf files, which are installed on your firewall module.
- **.pf:* This file contains "compiled" policy files. These files are not really compiled in the conventional sense, but they are turned into INSPECT code. You can edit this file directly if you would like; any changes you make to this file will be overwritten any time you reload this policy from the GUI.

Other files also make up your security policy in $FWDIR/lib/*.def. You can edit these files, but normally you do not edit these files unless instructed to do so by your support provider (or as directed in this book).

4.2: How Do I Edit `objects.C` and `rulebases.fws` Manually?

To modify objects.C and rulebases.fws manually (which several sections of this book tell you to do to enable or disable features), kill the "fwm" process on your management console using the command **fw kill fwm**, which terminates any GUIs that may be connected. Once you edit these files, make sure you delete objects.C.bak and objects.C.sav. If these files have a more recent timestamp, fwm will use these files instead of your edited objects.C. Check Point recommends executing **fwstop** on the management console, making the changes, and then typing **fwstart** to restart the software.

All modifications to these files, unless otherwise specified, will always occur on the management console only, not the firewall modules. Once you have made changes to these files, you need to reinstall the security policy for the changes to take effect on the firewall modules.

4.3: Does Any Service Really Mean Any Service?

Any service that requires INSPECT code within FireWall-1 to work properly (with the exception of FTP) will not work with service Any and, instead, must be explicitly listed to be properly allowed. Table 4-3 contains a nonexhaustive list of services that require explicit rules with the explicit service to be allowed correctly (i.e., Any will not allow these services). This list was derived from a cursory look at the INSPECT files included in $FWDIR/lib:

Table 4-3 Services that do not work with the Any service

RPC	sunRSH	REXEC	VDOLive	RealAudio	RTSP
SQL*Net2	FreeTel	CoolTalk	H.323	NetShow	
Winframe	Backweb	IIOP	CVP		

4.4: When Should I Reinstall My Security Policy?

You should reinstall your security policy anytime you make a change to a network object, the rulebase properties, the rulebase, or any of the files that make up the security policy.

4.5: Which Characters or Words Cannot Be Used When Naming Objects?

The most current list of characters or words that cannot be used when naming objects can be found in Check Point Support's Knowledge Base article number 464a027a-a2f7-11d4-b000-080020cf9075. Tables 4-4 through 4-6 list these words and characters.

Table 4-4 Illegal characters

Space	+	*	?	!	(
)	{	}	?	[	]
#	<	>	,	:	;
'	"	`	\	/	@
$	%	^	|	&	

Table 4-5   INSPECT reserved words

accept	all	and	any	apr	April
aug	august	black	blue	broadcasts	call
date	day	debug	dec	December	deffunc
define	delete	direction	do	domains	drop
dst	dynamic	expcall	expires	export	feb
February	firebrick	foreground	forest green	format	fri
Friday	from	fwline	fwrule	gateways	get
gold	gray	green	hashsize	hold	host
hosts	if	ifaddr	ifid	implies	in
inbound	interface	interfaces	intrap	ipsecdata	ipsecmethods
is	jan	January	jul	july	jun
june	kbuf	keep	limit	log	magenta
mar	march	may	mday	medium	modify
mon	Monday	month	mortrap	navy	netof
nets	nexpires	not	nov	November	oct
October	or	orange	origdport	origdst	origsport
origsrc	other	outbound	outrap	packet	packetid
packetlen	pass	r_arg	r_cdir	r_cflags	r_ckey
r_connarg	r_ctype	r_entry	r_pflags	r_proxy_action	r_tab_status
r_xlate	record	red	refresh	reject	routers
sat	Saturday	sep	September	set	skipmen
sr	src	static	sun	Sunday	sync
targets	thu	Thursday	to	tod	tue
Tuesday	ufp	vanish	wasskipped	wed	Wednesday
xlatedport	xlatedst	xlatemethod	xlatesport	xlatesrc	xor
year					

NOTE!   In Tables 4-5 and 4-6, any capitalization of these words is also illegal.

Table 4-6 Scoped reserved words

account	alert	auth	authalert	duplicate	gateways
host	long	mail	netobj	resourceobj	routers
servobj	servers	short	snmptrap	spoof	spoofalert
tracks	targets	ufp	userdefined		

4.6: Are the Rulebase Properties per Firewall or Global?

Rulebase Properties apply to all gateways managed by the management console. In the next major release, these properties can be set on a per-firewall basis.

4.7: How Do I Enable DNS Verification When I Use the Rulebase Property to Allow DNS Queries?

In FireWall-1 4.1 SP2 and later, you can enable verification of DNS queries via this property by adding the following to the :props(section of $FWDIR/conf/ objects.C on the management console:

```
:dns_verification (true)
```

See FAQ 4.2 for how to properly edit $FWDIR/conf/objects.C.

4.8: Why Are Some Services Slow in Connecting?

Some services are slow in connecting either because the remote server is not able to do a reverse DNS lookup on the IP address you are coming from (it's timing out while looking) or because they are expecting an answer to their query on the ident port. To fix the latter problem, add a rule rejecting ident (see Figure 4-39). To fix the former problem, you must ask your DNS administrator to modify the reverse lookup tables so that the IP address you are coming from is resolvable.

Troubleshooting

The Management GUI generally does not have too many issues. However, there are a few problems that come up from time to time. Note that the issues described in the following sections are numbered as well, continuing from the previous section.

4.9: Client Is a Non-VPN, Whereas Management Server Is a VPN Version

In FireWall-1 4.0 and earlier, there are two versions of the GUI: a VPN version and a non-VPN version. The VPN version has encryption in it. The non-VPN version has no encryption in it. This is to enable FireWall-1 to be used in those few countries where the importation of encryption software is prohibited. In effect, you are running the wrong version of the GUI and must install the proper VPN version of the GUI (or non-VPN as appropriate). Note that this has nothing to do with licensing, but rather the version of the binaries you are using.

4.10: My Rulebases Have Disappeared!

There are times when it appears that all of your rulebases have disappeared. This is because the `rulebases.fws` file is corrupt. You can simply re-create this file by closing any GUI connected to the management console and performing the following steps:

On UNIX:

```
# cd $FWDIR/conf
# fwm -g *.W
```

On Windows NT:

```
c:\> cd %FWDIR%\conf
c:\WINNT/FW/conf> for %i in (*.W) do fw m -g %i
```

The differences between these commands are:

- On UNIX, the * is interpreted as a wildcard and includes all .W files.
- On Windows NT, the * is not interpreted as a wildcard, so you must list the .W files individually (thus the *for* loop).

When importing rulebase files, if objects referenced in a specific rulebase no longer exist, then the rulebase in question will not be successfully imported. This happens with particularly old rulebases. You will see errors to this effect when you run this command: These errors are normal.

4.11: Log Viewer Does Not Show All Fields

Versions of FireWall-1 prior to 4.0 SP1 chronically had this problem. The problem occurs because the header of the log file has been corrupted. Executing `fw logswitch` will not solve the problem, because it does not write a completely new log file. It uses the headers from the old one, which is the part of the log that has been corrupted.

You may be able to work around this problem by simply loading another log in the GUI. Keep a "very small" log file handy for this purpose. Open this log, and then switch back to the "current" log. You may then be able to see all the fields. If this does not work, you will need to have FireWall-1 create a brand-new log file. The following commands need to be executed on a UNIX/IPSO platform:

```
# fw logswitch
# fw kill fwd
# rm $FWDIR/log/fw.log*
# rm $FWDIR/log/fw.alog*
# rm $FWDIR/log/fw.vlog*
# rm $FWDIR/log/fw.logtrack
# fwd `cat $FWDIR/conf/masters
```

On Windows NT, these commands are:

```
> fw logswitch
> fwstop
> del %FWDIR%\log\fw.log*
> del %FWDIR%\log\fw.alog*
> del %FWDIR%\log\fw.vlog*
> del %FWDIR%\log\fw.logtrack
> fwstart
```

These commands kill and restart fwd on UNIX. Although logging will not function momentarily, your security policy will remain in effect. On Windows NT, this requires stopping FireWall-1 entirely.

4.12: Using the GUI over Slow Links

If you are using the GUI over a particularly slow link or have a particularly large number of rulebases or network objects, you may see a lot of "Server Not Responding" messages when you attempt to use the GUI. The GUI tries to download objects.C and all the rulebases used. If this takes longer than the timeout value (which is 25 seconds), you will get this message.

Although not much can be done for the size of objects.C, the number of rulebases can certainly be reduced. Assuming your rulebase is called "rulebase," you can do the following to rewrite rulebases.fws to contain only "rulebase" and not all your other rulebases:

On UNIX:

```
# cd $FWDIR/conf
# mv rulebases.fws rulebases.fws.orig
# fwm -g rulebase.W
```

On Windows NT:

```
> cd %FWDIR%\conf
> move rulebases.fws rulebases.fws.orig
> fw m -g rulebase.W
```

FireWall-1 3.0b build 3072 and later can have the GUI timeout adjusted as follows:

UNIX: Set the environment variable SERVER_TIMEOUT before running fwpolicy (e.g., setenv SERVER_TIMEOUT 60 to set the timeout to 60 seconds).

Windows: Create the following Registry entry as a DWORD, specifying the desired number of seconds for the timeout: `HKEY_LOCAL_MACHINE/ software/CheckPoint/Firewall-1 GUI/ServerTimeout`.

In FireWall-1 4.1, this Registry key is `HKEY_LOCAL_MACHINE/SOFTWARE/ CheckPoint/Policy Editor/4.1/server_timeout`.

Another option is to run the GUI connection over a compressed SSH or ZeBeDee connection as mentioned previously in this chapter.

4.13: I Cannot Fetch a Host's Interfaces

When you are editing a workstation object, you may be trying to do a GET to automatically fill in the interfaces on the Interfaces tab. This may fail. You can only "fetch" the interfaces on a host that has either FireWall-1 installed or SNMP installed. FireWall-1 3.x and earlier use SNMP to obtain interface information. In version 4.x, SNMP is only used for objects that are not marked as having FireWall-1 installed; otherwise, it uses the normal FireWall-1 control connection to obtain interface information. Depending on the object in question and the version of FireWall-1 being used, you will either have to troubleshoot this as a remote management issue (see Chapter 6) or as an SNMP issue.

Summary

Although it is impossible to describe every situation you might encounter during the initial configuration of your security policy, this chapter covered the basic elements you need to know in order to configure your security policy. Each element that is written into your security policy was detailed, including the Rulebase Properties and anti-spoofing. Different situations you might commonly encounter along the way as well as some common configuration questions were answered.

Chapter

5

Logging and Alerts

Logs and alerts are critical aspects of your firewall; they tell you what is going on with various aspects of your firewall. In this chapter, I focus on how logging and alerting work. I also show you what you are likely to see in the Log Viewer and System Status Viewer as well as suggest some strategies for managing your log files.

By the end of this chapter, you should be able to:

- Determine what information is displayed in the System Status Viewer
- Determine what information is displayed in the Log Viewer
- Identify where logging and alerting actually occur

The System Status Viewer

The System Status Viewer application allows you to see the status of your firewall. The Status Viewer has changed quite a bit in version 4.1 in that it shows information in a much more readable form. There are actually two modes: Icons View and Details View. The Icons View (see Figure 5-1) shows the status of each module you manage.

Figure 5-1 System Status Viewer Icons View

Each module can display four different modes, which are described in Table 5-1.

Table 5-1   States for firewall objects in the Status Viewer

State	Description
Installed	Policy is installed on the module.
Not Installed	Policy is not loaded on this module, but is responding.
Disconnected	Module is not responding to requests for status update. The module might be disconnected from the network, a loaded security policy might be preventing the query, or some other condition might be causing the problem.
Untrusted	The management console is not the master of the firewall module being queried.

The Details View is shown in Figure 5-2.

General					Status	VPN-1 & FireWall-1					
Name	IP Address	Cluster Name	Comment	Updated	Status	Status	Policy Name	Installed At	Accepted	Dropped	Logged
mrhat	207.225.43.41	phoneboy-gc		26-11-2000 at 17:00:23	?	Disconnected					
mrtwig	207.225.43.42	phoneboy-gc		26-11-2000 at 17:00:36	?	Disconnected					
marvin	10.0.0.11			26-11-2000 at 17:00:36	✓	Installed	v35-test	18Nov2000 1:18:25	522	13941	4362

Figure 5-2   System Status Viewer Details View

The headings in this view are described in Table 5-2.

Table 5-2   Entries in the System Status Viewer Details View

Heading	Description
Name	The name of the workstation object representing the firewall.
IP Address	IP address of object.
Cluster Name	If the object is part of a Gateway Cluster, that name is shown in this column.
Comment	Comment that the object was given in the Policy Editor.
Updated	The time when the data shown for this object was last updated.
Status	A graphical and textual representation of the status as shown in Table 5-1.
Policy Name	The name of the policy loaded.
Installed At	The date and time that the policy was loaded. This can reflect when the policy was loaded from the management console or when the firewall last fetched the policy.
Accepted	The number of packets accepted since the "Installed At" date and time.
Dropped	The number of packets dropped or rejected since the "Installed At" date and time.
Logged	The number of log entries generated since the "Installed At" date and time.

You can also get this information in the Icons View mode by double-clicking the module you want to see the data for (see Figures 5-3 and 5-4).

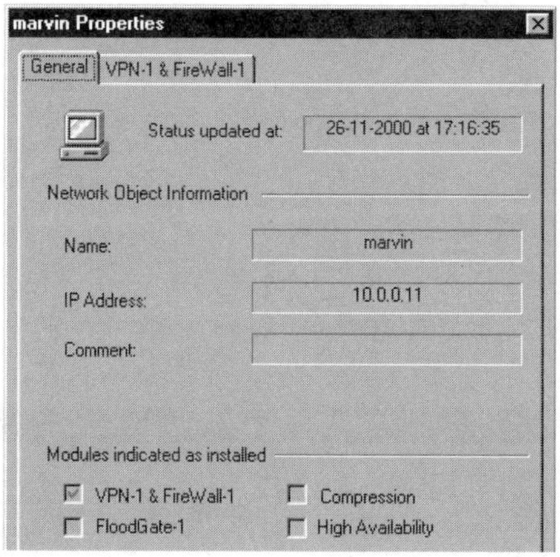

Figure 5-3   Firewall Properties, General tab

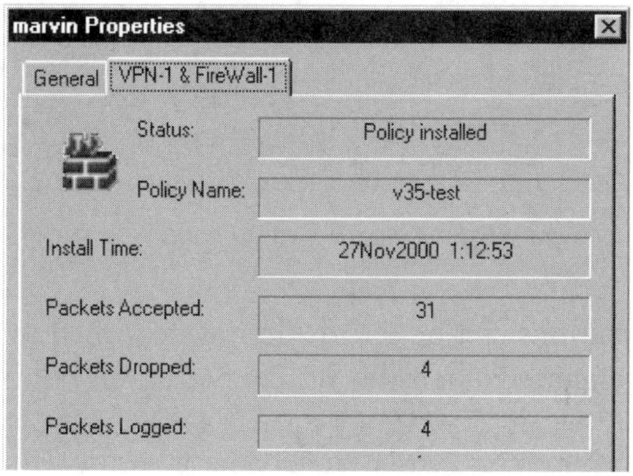

Figure 5-4   Firewall Properties, VPN-1 & FireWall-1 tab

System Status Viewer also displays alerts. Any rule that has a tracking type of alert shows up in a separate Alert window, which is shown in Figure 5-5.

Transitions in the state of policy on a module also generate an alert on the System Status Viewer. Note that this does not happen right away; it happens when the System Status Viewer updates the status of the module. You can determine when an alert is generated by selecting Options from the View menu, which is shown in Figure 5-6.

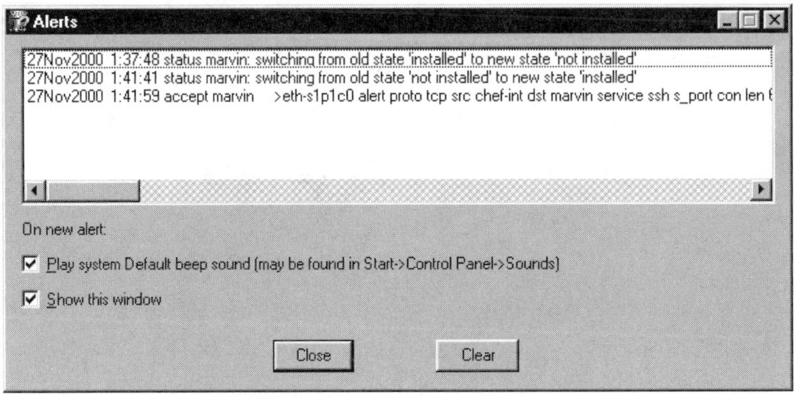

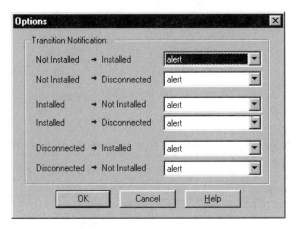

Figure 5-5 Alert Viewer

Figure 5-6 System Status Options screen

Each of these transitions can be set to Alert as described in Table 5-3. (Note that these alerts are only generated when the System Status Viewer is actually open.)

Table 5-3 Transition states in the System Status Viewer

Selection	Description
Blank	Do nothing
Alert	Generate an alert in the System Status Viewer only
Mail	Send an e-mail from the management console
SNMP Trap	Send an SNMP Trap from the management console
User Defined	Generate a User Defined alert from the management console

Note that for mail, SNMP Trap, and User Defined alerts, not only is an alert generated in the System Status Viewer, but the appropriate action is also taken as defined in the Log and Alert tab of the Rulebase Properties in the security policy. The Log and Alert tab is discussed in the "Alerts" section in this chapter.

Two other items of interest in the System Status Viewer are Show/Hide Objects and Automatic Update. Show/Hide Objects allows you to not show certain objects. From the View menu, select Show/Hide Objects (see Figure 5-7). To hide objects, clear the appropriate object check boxes, and click OK.

Figure 5-7   Show/Hide Firewalls in System Status Viewer

The Automatic Update tells the System Status Viewer how often it should poll modules to obtain their status (see Figure 5-8).

Figure 5-8   Automatic Update in System Status Viewer

To enable Automatic Update, set the update interval, select the objects on which this update will be performed, and click OK.

System Status Information from the Command Line

If you have command-line access to your management module, you can also get System Status information from the command line. If you are working with remote firewalls, these commands will only work if you have established an authenticated control connection with the remote firewall as described in Chapter 6.

To check the status of the local firewall, use the following command:

```
# fw stat
HOST        POLICY      DATE
localhost   template    21Dec2000 12:59:23 :   [>eth-s1p1c0] [<eth-s1p1c0]
```

To look at the status of a remote firewall, use:

```
# fw stat mrhat mrtwig
HOST        POLICY      DATE
mrhat       av          21Nov1999 15:23:59 :   [>eth-s1p4c0] [<eth-s1p4c0]
[>eth-s1p1c0] [<eth-s1p1c0] [>eth-s1p3c0]
mrtwig      av          21Nov1999 15:28:17 :   [>eth-s1p4c0] [<eth-s1p4c0]
[>eth-s1p1c0] [<eth-s1p1c0] [>eth-s1p3c0]
```

This output tells you which policy is loaded (av is loaded on both mrhat and mrtwig), the date the policy was loaded on each box, and which interfaces have seen traffic inbound and outbound. In this example, both firewalls have seen traffic on eth-s1p4c0 and eth-s1p1c0 in both directions. The eth-s1p3c0 interface has only seen traffic in the outbound direction.

To get more detailed statistics, run **fw stat -long**:

```
# fw stat -long mrhat
HOST     IF           POLICY   DATE                 TOTAL REJECT  DROP ACCEPT  LOG
mrhat    >eth-s1p4c0 av        21Nov1999 15:23:59   72    0       0    72      1
mrhat    <eth-s1p4c0 av        21Nov1999 15:23:59   57    0       0    57      0
mrhat    >eth-s1p1c0 av        21Nov1999 15:23:59   180   0       14   166     1
mrhat    <eth-s1p1c0 av        21Nov1999 15:23:59   170   0       0    170     0
mrhat    >eth-s1p3c0 av        21Nov1999 15:23:59   90    0       90   0       1
```

The eth-s1p2c0 interface is missing from this list because it has not seen any traffic. To show this interface, use the -inactive parameter:

```
# fw stat -long -inactive mrhat
HOST     IF           POLICY   DATE                 TOTAL REJECT  DROP ACCEPT  LOG
mrhat    >eth-s1p4c0 av        21Nov1999 15:23:59   72    0       0    72      1
mrhat    <eth-s1p4c0 av        21Nov1999 15:23:59   57    0       0    57      0
mrhat    >eth-s1p1c0 av        21Nov1999 15:23:59   184   0       17   167     1
mrhat    <eth-s1p1c0 av        21Nov1999 15:23:59   171   0       0    171     0
```

```
mrhat    >eth-s1p2c0 av    21Nov1999 15:23:59   0  0      0       0      0
mrhat    <eth-s1p2c0 av    21Nov1999 15:23:59   0  0      0       0      0
mrhat    >eth-s1p3c0 av    21Nov1999 15:23:59  90  0     90       0      1
mrhat    <eth-s1p3c0 av    21Nov1999 15:23:59   0  0      0       0      0
```

The Log Viewer

The Log Viewer allows you to view what the firewall has logged. When you start up and log on to the Log Viewer, you are presented with the screen shown in Figure 5-9.

The fields in the Log Viewer are listed in Table 5-4 (not all are shown in Figure 5-9).

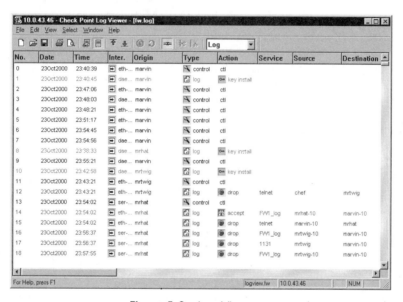

Figure 5-9 Log Viewer

 **NOTE!** Short log entries contain all entries from No. to Proto (see Table 5-4). Long log and alert entries contain all fields except the accounting-specific entries. Accounting log entries show up twice: once in the normal log as a long log entry and once in the accounting log with the accounting-specific information, which does not get written until approximately five minutes after the connection has closed.

If you have a serious amount of traffic flowing through the firewall, you will have many log entries to look through. It is very important that you examine your logs on a regular basis to make sure that proper security is maintained. However, a few thousand log entries can be difficult to look through. The following list contains a few hints that might save you some time:

Table 5-4 Entries in Log Viewer

Entry	Description
No.	The log entry number.
Date	The date the log entry was generated.
Time	The time the log entry was generated.
Inter.	The interface the packet being logged came in or went out (with direction).
Origin	The firewall module that generated the log entry.
Type	Log (for short or long log entries), alert (for alert log entries), or control (changes to policy or logging on a firewall).
Action	The action taken on the packet (drop, reject, accept, etc.).
Service	The "service" of the packet (HTTP, Telnet, etc.), which is usually based on the destination TCP/UDP port.
Source	The source IP address of the connection or packet.
Destination	The destination IP address of the connection or packet.
Proto	The protocol of the IP packet (TCP, UDP, ICMP, etc.).
Rule No.	The rule number that this connection or packet matched in the rulebase.
S_Port	The source port of the packet if TCP or UDP. For other protocols, this field is gibberish.
User	If the action was an authorize or de-authorize or was the result of an authenticated connection (with or without encryption), the appropriate user is listed.
SrcKeyID	If the action was encrypt or decrypt, this shows the source's KeyID.
DstKeyID	If the action was encrypt or decrypt, this shows the destination's KeyID.
Elapsed	Amount of time the connection was active (accounting mode only).
Bytes	Number of bytes for the connection in question (accounting mode only).
XlateSrc	The source IP address the connection will have *after* Network Address Translation (NAT) is applied.
XlateDst	The destination IP address the connection will have *after* NAT is applied.
XlateSPort	The source port the connection will have *after* NAT is applied.
XlateDport	The destination port the connection will have *after* NAT is applied.
Product	The product for which this log entry is relevant.
Info	More information about this log entry. For most packets or connections, it will simply show "len X" where X is the number of bytes in the packet. This entry also shows useful information on encrypt/decrypt log entries and drops or rejects on Rule 0.

- Limit the number of entries that appear in the log. Do not log on *every* rule, but instead log judiciously. Only log important information (e.g., all unauthorized traffic). Creating rules to catch noise services to drop and not log is one way to do this.
- Rotate your logs frequently. The Log Viewer does not function very well when the log contains more than a few hundred thousand entries. Although you can rotate your logs manually in the GUI, it is recommended that you set up a scheduled job via `cron` or Windows NT's scheduler to do this. This is discussed in the "Log Maintenance" section later in this chapter.
- Use the selection criteria to limit the displayed items or to find the entries you are most interested in.
- Use some of the third-party log analysis tools listed in Appendix J.

Selection criteria is chosen by right-clicking the column title in question and selecting Selection. The following list contains a few notes regarding selection criteria:

- Selection criteria are cumulative; if you use more than one selection criteria, they will be "anded" together.
- The Log Viewer *remembers* previous selection criteria, so you could possibly end up excluding all log entries. Before applying selection criteria, click the Current Selection Criteria button, and make sure all the selection criteria is deleted if necessary.
- The option Show Null Matches on the Options screen affects how log entries are displayed in the selection criteria. This option is explained in the following list.
- The Options screen (select Options from the Select menu) allows you to control what is displayed in the Log Viewer (see Figure 5-10).

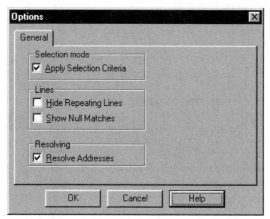

Figure 5-10   Log Viewer options

The Options screen includes the following choices:

Apply Selection Criteria: Shows only the log entries that match the selection criteria. Otherwise, all log entries are shown.

Hide Repeating Lines: Suppresses identical consecutive entries from the Log Viewer.

Show Null Matches: Shows entries that are neither included nor excluded by the current selection criteria. For example, if you are selecting entries based on "Action" and you have control entries in your log, they will neither be included nor excluded because control log entries do not have "Action" entries.

Resolve Addresses: Source and Destination addresses can appear either as names or IP addresses. FireWall-1 stores only the IP address in the logs; however, the management console can attempt to use DNS or WINS to resolve the IP addresses it has stored. If your DNS server is slow or your management console must use WINS to resolve names, this can slow down the Log Viewer considerably. In most cases, it is recommended that you disable this option in the Log Viewer.

Viewing Logs from the Command Line

You can also view logs from the command line on the management module using the command `fw log`. This command shows the logs in ASCII text. Note that not all fields are shown, only relevant fields. This format makes the output somewhat difficult to parse with a program, but it is fairly easy to look at. Output from `fw log` looks something like this:

```
Date: Dec 12, 2000
17:40:44 ctl    marvin      >daemon started sending log to localhost
17:51:18 accept mrhat       <eth-s1p1c0 proto udp src mrhat dst chef
service ntp-udp s_port ntp-udp len 76 rule 10
17:52:22 accept mrhat       <eth-s1p1c0 proto udp src mrhat dst chef
service ntp-udp s_port ntp-udp len 76 rule 10
17:53:26 accept mrhat       <eth-s1p1c0 proto udp src mrhat dst chef
service ntp-udp s_port ntp-udp len 76 rule 10
```

There are plenty of options you can use with `fw log` to help you find the log entries you are interested in. Table 5-5 lists the options for this command. Usage information for the `fw log` command is as follows:

```
fw log [-f[t]] [-c action] [-1] [-start time] [-end time] [-b stime
etime] [-h hostname] [log-file]
```

Table 5-5   Options for the `fw log` command

Flag	Description
`-f`	If no file is specified, shows the log forever. Entries are shown as they are generated.
`-t`	Used with `-f` to only show new log entries (i.e., entries added after `fw log` was executed).
`-l`	Instead of printing out the date separately, it is included in each line's log entry.
`-s start-time`	Used with `-f` to show log entries generated after the specified date or time (hh:mm format).
`-e end-time`	Used with `-f` to show log entries generated before the specified date or time (hh:mm format)
`-b timea timeb`	Used with `-f` to show log entries generated between the specified times.
`-h firewall`	Shows log entries generated by the firewall module named "firewall."
`-n`	Do not do name resolution for source and destination IP addresses.
`log-file`	Use the specified log file (otherwise, use `$FWDIR/log/fw.log`).

Active Mode and Blocking Connections

So far, I have only discussed the most commonly used mode: Log mode. Along the right side of the icon bar in the Log Viewer window there is a pull-down menu. This menu allows you to change to the other two modes in the Log Viewer: Accounting and Active. Accounting mode works much the same as the Active mode except it deals with Accounting Log entries. They are stored in a separate log file, which is why there is a separate view for those log entries. Because Active mode works differently from Log mode, let's take a look at how it works. Figure 5-11 shows a screen from Active mode.

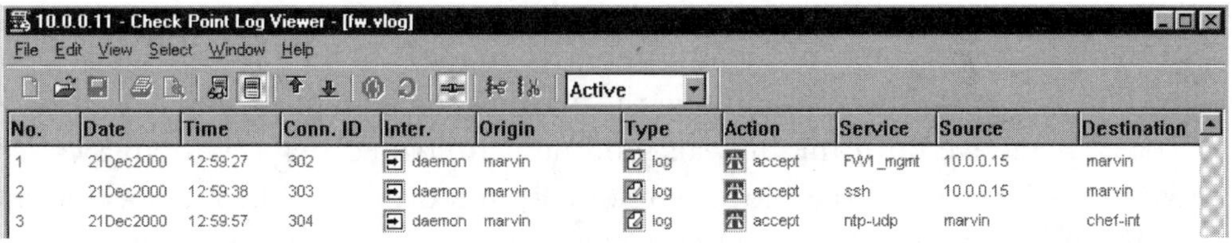

Figure 5-11   Log Viewer Active mode

Table 5-6   Fields in Log Viewer Active mode

Name	Description
No.	The log entry number.
Date	The date the log entry was generated.
Time	The time the log entry was generated.
Conn. ID	A number referencing this specific connection.
Inter.	Usually daemon.
Origin	The firewall module that generated the log entry.
Type	Log (for short or long log entries), alert (for alert log entries), or control (changes to policy or logging on a firewall).
Action	The action taken on the packet, usually accept.
Service	The service of the packet (HTTP, Telnet, etc.), which is usually based on the destination TCP/UDP port.
Source	The Source IP of the packet.
Destination	The Destination IP of the packet.
Proto	The IP Protocol of the packet. Usually, TCP, UDP, or ICMP, but could be any IP Protocol or a number.
S_Port	The Source Port of the packet if it is TCP or UDP.
Elapsed	For entries logged as type Accounting, the amount of time elapsed since the connection began.
Bytes	For entries logged as type Accounting, the number of bytes that have elapsed since the connection began.
Product	The product for which this log entry is relevant.
Info	More information about the entry. This is usually blank.

This mode shows connections that are currently active through the firewall (i.e., in its state tables). Table 5-6 lists the fields that are displayed and provides descriptions of each field.

The main function you can perform in Active mode is to temporarily block a connection. This is done without modifying the existing rulebase in the Policy Editor. All such blocks are active until the firewall module is unloaded (e.g., with an fwstop), the system is rebooted, or the block is manually removed. To block a specific connection, double-click the line showing the connection, and the dialog shown in Figure 5-12 appears.

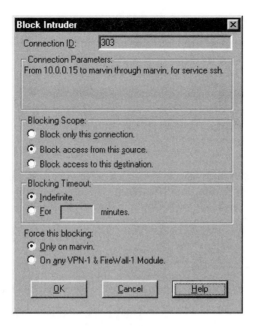

Figure 5-12   Block Intruder

You can then select what will actually be dropped by using the following options:

Block only this connection: Block only this specific connection. If the host attempts to connect to this destination and this service port again, it will be blocked.

Block access from this source: If the host listed as the source attempts to make any connection, it will be blocked.

Block access to this destination: If any host tries to reach this destination host, it will be blocked.

Blocking Timeout: Indicates how long this block will be active for. Indefinite really means until the firewall module is unloaded (via `fwstop`) or a reboot occurs.

Force this blocking: Indicates the firewalls that will enforce the block you are requesting. By default, only the firewall the connection went through will enforce this block. This function can be pushed to all firewalls managed by this management console.

Note that you can enable these actions from the command line of the management module or firewall module using the command `fw sam`. These command options are described in Table 5-7. Usage of the `fw sam` command is as follows:

Table 5-7 Options for the `fw sam` command

Option	Description
`-v`	Turn on verbose mode.
`-s sam_server`	The SAM server to be contacted. Default is localhost.
`-t timeout`	Timeout in seconds. Default is Never.
`-f fw_host`	The firewalls to run the operation on. This command option should contain either the name of a firewalled object, the name of a group of firewalled objects, or one of the predefined names: All and Gateways. The default is All.
`-C`	Cancel the specified option.
`-n`	Notify every time a connection that matches the specified criteria passes the firewall.
`-i`	Inhibit connections that match the specified criteria.
`-I`	Inhibit connections that match the specified criteria and close existing connections that match it.
`-D`	Delete all previous operations.

```
fw sam [-v] [-s sam_server] [-t timeout] [-f fw_host] [-C]
-n|-i|-I <criteria>
fw sam [-v] [-s sam_server] [-f fw_host] -D
```

The criteria for the `fw sam` command is described in Table 5-8.

The IP addresses in Table 5-8 may be resolvable hostnames or dotted decimal notation addresses. Service may be a resolvable service name (in the services file, like Telnet or WWW) or a service number (a TCP/UDP port number). Protocol may be a protocol name (like TCP) or a protocol number.

Table 5-8 Criteria for `fw sam` command

Format	Description
`src ipaddr`	Match the source address of connections
`dst ipaddr`	Match the destination address of connections
`any ipaddr`	Match the source or destination address of connections
`srv srcip dstip service protocol`	Match the specified source, destination, and service

For example, if you want to turn on additional notification for a specific action, say, accessing www.phoneboy.com, you would type:

```
# fw sam -n dst www.phoneboy.com
```

All notifications will appear as rule "sam" in the logs.

If you want to deny all connections to www.phoneboy.com for 60 seconds, you would type:

```
# fw sam -t 60 -i dst www.phoneboy.com
```

If you want to deny all connections to foo.bar.com and close any existing connections, you would type:

```
# fw sam -I dst foo.bar.com
```

If you want to close a specific Telnet connection from host.yoursite.com to foo.bar.com and prevent further requests from that host, you would type (23 is the port number for Telnet; 6 is the protocol number for TCP):

```
# fw sam -I srv host.yoursite.com foo.bar.com 23 6
```

To cancel the preceding operation, you would type:

```
# fw sam -C srv host.yoursite.com foo.bar.com 23 6
```

To cancel all previous operations (i.e., unblock all blocked connections), you would type:

```
# fw sam -D
```

Alerts

Now that I have discussed the two applications that let you look at logs and alerts, I will talk about alerts themselves; mainly, how they are generated. Aside from creating rules that have a Log Track of one of the Alert types, you need to configure the Log and Alert tab of the Rulebase Properties, which is shown in Figure 5-13. This tab allows you to configure exactly what is executed when each of the alerts is invoked. Note that all commands listed must be executable on the management console, *not individual firewalls.*

The options on the Log and Alert tab include:

Excessive Log Grace Period: To try and limit the number of entries logged to the log file, FireWall-1 keeps track of everything that is logged for a set period of time, and if a particular activity (by source, destination, service, and source port) occurs within the excessive log grace period multiple times, only one log entry is generated. By default, this option is set to 62 seconds, which in reality results in about 60 seconds. Whatever setting you choose, be sure to add two seconds to the value.

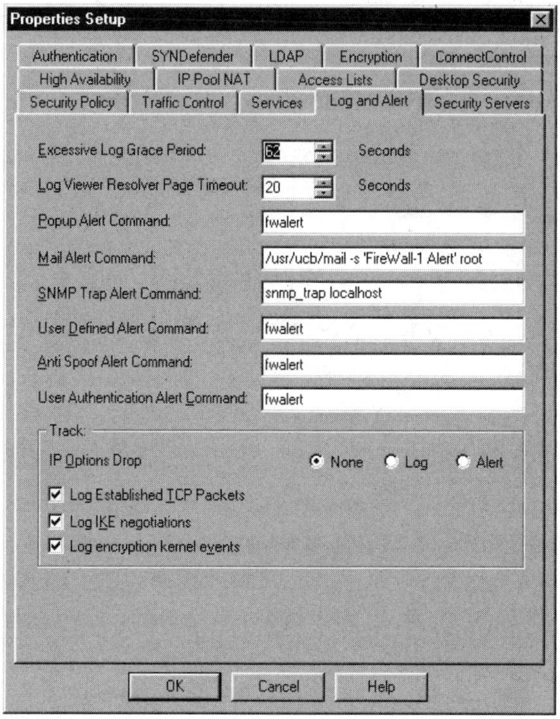

Figure 5-13 Policy Properties, Log and Alert tab

Log Viewer Resolver Page Timeout: This option indicates the number of seconds the Log Viewer spends on attempting to resolve entries shown in the Log Viewer. Note that this timeout does not always seem to be enforced on Windows NT when WINS is used to resolve names.

Pop-Up Alert, Mail, SNMP, User Defined Alert Commands: These commands control the commands that are executed with the following log actions: Alert, Mail Alert, SNMP Alert, and User Defined Alert. The default `fwalert` command (for most of these log actions) only generates an alert if the System Status Viewer happens to be running at the time. To execute Mail Alerts on a Windows NT management module, you need to change the command to:

```
%FWDIR%\bin\sendmail -s Alert -t smtp-server-ip -f from-email-addr
-t to-email-addr
```

On an IPSO-based management console, you need to change the command to:

```
/bin/mail -s Alert to-email-addr
```

and make sure that the Mail Relay function is correctly configured in Voyager.

Anti-Spoof Alert Command: This command is executed when anti-spoofing is violated and the track is set to Alert (see Chapter 4). The default is `fwalert`.

User Authentication Alert Command: This command is executed when either an authentication failure occurs for a service that requires authentication (see Chapter 7) or when a particular user logs in via SecuRemote (see Chapter 10). The default is `fwalert`.

Note that it is possible to write your own script or program that parses the input and performs an action based on that input. The script must take a single line of text from standard input (stdin). The format used is identical to how log entries are output via the command `fw log`. Once you have your program written, you simply replace the appropriate alert command with the complete pathname to the script or program on the management console.

Messages in the Log

This section will help you decipher some of the messages you might see in the logs associated with entries and decide what to do about them. Some messages are specific to certain features (such as encryption) and will be listed in their specific sections of the book.

Rule 0

If a packet is dropped, but it is not dropped as the result of a specific rule in the rulebase, it is usually dropped on Rule 0. There are several reasons why a packet might be dropped on Rule 0:

- *Anti-spoofing violation:* The connection may violate your anti-spoofing settings. More information on this is documented in Chapter 4.
- *Authentication Failures:* Whether or not this is logged is set on the Authentication tab of the Rulebase Properties.
- *SYNDefender warning:* The "Display Warning Messages" check box is disabled on the SYNDefender tab of the Rulebase Properties.
- *SecuRemote authentication (successful ones):* This is controlled on a per-user basis. See Chapter 10 for more details.
- *A security feature in FireWall-1 is dropping the packet:* The specific reason is listed in the Info field of the log entry.

Some of the more-common messages are explained in the following sections.

Local Interface Anti-Spoofing

Local Interface Anti-Spoofing is a different sort of anti-spoofing from the one configured in the workstation object for the firewall. As of FireWall-1 4.1 SP2 and FireWall-1
4.0 SP7, FireWall-1 will drop any packet it receives with a source IP address of one of
the firewall's local interfaces. This error message occurs on IPSO platforms running
FireWall-1 4.1 SP2 that use VRRP IP addresses for address translation. FireWall-1 4.1
SP3 and later do not appear to have this problem.

You can disable this anti-spoofing by changing the FireWall-1 kernel variable
`fw_local_interface_antispoofing` to zero. For more details on how to change
FireWall-1 kernel variables, see Appendix I.

Host Tried to Open TCP Service Port

The error message "Host tried to open TCP service port" shows up with services that
use multiple ports for their communication. It is most common with FTP but can
also occur with other services. By default, FireWall-1 does not allow any port that
FireWall-1 has defined as a service to be used for a data connection for certain services.
This check can be disabled by editing `$FWDIR/lib/base.def` on the management
console and reinstalling the security policy. In FireWall-1 3.x, `base.def` looks like
this:

```
#define NOTSERVER_TCP_PORT(p) ( p not in tcp_services
and p > 1024 )
```

You need to change it to read:

```
#define NOTSERVER_TCP_PORT(p) ( p > 1024 )
```

In FireWall-1 4.x, `base.def` looks like this:

```
// ports which are dangerous to connect to
define NOTSERVER_TCP_PORT(p) {
    (not
        (
            ( p in tcp_services, set sr10 RCODE_TCP_SERV, set sr11 0,
             set sr12 p, set sr1 0, log bad_conn)
        or
            ( p &lt; 1024, set sr10 RCODE_SMALL_PORT, set sr11 0, set
sr12 p,
            set sr1 0, log bad_conn)
        )
    )
} ;
```

which should be changed to:

```
// ports which are dangerous to connect to
define NOTSERVER_TCP_PORT(p) {
    (not
        ( p < 1024, set sr10 RCODE_SMALL_PORT, set sr11 0, set sr12 p,
        set sr1 0, log bad_conn)
    )
} ;
```

Unknown Established TCP Connection

"Unknown established TCP connection" means that FireWall-1 sees a TCP ACK packet, which occurs as part of a normal TCP connection, for which it does not have a matching entry in the state tables. This may occur because the connection was inactive for a period of time or the connection is no longer in the state tables because they were flushed (e.g., as part of a policy installation). Although most connections survive a policy installation, certain types of connections (Citrix, FTP Data, and SQLNet2) do not always survive.

FireWall-1 4.1 handles established TCP connections differently from previous versions. In version 4.0 and earlier, if FireWall-1 received a TCP ACK packet for which there was no corresponding entry in the connections table, FireWall-1 would strip off the data portion of the packet (make it harmless), mangle the TCP sequence number, and forward the packet on. This would cause the remote end of the connection to send a SYN packet to resynchronize the connection. The SYN packet would then go through the rulebase. If the rulebase permitted the packet, the connections table entry would be re-created, and the connection would go on as normal.

In FireWall-1 4.1 base and FireWall-1 4.1 SP1, FireWall-1 only allows the unsolicited TCP ACK packet if it comes from the server. If the TCP ACK packet comes from the client (i.e., the machine that originated the connection), the TCP ACK packet is dropped.

In FireWall-1 4.1 SP2 or any system with the ACK DOS fix applied, FireWall-1 drops all TCP ACK packets for which there are no valid connection entries and logs the message "unknown established TCP packet." In FireWall-1 4.0 or 3.0, it logs the message "unknown error code: 12."

You can disable logging of these packets in FireWall-1 4.1 base or 4.1 SP1 by commenting out the following line (place two forward slashes [//] in front of the line or enclose the line in C style comments (i.e., /* */) in $FWDIR/lib/fwui_head.def:

```
#define CLUSTER_RULEBASE_MATCH_LOG
```

In FireWall-1 4.1 SP2, you need to comment out the following line in `$FWDIR/lib/fwui_head.def`:

```
#define NON_SYN_RULEBASE_MATCH_LOG
```

In FireWall-1 4.0 or 3.0 systems where the ACK DOS fix is applied, you can disable the logging of these messages by adding the following line in `$FWDIR/lib/code.def` on the management console before the ACK DOS code:

```
#define NO_NONFIRST_RULEBASE_MATCH_LOG
```

You then need to reinstall the security policy.

The preceding changes cause the code that actually does the logging of this type of packet to be skipped, thus eliminating the error messages. To disable the code entirely on FireWall-1 4.1 SP2 and later, you can uncomment the line (remove the two forward slashes from the line) in `$FWDIR/lib/fwui_head.def` that reads:

```
#define ALLOW_NON_SYN_RULEBASE_MATCH
```

len xx

The "len xx" message simply indicates the length of the packet that was accepted or dropped.

The Service ident

When attempting to use certain services like SMTP or IRC, the server will try to send a communication back to the client on the ident service port. Ident is typically used to provide identification for certain services. In general, it is not necessary. It is highly recommended that you create a rule that rejects all ident traffic (instead of dropping) without logging so that services that rely on ident will start faster because they won't wait for the ident connection to "time out."

lvfile_open: failed to open logfile `c:\winnt\fw\log\fw.log` log ptrs problem

The "lvfile_open: failed to open logfile `c:\winnt\fw\log\fw.log` log ptrs problem" message isn't an error you will see in your logs, but rather one the Log Viewer may display when you are viewing logs. This message means the log pointers for that log file are corrupt. Fortunately, you can delete the existing log pointer files by removing the files `$FWDIR/log/*.logptr` and `$FWDIR/log/*.alogptr`. When you open these files for viewing again, FireWall-1 should re-create the log pointer files.

Log Maintenance

It is recommended that you look at your logs regularly to determine if people are attempting to violate your security policy. Also, log files themselves tend to get rather big and need to be switched every so often. In the Log Viewer application, you can use New under the File menu in the Log Viewer to rename the old log file, Purge under the File menu to simply delete the current log, or the command `fw logswitch` from the management console. People often rotate their logs daily or more frequently if logging is particularly heavy. I personally recommend doing a logswitch on a daily basis unless you log more than a few hundred thousand entries a day; in which case, I would rotate at a regular interval to keep the total number of log entries below 300,000. This can be automated with a `cron` job or the `at` scheduler in Windows NT.

Optionally, you can give `fw logswitch` an argument with a filename to switch the log to. The default is to simply stamp the previous `fw.log` file with the current date and time.

Automating `fw logswitch` on UNIX and IPSO

Using the `cron` facility, you can execute the `fw logswitch` command automatically on UNIX and IPSO. You need a `cron` entry that looks something like this (you edit your `crontab` file with the command `crontab -e`):

```
59 11 * * * /etc/fw/bin/fw logswitch > /dev/null 2>&1
```

This entry executes the command at 11:59 P.M. local time each day. Note that you should specify the complete path to the `fw` binary instead of using `$FWDIR` except on IPSO where it is possible to use `$FWDIR`.

Automating `fw logswitch` on Windows NT

Using the `at` command in Windows NT, you can execute the `fw logswitch` command automatically. The `at` command relies on the scheduler service, which is installed but not enabled on most Windows NT systems. Once you enable it, you can then set up an automatic task with a command like this:

```
at 11:59pm %FWDIR%\bin\fw logswitch
```

This entry executes the `fw logswitch` command at 11:59 P.M. local time each day (and yes, this command is persistent across reboots).

Rotate and Download Logs from Firewall to Management Console

There are times when the connection between the firewall and management console will be broken. During this time, the firewall will write log entries to a local log file.

This procedure shows you how to retrieve this data from the remote firewall and store it on the management console.

The following code assumes you have set up an authenticated connection between your firewall module and management console as described in Chapter 6. The command `fw logswitch` can be used to rotate logs on a remote firewall module that is logging locally as follows:

```
# fw logswitch -h mrtwig
Trying to switch logfile to 21Nov1999-16:28:08.log

Done
```

You can also use the `fw logswitch` command to perform a logswitch and download the switched logs from the remote firewall module as follows:

```
# fw logswitch -h mrtwig +
Trying to switch logfile to 21Nov1999-16:28:31.log
mrtwig.21Nov1999-16:28:31.log
mrtwig.21Nov1999-16:28:31.logptr
mrtwig.21Nov1999-16:28:31.alog
mrtwig.21Nov1999-16:28:31.alogptr
Done
```

This code performs a logswitch and downloads the log files to the management console's `$FWDIR/log` directory. Note that a copy is still kept on the remote firewall module. To do the logswitch, download the log files, and delete them on the remote module using the following command:

```
# fw logswitch -h mrtwig -
Trying to switch logfile to 21Nov1999-16:28:50.log
mrtwig.21Nov1999-16:28:50.log
mrtwig.21Nov1999-16:28:50.logptr
mrtwig.21Nov1999-16:28:50.alog
mrtwig.21Nov1999-16:28:50.alogptr
Done
```

You should be able to open these new log files via the Log Viewer application, which allows you to look at different log files.

Summary

Logging and Alerting are critical components of any security architecture. Logs tell you who did what when. Alerting gives you immediate notification of a defined action. This chapter explained how these components work in FireWall-1 as well as some ways to make better use of them.

Chapter

6

Remote Management

Large organizations often require multiple firewalls in order to keep the network secure. The ability to manage all these firewalls from a central place is desirable as is the ability to manage the firewalls from anywhere. FireWall-1 offers this ability via a centralized management console and a GUI that can be run on Solaris, AIX, HP/UX, and Windows 95, 98, or NT. Often, in smaller environments, the firewall and management console are on the same box. This configuration masks a lot of the complexity and power of FireWall-1.

This chapter explains each of these components in detail and how they interact with one another. Remote management is then discussed. Topics in this area include the ability to manage one or more remote firewalls from a single management console, scenarios that might come up, including management console migration, and how to troubleshoot these configurations.

By the end of this chapter, you should be able to:

- Understand the different components of FireWall-1 and how they interact
- Effectively manage several remote firewall modules
- Move your management console from one host to another
- Troubleshoot common problems with remote management

The Components

FireWall-1 can be broken down into three basic components:

- *Firewall module:* A device that enforces a security policy.
- *Management module:* A device that stores, compiles, and installs the security policy the firewall modules enforce. It also stores logs the firewalls send back and can send alerts.

- *Management GUIs:* Programs that talk to a management console and allow you to view logs and system status, and modify the security policy.

Each component can exist on completely separate systems, or they all can exist on the same system as shown in Figure 6-1.

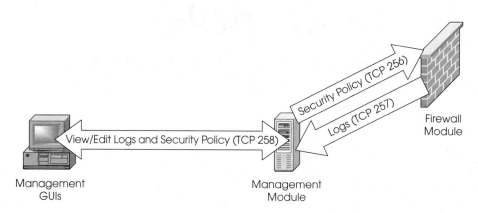

Figure 6-1 How modules interact

How do these processes communicate with each other? The GUI connects to fwm on the management console, which listens on TCP port 258. The IP address of the client, as well as the username and password that are supplied, are authenticated against a database of allowed IPs and users. If these match, the connection is allowed.[1] The network objects, security policies, and users are downloaded to the local GUI. Depending on the access privileges allowed, the user can view logs and system status, read, modify, and load new security policies to the firewall modules. With the exception of non-VPN versions of FireWall-1 (i.e., those binaries that contain no encryption at all), all communication between the management console and GUI are encrypted.

The management console stores configuration about your firewall modules. This includes network objects, users, security policies, and logs. It compiles and loads rule-bases to the firewall modules. The management console opens connections to the remote firewalls via TCP port 256 on-demand to load security policies and get status.

The firewall module enforces your security policy. It accepts, drops, rejects, authenticates, and encrypts traffic. The firewall module opens a connection to its management console on TCP port 257 to send logs. It also opens a connection via TCP port 256 to fetch the security policy at boot time. In addition, the firewall mod-

---

1. I personally find that redirecting the Management GUI connection through an SSH port redirection (as discussed in Chapter 4) provides greater security. It provides an extra layer of authentication and encryption. The authentication is even stronger if you use RSA/DSA keys.

ule communicates with antivirus servers, URL filters, and authentication servers as necessary.

The communication between the management and firewall module is authenticated and/or encrypted. The command `fw putkey` and the `control.map` file set up this authentication, which is discussed in the next section.

The Management Console to Firewall Module Connection

Because it is not desirable for just any management console to install a security policy on a firewall module or for any firewall module to send logs to a management console, all communication between the management console and firewall module should be authenticated. Setting up this authentication can be one of the trickier aspects of Fire-Wall-1. Despite all of the improvements in FireWall-1 over the years, this feature still causes even experienced FireWall-1 administrators some headaches. This section explains how this authentication works and how to set it up.

The authentication is dependent on three factors:

- The system's node name IP address (nnIP)
- The contents of `$FWDIR/conf/masters`
- The contents of `$FWDIR/lib/control.map`

The nnIP address is the IP address the node name resolves to. On a UNIX or IPSO platform, a `uname -n` gives you the system's node name. On Windows NT, the system's node name is defined in the Network configuration under the Identification tab. The command `hostname` returns the system's correct hostname. In either case, the nnIP should be routable with respect to any FireWall-1 nodes the system may have management type interactions with. For a firewall module, this means that the nnIP should be routable with respect to its management console. For a management console, this means that the nnIP should be routable to all of its firewall modules.

The reason the nnIP address is relevant is that even though FireWall-1 uses other IP addresses for communication, the authentication actually occurs using the system's nnIP. Although the nnIP address is important for management console traffic, it is also relevant for other parts of FireWall-1 (especially encryption), so it is important that the nnIP be routable.

The `masters` file contains the IP address of the management console that controls the firewall module. This file indicates where the firewall module will fetch its security policy on boot as well as where to send logs. It also has special relevance for the `control.map` file, which is described in the next section.

The `control.map` File

The `control.map` file specifies how and under what circumstances FireWall-1 will authenticate management communication. Lines of a `control.map` file either begin with a # (a comment) or have lines that look like the following:

```
hosts: commands/auth
```

The *hosts* variable can be an IP address, a list of IPs separated by commands, the word MASTERS, the word CLIENT, or * (to match all other hosts). The *commands* variable is a comma-delimited list of commands that can be performed (or * to match all commands), and the *auth* variable is the authentication that must be used for those commands. Note that multiple commands/auth pairs can be listed on a line if different levels of authentication are required.

A default FireWall-1 4.1 SP3 installation's `control.map` file looks like this (other versions have similar entries):

```
MASTERS: getkey,gettopo,gettopossl,certreq/none
fwn1_opsec/fwn1 ssl_opsec/ssl ssl_clear_opsec/sslclear    */fwa1
CLIENT : load,db_download,fetch,log/fwa1    fwn1_opsec/fwn1
ssl_opsec/ssl  ssl_clear_opsec/sslclear    */none
*      : getkey,gettopo,gettopossl,certreq/none
unload,load,db_download,fw logswitch/deny    fwn1_opsec/fwn1
ssl_opsec/ssl ssl_clear_opsec/sslclear */fwa1
```

The first line defines what happens when the master (as defined in `$FWDIR/conf/masters`) talks to this host. In this case, FireWall-1 will:

- Allow encryption keys, network topology (with and without Secure Sockets Layer [SSL]), and certificate request functions without authentication.
- Require fwn1 authentication for OPSEC-related functions.
- Require fwa1 authentication for all other functions.

The second line defines what happens when this hosts talks to its master, or how a master would talk to one of its managed firewalls. In this case, FireWall-1 will:

- Authenticate with fwa1 for policy load, user database download, policy fetch, and establishing a log connection.
- Authenticate via fwn1 for OPSEC-related functions (see the "Security Server" section in Chapter 8).
- Authenticate via ssl for OPSEC encrypted with SSL.
- Authenticate via ssl_clear (unencrypted SSL) for OPSEC with unencrypted SSL.
- Not authenticate for other functions.

The third line defines what happens when this hosts attempts to talk to all other hosts (or other hosts attempt to talk to it). In this case, FireWall-1 will:

- Give (or require) no authentication for encryption keys, network topology (with and without SSL), and certificate request functions.
- Give deny authentication (i.e., will not be allowed) to perform a policy load or unload, user database download, or a logswitch.
- Give (or require) fwn1 authentication for OPSEC functions.
- Give (or require) ssl authentication for OPSEC encrypted with SSL.
- Give (or require) ssl_clear (unencrypted SSL) for OPSEC with unencrypted SSL.
- Give (or require) fwa1 or all other functions.

Commands and Authentication Types Supported in `control.map`

Many different commands can be listed in `control.map`. Improper use of `control.map` can have an effect beyond management communication, so edit this file with extreme care. Table 6-1 lists some of the commands that can be used in `control.map`.

Table 6-1   Commands in `control.map`

Command	Description
certreq	Used to fetch a certificate from a certificate server
db_download	Used to load databases (user, objects) to a firewall module
fetch	Used by a firewall module to obtain the last installed security policy from the management console
fwn1_opsec	Used between OPSEC-compliant products for authentication (4.1)
get_logdom	Used to get the log format or log domain from a management console
get_tab_name	Allows for a management console to request table names and ID numbers
getkey	Used to fetch a public encryption or certificate authority key
gettopo	Used by SecuRemote/Secure Client to fetch the topology (encryption domain)
gettopossl	gettopo with SSL encryption
ioctl	Used to control kernel module functions on the firewall module (4.1 SP1 and earlier)
load	Used to load a security policy to a firewall module
log	Used by a firewall module to send logs to the management console

(continued)

Table 6-1   (cont.)

Command	Description
logswitch	Used to remotely switch log files and/or download them to a management console
opsec	Used between OPSEC-compliant products for authentication (3.0 and 4.0)
ssl_opsec	Used between OPSEC-compliant products for authentication and SSL encryption (4.1)
stat	Allows for a management console to request status from the firewall module
sync	Used to synchronize state tables between firewall modules
tab_stat	Allows for a management console to request table information
unload	Used to remotely unload a security policy from a firewall module

The types of authentication supported in control.map are listed in Table 6-2.

Table 6-2   Authentication schemes in `control.map`

Type	Description
none	Require no authentication.
deny	Do not allow (i.e., deny) the following action.
fwa1	A Check Point proprietary scheme involving authentication and encryption. In versions of FireWall-1 prior to 4.1 SP1, an encryption license is required to make use of this authentication method.
fwn1	Same as fwa1, but without encryption.
skey	An authentication scheme based on S/Key (one-time password scheme).
ssl	Authentication and encryption with SSL.
sslclear	Authentication with SSL.

The Workings of Different Authentication Schemes

All of the authentication schemes perform authentication differently, but they all have a similar basis for authentication: a seed password.[2] This password is shared between the management console and firewall module by a process called "putkey," which is explained in the next section.

---

2.   With SSL, the putkey password is only used when the SSL connection is first established. After it has been established the first time, SSL certificates are negotiated and the putkey password is no longer needed.

Fwa1 is an encrypted authentication scheme. All management traffic communication between sites that use fwa1 authentication will be authenticated *and* encrypted. In versions of FireWall-1 prior to 4.1 SP1, an encryption license is required to use fwa1. Because Check Point is based in Israel and their laws forbid it, Check Point cannot divulge many details about the encryption algorithm used for fwa1. However, someone on the Usenet group comp.sci.crypt claims to have reverse engineered the algorithm and has posted the source code.

Skey is an authentication scheme that is similar to the S/Key authentication system used for authentication of users. Each side of the connection uses a chain of 100 passwords based on the seed password chosen. After the one hundredth password is used, a new seed password is generated automatically. Both sides of the connection generate the same seed password because they use the same algorithm. This process continues until a new seed password is set with the command `fw putkey`.

Because skey is based on a chain of passwords, it is possible that the two sides of the connection can become out of sync. This happened quite a bit on the first versions of FireWall-1 on Windows NT. Even on current versions, putkeys have been known to "go bad." This makes it unsuitable for situations where connections are asymmetric.

Fwn1 is an unencrypted version of fwa1 that does not encrypt the data communication. It was designed for authentication with OPSEC products, particularly in cases where the connections can be asymmetric in nature. It provides a similar level of authentication to S/Key.

In versions of FireWall-1 earlier than 3.0, skey authentication was required in cases where an encryption license was not available on either the management console or the firewall module. In FireWall-1 3.0 and later, you can either use skey or fwn1 for authentication. In version 4.0 SP5 and later, it is not possible to use fwn1 for authenticating a control connection between a management console and a firewall module. In version 4.1 SP1 and later as well as FireWall-1 4.0 SP7 and SP8, Check Point allows you to use fwa1 for authentication, even if you do not have an encryption license.

Vulnerabilities were discovered in fwa1 and fwn1, which were made public at the Black Hat 2000 Conference. Perhaps as a result of this, FireWall-1 4.1 SP2 and later now support the use of industry standard SSL for authentication and encryption of authenticated control connections. Because this is not supported in previous versions, you must specifically enable this support. In future major releases, Check Point will make SSL the default scheme.

To change the type of authentication used, you simply need to modify the `control.map` file and restart FireWall-1.

The `fw putkey` Command

The `fw putkey` command is used to establish authentication between two hosts for the purposes of a control connection. It establishes a seed password that the hosts use as a basis for authentication. How this password is used will vary with the authentication scheme used. This section describes how to use this command.

The most common form of the `fw putkey` command is as follows:

```
# fw putkey a.b.c.d
```

The variable *a.b.c.d* is the host with which you want to set up the authentication. This command then prompts you for a password, which you need to type in twice as prompted. If password input needs to be done noninteractively (e.g., as part of a script), you can use this form:

```
# fw putkey -p password a.b.c.d
```

The password chosen should be eight characters or less. Passwords with more than eight characters have historically had problems (putkeys based on these passwords fail to work). You can use the same password for multiple IP addresses as follows:

```
# fw putkey -p password a.b.c.d e.f.g.h i.j.k.1
```

To do a putkey for SSL authenticated connections, use the following –ssl option:

```
# fw putkey -ssl -p password a.b.c.d e.f.g.h i.j.k.1
```

The only other option you are likely to use is the –n option, which forces the IP used for authentication to the specified IP address. If for some reason the systems cannot communicate via the nnIP addressees, perhaps because the nnIP on one box must be tied to a nonroutable or nonreachable IP address, you can use the –n flag to "override" the nnIP address of the local system:

```
# fw putkey -n local-ip remote-ip
```

The variable *local-ip* refers to the local IP used for communication (e.g., the value that "overrides" the local nnIP), and *remote-ip* is the remote system's IP address.

WARNING!   If you must use `fw putkey –n` for multiple sites, you can only use **one** distinct IP address for the *local IP* for all sites. The minute you use a different IP for –n, all the other putkeys performed with –n will cease to work.

Establishing an Authenticated Control Connection

Now that all the background information has been covered, let's talk about how to establish an authenticated control connection between a firewall module and a management console. Consider the situation shown in Figure 6-2.

The steps taken to configure the network in Figure 6-2 are as follows:

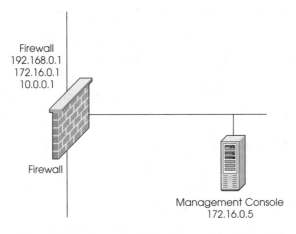

Figure 6-2 Sample network configuration #6-1

1. On your firewall module, edit `$FWDIR/conf/masters` so that it contains the IP address of the management console. In this case, it is 172.16.0.5.
2. Execute `fwstop` on both the management and firewall modules.
3. Run `fw putkey` on the management console to establish authentication with the firewall module:

   ```
   # fw putkey -p password 172.16.0.1 10.0.0.1 192.168.0.1
   ```

4. Run `fw putkey` on the firewall module to establish authentication with the management console:

   ```
   # fw putkey -p password 172.16.0.5
   ```

5. Execute `fwstart` on your management console, and allow FireWall-1 to complete start up.
6. Execute `fwstart` on your firewall module.

If the configuration is successful, you should see the message "connected to log server 172.16.0.5" on your console, in the `$FWDIR/log/fwd.log` file on your FireWall-1 4.0 or earlier firewall module, or in the `$FWDIR/log/fwd.elg` file on your FireWall-1 4.1 or later firewall module. On your management console, you should see a similar message about your firewall being connected.

Special Remote Management Conditions

The preceding steps work if both modules are at the same encryption level and if NAT is not involved. There are situations where you may need to manage a firewall over the Internet, and your management console will require NAT to get to the Internet. You may also need to manage a firewall in a place where encryption capabilities may not be necessary or even legal. For these cases, you will have to perform additional steps.

Forcing a Firewall Module to Log Locally

By default, when a firewall module is remotely managed, any logging is automatically sent to the management console. There are some cases where this may not be desirable. One example is when a remote firewall module is only accessible via a relatively slow link, and the overhead imposed by logging across the network is undesirable. Logging is desirable, but it would be far better to do it locally.

Once you have set up the system to log locally, you will only be able to view the active logs via the command line of the firewall module. You can set up an `fw logswitch` command to rotate the logs and download them to your management console at regular intervals as discussed in the "Log Maintenance" section of Chapter 5.

Aside from the usual steps to establish remote management, an additional step needs to be performed, as shown in the next two sections.

FireWall-1 4.0 SP3 and Earlier

To log locally on FireWall-1 4.0 SP3 and earlier, you need to modify the following script.

NOTE!   These modifications can only be done on a UNIX platform. On Windows NT, you need to upgrade to version 4.0 SP4 or later.

The `fwstart` script (in `$FWDIR/bin`) should contain lines that look like this:

```
echo 'FireWall-1: Starting fwd'
if ($fw1_firewall) then
        fwd $masters
else
        fwd -n $masters
endif
```

In this case, you simply edit the line `fwd $masters` so that it reads `fwd`. Whenever `fwstart` runs, fwd will be started in such a way as to force it to log locally.

FireWall-1 4.0 SP4 and Later

FireWall-1 4.0 SP4 and later have the file `$FWDIR/conf/loggers`, which can be set up to log locally instead of logging to the management console. If this file does not exist, FireWall-1 simply sends logs to the hosts listed in `$FWDIR/conf/masters`. If this file exists, FireWall-1 sends logs only to the hosts in these files, not `$FWDIR/conf/masters`. To log locally, add the IP address "127.0.0.1" to the top of this file and restart FireWall-1.

Remote Management with NAT

There are situations where you may need to manage your firewall module from a management console subject to address translation. In this case, FireWall-1's dependence on nnIP for authentication will rear its ugly head and cause a problem. In order to work in this configuration, the management console needs to have its own statically translated IP address. You also need to make use of `fw putkey -n` to override the system's nnIP.

Consider the situation in Figure 6-3.

When accessing the Internet, the management console will have a translated IP address of 192.168.0.5.

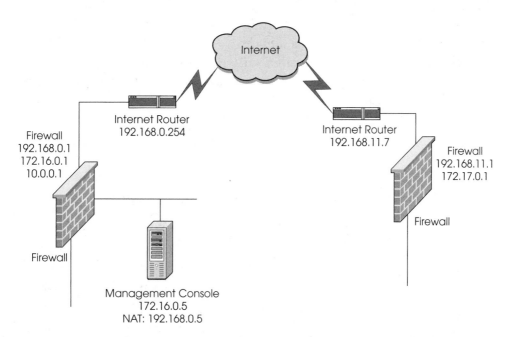

Figure 6-3   Sample network configuration #6-2

To establish an authenticated control connection between the management console and the remote firewall as shown in Figure 6-3, follow these steps:

1. On your firewall module, edit `$FWDIR/conf/masters` so that it contains the translated IP address of the management console. In this case, it is 192.168.0.5.

2. Execute `fwstop` on both the management and firewall modules.

3. Run `fw putkey` on the management console to establish authentication with the firewall module. Note that because address translation is involved, the -n option is necessary to ensure that the correct IP address is used for authentication:

   ```
   # fw putkey -n 192.168.0.5 -p password 192.168.11.1 172.17.0.1
   ```

4. Run `fw putkey` on the firewall module to establish authentication with the management console. Use the following translated IP address:

   ```
   # fw putkey -p password 192.168.0.5
   ```

5. Execute `fwstart` on your management console, and allow FireWall-1 to complete start up.

6. Execute `fwstart` on your firewall module.

Neither Firewall nor Management Console Have Encryption Licenses

If both modules are running FireWall-1 4.1 SP1 or later, or running 4.0 SP7 or SP8, this section is not relevant, because fwa1 is supported without an encryption license in these versions. However, if you are using earlier versions of FireWall-1 and you lack encryption licenses on both your management and firewall module, this section is relevant.

Consider the situation in Figure 6-4.

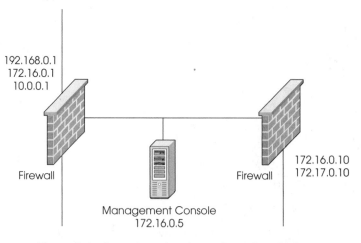

192.168.0.1
172.16.0.1
10.0.0.1

Firewall

Firewall

172.16.0.10
172.17.0.10

Management Console
172.16.0.5

Figure 6-4   Sample network configuration #6-3

The steps taken in Figure 6-4 are as follows:

1. On your firewall module, edit `$FWDIR/conf/masters` so that it contains the IP address of the management console. In this case, it is 172.16.0.5.
2. Execute `fwstop` on both the management and firewall modules.
3. Edit `$FWDIR/lib/control.map` on both the management and firewall module. Change all occurrences of "fwa1" to "skey."
4. Run `fw putkey` on the management console to establish authentication with the firewall module:

   ```
   # fw putkey -p password 172.16.0.1 10.0.0.1 192.168.0.1
   ```

5. Run `fw putkey` on the firewall module to establish authentication with the management console:

   ```
   # fw putkey -p password 172.16.0.5
   ```

6. Execute `fwstart` on your management console, and allow FireWall-1 to complete start up.
7. Execute `fwstart` on your firewall module.

Management Console Has Encryption, Firewall Module Does Not

If both modules are running FireWall-1 4.1 SP1 or later, or running 4.0 SP7 or SP8, this section is not relevant, because fwa1 is supported without an encryption license in these versions. However, if you are using earlier versions of FireWall-1 and you lack encryption licenses on both your management and firewall module, this section is relevant.

Consider the situation where a management console licensed for encryption needs to manage a firewall module that is not licensed for encryption. The reverse situation is not a realistic situation, because you need a management console with encryption in order to manage a firewall module with encryption. Let's assume the same network diagram as shown in Figure 6-3 except that one of the firewalls (172.16.0.10) does not have encryption.

To establish an authenticated control connection between the management console and the nonencryption firewall as shown in Figure 6-3, follow these steps:

1. On your firewall module, edit `$FWDIR/conf/masters` so that it contains the IP address of the management console. In this case, it is 172.16.0.5.
2. Execute `fwstop` on both the management and firewall modules.

3. Edit `$FWDIR/lib/control.map` on the firewall module. Change all occurrences of "fwa1" to "skey." (Note that this is not necessary if the firewall and the management console are running version 4.1 SP1 or later.)

4. Edit `$FWDIR/lib/control.map` on the management console. In this case, you need to add a line to allow the firewall without encryption to be managed while maintaining encryption between the firewalls that have it. The newly modified `control.map` file should look something like this:

```
172.16.0.10, 172.17.0.10: */skey
MASTERS:    getkey,gettopo,gettopossl,certreq/none
opsec/fwn1    */fwa1
CLIENT :    load,db_download,fetch,log/fwa1   opsec/fwn1    */none
*       :    getkey,gettopo,gettopossl,certreq/none
unload,ioctl,load,bb_download,fw logswitch/deny
opsec/fwn1    */fwa1
```

The line should be added above the MASTERS, CLIENT, and * lines.

5. Run `fw putkey` on the management console to establish authentication with the firewall module:

   # fw putkey -p password 172.16.0.10 172.17.0.10

6. Run `fw putkey` on the firewall module to establish authentication with the management console:

   # fw putkey -p password 172.16.0.5

7. Execute `fwstart` on your management console, and allow FireWall-1 to complete start up.

8. Execute `fwstart` on your firewall module.

What You Can Do with Remote Management

This section explains what you can do with the command line once remote management is configured correctly. Note that many of these commands can be executed when the management console and firewall module are on the same machine as well. See also the various command-line functions documented in Chapter 5.

Control Policy on a Firewall Module

A management console can load or unload a policy from a firewall module. The Security Policy Editor is normally used to do this, but this can also be initiated from the command line on the management console. With a large and/or complex policy, you should load the policy from the command line because it takes far less time than using the GUI.

To load a policy from the management console to the firewall module, use the command fw load as in the following example:

```
# fw load av.W mrtwig
av.W: Security Policy Script generated into av.pf
av:
Compiled OK.
Installing Security Policy av.pf on all.all@mrtwig
Installing Security Policy on mrtwig succeeded
Done.
```

To unload the policy on the remote firewall module from the management console, use the command fw unload as in the following example:

```
# fw unload mrtwig
Uninstalling Security Policy from all.all@mrtwig
Done.
```

On the remote firewall module, you can fetch the last installed policy from the management console using the fw fetch command as in the following example:

```
# fw fetch mrhat
Trying to fetch Security Policy from mrhat:
Installing Security Policy av on all.all@mrtwig
Fetching Security Policy from mrhat succeeded
```

View State Tables of Firewall Modules

The fw tab commands can be run from the management console to check the state tables on a firewall module. A few tables of interest include the connections table and the address translation tables. The following command shows you the contents of the connections table on mrtwig:

```
# fw tab -t connections mrtwig
mrtwig:
——— connections ———
attributes: refresh, sync, expires 60, free function 4066157116
4, kbuf 1, hashsize 32768, limit 25000
<0a002b29, 0000046f, 0a002b2a, 00000100, 00000006; 00000000,
00007001, ffff0800; 50/50>
<0a002b29, 00000470, 0a002b2a, 00000100, 00000006; 00000000,
00004001, ffff0800; 300/300>
<0a002b2a, 0000007b, ac1f0001, 0000007b, 00000011; 00000000,
00004002, ffff0600; 11/40>
<0a002b2a, 0000007b, ac1f0001, 00000000, 00000011; 00000000,
00004002, ffff0600; 11/40>
```

NOTE! The first five entries in each connections table entry are source IP, source port, destination IP, destination port, and IP proto number. They are all in hexadecimal.

You can also just get a count of a few tables if that is all you are interested in (the number under #VALS is the number of entries):

```
# fw tab -s -t connections -t fwx_forw -t fwx_backw mrtwig
HOST                NAME                  ID   #VALS
mrtwig              connections           18       8
mrtwig              fwx_forw            8189       0
mrtwig              fwx_backw           8188       0
```

Updating Licenses

A new feature added to FireWall-1 4.1 SP1 is the ability to view, retrieve, and edit licenses for remote firewall modules from a management console. These functions can only be used with modules running FireWall-1 4.1 SP1 or later. They are especially useful for Windows NT firewall modules because getting remote access to a Windows NT server can be difficult and requires third-party software.

The new commands are as follows:

```
fw rputlic object-name [putlic flags and license]
fw rgetlic object-name
fw rprintlic
```

The first command installs a license onto the remote module in $FWDIR/conf/cp.license (the normal license file in FireWall-1 4.1). The second command gets the license installed on that platform. The third command shows licenses either installed via fw rputlic or retrieved via fw rgetlic. The licenses fetched or installed via these commands are located in $FWDIR/conf/RemoteLicenses.dat.

The following example shows how to use these commands. If you have never executed fw rgetlic or fw rputlic commands, you will receive this error:

```
tweek[admin]# fw rprintlic
Remote licenses repository file /opt/pkg/FireWall-1-
strong.v4.1.SP-2/conf/RemoteLicenses.dat NOT FOUND
```

The following command shows how to get the licenses off the remote firewalls (mrtwig and mrhat in this example):

```
tweek[admin]# fw rgetlic mrtwig
Got next licenses from mrtwig:
Host                      Exp. Date        Features
-----------------------------------------------
10.0.43.42                30May2000        CPSUITE-EVAL-3DES-v41
tweek[admin]# fw rgetlic mrhat
Got next licenses from mrhat:
Host                      Exp. Date        Features
-----------------------------------------------
10.0.43.41                30May2000        CPSUITE-EVAL-3DES-v41
```

An `fw rprintlic` command will then show something like this:

```
tweek[admin]# fw rprintlic
Host                      Exp. Date        Features
-----------------------------------------------
10.0.43.41                30May2000        CPSUITE-EVAL-3DES-v41
10.0.43.42                30May2000        CPSUITE-EVAL-3DES-v41
```

Because these evaluation licenses are about to expire, you need to install new licenses. To overwrite the existing license while installing the new license, use the `-o` flag. This flag works with both `fw putkey` and `fw rputkey`:

```
tweek[admin]# fw rputlic mrhat -o 10.0.43.41 30Aug2000 aBcDeFgH-
iJkLmOpQ-rStUvWxY-z1234567 CPSUITE-EVAL-3DES-v41
Remote license installation on mrhat completed successfully.
License Storage completed successfully.
tweek[admin]# fw rputlic mrhat -o 10.0.43.41 30Aug2000 aBcDeFgH-
iJkLmOpQ-rStUvWxY-z1234567 CPSUITE-EVAL-3DES-v41
Remote license installation on mrhat completed successfully.
License Storage completed successfully.
tweek[admin]# fw rprintlic
Host                      Exp. Date        Features
-----------------------------------------------
10.0.43.41                30Aug2000        CPSUITE-EVAL-3DES-v41
10.0.43.42                30Aug2000        CPSUITE-EVAL-3DES-v41
```

Now let's say that mrtwig has to be rebuilt from scratch. You can use `fw rputlic` with an `-r` option to reinstall the license you have saved on the management console:

```
tweek[admin]# fw rputlic -r mrtwig
Remote license installation on mrtwig completed successfully.
License Storage completed successfully.
```

Moving Management Consoles

As a company grows from needing one firewall to several, it may be desirable to move the management functions from the firewall platform to a separate box that only functions as a management console. Moving a management console from one platform to another usually requires little more than copying a few files and establishing new putkeys with the new management console. However, in certain situations, it can be more complicated.

Moving the Firewall Module off the Management Console

Let's assume you have a machine with both a management console and a firewall module. Your goal is to use a different system for the firewall portion and use the existing one for the management console. No data needs to be copied between systems because the existing system can install the policies and user databases on the new system. To move the firewall module off the management console, you need to do the following:

1. Determine the IP address that the existing system will use in its new role as purely a management console.
2. Configure the new system identically to the existing system. This means it should have the same interfaces and routing table as the existing system.
3. Load FireWall-1 on the new system, ensuring that the software revision level is the same level as the one currently on the existing system.
4. Configure the new system as a firewall module only.
5. License the new firewall module.
6. `fwstop` the existing firewall module.
7. Reconfigure the IP addresses and routing on the existing system to be consistent with its new role as a management console. Make sure you disable the unused interfaces.
8. Modify `$FWDIR/conf/product.conf` on the existing system (if you are using Windows NT, look in the Registry entry `\HKEY_LOCAL_MACHINE\SOFTWARE\CheckPoint\FW1\4.1`) so that FireWall=0 and Auth=0.
9. Connect the new firewall module in place of the old one.
10. Perform putkeys on the firewall module (new system).
11. Modify `$FWDIR/conf/masters` on the firewall module to point to the new management console.
12. Perform putkeys on the management module (old system).
13. `fwstart` the management console.
14. `fwstart` the firewall module.

If this process is done correctly, you should be able to load your existing security policy on the new firewall module.

Moving the Management Console off the Firewall Module

Although moving the management console off the firewall module may sound like the previous situation, it is very different. In this case, the goal is to use a different system for the management portion and use the existing system as a firewall module. Follow these steps to accomplish this move:

1. Configure the new system as appropriate.
2. Load FireWall-1 on the new system, ensuring that the software revision level is the same level as the one currently on the existing system.
3. Configure the new system as a management module only.
4. License the new management module.
5. Copy the appropriate files from the firewall module. The files you need include:

   - `$FWDIR/conf/objects.C`: This contains all of your network objects, services, resources, servers, and so on.
   - `$FWDIR/conf/rulebases.fws`: This contains all of your recently used rulebases. You can reconstruct this file from `$FWDIR/conf/*.W` if you have to.
   - `$FWDIR/conf/fwauth.NDB`: This contains all of your users and user groups.
   - `$FWDIR/conf/xlate.conf`: This is needed if you still use xlate.conf to manage your address translation. Most people use the GUI, but a few people still use this deprecated method.
   - `$FWDIR/conf/snmp.C`: This is needed if you changed the SNMP Community Strings for FireWall-1's SNMP Agent.
   - `$FWDIR/lib/setup.C`: This is needed if you have modified this file for any reason. See FAQ 6.6 in this chapter for a reason you might modify this file.
   - `$FWDIR/lib/control.map`: This is needed if you have modified this file for any reason.
   - Any other files you may have modified in `$FWDIR/lib` for changes to the INSPECT code.

6. Modify `$FWDIR/conf/product.conf` on the old system (or `\HKEY_LOCAL_MACHINE\SOFTWARE\CheckPoint\FW1\4.1` on Windows NT) so that Management=0.
7. `fwstop` the firewall module.

8. Perform putkeys on the firewall module (old system).

9. Modify `$FWDIR/conf/masters` on the firewall module to point to the new management console.

10. Perform putkeys on the management module (new system).

11. `fwstart` the management console.

12. `fwstart` the firewall module.

If this process is done correctly, you should be able to load your existing security policy on the firewall module from your new management console.

Troubleshooting Remote Management Issues

This section covers how to troubleshoot issues related to remote management.

6.1: General Tips

The following list contains some general tips to ensure a smooth remote management configuration:

- Ensure that both the management console and the firewall module can resolve hostnames to their IP addresses. Place the appropriate entries in the system's localhosts file. The inability for FireWall-1 to resolve a hostname to an IP address is usually the reason that an authenticated connection between management consoles and firewall modules fail.

- Putkey passwords should be eight characters or less. You may have trouble with passwords longer than eight characters, especially if you use different platforms for your management console and firewall module.

- If there are other firewalls or routers in place, ensure that the FireWall-1 control traffic (TCP ports 256 and 257) is not being blocked by any rules or access control lists on intermediary routers.

6.2: Peer Asked for Deny Authentication or Authentication for Command X Failed

This error means that the remote module does not recognize the client's authority to execute the requested command. It can also be that the authentication is out of sync (which is common with skey).

In the case of a management console attempting to install a policy on a firewall module, it means the firewall module does not have an entry for that management console in `$FWDIR/conf/masters`. Make sure that the authentication between the firewall module and management console is established.

If the authentication is out of sync, you will have to perform the putkeys once again. In other cases, this error may occur because the wrong entry is being matched in `$FWDIR/lib/control.map`. You may need to add an entry in this file for the IPs that are attempting to establish an authenticated control connection and restart FireWall-1.

6.3: IP Address a.b.c.d Tries to Exchange a Control Security Key, but Has One (or Doesn't Have Any)

This error means that one end of the connection is out of sync with the other. Perform the steps necessary to establish an authenticated control connection between the management console and the firewall module once again.

6.4: WARNING: Using S/Key Authentication Instead of FWA1: No Encryption License

This error means that you are using a version of FireWall-1 prior to the 4.1 SP1 release or 4.0 SP5 and earlier, and you do not have an encryption license. You can upgrade all affected management consoles and firewall modules to version 4.1 SP1 or later, or use the steps documented previously in either the "Neither Firewall nor Management Console Have Encryption Licenses" or the "Management Console Has Encryption, Firewall Module Does Not" sections to resolve the issue.

6.5: Failed to Install xxxx Control Key: Bad Signature

This error points to a mismatch in passwords between the management console and the firewall module. Perform the steps necessary to establish an authenticated control connection between the management console and the firewall module once again.

6.6: Operation Would Block

This error means that the connection between the management and firewall modules would time out. This timeout does not normally need to be adjusted. You can adjust the timeout value by adding the following to the top of `$FWDIR/lib/setup.C` on the management console:

```
:fwd_conn_tout (###)
```

The variable ### is the number of seconds you want the timeout to be (25 seconds is the default). After you have changed the value, the file will look like this:

```
(
    :fwd_conn_tout (###)
    :setup_version (300)
    :has_iiicom (true)
```

This file may be overwritten during upgrades, so if you perform an upgrade of any sort, you may have to reapply this change.

> **WARNING!**   There is a known issue in FireWall-1 4.1 SP2 and earlier where this value is ignored in some instances. FireWall-1 4.1 SP3 and FireWall-1 4.0 SP8 resolve this issue.

6.7: If You Have Recently Changed IP Addresses for One of Your Modules

You may need to use `fw putkey -n` to force the nnIP for authentication.

6.8: If All Else Fails

You have performed the steps necessary to establish an authenticated control connection between the management console and the firewall module again. You have also followed all the tips in the previous "General Tips" section, and still nothing has worked. The following advanced troubleshooting suggestion should assist you in uncovering the problem.

The authentication sequence is stored in the following files:

- `$FWDIR/database/authkeys.C`
- `$FWDIR/database/opsec_authkeys.C`
- `$FWDIR/database/ssl*.C`
- `$FWDIR/conf/fwauth.keys`
- `$FWDIR/conf/serverkeys.*`

Deleting these files before executing the `fw putkey` command should flush out any old data in these files.

You can also run certain commands using a `-d` flag for debug (e.g., `fw load -d`, `fw fetch -d`), which can assist you in troubleshooting authentication problems. Your support provider may request that you run these commands in debug mode.

The following is an example of `fw fetch -d mrhat` (tries to fetch a policy from mrhat). Because the debug output can be quite long, only relevant parts of the debug output are shown.

```
[204@mrtwig] peers addresses are
[204@mrtwig] 192.168.43.41
[204@mrtwig] 192.168.43.43
[204@mrtwig] 192.168.43.44
[204@mrtwig] 172.29.0.41
```

```
[204@mrtwig] 172.29.0.40
[204@mrtwig] 172.29.0.43
[204@mrtwig] 172.16.32.1
```

This information is useful to determine what IP addresses the other module is seeing. It can be used as a sanity check to ensure that you are connecting to the right hosts.

```
[204@mrtwig] readstring: got a string at efbfc5b0 : 'none'. v = 5
[204@mrtwig] al_call: identifying to none authentication
[204@mrtwig] Peer asked to perform none authentication
[204@mrtwig] fwusr_init: creating user commands authentication
table
[204@mrtwig] fwusr_init: authentication table created
[204@mrtwig] fwusr_get: looking for client scheme for service
fetch
[204@mrtwig] fwusr_get: auth method for CLIENT & command fetch:
none
[204@mrtwig] I want to perform none authentication
[204@mrtwig] actual authentication I would perform is none
```

The preceding sequence allows you to ensure that both sides are asking for the same sort of authentication. In the preceding example, none authentication is being used. If there is a mismatch, you might see something like this:

```
[204@mrtwig] fwusr_get: looking for client scheme for service
fetch
[204@mrtwig] fwusr_get: auth method for CLIENT & command fetch:
deny
[204@mrtwig] I want to perform skey authentication
[204@mrtwig] actual authentication I would perform is deny
```

The preceding example shows that the host is likely matching the * line in `control.map`, which would deny a fetch by default.

Large-Scale Management Issues

One function that Check Point has not addressed well to date is managing a large number of firewalls. Although Provider-1 does help somewhat, there are some inherent weaknesses in how FireWall-1 does things and how well it scales. Thus far, there are not any really good solutions to these problems; however, knowing about them is half the battle, which is the purpose of this section.

Security Policies

I first need to address security policies. Although a single policy can actually be enforced on numerous firewalls, there are several limitations that affect the ability to manage security policies in general.

Number of Network Objects

The Management GUI and the fwm process on the management console do not deal with a large number of objects very well (above 10,000 or so). Having lots of memory on your management console can mitigate this, but the fewer network objects you have, the better.

Number of Rules

Although FireWall-1 can (theoretically) handle any number of rules, large security policies (over 150 rules) on the whole take an extremely long time to compile and install on the various modules. Even managing the rules themselves becomes problematic.

Number of Rulebases

The Management GUI is somewhat inefficient in that each rulebase, whether or not it is actually being used on a firewall, is downloaded to the GUI. This causes some problems within the GUI, particularly if you have a large number of rulebases, or even a small number of large ones. Although there are timeouts you can adjust to increase the amount of data that can be transferred, there are inherent limitations to downloading everything to the Management GUI.

Hierarchical Management

As it stands right now, there is only one rulebase, and anyone with read-write access to the Policy Editor can change the policy. For large organizations with a number of sites, it is reasonable to assume there will be different needs at the different sites. The ideal structure would be to have three classes of rules in the following order:

1. *Organization-wide rules:* A "global" administrator would set these rules. A local site administrator would not be able to override these rules.
2. *Site-specific additions:* These are rules that a local administrator could tweak to his or her liking. Anything not denied in the organization-wide rules would be placed within these rules.
3. *Organization-wide default rules:* A global administrator would also set these rules. These rules could contain rules that take effect if neither of the two previous sets of rules apply.

Number of Firewalls

Although there is no theoretical limit to the number of firewalls that can be managed by a single management console, there is a realistic limit to the number of firewalls that can be managed. In most cases, this number is 12; however, it varies depending on the amount of logging that is taking place, the processing speed of the management console, and the network bandwidth. Many sites employ local logging on the firewalls and regular downloads of the logging information to increase the number of firewalls that can be managed.

Having a Large Amount of Logs

Having a large amount of logs is not an easy problem to solve, regardless of what you use as a firewall. However, with FireWall-1, the Log Viewer itself becomes a bottleneck. Some reports have suggested that more than 300,000 log entries will cause the Log Viewer to lock up or even for FireWall-1 to stop logging. Frequent log switches can mitigate this. Even if you could view this many log entries, would you want to? How could you analyze such large log files, or even search through such log files to find events you are interested in?

Summary

Being able to manage multiple firewalls is important in any organization. You should now understand how to establish an authenticated control connection between a firewall and a management console in a variety of situations. There are a number of tasks you can perform once this connection is established. When something goes wrong with this connection, you can now troubleshoot it. You also know how to move your management console from one system to another. Additionally, you understand some of the issues that come into play when managing multiple firewalls within a large network.

Sample Configurations

The following four situations presented are representative of situations I have come across in the real world. Each is designed to demonstrate what people typically do with Remote Management and show how to configure each situation on the chosen platform.

Adding a New Firewall Module to Manage

The Situation

You work for a midsize company that currently has an Enterprise firewall and management console running on a Nokia Security Platform. The current firewall has encryption as SecuRemote is being used to access the site across the Internet. The new firewall is designed to protect some publicly accessible servers off-site. Because the current and new firewall will be running version 4.1 SP3, you do not have to worry about changing the default authentication scheme from fwa1. Figure 6-5 shows what the network looks like.

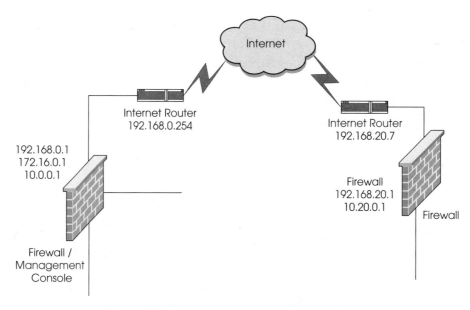

Figure 6-5   Sample network configuration #6-4

The Goals

- Configure the firewall modules for management console.
- Establish an authenticated control connection between the management console and the firewall module.

Checklist

- Obtain the appropriate licenses from your Check Point reseller.
- Establish an authenticated control connection between the management and firewall modules.
- Install the security policy.

Implementation

Before proceeding, you should ensure that you have the proper licenses. If you do not, you could get into trouble when trying to implement this network configuration. Work with your resellers to get permanent or temporary licenses, and have them on hand before beginning this process.

You can then establish the authenticated control connection between the management console and the firewall module.

1. On your remote firewall module, edit `$FWDIR/conf/masters` so that it contains the IP address of the management console. In this case, it is 192.168.0.1.
2. Execute `fwstop` on both the local and remote firewall modules.
3. Run `fw putkey` on the management console to establish authentication with the firewall module:

    ```
    # fw putkey -p password 192.168.20.1 10.20.0.1
    ```

4. Run `fw putkey` on the remote firewall module to establish authentication with the management console:

    ```
    # fw putkey -p password 192.168.0.1 172.16.0.1 10.0.0.1
    ```

5. Execute `fwstart` on your management console, and allow FireWall-1 to complete start up.
6. Execute `fwstart` on your firewall module.

Changing the Default Authentication Scheme to SSL
The Situation

In the previous situation, you decided that relying on fwa1 for authentication is a bad idea. Instead, the authentication scheme will be changed to SSL, but only for the remote firewall in question.

The Goals
- Change the authentication scheme to SSL between the remote firewall and the management console.
- Reestablish an authenticated control connection between the management console and the firewall modules.

Checklist
- Edit `$FWDIR/conf/control.map` on both the firewall and management consoles.
- Perform new `fw putkey` commands with the `-ssl` option.
- Bounce firewalls.

Implementation

You should first `fwstop` the management console and the firewall module. Next, modify `$FWDIR/lib/control.map` on the management console. Make a copy of the line that reads MASTERS. In one copy, change MASTERS to the IP addresses of the remote module. Also change all occurrences of fwa1 in this line to ssl. This new line should be placed above the existing MASTERS line as such:

```
192.168.20.1,10.20.0.1: getkey,gettopo,gettopossl,
certreq/none    fwn1_opsec/fwn1 ssl_opsec/ssl
ssl_clear_opsec/sslclear    */ssl
MASTERS: getkey,gettopo,gettopossl,certreq/none
fwn1_opsec/fwn1 ssl_opsec/ssl ssl_clear_opsec/sslclear
*/fwa1
```

Likewise, on the firewall module, modify `$FWDIR/lib/control.map`. Make a copy of the line that reads CLIENT. In one copy, change CLIENT to the IP addresses of the management module. Also change all occurrences of fwa1 in this line to ssl. This new line should be placed above the existing CLIENT line as such:

```
192.168.0.1,172.16.0.1,10.0.0.1: load,db_download,fetch,
log/ssl    fwn1_opsec/fwn1 ssl_opsec/ssl  ssl_clear_
opsec/sslclear    */none
CLIENT : load,db_download,fetch,log/fwa1    fwn1_opsec/
fwn1 ssl_opsec/ssl  ssl_clear_opsec/sslclear    */none
```

Execute the following commands on your management module:

```
fw putkey -p test123 192.168.20.1 10.20.0.1
fw putkey -ssl -p test123 192.168.20.1 10.20.0.1
```

Execute the following commands on your firewall module:

```
fw putkey -p test123 192.168.0.1 172.16.0.1 10.0.0.1
fw putkey -ssl -p test123 192.168.0.1 172.16.0.1 10.0.0.1
```

Bounce your management console (`fwstop; fwstart`). Wait for it to completely come up, and then bounce your firewall module. Verify that the firewall module can fetch security policy and is logging to the management console, and that the management console can push policy.

Notes

Do both a normal `fw putkey` and an `fw putkey -ssl`. For some reason, ssl authentication requires that normal putkeys are done as well, and that they use the same password as the ssl putkeys.

Moving the Firewall off the Management Console

The Situation

You work for a growing company that currently has a 250-user Single Gateway firewall running on a Windows NT platform (i.e., the management console and the firewall module must be on the same box). The company is rapidly outgrowing this network and needs to upgrade to an Enterprise (unlimited) license. To handle future growth, it is desirable to move the firewall to a Nokia Security Platform. The existing Windows NT platform will be used as the management console. Due to the nature of this change, downtime is required to accomplish these modifications (see Figure 6-6).

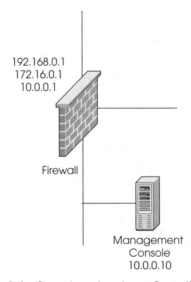

192.168.0.1
172.16.0.1
10.0.0.1

Firewall

Management
Console
10.0.0.10

Figure 6-6   Sample network configuration #6-5

The Goals

- Configure the Nokia Security Platform to be identical to the existing Windows NT platform with respect to routing and interface configuration.
- Reconfigure the existing Windows NT platform as appropriate for its new role as purely a management console.
- Establish an authenticated control connection between the Windows NT management console and the Nokia Security Policy.

Checklist

- Obtain the appropriate licenses from your Check Point reseller.
- Configure the Nokia Security Platform for its role as a firewall.
- Reconfigure the Windows NT management console for its new role.
- Establish an authenticated control connection between the management and firewall modules.
- Install the security policy.

Implementation

Before proceeding, you should ensure that you have the proper licenses. If you do not, you could get into trouble when trying to implement this configuration. Work with your resellers to obtain either permanent licenses or temporary licenses. You should have these on hand before beginning this process.

The Nokia Security Platform needs to be configured with the correct interfaces and IP addresses via Voyager. It should match the existing firewall. Obviously, this system should not be connected to a live, production network. You should then configure any necessary static routes, proxy-ARPs, and so on. Next, load FireWall-1, ensuring that the software revision level is the same level as the one currently on the existing system. Make sure you configure the Nokia as a firewall module only. License the platform.

You then need to `fwstop` the existing firewall module. Modify `\\HKEY_LOCAL_MACHINE\SOFTWARE\CheckPoint\FW1\4.1` in the Windows NT systems Registry so that FireWall=0 and Auth=0. Reconfigure the IP addresses and routing on the existing system to be consistent with its new role as a management console. This means disabling the two unused NICs in the Windows NT box and renumbering the system with 10.0.0.10. This requires rebooting the Windows NT box.

At this point, you can connect the Nokia Security Platform in place of the Windows NT platform. Modify `$FWDIR/conf/masters` on the Nokia Security Platform to point to the Windows NT management console. Run `fw putkey` on the Security Platform to establish authentication with the firewall module:

```
# fw putkey -p password 10.0.0.10
```

Run `fw putkey` on the remote firewall module to establish authentication with the management console:

```
# fw putkey -p password 192.168.0.1 172.16.0.1 10.0.0.10
```

Execute `fwstart` on your Windows NT management console, and allow FireWall-1 to complete start up. Then execute `fwstart` on your Nokia Security Platform.

Notes

If you were going to make a Nokia Security Platform purely a management console, be aware that there is a problem in the `fwstart` script in the IPSO version that prevents FireWall-1 from functioning purely as a management console. Resolution 2043 in the Nokia Knowledge Base discusses this issue.

Moving the Management Console off the Firewall

The Situation

You work for a midsize company that currently has an Enterprise firewall and management console running on a Solaris Platform (see Figure 6-7). This management console currently manages one firewall at a remote site. To handle future growth, the management console needs to be moved to a separate Solaris Platform. Minimal downtime is necessary to accomplish this change. For simplicity, assume NAT is done via the GUI, no changes have been made to any INSPECT files or `control.map`, and all IP addresses are routable.

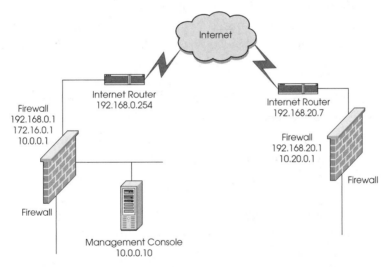

Figure 6-7   Sample network configuration #6-6

The Goals

- Set up the new management console.
- Copy files from the existing management console to a new management console.
- Configure the firewall modules for the new management console.
- Establish an authenticated control connection between the management console and the two firewall modules.

Checklist

- Obtain the appropriate licenses from your Check Point reseller.
- Copy the management console information from the firewall module to the new management console.
- Configure the current firewall/management console for its new role as purely a firewall module.
- Configure the new management console for its new role.
- Establish an authenticated control connection between the management and firewall modules.
- Install the security policy.

Implementation

Before proceeding, you should ensure that you have the proper licenses. If you do not, you could get into trouble when trying to implement this configuration. Work with your resellers to obtain either permanent licenses or temporary licenses. You should have these on hand before beginning this process.

Once the new management console is set up with the proper IP addresses and FireWall-1 is configured, you need to copy a few files from the existing management console/firewall module. The files needed include:

- *$FWDIR/conf/objects.C*: This contains all of your network objects, services, resources, servers, and so on.
- *$FWDIR/conf/rulebases.fws*: This contains all of your recently used rulebases. You can reconstruct this from $FWDIR/conf/*.W if you have to.
- *$FWDIR/conf/fwauth.NDB*: This contains all of your users and user groups.

Next, fwstop both the local and remote firewall modules. Then modify $FWDIR/conf/product.conf on the local firewall module so that the management functionality is disabled. You can do this by setting Management=0. You also need to tell the local firewall module that it needs to get its security policy from the new management console, so modify $FWDIR/conf/masters using the IP of the new management console, 10.0.0.10. Modify $FWDIR/conf/mastersend on the remote firewall so that it thinks that 10.0.0.10 is the management console.

Once you have established where the new management console is, you need to do putkeys. On the new management console, do the following sets of putkeys:

```
# fw putkey -p test123 192.168.0.1 172.16.0.1 10.0.0.1
# fw putkey -p abc123  192.168.20.1 10.20.0.1
```

On the local firewall module, you need to do the following:

```
# fw putkey -p test123 10.0.0.10
```

On the remote firewall module, you need to do the following:

```
# fw putkey -p abc123 10.0.0.10
```

At this point, you can `fwstart` all the systems. Perform this step first on the management console, and let it start up completely. Then perform it on the remote firewall modules. Note that it should fail to load a policy from the management console the first time because no policy has ever been installed from the new management console (i.e., a "no state saved" message should appear). Load a policy from the new firewall module, and your task is complete.

Notes

In the preceding situation, two different passwords were used in the putkeys. As long as you are consistent (i.e., use the same password on both ends of the authenticated connection), this is not a problem.

Chapter

7

Authentication

It is unfortunate that some people cannot be trusted to only do what they are supposed to do. If it were not for these people, you would not need to take security measures to protect your networks. Authentication provides a mechanism for validating user identities and also provides different levels of access. FireWall-1 provides several different mechanisms for authenticating users.

In this chapter, I cover the key to all authentication schemes used within FireWall-1 today: passwords. Next, I cover the three methods of authentication supported by FireWall-1 for users, complete with a demonstration of each: User Authentication, Session Authentication, and Client Authentication. I then discuss how to actually set up FireWall-1 so it can perform authentication including how to integrate FireWall-1 with various external authentication servers. Finally, I discuss how to troubleshoot authentication-related problems.

By the end of this chapter, you should be able to:

- Understand the difference between static and one-time password systems
- Use User, Client, and Session Authentication as a user
- Understand which authentication mechanism is the most appropriate for a given situation
- Set up User, Client, and Session Authentication
- Integrate supported third-party authentication servers into FireWall-1
- Troubleshoot problems with authentication

Passwords

All multiuser computer systems have some form of login identification (or username) and some sort of password. This has been the basis for authentication on computers since multiuser computer systems came into existence. All authentication mechanisms in FireWall-1 rely on some sort of username and password. Before proceeding, let's briefly discuss passwords.

To date, the vast majority of authentication is done with a static password. Most users, when left to their own devices, choose very simple passwords that are easy to guess. Even if a complicated password is chosen, the password, as it is being typed, can easily be picked off the wire with a packet sniffer. For these reasons, static passwords are not recommended. The risks these passwords create are somewhat mitigated by encrypting the passwords as part of the data stream (e.g., as part of SSH or HTTPS). However, most applications do not use encryption. Also, there is no point to encryption if the password is easy to guess.

One-Time Password (OTP) schemes were developed to solve these problems. They require a different password each time the user authenticates. Even though the network may be subject to packet tracing and may be able to see the entire challenge/response session, no information is divulged, so a hacker cannot pretend to be a particular user. OTP schemes use a secret key along with a cryptographic hash function. As long as the secret key is not divulged, the scheme is not compromised.

Passwords, regardless of whether or not they are OTP or static, can be managed a number of different ways, some inside FireWall-1 and others on external authentication servers.

FireWall-1 Password

FireWall-1 Password is a simple, static password that is maintained internally by FireWall-1. The password can be up to eight characters in length. No additional software is needed to use FireWall-1 Password. Due to the fact that FireWall-1 Passwords are static, use outside of a test environment is not recommended.

OS Password

FireWall-1 can use the login and password information stored in the OS of the firewall for authentication. You are limited to what the specific OS will provide in terms of usernames and password, which is usually a static password of limited length. No additional software is needed to use OS Password.

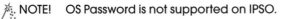 NOTE!   OS Password is not supported on IPSO.

S/Key

S/Key is an OTP system that uses an MD4 or MD5 cryptographic hash function. It uses three values: a password number, a seed value (usually the same as the username), and a secret key. The password number and the seed value are transmitted in the clear as the challenge. The challenge, along with the secret key, is typed into an *S/Key generator* (S/Key generators are freely available on the Internet) that resides on the user's local system. The S/Key generator then generates a response to that challenge, which users type in to authenticate themselves.

Given the challenge and the response, it is impossible to determine what future responses need to be without knowing the secret key used to generate the *S/Key chain*. However, if you choose an easy-to-guess secret key, your login can easily be compromised. It is important that you choose a secret key that is difficult to guess. As of version 4.1, FireWall-1 requires a secret key of at least ten characters to try to enforce a difficult-to-guess secret key.

When you log on and use S/Key, you are given a challenge such as:

```
SKEY CHALLENGE: 98 username
```

The number is the password number, which decrements after each successful login. The seed (in this case `username`) always stays the same. You would type this information into an S/Key generator along with your secret key. This generates a one-time password, which you then use as the response.

On a UNIX platform, the interaction with an S/Key generator looks something like this:

```
$ key 98 username
Reminder - Do not use this program while logged in via telnet or
rlogin.
Enter secret password: test123
SNOW SON TECH FARM DOME BEG
```

On a Windows platform, the interaction with an S/Key generator might look similar to Figure 7-1.

S/Key can be used natively in FireWall-1 without having to purchase additional software. S/Key generators, and where to obtain them, for Windows and UNIX platforms are listed in Appendix J.

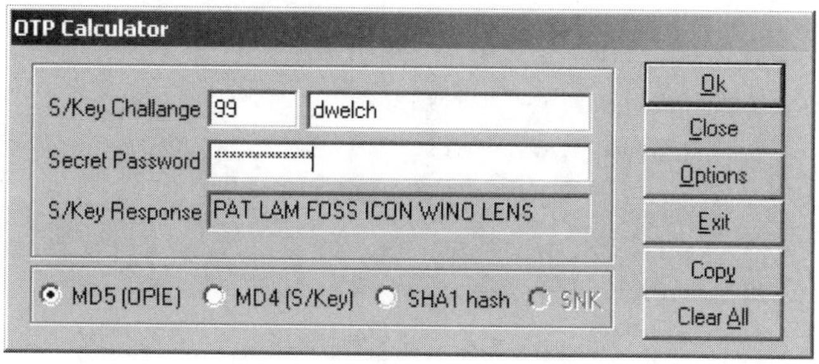

Figure 7-1   S/Key generator on Windows

SecurID

SecurID uses a hardware token with a value that changes every minute or so. The card is synchronized with an ACE/Server, which validates the authentication attempt. So long as you do not lose this card, your authentication will be secure.

When you are prompted for authentication, you will be given a "passcode" prompt. Depending on the type of SecurID card you have, you will either type in a PIN (4–8 alphanumeric digits in length) followed by the six-digit number currently displayed on your SecurID card, or you will enter the PIN on your SecurID card, press the diamond key, and type in the number displayed on the SecurID card. Because the SecurID card and ACE/Server are in sync, the ACE/Server knows what the SecurID card should read at any given moment.

Using SecurID involves purchasing both the ACE/Server (which runs on UNIX or Windows NT workstations) and SecurID keys. The hardware keys expire after a period of time. A sample SecurID token is shown in Figure 7-2.

Axent Pathways Defender

Axent Pathways Defender is also a hardware token-based solution. Instead of a changing value like SecurID, you use a numeric keypad on the hardware key to punch in a challenge and a user-definable PIN, which gives you a response. The hardware key is programmed with an ID that is also specified on the Defender Authentication Server. This key is tied to a specific login ID and cannot be used with anyone else's login ID.

When you log in, you are prompted with a challenge (a number). You enter this number along with your PIN into the hardware key. This generates your response, which you then type into the computer.

Figure 7-2 SecurID token

Axent Pathways Defender requires the purchase of the hardware keys and special server software. A sample Defender token is shown in Figure 7-3.

NOTE! Axent Pathways Defender authentication is not supported on IPSO.

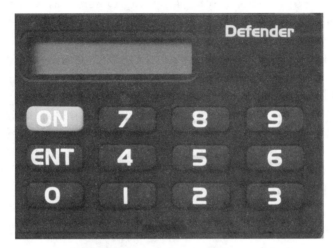

Figure 7-3 Defender token

Remote Access Dial-In User Service (RADIUS)

Originally developed by Livingston (now a part of Lucent), RADIUS is an authentication server usually used by those providing dial-up access for authentication. RADIUS typically employs static passwords, but recent versions of SecurID have a built-in RADIUS server that allows for easier integration. RADIUS can theoretically support any sort of password scheme, static or OTP. A few different types of RADIUS servers can integrate with UNIX or Windows NT password schemes. It is often far easier and more secure to use RADIUS to authenticate against a Windows NT domain versus using actual Microsoft protocols to do it.

Terminal Access Controller Access Control System (TACACS / TACACS+)

TACACS provides access control for routers, network access servers, and other networked computing devices via one or more centralized servers. TACACS was originally developed by BBN Technologies for use on MILNET. Cisco has built upon and enhanced TACACS. The original TACACS is no longer supported by Cisco. A newer version, called TACACS+, provides several enhancements to the original protocol including the use of TCP (instead of UDP) and separation of functions (authentication, authorization, and accounting).

Lightweight Directory Access Protocol (LDAP)

LDAP Directories are becoming popular in midsize to large enterprises as a way to centrally store and manage information about people, places, and things. FireWall-1 allows you to utilize information stored in an LDAP server as well as store FireWall-1 specific data there. This allows you to use existing LDAP tools to manage users as well as the included Account Management Client. All authentication schemes previously mentioned can be used with users defined in an LDAP server in addition to the password that is stored in each LDAP record (typically a fixed password). You also have additional flexibility insofar as groups can be defined in terms of existing hierarchies that may already exist in your LDAP Directory. Users can also be defined in terms of templates. All an administrator has to do is change the template, and all the users who use that template will have their attributes changed accordingly. LDAP requires the purchase of additional licenses in FireWall-1 in order to make use of it, not to mention having an LDAP server.

How Users Authenticate

Now that I have discussed passwords, I can talk about the various ways FireWall-1 can ask users for passwords. Demonstrations of each method are provided in the following sections.

User Authentication

User Authentication allows you to provide authentication for five different services: Telnet, rlogin, HTTP, HTTPS, and FTP. FireWall-1 provides user authentication via the appropriate Security Server processes. These processes are invoked when FireWall-1 needs to authenticate a connection. The Security Server authenticates the session, and then passes it on to the remote server.

For example, if you want to Telnet to 172.29.0.44 and you want FireWall-1 to require authentication, the following exchange would occur:

```
$ telnet 172.29.0.44
Trying 172.29.0.44...
Connected to 172.29.0.44.
Escape character is '^]'.
Check Point FireWall-1 authenticated Telnet server running on
mrhat
User: dwelch
FireWall-1 password: ******
```

```
User dwelch authenticated by FireWall-1 authentication
Connected to 172.29.0.44
Red Hat Linux release 6.0 (Hedwig)
Kernel 2.2.12-20 on an i486
login:
```

The following list explains the steps taken in the previous code:

1. FireWall-1 intercepts the communication between the client and the server.
2. FireWall-1 prompts for a username and password.
3. If the user successfully authenticates with FireWall-1, the connection is then passed on to the destination host. The remote host then prompts for a username and password, which will likely be different from the one given to the firewall.

Because rlogin works in almost exactly the same way, a specific rlogin example is not needed. HTTP uses the standard HTTP authentication screen you would see when accessing a password protected site (see Figure 7-4).

You must enter your username and password. If a specific challenge is needed before you can enter your password, simply enter your username and click OK. You are then presented with the challenge as the "reason" shown in the dialog box.

FTP is a bit more complicated. Even though you can FTP directly to a specific host and FireWall-1 will intercept it, you must still tell the FTP Security Server where to go:

```
$ ftp 172.29.0.44
Connected to 172.29.0.44.
220 aftpd: Check Point FireWall-1 Secure FTP server running on
mrhat
Name (172.29.0.44:dwelch):
```

At this point, you must enter a username in the following format:

```
FTP Site User@FireWall-1 User@Remote Host
```

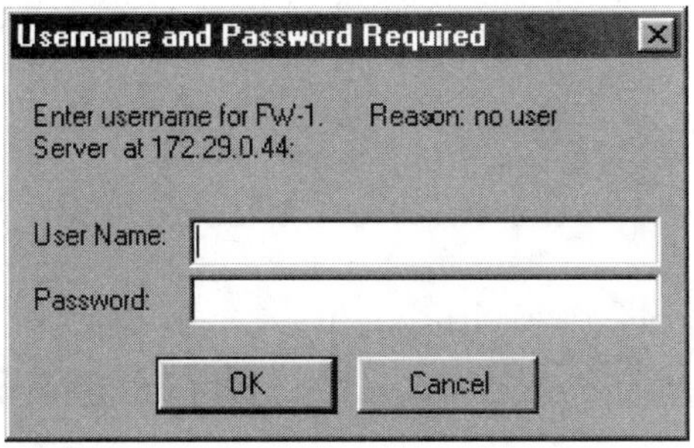

Figure 7-4 User authentication with HTTP

If the FireWall-1 user and the FTP site user are the same, you can enter the user-name in this format:

```
user@Remote Host
```

Here is an example of an FTP authentication:

```
Name (172.29.0.44:dwelch): anonymous@dwelch@172.29.0.44
331 aftpd: FireWall-1 password: you can use password@FW-1-pass-
word
Password:
```

The password is in the following format:

```
FTP Site Password@FireWall-1 Password
```

Anonymous login to an e-mail server usually asks for an e-mail address; dwelch@phoneboy.com is the e-mail address used in this example. Note that if either the username or password contains an @ symbol, you need to enter the @ twice as follows:

```
Password: dwelch@@phoneboy.com@abc123
230-aftpd: User dwelch authenticated by FireWall-1
authentication
230-aftpd: Connected to 172.29.0.44. Logging in...
230-aftpd: 220 stinkpot Microsoft FTP Service (Version 3.0).
230-aftpd: 331 Anonymous access allowed, send identity (e-mail
name) as password.
230 aftpd: 230 Anonymous user logged in.
Remote system type is Windows_NT.
ftp>
```

As of FireWall-1 3.0b build 3064, a new interface is available by adding or modifying a line in `objects.C`. See Chapter 4, FAQ 4.2 for instructions on how to do this. After the ":props (" line, add or modify this line to read:

```
:new_ftp_interface (true)
```

In this case, the FTP to 172.29.0.44 is a bit easier to access via the command line:

```
$ ftp 172.29.0.44
Connected to 172.29.0.44.
220 aftpd: Check Point FireWall-1 Secure FTP server running on
mrhat
Name (172.29.0.44:dwelch):
```

At this point, you must enter a username in the following format:

```
FireWall-1 User@Remote Host
```

The format is used in the following example:

```
Name (172.29.0.44:dwelch): dwelch@172.29.0.44
331 aftpd: FireWall-1 password: you can use FW-1-password
```

Next, simply enter the FireWall-1 Password:

```
Password: abc123
230-aftpd: User dwelch authenticated by FireWall-1 authentication
230-aftpd: Connected to 172.29.0.44. Logging in...
230-aftpd: 220 stinkpot Microsoft FTP Service (Version 3.0).
ftp>
```

You should then be connected to the remote FTP server. You must log in by using the `user` command as follows:

```
ftp> user anonymous
331 Anonymous access allowed, send identity (e-mail name) as
password.
Password: dwelch@phoneboy.com
230 Anonymous user logged in.
ftp>
```

Session Authentication

Session Authentication can be used for any service. Authentication relies on the presence of an agent on the client, which prompts users for authentication as they make the connection request. When necessary, the firewall contacts the agent, which either transparently provides authentication to the firewall or prompts the user for authentication if it cannot provide authentication. Check Point includes agents for all supported platforms (Windows, Solaris, AIX, and HP). Figure 7-5 illustrates an example of what happens when a user tries to use Session Authentication on a Windows

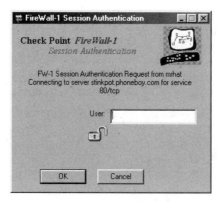

Figure 7-5   Session Authentication logon screen #1

platform. In the figure, the user tries to access 172.29.0.44 (stinkpot.phoneboy.com) via HTTP.

Once you type in your username, you are prompted for your password, as shown in Figure 7-6.

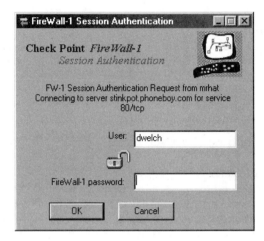

Figure 7-6   Session Authentication logon screen #2

Client Authentication

Client Authentication can be used to authenticate any service. The user must authenticate with the firewall before using the service. The service is then provided to the user a specific number of times and/or for a specific period of time. A user can authenticate in three ways, depending on how Client Authentication is configured:

- A Telnet connection to the firewall on port 259
- An HTTP connection to the firewall on port 900
- Using User or Session Authentication

For the latter case, the authentication looks no different from the example shown earlier in the "User Authentication" section. However, you have two other choices to make with respect to Client Authentication:

- Standard Sign-On
- Specific Sign-On

Standard Sign-On simply allows users to authenticate once and be allowed to do whatever the authentication allows. Specific Sign-On requires users to specify each destination and service they want to use when they authenticate. Users are only allowed to access those services and destinations they specify, even if the rule allows for more. For simplicity's sake, most administrators are satisfied with simply allowing users to use Standard Sign-On, because it requires less end-user training.

Manual authentication via Telnet using Standard Sign-On looks like this:

```
$ telnet mrhat 259
Trying 172.31.0.41...
Connected to mrhat
Escape character is '^]'.
Check Point FireWall-1 Client Authentication Server running on
mrhat
User: dwelch
FireWall-1 password: ******
User dwelch authenticated by FireWall-1 authentication
Choose:
        (1) Standard Sign-on
        (2) Sign-off
        (3) Specific Sign-on
Enter your choice: 1
User authorized for standard services (1 rules)
Connection closed by foreign host.
$
```

With Specific Sign-On, users must specify each service and destination they want to access. The following example sets up HTTP and FTP access to stinkpot.phoneboy.com:

```
$ telnet mrhat 259
Trying 172.31.0.41...
Connected to mrhat
Escape character is '^]'.
Check Point FireWall-1 Client Authentication Server running on
mrhat
User: dwelch
FireWall-1 password: ******
User dwelch authenticated by FireWall-1 authentication
Choose:
        (1) Standard Sign-on
        (2) Sign-off
        (3) Specific Sign-on
Enter your choice: 3
Service (^D to Quit): http
Host: stinkpot.phoneboy.com
Client Authorized for service
Service (^D to Quit): ftp
Host: stinkpot.phoneboy.com
Client Authorized for service
Service (^D to Quit): Connection closed by foreign host.
$
```

HTTP authentication to port 900 on the firewall is shown in Figure 7-7.

Note that a username has already been entered into the form. When you click Submit, the screen shown in Figure 7-8 appears.

Type in your password, and click the Authentication button. You are then presented with the screen shown in Figure 7-9.

Figure 7-7   Client Authentication via HTTP port 900 username

Figure 7-8   Client Authentication via HTTP port 900 password

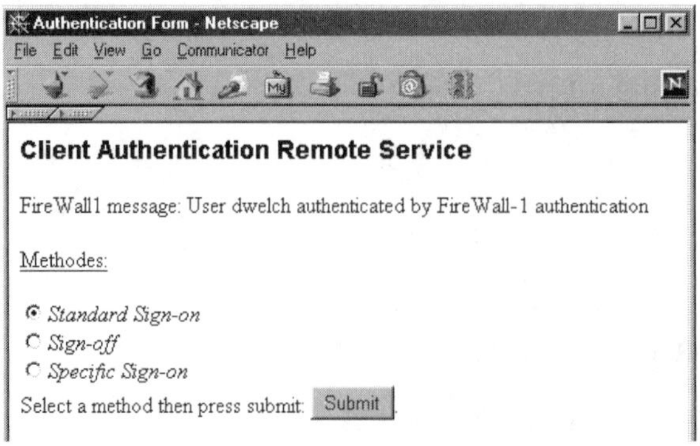

Figure 7-9   Client Authentication via HTTP port 900 Sign-On scheme

If you select Standard Sign-On, the authentication is complete, as shown in Figure 7-10.

If you click Specific Sign-On, a screen appears allowing you to enter the services and hosts you want to access. Figure 7-11 shows how access is being asked for using both FTP and HTTP to host 172.29.0.44.

Figure 7-10   Client Authentication via HTTP port 900 Standard Sign-On

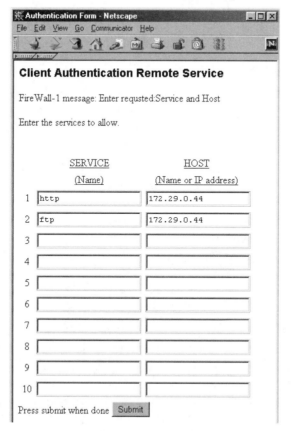

Figure 7-11   Client Authentication via HTTP port 900 Specific Sign-On

Which Authentication Type Should You Use?

Usually, the application you need to authenticate and the OS of the client in question dictate the type of authentication you need to perform. Table 7-1 provides you with a guide to the various authentication schemes.

Client and Session Authentication have a limitation whereby only a single user can come from an IP address you want to authenticate from. Typical UNIX systems and NAT gateways present situations where more than one person can potentially come from a single IP address. In the case of Client Authentication, a user who authenticates from such an IP address could potentially be letting in more users than just himself. Client Authentication can be dangerous in this situation. In the case of Session Authentication, the problem is that it is not clear whom to prompt for Session Authentication on a multiuser system. Because the Session Authentication agent typically caches the login and password information, you either have a situation where the user is constantly entering in (or having to cancel) authentication requests for connections he is not making or more than just the "authorized" user is allowed to perform a service. In these cases, the only appropriate authentication mechanism is User Authentication because each individual session is authenticated in-band, which means you are limited to what you can reasonably authenticate in these cases.

Setting Up Authentication

Now that I have discussed passwords and how the various forms of authentication work, I will discuss how to set up authentication.

Table 7-1   Authentication schemes

Use This Method	Under These Circumstances
User Authentication	• The protocol in question is FTP, HTTP, HTTPS, rlogin, or Telnet. • You want to authenticate each session. • If the protocol is HTTP, authenticate for a specific period of time. • You want to perform content security. • You need the proxy capabilities of the Security Servers.
Client Authentication	• The protocol in question is not FTP, HTTP, HTTPS, rlogin, or Telnet. • You want to authenticate for a specific period of time. • When you want better performance than the Security Servers can provide. • Only one user can come from a given IP address at a time.
Session Authentication	• The protocol in question is not FTP, HTTP, HTTPS, rlogin, or Telnet. • Only one user can come from a given IP address at a time. • You want to authenticate each session. • You have a Session Authentication agent for the client platform you want to authenticate against.

Creating Users

Before you can even begin to authenticate people, you need to know how to create users. In Policy Editor, select Users from the Manage menu. A dialog box similar to Figure 7-12 appears.

Figure 7-12 Manage Users main screen

The buttons on the Manage Users main screen are described as follows:

New: Create a new user, group, or template.

Remove: Remove the user, group, or template selected.

Edit: Edit the user, group, or template selected.

Close: Close the window.

Install: Install the user database on managed firewalls. This must be done anytime the user database has been modified.

When you click New, a pop-up menu shown in Figure 7-13 appears. The options on this menu are described as follows:

Group: Used to create a new group within FireWall-1.

External group: Used to reference a branch of an LDAP Directory for use in Fire-Wall-1. This is discussed in the "LDAP" section of this chapter.

Template: Used to create a template user. Pretty much all the screens you see in Figure 7-14 through 7-23 also apply to templates with the exception of actually setting a password.

Figure 7-13   Manage Users, create New

Default: All users are created as templates. Other templates would be listed below the Default option if they existed. In this case, they do not. Therefore, to create a user, select Default.

For this example, select Default. You are then presented with the dialog shown in Figure 7-14.

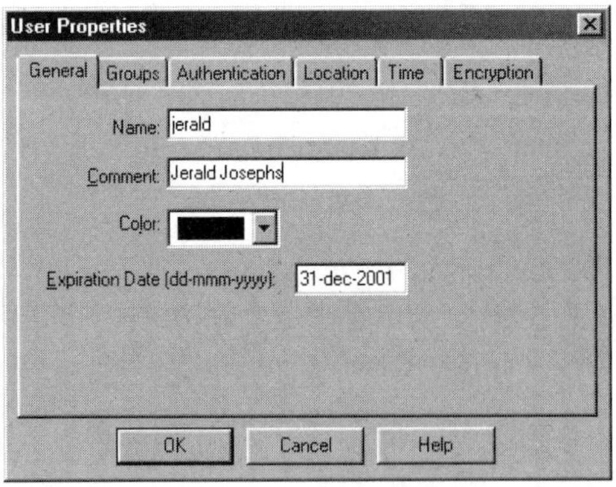

Figure 7-14   Edit User, General tab

The fields on this dialog are described as follows:

Name: Enter the username that the user will use to log on to the system.

Comment: Enter any information you would like. It is strongly suggested that you enter the user's full name in this field.

Expiration Date: After this date, the user cannot authenticate through the firewall.

Next is the Groups tab (see Figure 7-15), where you list the groups the user is a member of.

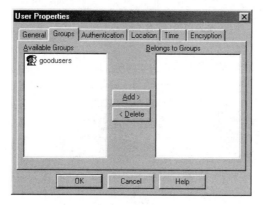

Figure 7-15   Edit User, Groups tab

NOTE!   All users belong to the default group "All Users," which is never shown on the Groups tab.

NOTE!   There is a bug in the version 4.0 SP3 GUI (build 4050). If you make users a member of a group via this dialog, the user will not be treated as part of that group. This bug is fixed in later versions of the GUI, which you can obtain through Check Point Software subscription and/or from your reseller.

Next, let's look at the Authentication tab (see Figure 7-16).

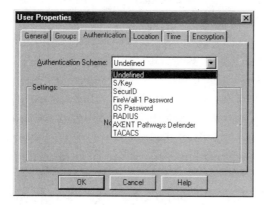

Figure 7-16   Edit User, Authentication tab

A user must have a form of authentication defined. Recall that the authentication types were described earlier in this chapter, although specific settings for some of these types are discussed in this section. I'll start with S/Key (see Figure 7-17).

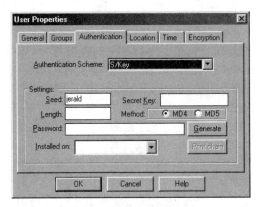

Figure 7-17   Edit User, Authentication tab, S/Key

The fields on this tab are described as follows:

Seed: This field usually contains the username, but can be anything. It is used as part of calculating the S/Key chain.

Secret Key: This field contains the password the user enters into an S/Key generator to generate the response to the S/Key challenge. It must be at least ten characters long.

Length: This field contains the number of passwords in the chain. This value also indicates the number of times the user can authenticate before his S/Key chain needs to be regenerated. It is actually one less than this number because the first password in the chain is displayed in the GUI, so you can match the user with the printed S/Key chain (see Print Chain at the end of this list). As a result, the first password in the chain is not used.

Method: MD4 or MD5 is used to generate the proper S/Key response. MD5 is stronger, but not all S/Key generators support it. If your version of FireWall-1 does not ask you which method you want to use, it uses MD4.

Installed on: With S/Key users, the user can only exist on a single FireWall-1 gateway. This is to ensure that each password is only used once. The only easy way to do this is to only allow you to install the user on a single gateway.

Password: Leave this field blank. It will be filled in once the Generate button is clicked.

Generate: Once the Installed on, Seed, Length, and Password fields are filled in, click Generate. A password then appears in this field. If none of the fields are filled in (except for Installed on, which must be filled in), FireWall-1 will make up a secret key and generate a chain of 100 passwords. FireWall-1 does not tell you what the key is, so you need to click the Print Chain button. If a user loses the printout, there is no way to recover the chain, and a new chain will have to be generated.

Print Chain: Once you have all the fields filled in, click Print Chain to print out the entire chain of passwords. This printout allows a user to use S/Key authentication in situations where having an S/Key generator is not desirable. Do not lose this piece of paper!

If you decide to use FireWall-1 Password as your authentication type, see Figure 7-18.

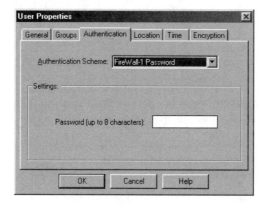

Figure 7-18   Edit User, Authentication tab, FireWall-1 Password

Enter your password in the Password field. Your password is stored locally and encrypted with a mechanism similar to the one used to store UNIX passwords in `/etc/passwd`.

If you decide to use RADIUS as your authentication type, see Figure 7-19.

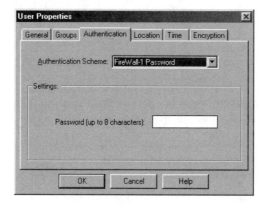

Figure 7-19   Edit User, Authentication tab, RADIUS

This screen presents you with any server objects of type RADIUS or any groups that might contain them. By default, all RADIUS servers will be queried. For TACACS, you will receive a dialog similar to the one shown in Figure 7-20.

Only server objects of type TACACS will be shown on this screen.

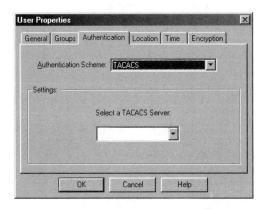

Figure 7-20   Edit User, Authentication tab, TACACS

Let's move on to the Location tab (see Figure 7-21).

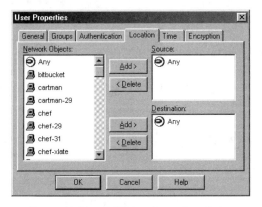

Figure 7-21   Edit User, Location tab

On this screen, you can specify which sources and destinations are permitted for a particular user. Note that the rulebase can specifically override this designation on a per-rule basis, as I will describe in more detail in the next section.

The Time tab defines when a user is allowed to authenticate (see Figure 7-22).

The user must still be permitted by the rulebase.

The Encryption tab (see Figure 7-23) is not used at this point. This tab is discussed in Chapter 11.

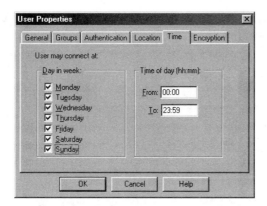

Figure 7-22   Edit User, Time tab

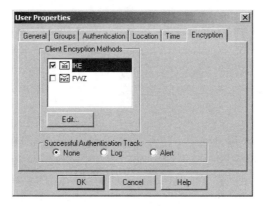

Figure 7-23   Edit User, Encryption tab

Creating Groups

Creating a new group is necessary if you only want to permit some of your users to do certain things. FireWall-1 does not allow you to define rules in terms of individual users, but rather as groups. The dialog looks similar to the one shown in Figure 7-24.

Setting Supported Authentication Schemes

You must configure the workstation object representing your firewall so that the authentication schemes you intend to use are enabled on your firewall object. Edit the object, and then select the Authentication tab (see Figure 7-25).

By default, OS and FireWall-1 Password are disabled. If you want to use these authentication schemes, you need to select them on this tab.

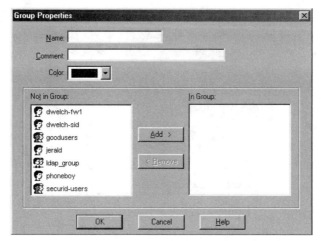

Figure 7-24   Creating a new group

Figure 7-25   Workstation Properties, Authentication tab

User Authentication

The steps for setting up User Authentication are as follows:

1. Create the necessary users and groups required for authentication, and then install the user database.
2. Ensure that the appropriate Security Servers are enabled in `$FWDIR/conf/fwauthd.conf`.
3. Create the appropriate rule(s) in the rulebase.
4. Configure the User Authentication Action Properties.
5. Configure the Rulebase Properties Authentication tab.
6. Verify and install the policy.

After creating your users, verify that the appropriate Security Servers are enabled in `$FWDIR/conf/fwauthd.conf`. The lines for the servers you want to enable should be present and not commented out (i.e., line begins with a #). The FTP, HTTP, Telnet, and rlogin servers are enabled if these lines are present in `fwauthd.conf`:

```
21              in.aftpd        wait    0
80              in.ahttpd       wait    0
23              in.atelnetd     wait    0
513             in.arlogind     wait    0
```

You then need to create the appropriate rule in the rulebase. When adding the source of the rule, right-click the source field, and select Add User Access. This screen is shown in Figure 7-26.

Select the appropriate group. The Location must also be set. The No restriction option means *any* in the rulebase. The Restrict option allows you to select a network object or group that represents where you want to authenticate the connections from.

Figure 7-26 Add User Access

For example, if you want to authenticate all users in the group "knights-of-the-roundtable" from the network camelot to the host castle-anthrax via Telnet and HTTP, the rule would look like the one shown in Figure 7-27.

Figure 7-27 Sample User Authentication rule

You must then edit the User Auth properties. You do this by right-clicking the Action field of the rule and selecting Edit Properties. Figure 7-28 shows the screen that appears.

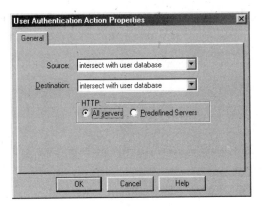

Figure 7-28   User Authentication Action Properties

For both the source and destination, you will be able to select one of two options:

Intersect with user database: This option means that if the user who authenticates is coming from a source or destination (as appropriate) that is not allowed as defined in the user's record, the user will actually be denied, even if the rule says the user should be allowed access. This option allows you to set up fairly granular access.

Ignore user database: This option means that users who would otherwise be denied as a result of the allowed sources or destinations defined in their user record are allowed anyway.

To illustrate the way these options work, let's use the users sir-gallahad and sir-lancelot with the rule created earlier. The allowed sources and destinations for sir-gallahad are both *any*. The allowed sources for sir-lancelot are *any*, but his allowed destination does not include castle-anthrax (i.e., it is not "any" or a group that includes castle-anthrax). If the User Authentication properties for the rule were defined using "intersect with user database" for the destination, then when sir-robin tried to authenticate to access castle-anthrax, he would be denied, even if he were coming from camelot[1] and presented correct authentication. If the setting were "ignore user database," sir-robin would be permitted to go to castle-anthrax provided he supplied the correct authentication and were coming from camelot.

For the HTTP section of this screen, there are two options:

- *Predefined Servers:* This option is the default. It means you can only go to servers defined in the Policy Properties Security Servers tab. Using this setting only makes sense if you are using FireWall-1 as a reverse proxy server.

---

1.   It's only a model.

- *All servers:* This setting *should* be the default for this screen. It allows you to authenticate and go to any HTTP server without having to define it in the Policy Properties Security Servers tab. Of course, it still must match the rulebase. Unless you are using this rule to authenticate access to internal servers only, it is *highly recommended* that you use this setting (otherwise, the rule won't work).

Finally, you must configure the Policy Properties Authentication tab (see Figure 7-29), which contains two important settings.

Figure 7-29   Rulebase Properties, Authentication tab

The User Authentication timeout is used for two purposes:

- Inactive authenticated Telnet, FTP, and rlogin connections are terminated after the amount of time specified.
- For HTTP authentication used with an OTP scheme, the specified time indicates how long the user will be authenticated before requesting a new password. *If a static password scheme is used with HTTP, this setting has no effect because Web browsers cache passwords.*

The Authentication Failure Track provides three options that determine what happens when a user fails to authenticate successfully:

None: Nothing is logged when a user fails to authenticate successfully.

Log: A long log entry is generated when a user fails to authenticate successfully.

Alert: A long log entry is generated plus an Alert is sent as defined in the Rulebase Properties.

Once the rules and the Rulebase Properties are set up to your liking, install the security policy.

NOTE!   Because the authenticated connections will appear to originate from the firewall upon successful authentication, make sure that your security policy outbound from the firewall permits the connection. If "Apply Gateway Rules to Interface Direction" is set to Inbound and "Allow Outgoing Packets" is enabled, this generally will not be a problem.

The Importance of Rule Order in User Authentication

There is one case where FireWall-1 does not process the rules in order but instead uses the rule that is most permissive. This occurs when User Authentication for HTTP, FTP, Telnet, and rlogin is used and such a rule is matched in the rulebase. If during the in-order rulebase evaluation the rule that matches the connection (based on source, destination, and service) is User Authentication; then all rules in the rulebase are evaluated and the least restrictive one will apply.

To give you an idea of what this means, consider the security policy shown in Figure 7-30.

No.	Source	Destination	Service	Action	Track	Install On
1	Any	Web_Server	http https	accept		Gateways
2	Any	Email_Server	smtp	accept		Gateways
3	Any	ftp_server	ftp	accept		Gateways
4	DMZAdmins@internal-networks	DMZ_net	telnet ftp	User Auth	Long	Gateways
5	FWAdmins@internal-networks	Local_Gateway	telnet	User Auth	Long	Gateways
6	Any	Local_Gateway	Any	drop	Long	Gateways
7	internal-networks	Any	telnet ftp http https	accept	Long	Gateways
8	Any	Any	Any	drop	Long	Gateways

Figure 7-30   Sample rulebase with User Authentication

Based on the rules and how the rulebase rules are applied, the following list details how these rules will apply themselves:

- Everyone on the Internet will be able to access the HTTP, HTTPS, and SMTP servers without any authentication from the firewall.
- Everyone will have access via FTP to the ftp_server. There are other rules (Rule 4 and Rule 7) that could match this rule as well, but Rule 3 will match first because it is listed first and does not involve User Authentication. This is not a major problem, but worth noting.
- Users in the DMZAdmins group who Telnet or FTP from the internal-nets to the DMZ-net will not have authenticated access to all servers in the DMZ-net for two reasons: Rule 3 and Rule 7. Rule 3 will match FTP connections to the FTP server

before Rule 4. When Rule 4 is matched, because it is a User Authentication rule, the least restrictive rule will apply and Rule 7 will permit access.

- When people Telnet to the firewall, Rule 5 will match initially, but again because of the least restrictive rule for User Authentication, Rule 7 will actually permit the communication without authentication.
- Rule 7 also permits these services to the firewall as well, which may not be desirable.

The major problem in this rulebase is that Rule 4 and Rule 5 are not providing authentication in cases where you would expect them to, because Rule 7 is too permissive. You can fix this by making Rule 7 a bit less permissive by excluding the DMZ and Local_Gateway from the allowed destination, as shown in Figure 7-31.

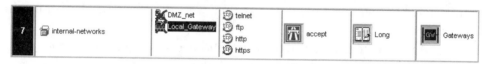

Figure 7-31 Corrected Rule #7 from Figure 7-30

Session Authentication

The basic steps for setting up Session Authentication are the same as the previous steps for setting up User Authentication:

1. Create the necessary users and groups required for authentication, and then install the user database.
2. Create the appropriate rule(s) in the rulebase.
3. Configure the Session Authentication Action Properties.
4. Configure the Rulebase Properties Authentication tab.
5. Verify and install the policy.

The source and destination for the rule are defined in the same way as those in the preceding section. A Session Authentication rule might look like the screen shown in Figure 7-32.

Figure 7-32 Sample Session Authentication rule

You then configure the Session Authentication Action Properties by right-clicking Session Auth and selecting Edit Properties. A screen similar to the one shown in Figure 7-33 appears.

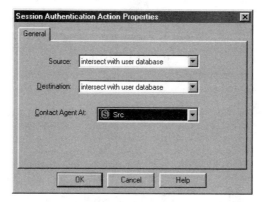

Figure 7-33 Session Authentication Action Properties

Source and Destination are defined as they were for User Authentication in the previous section.

Contact Agent At tells FireWall-1 on which host to attempt to contact a Session Authentication Agent. The possibilities are as follows:

Src: The IP address that is originating the connection will be contacted. This is the default and the most common.

Dst: The IP address that the connection is destined for will be contacted. Use this option for protocols where the client/server model is reversed, such as X Windows.

Other Host: You can select which workstation will receive the authentication request.

Once the rules are set up to your liking, verify that the Authentication Failure Track is set appropriately in the Policy Properties Authentication tab, and install the security policy.

 **NOTE!** Because the firewall will be originating a connection to port 261 on a remote host, make sure that your outbound security policy does not prohibit this. If "Apply Gateway Rules to Interface Direction" is set to Inbound and "Allow Outgoing Packets" is enabled, this generally will not be a problem.

Client Authentication

The basic steps for setting up Client Authentication are the same as the steps used to set up the User and Session Authentication:

1. Create the necessary users and groups required for authentication, and then install the user database.

2. Create the appropriate rule(s) in the rulebase.
3. Configure the Client Authentication Action Properties.
4. Configure the Rulebase Properties Authentication tab.
5. Verify and install the policy.

The source and destination for the rule are defined in the same way as those in the "User Authentication" section. A Client Authentication rule might look similar to the screen shown in Figure 7-34.

Figure 7-34 Client Authentication rule example

You then configure the Client Authentication Action Properties by right-clicking Client Auth and selecting Edit Properties. A screen similar to the one shown in Figure 7-35 appears.

Source and Destination are defined as they were in the "User Authentication" section. Due to the nature of Client Authentication, it is not possible for the Client Authentication process to know where the client may be connecting to when the Required Sign On is set to Standard, so the user's allowed destinations cannot be checked.

Required Sign On can be set to Standard or Specific. Standard allows the user to log in and be automatically authorized for all services that the rule(s) allows for. The Specific selection means that the user must manually request each service and each host he will be trying to contact. Examples of each of these methods were provided in the "User Authentication" section of this chapter.

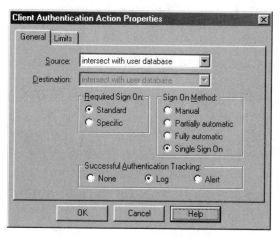

Figure 7-35 Client Authentication Action Properties, General tab

The Sign On Method (which is displayed in version 4.0 and later) can be set to one of the following options:

Manual: Authentication can only occur via a Telnet to the firewall on port 259 or via HTTP to the firewall on port 900. Note that the other methods in this list also allow for manual authentication.

Partially Automatic: FireWall-1 allows you to use User Authentication to perform a Standard Sign On. This means you can Telnet, FTP, rlogin, or HTTP to a destination permitted by the rule, and FireWall-1 will use User Authentication to authenticate you when necessary.

Fully Automatic: FireWall-1 attempts to use Session Authentication when the rule is matched and the user has not previously been authenticated. If the user successfully authenticates, FireWall-1 performs a Standard Sign On.

Single Sign On: When used with Meta IP, this option allows users to sign on as a result of authenticating with Windows NT. Otherwise, this option has no effect.

You can enable Partially or Fully Automatic Client Authentication in FireWall-1 3.0 by adding or modifying the following line in `$FWDIR/conf/objects.C`:

```
:automatically_open_ca_rules (true)
```

See Chapter 4, FAQ 4.2 for information on how to modify `objects.C`. Successful Authentication Tracking can be set to one of the following options:

None: Nothing is logged when a user authenticates successfully against this rule.

Log: A long log entry is generated when a user successfully authenticates against this rule.

Alert: A long log entry is generated plus an Alert is sent as defined in the Rulebase Properties.

You also need to set the timeout period for the authentication in the Limits tab (see Figure 7-36).

Authorization Timeout can be set to a specific period of time or indefinite. If you choose indefinite, either the user must explicitly sign off and reload the security policy or stop and start FireWall-1 in order for the user to no longer be permitted. If you select Refreshable timeout, the timeout resets every time the user makes a successful connection against this rule, which means that the user only has to re-authenticate if the user has not made any new connections for a period of time.

The Number of Sessions Allowed refers to the number of individual connections the user is allowed to make through the firewall before the authentication expires. With HTTP (or any other service that makes lots of individual connections), the

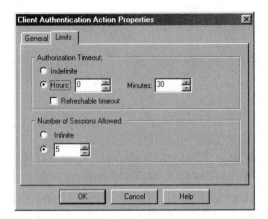

Figure 7-36   Client Authentication Action Properties, Limits tab

default of five connections will be used very quickly. With Telnet, the user is allowed to make five Telnet connections before his authentication expires.

NOTE!   If Partially Automatic Authentication is enabled and a user uses HTTP to authenticate, there must not be a rule (such as a stealth rule) listed, before the Client Authentication rule, that prohibits HTTP to access the firewall .

Once the rules are set up to your liking, verify the Policy Properties settings on the Authentication tab (see Figure 7-29). The Authentication Failure Track is described in the "User Authentication" section of this chapter. Enable Wait Mode changes the behavior of Client Authentication via Telnet. What normally happens is that once authentication is successful, the Telnet connection to the firewall closes. With Enable Wait Mode, the connection stays open. The authentication is active as long as this connection is open. Once this connection is closed, the authentication is no longer valid. This particular option does not scale well because the firewall has to keep a connection open to each client that authenticates. At least in my experience, FireWall-1 is unable to handle more than about 20 to 30 users authenticated with this option enabled.

Once these properties are set as desired, install the security policy.

Integrating External Authentication Servers

The following sections describe how to integrate the various supported authentication servers with FireWall-1. Note that if you do an eitherbound security policy, you must ensure that the firewall module can talk to the external authentication server on the appropriate port. Figure 7-37 shows an example using SecurID.

Figure 7-37 Rule allowing a firewall to access SecurID server

SecurID

To configure FireWall-1 for SecurID authentication, you simply need to copy the `sdconf.rec` file from the ACE/Server to `/var/ace/sdconf.rec` on UNIX or IPSO or to `%SystemRoot%\System32\sdconf.rec` on Windows NT. Generating a proper `sdconf.rec` file on the ACE/Server is the tricky part of this process.

Your firewall will be defined as an ACE/Client within the ACE/Server. Be sure that the client hostname and IP address of the firewall defined in the ACE/Server agree with the firewall's own definitions. This means that the client hostname specified should be the same as the UNIX, Windows NT, or IPSO command `hostname` and that the IP address that this name resolves to is the same on both systems. The other IP addresses associated with the firewall should be listed as Secondary Nodes. These Secondary Nodes must be listed in order for the ACE/Server to accept authentication requests from the firewall. For IPSO systems, do not include the VRRP IP addresses.

SecurID is predefined on most versions of FireWall-1. SecurID uses UDP port 5500 and TCP port 5510.

Axent Pathways Defender

To configure FireWall-1 for Defender authentication, create a server object of type Defender. The configuration options shown in Figure 7-38 appear.

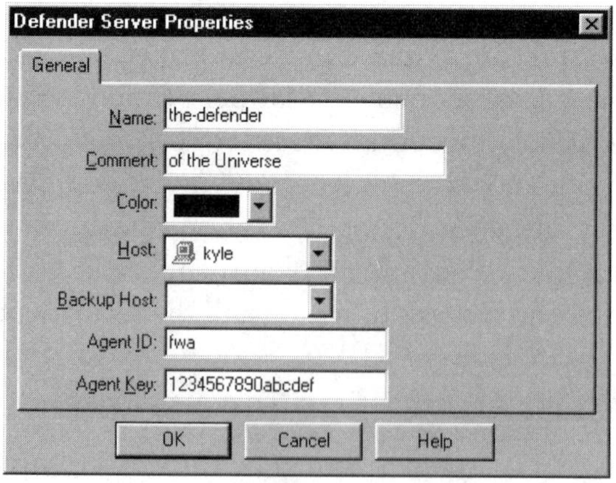

Figure 7-38 Defender Server Properties

The fields on this screen are described as follows:

Name: Enter the name you want to give the object. It should be unique.

Comment: Enter any information you would like in this field.

Color: Select whichever color is appropriate.

Host: Indicate the workstation object that the Defender server runs on.

Backup Host: Indicate the workstation object that the backup Defender server runs on.

Agent ID: Enter the Agent ID that FireWall-1 uses to identify itself to the Defender server.

Agent Key: Enter the Agent Key that FireWall-1 uses to encrypt data between FireWall-1 and the Defender server.

Once this screen has been completed, you should be able to create users of type Defender.

NOTE! The IPSO versions of FireWall-1 do not support Axent Pathways Defender authentication and probably will not for the foreseeable future. Unfortunately, the software itself does not tell you this—authentication just fails. However, the latest versions of the Defender server come with a RADIUS add-on that allows Defender authentication to work via RADIUS, which does work with IPSO versions of FireWall-1.

RADIUS

FireWall-1 3.0 integrates with any Radius 1.x-compliant server using simple password authentication. FireWall-1 4.0 onwards will work with any 1.x or 2.x server.

Adding a Firewall to RADIUS Server's Clients File

The clients file (in `/etc/raddb` on UNIX stations) contains entries that are of the following format:

```
radius-client       shared-secret
```

The *radius-client* in this case is your firewall. Note that this name should reflect the hostname your firewall resolves as on your RADIUS server. You may need to do some debugging to determine the correct hostname.

The *shared-secret* is a password that both the RADIUS client (your firewall) and the RADIUS server will use for encryption when communicating with each other. In FireWall-1 3.x, shared secrets beginning with a number or the letter *f* have problems.

Adding Users in RADIUS Server's Users File

You may not need to add users in the users file if you already have existing RADIUS users in your database file (typically in `/etc/raddb` on UNIX). If you are setting up new users, your user entries should look something like this:

```
phoneboy      Password = "abc123", Expiration = "Dec 31 2001"
              User-Service-Type = Login-User
```

Note that there are other entries you can put in the users file, which are not used by FireWall-1. The only entries that FireWall-1 cares about are the entries listed in the previous example. Note that if you install a RADIUS server on a UNIX or Windows NT machine and you want to use the existing users configured in the OS for authentication, make sure you have an entry in the users file that looks similar to this:

```
DEFAULT   Auth-Type = System, User-Service-Type =
Login-User
```

Creating a RADIUS Service (Optional)

In FireWall-1 4.0 and later, you can use RADIUS on a nonstandard port. You will need to create the RADIUS service as appropriate. The default port for RADIUS is UDP 1645.

Creating a RADIUS Server Object

You will need to create a workstation object for your RADIUS server in your Security Policy Editor. You then need to create a new server object of type RADIUS. The dialog in Figure 7-39 shows the RADIUS Server Properties.

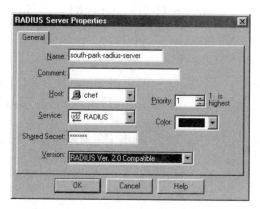

Figure 7-39   RADIUS Server Properties

The fields on this screen are described as follows:

Name: Enter the name you want to give the object. It should be unique.

Comment: Enter any information you would like in this field.

Host: Indicate the workstation object that the RADIUS server runs on.

Priority: If you have multiple RADIUS servers, you can prioritize the order in which they are queried. The default is 1, which is the highest priority, meaning it will be queried first. Check Point recommends only having one server defined with each priority.

Service: Indicate the port on which RADIUS will run. By default, this is port 1645 (i.e., the default RADIUS port). Note that this option is not available in FireWall-1 3.0.

Color: Select whichever color is appropriate.

Shared Secret: Indicate the shared secret. This should be the same shared secret configured on the RADIUS server.

Version: Choose the appropriate version of the RADIUS server. Note that this option is not available in FireWall-1 3.0.

Once these fields have been completed, you should be able to create users of type RADIUS.

TACACS/TACACS+

The TACACS configuration is very similar to RADIUS, although it is much simpler. As with RADIUS, you must configure a server object of type TACACS after defining the workstation object on which your TACACS server runs (see Figure 7-40).

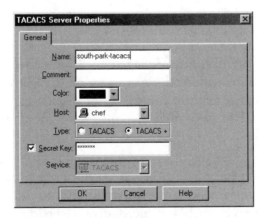

Figure 7-40   TACACS Server Properties

The fields on this screen are described as follows:

Name: Enter the name you want to give the object. It should be unique.

Comment: Enter any information you would like in this field.

Color: Select whichever color is appropriate.

Host: Indicate the workstation object that the TACACS server runs on.

Type: Choose TACACS or TACACS+ as necessary.

Secret Key: Enter the secret key. This should be the same as the NAS Key defined on your TACACS+ server (only active when TACACS+ is used).

Service: Indicate the port on which TACACS is being used (only active when TACACS is used).

Once these fields are complete, you should be able to create users of type TACACS.

NOTE! TACACS uses UDP port 49, and TACACS+ uses TCP port 49.

LDAP

In order to integrate FireWall-1 into an LDAP server, you need to have certain items:

- The suffix of the directory. Your LDAP administrator should be able to tell you the suffix of the directory. For the following examples, I will use `"o=acmelabs, c=us."`

- An account on the LDAP server that has at least read access to the parts of the directory FireWall-1 will use.

If you want to use the Account Management Client to edit users on the LDAP server, you need an account with read/write access on the LDAP server.

Once you have this information, you will want to configure the LDAP server with the schema for FireWall-1. Note that although you could simply disable schema checking, this makes your directory far less manageable. Schema checking ensures that the data you import into the directory server follows a particular format. Check Point includes a schema file in `$FWDIR/lib/ldap/schema.ldif`. However, it is coded in LDIF format and thus can only be imported into directory servers that support modifying schemas via an LDIF file. Current versions of Netscape Directory Server (and possibly others) support this using the following command:

```
ldapmodify -D "cn=root" -w password -f schema.ldif
```

When using this command, replace `cn=root` with your rootdn name, and replace `password` with your actual password. The output of this command should continually print "modifying entry cn=schema" over and over without any errors.

Other LDAP servers, such as OpenLDAP v1 and v2, do not support schema modifications in this manner. As a result, you have to modify your schema so that it includes the FireWall-1 schema. Instructions on how to do this are provided in Appendix B for OpenLDAP v1 and Appendix C for OpenLDAP v2.[2]

Once all of the previous requirements are met, you can begin to configure FireWall-1 to use LDAP. The first change you need to make is in the Policy Properties LDAP tab (see Figure 7-41).

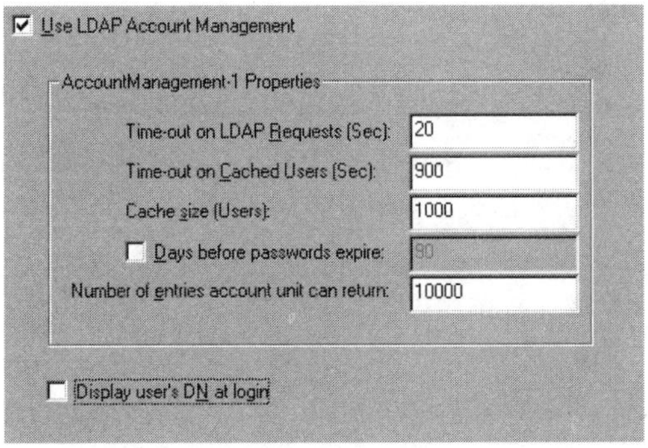

Figure 7-41   Policy Properties, LDAP tab

The options for LDAP Account Management are described as follows:

Use LDAP Account Management: Select this check box if you want to allow FireWall-1 to use LDAP.

Time-out on LDAP Requests (Sec): Indicate the length of time FireWall-1 will wait for a response from the LDAP server before giving up.

Time-out on Cached Users (Sec): Indicate the amount of time FireWall-1 will cache an entry it has read from the LDAP server before it attempts to reread the entry from the LDAP server.

Cache size: Indicate the number of users FireWall-1 will attempt to keep cached in memory.

Days before passwords expire: If this box is selected, passwords specified in the General tab of the Account Unit Properties window expire after this number of days and a new password must be chosen.

Number of entries account unit can return: Specify the maximum number of entries a particular account unit will return.

---

2. All of the LDAP examples in this book were done against an OpenLDAP server.

Display user's DN at login: If this box is selected, FireWall-1 displays the user's Distinguished Name in the LDAP server before asking for a password. This is used to ensure that the user is authenticating against the correct record in the LDAP server, thus making it a useful diagnostic tool.

Once you have configured these properties, you can then define an LDAP Account Unit, which is created as an object of type Server. The screens to create an LDAP Account Unit start with Figure 7-42.

The fields on this screen are described as follows:

Name: Enter the name you want to give to the LDAP Account Unit. It should be unique.

Comment: Enter any information you would like in this field.

Account Unit Usage: This screen is only available in version 4.1 and later. You can use the Certificate Revocation Lists (CRLs are used in a Public Key Infrastructure) stored in the LDAP server. If you are only using the CRL Retrieval function, you do not need to fill in the Login DN or Password, because CRLs can be obtained through an anonymous bind with the LDAP server. User Management allows you to use accounts stored in the LDAP server for authentication.

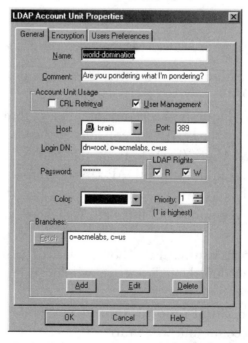

Figure 7-42 LDAP Account Unit Properties, General tab

Host: Indicate the workstation object that represents the machine the LDAP server runs on.

Port: Indicate the port on which the LDAP server is listening. Usually, this is port 389.

Login DN: Indicate the Distinguished Name that FireWall-1 will use to bind to the LDAP server to obtain information.

Password: Indicate the password needed to bind as the specified DN.

LDAP Rights: Specify the rights the specified DN will have. R equals read access; W equals write access.

Color: Select the appropriate color.

Priority: Specify this particular account unit's priority in relation to other account units.

Branches: Indicate the branches (or suffixes) this LDAP account unit refers to. Depending on the LDAP server you are using, you may be able to fetch this information by clicking on the Fetch button. Use the Add, Delete, and Edit buttons as appropriate.

The Encryption tab is shown in Figure 7-43.

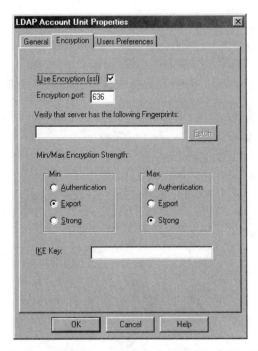

Figure 7-43   LDAP Account Unit Properties, Encryption tab

The fields for this screen are described as follows:

Use Encryption (ssl): If you need to use SSL to access your LDAP server, select this check box.

Encryption port: Indicate the port used to make the encrypted connection to the LDAP server. The default is port 636.

Verify that server has the following Fingerprints: Because FireWall-1 does not use a certificate authority (CA) to verify keys, you should obtain the server key fingerprints via some non-network method and enter them in this box. If you do not, FireWall-1 will fill in this information the first time an SSL connection is made to the LDAP server. On subsequent attempts to connect, FireWall-1 compares what it receives with what is in this box and displays an error message if there is a discrepancy.

Min/Max Encryption Strength: Set the minimum and maximum level of encryption you want to allow for the SSL connection to the LDAP server. Export refers to 40-bit encryption. Strong refers to 128-bit encryption.

IKE Key: Indicate the IKE Shared Secret when IKE is used between the firewall and LDAP server.

The User Preferences tab is shown in Figure 7-44.

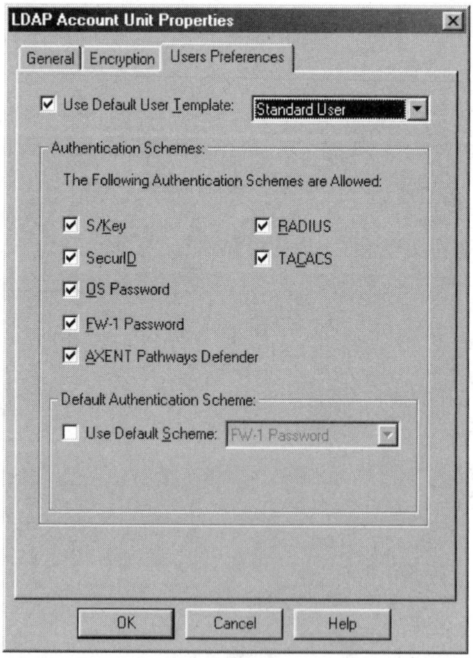

Figure 7-44 LDAP Account Unit Properties, User Preferences tab

The fields on this tab are described as follows:

Use Default User Template: This option exists in FireWall-1 4.1 and later. If the LDAP server does not provide a default user template, the template specified in this field is used.

Authentication Schemes: This field defines the authentication schemes this account unit will allow. It is very similar to the specifications listed in the Workstation Properties for your firewall object(s).

Default Authentication Scheme: If you are using an existing LDAP Directory where a particular DN does not have FireWall-1-specific information as part of the record, this option can be used to give these users an authentication scheme. Without this option selected, authentication would fail for that particular DN. Note that S/Key is not allowed as an option, because more information is needed to establish an S/Key chain.

Once you have defined the LDAP Account Unit, you then need to create an External Group via the Manage Users interface. Figure 7-45 shows this screen.

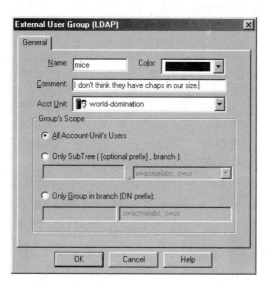

Figure 7-45 Create External Group

The fields on the General tab are described as follows:

Name: Enter the name you want to give this external group.

Color: Choose the appropriate color for this group.

Comment: Enter any information you would like in this field.

Acct Unit: Choose the LDAP Account Unit you defined earlier.

Group's Scope: You can further narrow down the Account Unit specified by either designating a certain subtree or by designating an existing LDAP group using a DN prefix.

Once you have completed these fields, you can create a rule in terms of this new external group (see Figure 7-46).

Figure 7-46 Sample rule with LDAP External Group

Frequently Asked Questions

Now that you have learned the basics of setting up authentication, take a look at the following FAQ for more information. As in previous chapters, the FAQ are numbered for easy reference.

7.1: How Do I Use All the Users in My External Authentication Server without Entering Them into FireWall-1?

Because of the way you configure LDAP into FireWall-1, LDAP does this automatically. However, if you are using RADIUS, SecurID, Defender, TACACS, or even a Windows NT domain, you need to create a user with the username "generic*" (only one such user can be defined). FireWall-1 queries the external authentication mechanism defined in generic* for users that are not defined in FireWall-1. You configure this user as you would any other user, keeping in mind that the parameters you set for generic* apply to all users not otherwise defined in FireWall-1. For users that require different parameters (for example, those that need to be in different groups), you still need to define these users individually in FireWall-1.

7.2: How Do I Integrate FireWall-1 into a Windows NT Domain?

If you have FireWall-1 on Windows NT, you can simply make the firewall system part of your Windows NT domain and set the generic* user up to use OS Authentication. However, it is generally not recommended that you run any of the Microsoft Networking services on your firewall.

If your FireWall-1 does not run on Windows NT or you decide not to run the Microsoft Networking services on your Windows NT firewall, you can set up a RADIUS server that pulls its authentication information from Windows NT, which requires running a RADIUS server on a Windows NT server. You can easily set up FireWall-1 to authenticate against the RADIUS server. This configuration is far more secure than running Microsoft Networking services on your Windows NT firewall.

7.3: How Do I Allow People Access Based on What They Are Logged in as on Their Windows Workstation?

This involves using a product by Check Point called Meta IP. It is outside the scope of this book to discuss this product. For more details on this product, visit Check Point's Web site at www.checkpoint.com.

7.4: How Do I Import or Export Users from a FireWall-1 User Database?

The commands in question are `fw dbimport` and `fw dbexport` respectively. The options for `fw dbimport` are described in Table 7-2. The usage is as follows:

```
fw dbimport [-m] [-s] [-v] [-r] [-k errors] [-f file]
[-d delim]
```

Table 7-2 `fw dbimport` Options

Parameter	Description
`-m`	If an existing user is encountered in the import file and this option is specified, the user's default values will be replaced by the values in the template (the default value or the value given in the attribute list for that user in the import file), and the original values will be ignored. If this option is not specified, an existing user's original values will not be modified.
`-s`	Suppress the warning messages issued when an existing user's values are changed by values in the import file.
`-v`	Verbose mode.
`-r`	All existing users in the database will be deleted (but not groups or templates).
`-k nerrors`	Continue processing until nerror errors are encountered. The line count in the error messages starts from 1 including the attributes line and counts empty or commented out lines.
`-f file`	Specifies the name of the import file. The default import file is `$FWDIR/conf/user_def_file`.
`-d`	Specifies a delimiter different from the default value (;).

The `fw dbexport` options are documented in Table 7-3. The usage is as follows:

```
fw dbexport [ [-g <group> | -u <user>] [-d <delim>]
[-a {attrib1, attrib2, ...} ] [-f <file>] ]
```

Table 7-3 `fw dbexport` Options

Parameter	Description
`-g`	Specifies a group of users to be exported (others are not exported).
`-u`	Specifies that only the specified user be exported.
`-d`	Specifies a delimiter different from the default value (;).
`-a`	Specifies the attributes to export in the form of a comma-separated list between {} characters, for example, -a {name,days} . If there is only one attribute, the {} may be omitted.
`-f`	Specifies the name of the output file. The default output file is `$FWDIR/conf/user_def_file`.

NOTE! FireWall-1 Passwords are stored in the output encrypted with the UNIX `crypt()` function using the first two characters of the actual password as the "salt" argument.

NOTE! The `fw dbimport` function will not import users who are assigned to groups that do not exist in the User Database. You need to create these groups manually before importing the users.

7.5: How Do I Add My Own Custom Message for Authentication?

Go to the Policy Properties Security Servers tab, which is shown in Figure 7-47.

You can specify welcome files for Telnet, FTP, rlogin, and Client Authentication. Specify the full path to the file, which must exist on the firewall module.

7.6: How Do I Forward Authenticated HTTP Requests to an HTTP Proxy?

As shown in Figure 7-47, there is a field called HTTP Next Proxy. If you want Fire-Wall-1 to send requests to a proxy server, fill in the host and port number of the proxy server. Note that this only works when FireWall-1 is configured as the proxy server for your Web-browsing clients.

7.7: Can I Use FireWall-1 as a "Reverse HTTP Proxy"?

FireWall-1 can act as a Reverse Proxy for HTTP. It does not cache the content like a true proxy server, but it does provide authentication.

If you go to the Policy Properties Security Servers tab, you will see a field called HTTP Servers, as shown in Figure 7-47. Let's assume the firewall has the fully quali-

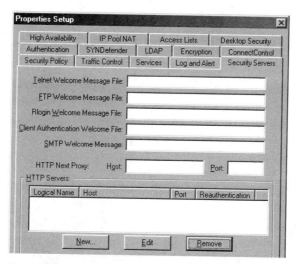

Figure 7-47   Policy Properties, Security Servers tab

fied name hellonurse.animaniacs.com. There are three servers that need to made accessible: yakko, wacko, and dot. Each one of them is defined as an HTTP server, as shown in Figure 7-48.

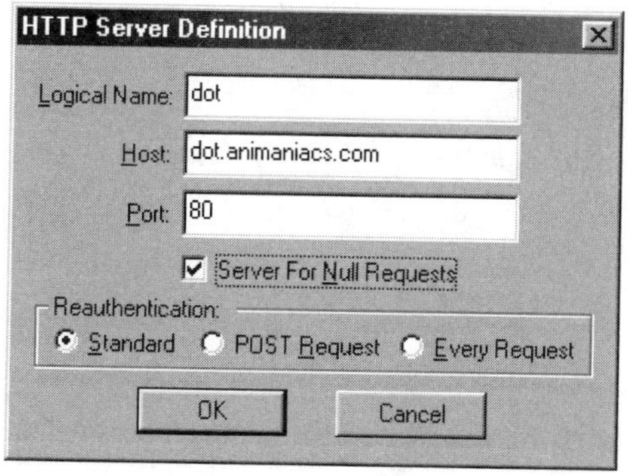

Figure 7-48   Sample HTTP Server Definition

The fields on the HTTP Server Definition screen are described as follows:

Logical Name: Enter the name you want to give the logical server. The server will be accessible as http://firewall-name/logical-name.

Host: Indicate the hostname or IP address of the host that FireWall-1 will connect to when this logical server is accessed.

Port: Indicate the port of the host to access using the host in the previous field.

Server for Null Requests: Only one logical server can be defined in this manner. Simply accessing http://firewall-name can access the server that is the Null server.

Reauthentication: Authentication can be asked for per the normal rules. You can also ask for authentication on every request or only ask for authentication on a POST command.

After all three servers are defined, this information will appear in the Policy Properties Security Servers tab under HTTP Servers (see Figure 7-49).

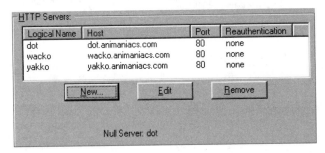

Figure 7-49 Policy Properties, Security Servers tab, HTTP Servers

NOTE! The *none* value in Figure 7-49 corresponds to "Standard" Reauthentication.

The servers will be accessible via the URLs in Table 7-4.

Table 7-4 Logical servers and their URLs

Logical Server	URL
dot	http://hellonurse.animaniacs.com/ and http://hellonurse.animaniacs.com/dot
yakko	http://hellonurse.animaniacs.com/yakko
wacko	http://hellonurse.animaniacs.com/wacko

The rule to enable access to these servers is shown in Figure 7-50.

Figure 7-50 HTTP Security Server Reverse-Proxy rule

7.8: How Do I Remove the Check Point Banner from Authentication?

The authentication daemons all show a banner identifying them as Check Point firewalls. Some people, at least those who believe in the concept called "security through obscurity," think that it is not a good idea to reveal the kind of firewall you are running. To disable these banners, modify `$FWDIR/conf/objects.C`. After the `:props (` line, add or modify this line to read as follows:

```
:undo_msg (true)
```

See Chapter 4, FAQ 4.2 for instructions on how to modify `objects.C` properly.

7.9: Can I Use FireWall-1 as a Proxy?

In FireWall-1 version 2.1 and earlier, in order to even do authentication for Telnet, FTP, and HTTP, you had to use FireWall-1 as a proxy. As of FireWall-1 3.0, FireWall-1 can authenticate these connections without having to proxy. There may be environments where using FireWall-1 in a proxy capacity is necessary. FireWall-1 requires authentication for Telnet, FTP, and rlogin. HTTP can be used as a proxy without authentication using a resource.

For proxy mode to work correctly, you must enable the "Prompt for Destination" mode in `objects.C`. See Chapter 4, FAQ 4.2 for instructions on how to do this. After the `:props (` line, add or modify this line to read:

```
:prompt_for_desination (true)
```

For HTTP, if you do not want to perform authentication, but want to use HTTP in proxy mode, you need to create a matchall resource, as discussed in Chapter 8, and use HTTP with this resource instead of just HTTP.

7.10: Can I Use FireWall-1 as an FTP Proxy for My Web Browser?

FireWall-1 supports proxying FTP using an FTP interface. However, Web browsers expect the FTP proxy to act like an HTTP proxy. FireWall-1 3.x and earlier do not support FTP in proxy mode. In FireWall-1 4.0 and later, it can be done via the HTTP Security Server. Just make sure you set your browser's FTP proxy to the firewall on port 80 instead of port 21.

Note that because FireWall-1 can be used as an FTP proxy with User Authentication, FTP or HTTP cannot be denied from the firewall, because the firewall has to originate these connections. In some cases, you may even have to put in an explicit rule installed as eitherbound, such as the rule shown in Figure 7-51.

Figure 7-51   Allow HTTP and FTP from the firewall

7.11: How Do I Authenticate HTTP over Different Ports?

There are five steps necessary to enable filtering on other ports:

1. Create a service for the ports in question (e.g., http8000).
2. Add a rule with the new service.
3. Install the security policy.
4. Reconfigure $FWDIR/conf/fwauthd.conf.
5. Bounce the firewall.

Creating the services is straightforward. Create a new service of type TCP. Set the Protocol Type to URI and the port as necessary (e.g., port 8000), as shown in Figure 7-52.

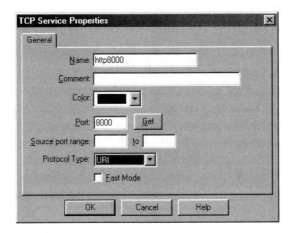

Figure 7-52   HTTP port 8000 definition

To reconfigure $FWDIR/conf/fwauthd.conf, you need to add a line to this file for each "unusual" port you want to filter on. For port 8000, for instance, the line would read:

```
8000  in.ahttpd   wait   0
```

Reinstall the security policy and bounce the firewall after making these changes (e.g., fwstop; fwstart). You can then use HTTP port 8000 in a service, authenticate against it with User Authentication, and do content security on that port.

7.12: How Do I Authenticate Outbound HTTPS Traffic?

As of FireWall-1 4.0, FireWall-1 can authenticate outbound HTTPS traffic. However, it can only do so when FireWall-1 is the proxy server for HTTPS requests from the Web browser.

The following line must be added to `$FWDIR/conf/fwauthd.conf`:

```
443 in.ahttpd wait 0
```

This line ensures that the HTTP Security Server is listening on port 443 to handle HTTPS requests. Once this line is added to `fwauthd.conf`, FireWall-1 must be restarted (`fwstop; fwstart`). Next, modify the HTTPS server so that the protocol type is URI (instead of None). You should then be able to add the appropriate rule and install the policy.

Note that no special certificate is necessary to authenticate outbound traffic.

7.13: Can I Authenticate Access to Internal HTTPS Servers?

Yes, you can. The following steps work with FireWall-1 4.1 SP1 and later:

1. Generate a CA key for the management console.
2. Distribute the CA key to the firewalled gateway.
3. Certify the relationship between the firewall and the management console.
4. Modify `$FWDIR/conf/fwauthd.conf` so that the HTTP Security Server is running in SSL mode.
5. Modify the HTTPS service to be of type URI.
6. Add in the appropriate rule, and install the security policy.

Generate the CA key for the management station as follows:

```
# fw ca genkey "ou=<machine name>, o=<org name>,
c=<country>"
```

The machine name should be the fully qualified domain name of the machine. For example:

```
# fw ca genkey "ou=roger.pinkfloyd.com, o=pinkfloyd, c=uk"
```

Distribute the CA key to the firewall gateway using:

```
# fw ca putkey <target>
```

You are then prompted for a password after this command. If you have multiple firewalls, issue this command multiple times. For example:

```
# fw ca putkey thewall
# fw ca putkey animals
```

On the firewall, issue the following command:

```
# fw certify ssl <management> <target>
```

For the target, make sure you use the fully qualified domain name of the firewall. When you enter this command, you are prompted for a password. Use the same password as entered previously. So, for example, on `thewall`, you would execute the command:

```
# fw certify ssl roger thewall.pinkfloyd.com
```

Next, modify the file `$FWDIR/conf/fwauthd.conf` by adding a line that enables the HTTP Security Server to run on an additional service port dedicated to HTTPS:

```
443            in.ahttpd      wait    0 eb
```

The `eb` at the end of this line ensures that communication between both the client and firewall and the firewall and the server is encrypted.

Modify HTTPS Service Properties so that the protocol type is URI, as shown in Figure 7-53.

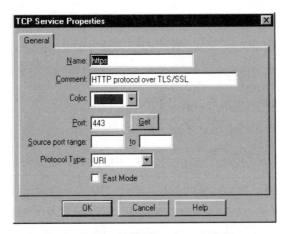

Figure 7-53   HTTPS Service definition

Then add an appropriate rule to the rulebase (such as the rule shown in Figure 7-54), and install the security policy.

Figure 7-54   Sample HTTPS authentication rule

NOTE!   When you connect to the server, you may get a message about the certificate not matching the name. Just accept the certificate when prompted. This is unavoidable.

7.14: How Can I Authenticate with HTTP to a Site Requiring Its Own Authentication?

Enter your login as follows: remoteuser@fw1user
Enter your password as follows: remotepass@fw1pass

7.15: How Can Users Change Their Own Passwords?

The short answer is they can't, at least not directly. One site I know of uses OS Password as its authentication mechanism. The company then allows its users to Telnet to the firewall, authenticate, and then change their password via the OS of the firewall. This has all kinds of potential security risks involved, so it is not recommended.

If you are using an external authentication server and it has its own remote password changing utility, you may be in luck. You may also be able to utilize the data from an `fw dbexport`, massage it with another application that allows you to change your password, and `fw dbimport` again.

7.16: Can a User Reset His or Her Own S/Key Chain?

When a user has less than ten S/Key passwords left, FireWall-1 will prompt the user to create a new S/Key chain if the user authenticates via Telnet, rlogin, or Client Authentication. The user will need to specify a different seed value (the default seed is the username), a new chain length to FireWall-1, and the last password in the chain.

On a UNIX machine, you would generate the new key chain as follows (assuming you want to use *seed* as the new seed value and 1000 as the chain length):

```
~ $ key 1000 seed
Reminder - Do not use this program while logged in via telnet or
rlogin.
Enter secret password: foobar
JOG WAKE SUN MEND ILL COWL
```

After generating the new key chain, you can input this information into your Telnet User Authentication or Client Authentication session as follows:

```
Check Point FireWall-1 authenticated Telnet server running on
mrhat
User: phoneboy
SKEY CHALLENGE: 9 phoneboy.
Enter SKEY string: MUG EMMA PI PRY HOYT MANN
User phoneboy authenticated by S/Key system

You have only 8 one-time passwords left. A new S/Key chain should
be created.
```

```
If you have a new chain, you can enter it now by typing the chain
length and the last password in the chain.
Enter New Chain (y/n) ? y
Enter S/Key chain length: 1000
Enter the last string of the new chain: JOG WAKE SUN MEND ILL
COWL New S/Key chain accepted
Connected to foo
```

The password generated and entered in the preceding example is only used to ini-tialize the S/Key chain. Future passwords will decrement from that point in the chain. Also, FireWall-1 always prompts you to use the old seed value, not the new one you entered in the previous example. You need to remember to use the new seed value when using an S/Key generator or when generating your own list.

7.17: Can I Customize the HTTP Client Authentication Pages?

It may be desirable for a variety of reasons to customize these pages with a different look. The HTML files that FireWall-1 uses are located in `$FWDIR/conf/ahclientd` on the firewall module. The files in this directory are as follows:

- `ahclientd1.html` is the first page users are greeted with (i.e., this page prompts users for a username).
- `ahclientd2.html` is the end-of-session page after a successful authentication.
- `ahclientd3.html` is the page for signing off.
- `ahclientd4.html` is the successful-login page where users choose the kind of sign-on or sign-off they desire.
- `ahclientd5.html` is the Specific Sign-On page.
- `ahclientd6.html` is the page for authentication failure.
- `ahclientd7.html` is the page that prompts users for their passwords.

These files contain "%s" or "%d" where FireWall-1 inserts information into these pages. Do not delete these symbols, as unpredictable results will occur. You certainly can change where they appear, but do not change the order in which they appear. You must also keep the files less than 1024 bytes in size.

Note that if you want to include any graphics, the graphics need to be included from a different Web server.

Troubleshooting Authentication Problems

The following sections contain some problem situations that you may run into and suggestions on how to resolve them. You should also see Chapter 8 for more trouble-shooting hints. The troubleshooting headings are numbered for easy reference.

7.18: This Gateway Does Not Support X

When trying to log in as a specific user, the following error might appear:

```
This gateway does not support X
```

The X represents an authentication scheme (SecurID, RADIUS, etc.). This error message occurs for one of two reasons:

- Your firewall workstation object is not defined with this authentication scheme enabled.
- If an LDAP user is trying to authenticate, the LDAP Account Unit does not have this authentication scheme configured as supported. Correct this problem, reinstall the security policy, and try again.

7.19: The Connection Is Closed by a Session Authentication Agent

If you are using Session Authentication with a protocol that opens lots of connections (like HTTP), you will see this error in your logs. In these cases, it is advisable to use Client Authentication with Fully Automatic authentication instead of using Session Authentication by itself.

7.20: Authenticated FTP Connections Stop If a Download Takes Longer than 15 Minutes

Short of increasing the authentication timeout, you will have to set the timeout for hidden connections. On FireWall-1 4.1, these steps are not necessary, as the NAT timers are taken into account whenever the timeouts are increased. On FireWall-1 4.0 and earlier, you need to increase these timers manually. On UNIX machines, increasing the timers is done as follows:

```
echo "fwx_tcp_expiration?W 0x<num>" | adb -w -k /dev/ksyms
     /dev/mem
```

The <num> variable represents the number of seconds in hex that the timeout needs to be. For example, to set the timeout to an hour, use the command:

```
echo "fwx_tcp_expiration?W 0xE10" | adb -w -k /dev/ksyms /dev/mem
```

On an IPSO platform, you can do something similar using the modzap utility, which can be obtained from Nokia's Knowledge Base, Resolution 1261. The command line to change the value to an hour is as follows:

```
modzap _fwx_tcp_expiration $FWDIR/boot/modules/fwmod.o 0xe10
```

You need to reboot after executing this command for the change to take effect.

On most UNIX platforms, this value is reset whenever a security policy is reloaded. It is recommended that this command be run from a `cron` job. On IPSO, it is zapped into the kernel module permanently, so this is not necessary.

7.21: Authentication Services Are Unavailable. Connection Refused.

This message occurs in one of two situations:

- The appropriate Security Server is not enabled in `$FWDIR/conf/fwauthd.conf`.
- There is more than one object with the firewall's IP address.

Fix these situations, reload the policy, restart FireWall-1, and try again.

7.22: Session Authentication Is Not Secure

This message means that communication between the firewall and the Session Authentication Agent is cleartext. The same thing goes for User Auth for Telnet, FTP, HTTP, and rlogin and Session Auth—the password is not encrypted. If you are concerned with passwords being sniffed over the wire, use a one-time password scheme like S/Key or SecurID. This way, even if the password is captured over the wire, it will not be useful.

FireWall-1 4.1 SP1 and later support using Session Authentication over SSL. This requires the use of the Session Authentication Client version 4.1 or later. It also requires a change to `$FWDIR/conf/objects.C`. In the `:props (` section, add or modify the line to read:

```
:snauth_protocol ("ssl")
```

The snauth_protocol can be set to one of the following:

- **none:** No encryption is performed.
- **ssl:** Only SSL encryption is supported (i.e., unencrypted Session Authentication is not supported).
- **none+ssl:** Both SSL and non-SSL versions are supported.

See Chapter 4, FAQ 4.2 for instructions on how to modify `objects.C`.

7.23: Using Session Authentication with Content Security

FireWall-1 does not support this because User Authentication can be used for any service that Content Security is available for.

7.24: Authenticating on Each URL

If FireWall-1 is used for User Authentication and the firewall is not set as the proxy in the client browser, this event will occur because FireWall-1 has to authenticate as each new site is accessed. In these situations, you should use Client Authentication with Partially Automatic Authentication.

7.25: No Client Auth Rules Available

This error appears when a user attempts to authenticate and there is no Client Authentication rule that matches. The source IP, user's group, and the user's allowed sources must match the rule. The user should not have a "blank" allowed.

7.26: Policy Install Logs out Client Auth Users

A policy reinstall flushes certain tables, of which the client_auth table is one. Although this is not generally recommended for security reasons, you can open `$FWDIR/lib/table.def` on the management console and modify the following entry:

```
client_auth = dynamic sync expires AUTH_TIMEOUT;
```

A "`keep`" needs to be added to the end of this line. It should read:

```
client_auth = dynamic sync expires AUTH_TIMEOUT keep;
```

The `keep` prevents the client_auth table from being flushed on a policy reinstall. You must reinstall the security policy in order for this change to take effect. The only way to flush this table is to bounce FireWall-1 (`fwstop; fwstart`).

7.27: Partially Automatic Client Authentication Redirects Site to an IP Address

This particular issue can cause a problem that exists in version 4.0 SP4 and earlier and in version 4.1 (no service pack). This can be a problem for sites that use virtual domains and/or cookies. The problem is fixed in FireWall-1 4.1 SP1 or 4.0 SP5 (and later) with the following modification made to `$FWDIR/conf/objects.C` in the `:props (` section:

```
: http_use_host_h_as_dst (true)
```

See Chapter 4, FAQ 4.2 for instructions on how to modify `objects.C`.

7.28: Using @ in a Username or Password with Client Auth via HTTP

Usernames containing the @ character (as in "foo@bar.net") are not supported for Client Authentication from a Web browser in versions of FireWall-1 prior to versions 4.0 SP5 and 4.1 SP1. The entry in the firewall log appears as a user named "foo%40bar.net," and the authentication shows as failed because there is no such user.

The Web browser correctly encodes "foo@bar.net" to "foo%40bar.net" (the @ character is hex 40), but the firewall does not decode it back to @ before processing the authentication.

7.29: FW-1 Form Has Expired

This error message may appear when using Partially Automatic Client Authentication in version 4.0 SP1 or 4.0 SP2. Upgrade to at least version 4.0 SP3.

7.30: Users Are Not Being Prompted for Authentication

The likely reason for this problem is that there is a rulebase rule that is less restrictive than the User Authentication rule actually matched. Long logging on all rules should allow you to discover which rule this is. Make this rule less restrictive, and/or reorder the rules to resolve this problem.

7.31: Request to Proxy Other Than Next Proxy Resource http://proxy.foo.com

This message is a result of trying to filter traffic going to a proxy server. You need to set the HTTP Next Proxy server and port as described in FAQ 7.6. You can only go to one proxy server because it is impossible to set more than one server in the HTTP Next Proxy setting.

7.32: Cannot Telnet to the Firewall

While trying to Telnet to the firewall with User Authentication, you get the Check Point Telnet banner; you authenticate successfully, but then lose the connection. If you are attempting to allow users to Telnet to the firewall for the purpose of proxy authentication, make sure prompt_for_destination is set to true in `objects.C`. If you want to allow people to Telnet to the firewall to log on to the firewall itself, you need to make sure that the Telnet daemon is running on the firewall box. Check `/etc/inetd.conf` to see if the Telnet daemon was commented out by FireWall-1 upon installation. If it was, uncomment it, and send the inetd process a hangup (HUP) signal.

 NOTE!   It is not recommended that you allow users to Telnet to your firewall directly. For enhanced security, use an encrypted login mechanism like SSH.

7.33: My User's Group Association Is Being Ignored

There is a bug in the version 4.0 SP3 GUI and, depending on how the user is added, FireWall-1 may not recognize a user's group membership. The following is an excerpt from the version 4.0 SP3 release notes in FireWall-1:

> When editing a user object and defining from the user dialog to which groups the user belongs, this definition will not take effect on the FireWall-1 module. This means that the user may not be allowed to connect although the user was defined as a member of the source group of an authentication rule. To overcome this limitation, you must define the membership of users in groups through the group dialog (i.e., edit the user group and choose which users are members of the group).

You can either upgrade the GUI to the latest 4.0 version, upgrade to a later version of FireWall-1, or edit the group to add the users to the group instead of editing the user to add them to a group.

7.34: When Accessing Certain Sites, the Connections Are Dropped with the Following in the Logs: Content-Encoding Type Not Allowed

You will see this problem in FireWall-1 4.1 SP2 or later when using either User Authentication or Content Security and accessing sites that support compressed encoding types. To resolve this problem, add the following to the `:props (` section of `$FWDIR/conf/objects.C` on the management console:

```
:http_disable_content_enc (true)
:http_disable_content_type (true)
```

This causes the HTTP Security Server to wait for an okay from the Content Vectoring Protocol server (CVP is described in Chapter 8) before allowing the compressed encoding methods. For more information about editing `objects.C`, see Chapter 4, FAQ 4.2.

You also need to go to the firewall modules and make a change to `$FWDIR/conf/fwopsec.conf`. Change the line that reads

```
server          127.0.0.1          18181          auth_opsec
```

so that it reads:

```
server          127.0.0.1          18181          opsec
```

This change tells FireWall-1 not to use the auto_sense mechanism while communicating with the CVP server. This mechanism used to be efficient when the Security Servers had to communicate with a CVP server that knew to work only with the old

CVP protocol. However, now all the certified CVP servers work with the new OPSEC protocol.

Bounce your firewall modules (`fwstop; fwstart`) and reload the policy.

Summary

Authentication is an important part of any security infrastructure. You now know the three methods used by FireWall-1 to provide authentication, the conditions under which you can apply each method, how to configure each method, and how to trouble-shoot when things go wrong. You can also integrate FireWall-1 with various external authentication servers.

Sample Configurations

The following sections present three situations that build on each other as the network and the needs of the enterprise change. Each type of authentication is demonstrated.

A User Authentication Example

The Situation

Consider the situation pictured in Figure 7-55.

Assuming that all IPs used are routable (i.e., no NAT is necessary), implement the security policy listed in "The Goals" section.

The Goals

- The Web Server in the DMZ will be accessible via HTTP from anywhere.
- The E-mail Server in the DMZ will be accessible via POP3 and SMTP from anywhere.
- bob and dan can FTP or Telnet from the internal network to any host on the DMZ segment provided they authenticate.
- bob, dan, doug, and joe can access the Intranet Web server from anywhere via HTTP provided they authenticate.
- Internal users on Segment A and B (dubbed "Internal") can access hosts on the Internet via HTTP, FTP, and HTTPS.
- All other traffic should be denied.
- Authentication timeouts should be enabled for at least 30 minutes.
- All users will authenticate with S/Key and have a chain length of at least 1000.

Checklist

- Create the necessary network objects.
- Create the necessary users and groups required for authentication, and install the user database.

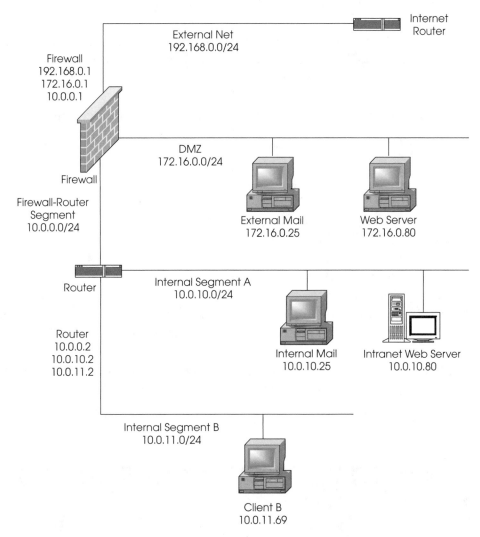

Figure 7-55 Sample network configuration for User Authentication

- Ensure that the appropriate Security Servers are enabled in `$FWDIR/conf/fwauthd.conf`.
- Create the appropriate rule(s) in the rulebase.
- Configure the User Authentication Action Properties.
- Configure the Rulebase Properties Authentication tab.
- Verify and install the policy.

Implementation

After creating all the network objects that represent your network, create the users bob, dan, doug, and joe. Make sure the expiration date for each user is set sufficiently far enough in the future. Next, create the group "WebAdmins" and add bob and dan to this group. Install the user database.

In this situation, the Security Servers you will be using are for Telnet, FTP, and HTTP. As such, you should verify in `$FWDIR/conf/fwauthd.conf` that these servers are enabled:

```
21              in.aftpd        wait    0
80              in.ahttpd       wait    0
23              in.atelnetd     wait    0
```

If you see the preceding lines without a comment in front of them (i.e., a #), the servers are enabled. If the lines are missing or commented out, add them or uncomment them, and bounce FireWall-1 (`fwstop; fwstart`).

As for the rulebase, you need to make sure that the rules do not allow more than they should. These rules should allow authenticated access to the appropriate hosts without permitting nonauthenticated access where appropriate. The proper rulebase is shown in Figure 7-56.

Next, you need to configure the User Authentication Action Properties for both rules. Right-click the User Authentication action for the two rules. The screen that appears is shown in Figure 7-57.

No.	Source	Destination	Service	Action	Track	Install On
1	Any	Web_Server	http	accept		Gateways
2	Any	Email_Server	smtp	accept		Gateways
3	DMZAdmins@internal-networks	DMZ_net	telnet ftp	User Auth	Long	Gateways
4	Any	Local_Gateway	Any	drop	Long	Gateways
5	All Users@Any	intranet-web-server	http	User Auth	Long	Gateways
6	internal-networks	Email_Server	pop-3	accept		Gateways
7	internal-networks	DMZ_net	telnet ftp http https	accept	Long	Gateways
8	Any	Any	Any	drop	Long	Gateways

Figure 7-56 Sample rulebase for User Authentication

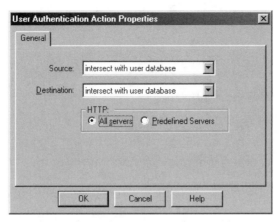

Figure 7-57 User Authentication Action Properties

You also need to configure the Policy Properties Authentication tab, so that the User Authentication timeout is 30 minutes, as shown in Figure 7-58.

Once this configuration is set up, verify and install the security policy.

Figure 7-58 Policy Properties, Authentication tab

A Session Authentication Example

The Situation

The same network as in the previous example is used in this situation except a new server has been added to the DMZ (172.16.0.42). This server needs to be administered via a program called VNC, which uses TCP port 5900. VNC does not provide for strong enough authentication, so it has decided to use Session Authentication to authenticate this service. A new user ("michael") will be the only user permitted to access this service on the internal network. "Michael" will also be able to administer the FTP or Telnet from the internal network to any host on the DMZ segment provided he authenticates.

The Goals

- Create new user "michael."
- Create a new group for michael called VNCAdmins.

- Add "michael" to the groups "VNCAdmins" and "WebAdmins."
- Permit "michael" to use VNC to the new machine via Session Authentication.

Checklist

- Create necessary network objects.
- Create necessary users and groups.
- Create the appropriate rule(s) in the rulebase.
- Configure the Session Authentication Action Properties.
- Verify and install the policy.

Implementation

Create a new workstation object for 172.16.0.42. Create the group "VNCAdmins." Create user "michael." Add "michael" to group "VNCAdmins" and "WebAdmins."

Only one new rule needs to be added. The modified rulebase is shown in Figure 7-59.

The Session Authentication Action Properties should be the defaults, as shown in Figure 7-60.

Verify and install the security policy.

No.	Source	Destination	Service	Action	Track	Install On
1	Any	Web_Server	http	accept		Gateways
2	Any	Email_Server	smtp	accept		Gateways
3	DMZAdmins@internal-networks	DMZ_net	telnet ftp	User Auth	Long	Gateways
4	VNCAdmins@internal-networks	VNCServer	VNC	Session Auth	Long	Gateways
5	Any	Local_Gateway	Any	drop	Long	Gateways
6	All Users@Any	intranet-web-server	http	User Auth	Long	Gateways
7	internal-networks	Email_Server	pop-3	accept		Gateways
8	internal-networks	DMZ_net	telnet ftp http https	accept	Long	Gateways
9	Any	Any	Any	drop	Long	Gateways

Figure 7-59 Sample rulebase for Session Authentication

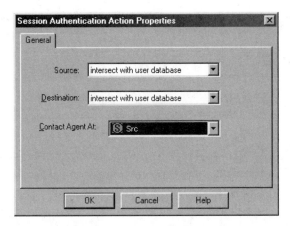

Figure 7-60   Session Authentication Action Properties

A Client Authentication Example

The Situation

Once again, the same network shown in Figure 7-55 is used in this situation. Due to a recent change in company policy, all outbound Internet access must be authenticated. Because of the way User Authentication works with HTTP and because it is not desirable to set the proxy in the browser, Client Authentication seems the most appropriate choice. It is also desirable to switch the existing User Authentication rules to Client Authentication. Users should reauthenticate after 30 minutes of inactivity. Also, michael would like to be authenticated to use VNC as a result of authenticating for HTTP as well as via the Session Authentication agent.

The Goals

- Change Rules 3, 6, and 8 from the previous situation to Client Authentication.
- Allow both Client and Session Authentication for VNC.

Checklist

- Change the actions of Rules 3, 6, and 8 to Client Authentication.
- Add a new rule allowing VNC to be authenticated by Client Authentication.
- Configure Client Authentication Action Properties for each of these rules.
- Verify and install the policy.

Implementation

After changing the action of the rules, your rulebase should look like the one shown in Figure 7-61.

No.	Source	Destination	Service	Action	Track	Install On
1	Any	Web_Server	http	accept		Gateways
2	Any	Email_Server	smtp	accept		Gateways
3	DMZAdmins@internal-networks	DMZ_net	telnet ftp	Client Auth	Long	Gateways
4	VNCAdmins@internal-networks	VNCServer	VNC	Client Auth	Long	Gateways
5	VNCAdmins@internal-networks	VNCServer	VNC	Session Auth	Long	Gateways
6	Any	Local_Gateway	Any	drop	Long	Gateways
7	All Users@Any	intranet-web-server	http	Client Auth	Long	Gateways
8	internal-networks	Email_Server	pop-3	accept		Gateways
9	internal-networks	DMZ_net	telnet ftp http https	Client Auth	Long	Gateways
10	Any	Any	Any	drop	Long	Gateways

Figure 7-61   Sample rulebase with Client Authentication

Each of the Client Authentication actions should have the properties set as shown in Figures 7-62 and 7-63.

Verify and install the policy.

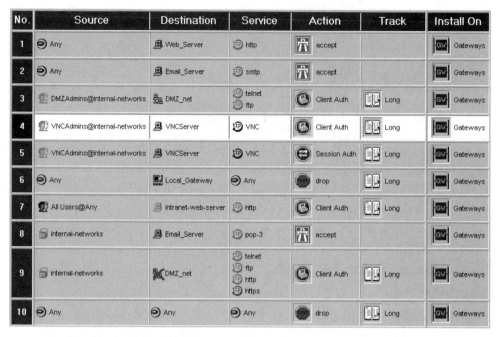

Figure 7-62   Client Authentication Action Properties, General tab

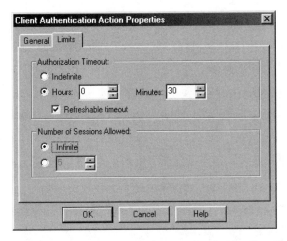

Figure 7-63   Client Authentication Action Properties, Limits tab

Notes

The Client Authentication rule is listed before the Session Authentication rule, as there is no reason to ask for Session Authentication if "michael" is already authenticated via Client Authentication.

Chapter

8

_____

Content
Security

In the last chapter, I talked about restricting access based on the user; in this chapter, I talk about restricting access to certain kinds of content. Such restrictions include not allowing people to access certain kinds of sites (e.g., pornography, news), preventing people from accessing specific types of content (e.g., RealAudio, MP3), or scanning content for viruses. I also discuss the various Security Servers for HTTP, FTP, SMTP, and the recently added TCP Security Server in some detail.

By the end of this chapter, you should be able to:

- Know what CVP and UFP are used for
- Restrict content for HTTP, FTP, SMTP, and generic TCP services
- Understand the performance issues inherent in content security
- Understand how to tune your FireWall-1 installation to perform well
- Troubleshoot problems with Content Security

The Security Servers

FireWall-1 normally relies on Stateful Inspection. However, like authentication, the business of virus and content filtering requires more capabilities than can be provided by Stateful Inspection alone. In these cases, FireWall-1 uses the various Security Servers to perform the necessary tasks. In the last chapter, I discussed how they were used for authentication. In this chapter, I look at each individual Security Server a bit more closely and explain how to configure them.

A Word about Licensing and Third-Party Products

All firewall modules can use Content Security. Inspection Modules or Embedded firewalls cannot use Content Security (although the recently introduced small-office products can). However, in order to use more than the rudimentary functions of Content Security in FireWall-1, third-party software is required. Check Point maintains a list of compatible applications and software vendors at www.opsec.com.

CVP and UFP

Inevitably, Check Point recognized that it could not do everything in terms of providing security. Consequently, Check Point created a program called Open Platform for Security (OPSEC), which allows third-party products to "hook in" to Check Point FireWall-1 and provide services. Two of these protocols, Content Vectoring Protocol (CVP) and URL Filtering Protocol (UFP) are discussed in this section. Some of the other functions OPSEC provides include:

- *Suspicious Activity Monitoring Protocol (SAMP):* Provides for Intrusion Detection
- *Log Export API (LEA):* The ability to analyze firewall logs
- *Event Log API (ELA):* The ability for other applications to tie into Check Point's alerting mechanisms
- *OPSEC Management Interface (OMI):* Allows third-party products to access the security policy
- *Public Key Infrastructure (PKI):* The ability for Check Point to tie into a Public Key Infrastructure
- *Secure Authentication API (SAA):* The ability for Check Point to use a variety of authentication mechanisms such as hardware-based tokens and biometric authentication
- *High Availability (HA):* The ability to provide highly available firewall servers
- *User-to-Address Mapping (UAM):* Helps authenticate and track users more effectively
- *User Authority API (UAA):* The ability to pass authentication information to other servers in order to reduce the number of authentication prompts

CVP is used to scan content. It is typically used to scan for viruses, but can also be used to scan for malicious Java or ActiveX applets, depending on which CVP server you decide to use. CVP works in this way: A content stream is intercepted by one of the Security Servers. FireWall-1 determines that the content needs to be scanned by the CVP server before allowing the content to be given to the end user. As the content is downloaded through the firewall, it is sent to the CVP server, which typically runs on a separate server from the firewall. The CVP server then takes one of three actions toward the content (this action is configured in the security policy):

- Send the content as-is, that is, without any modifications
- Send the content corrected, that is, with the virus or other offending content removed
- Do not send the content at all

UFP is used to filter HTTP traffic destined for the Internet based on URLs and the categories those URLs fall under. As a user requests a URL in his Web browser, FireWall-1 uses the HTTP Security Server to check that URL against a UFP server, which returns the category under which the URL falls. Based on that category and the defined security policy, FireWall-1 either allows the connection to the URL or rejects it. This allows for, say, Christian organizations to filter non-Christian content or for workplaces to filter pornography.

Resources and Wildcards

Resources are simply a way to match a specific kind of content, and then perform some action on it. Some resources are matched based on a query to a UFP server. Others are matched based on specific resources that you define.

The wildcards listed in Table 8-1 can be used in all resources. SMTP provides an additional wildcard, which is discussed in the "SMTP Security Server" section.

Table 8-1   Wildcards usable in resources

Character	Description
*	Matches any string of any length. For example, *@phoneboy.com matches all e-mail addresses at phoneboy.com.
+	Matches any single character. For example, pink+@acmelabs.com would match pinky@acmelabs.com, but not pinkie@acmelabs.com.
{ , }	Matches any of the listed strings. For example, brain@{acmelabs, animaniacs} .com would match both brain@acmelabs.com and brain@animaniacs.com.

HTTP Security Server

Of all of the Security Servers in FireWall-1, the HTTP Security Server is used most often. Because the HTTP Security Server can be used with both CVP and UFP, I will cover how to set up both types of Content Security.

The HTTP Security Server is enabled when the following situations are true:

- There is a line that permits in.ahttpd to start up in `$FWDIR/conf/fwauthd.conf`.
- A resource is used in your security policy or a rule involving User Authentication for HTTP.

Refer to Chapter 7 for information on authentication. Defining resources is discussed in the next section. The proper line for the HTTP Security Server in `$FWDIR/conf/fwauthd.conf` looks like this (without a comment "#" symbol at the beginning of the line):

```
80              in.ahttpd      wait   0
```

The first argument is the port the HTTP Security Server runs on (port 80). The second argument states that it is the HTTP Security Server (i.e., in.ahttpd). The third argument is always `wait`, and the fourth argument is used to indicate one of two items: which port it listens on (if greater than or equal to zero) or how many instances of the server to run (if negative). I discuss the latter point in the "Performance Tuning" section. The only time you want the Security Server listening on a particular port is when users will use the firewall as a nontransparent proxy for HTTP. If this line is not present or commented out, the HTTP Security Server will not run, and any process that relies on it will fail.

Filtering HTTP without a UFP or CVP Server

FireWall-1 has some rudimentary filtering features that can be utilized without using a UFP or CVP server. These features should only be used for the most basic of filtering needs. Anything too complex should be done with a UFP or CVP server. You can use these features by creating URI resources. From the Policy Editor, select Manage, and then choose Resources. Next, select New, and then choose URI. You are presented with the window shown in Figure 8-1.

The options on the URI Definition General tab are described as follows:

Name: Name of the resource (must be unique).

Comment: Enter any information you would like in this field.

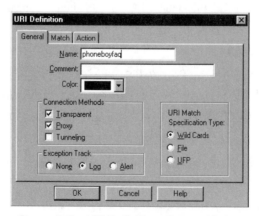

Figure 8-1   URI Definition, General tab

Color: Select whichever color you would like.

Connection Methods: Specifies when this resource is applied. Transparent means that the user will use the service normally, and FireWall-1 will transparently intercept the communication. Proxy means that this resource is applied when people specify the firewall as the proxy in their browser. Tunneling is used when FireWall-1 is defined as the proxy to the client's Web browser, but is used for services where FireWall-1 cannot examine the content of the request, only the hostname and port number. An example of this is HTTPS. Only the hostname and port number are sent in cleartext, the rest of the content is encrypted. The hostname and port number are the only specifications that can be filtered on using the Tunneling connection method. If Tunneling is specified, all Content Security options in the URI specification are disabled.

URI Match Specification Type: Specifies how you define this resource in terms of: Wild Cards, a URI File (which you must create), or with UFP. The first two methods are discussed later in this section. The last method is discussed in the "UFP with the HTTP Security Server" section.

Exception Track: Specifies how you log anything this resource acts upon.

You must then specify which URLs to filter by clicking on the Match tab, as shown in Figure 8-2.

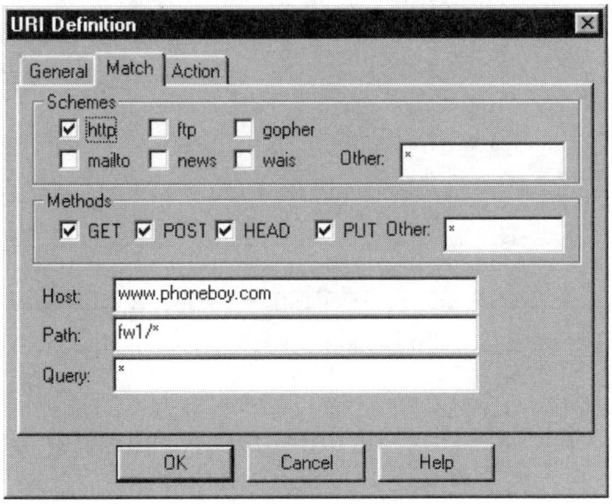

Figure 8-2   URI Definition, Wild Card Type, Match tab

The parameters that you can configure on the Match tab are described as follows:

Schemes: This parameter matches the different protocols you can use through the HTTP Security Server. It is only relevant if the firewall is specified as the proxy for these protocols. Normally, it is safe to just select HTTP.

Methods: This parameter specifies methods for HTTP. GET is used when you request a particular page (or element on a page); POST is used when sending data to a Web site (filling out forms, etc.); HEAD is usually used by caching servers and Web browsers to determine whether or not an element has changed to decide whether or not to download it; PUT is a less commonly used method for uploading files via HTTP. If another method is required, you can specify it in the "Other" field. To allow any method, use * in the "Other" field.

Host, Path, Query: This parameter takes the various parts of the URL and breaks them down into filterable components. For example, in the following URL: http://www.phoneboy.com/search/wwwwais/wwwwais.cgi?keywords=content+ security, the "host" part of the URL is www.phoneboy.com, the path is /search/ wwwwais/wwwwais.cgi, and the query is basically everything else (usually for CGI scripts such as search engines). You can filter on any part of the URL.

If you want to create a resource of type File rather than Wild Card Type (i.e., to filter URIs based on a file), the Match tab shown in Figure 8-3 appears.

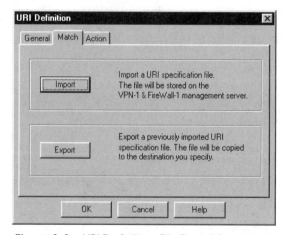

Figure 8-3 URI Definition, File Type, Match tab

A URI specification file is a series of lines in the following format:

```
ip-addr    /path    0
```

`ip-addr` is the IP address of the Web server you want to match against. For sites that resolve to multiple IPs, you need to list each one specifically. FireWall-1 4.1 and later also allow you to use names in this file, though it requires that DNS be enabled and configured on the firewall.

`/path` is optional. If you want to restrict a certain subdirectory of a site (or a certain URL), enter it here.

0 (or any hexadecimal number) is required on the end of each line. Here is a sample file:

```
10.0.146.201 0
10.251.29.12 0
10.91.182.100 /support.d 0
10.184.151.198 /support 0
```

There must also be a blank line at the end of the file. Once you have created this file, click the Import button and specify the path to this file on your Management GUI station. It will then be uploaded to your management console.

You then need to specify the action to take if this resource matches, so click the Action tab. Figure 8-4 displays the Action tab screen.

Figure 8-4   URI Definition, Action tab

The parameters that you can configure on the Action tab are described as follows:

Replacement URI: If the rulebase action this resource is used in is dropped or rejected, the user should be redirected to this URL. This could, for instance, be a policy document telling people the rules and regulations of Web usage.

HTML Weeding: If the action is accepted, strip out the tags selected. The HTTP Security Server does not really strip them, but rather comments out the offending HTML so that the tags are not run when downloaded. A user could theoretically save the HTML and reload a modified, local copy.

Response Scanning / Block JAVA Code: FireWall-1 can block the download of any Java code if this checkbox is selected. It does not match JavaScript, which is done with the HTML Weeding option.

CVP: If you have a CVP server and you want to scan all documents that match the resource, you would use this parameter to tell it which CVP server to use and whether to simply check the content and reject it if it contains inappropriate content (e.g., viruses; the Read Only setting), or rewrite the content so that it does not contain the offending content (the Read/Write setting).

You can then use this resource in a rule, as shown in Figure 8-5.

Source
Destination
Service
Action
Track
Install On
Local_Net
Any
http->phoneboyfaq
reject
Long
Gateways

Figure 8-5 Sample CVP rule

UFP with the HTTP Security Server

The UFP server is a third-party application that should be run on a different platform from the firewall. There are a variety of UFP servers available for FireWall-1 that run on Windows NT or Solaris. I will not cover their setup in this book. It is sufficient to say that once they are set up correctly, FireWall-1 is then able to communicate with them on TCP port 18182.

To configure UFP to work with FireWall-1 and the HTTP Security Server, the following steps need to be performed:

1. Define the workstation object that the UFP server is running on (if necessary).
2. Define the server object that represents the UFP server.
3. Define a resource of type UFP.
4. Use the rule with the resource, install policy.

Let's assume you have created a workstation object named "kyle" where the UFP server is installed. You select Manage and then choose Servers from the Policy Editor. You then create a new URI called url-filter, as shown in Figure 8-6.

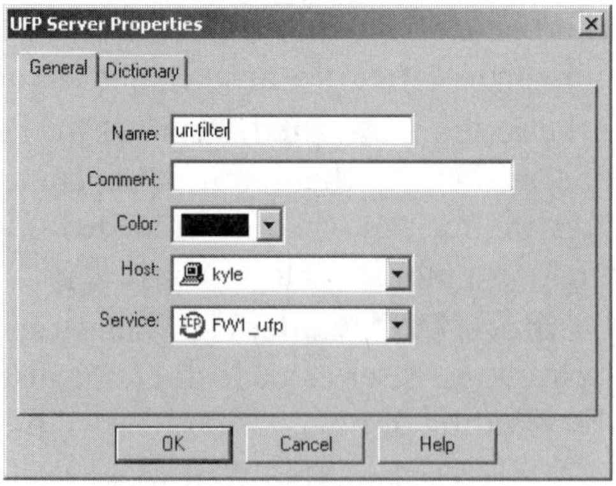
UFP Server Properties
General
Dictionary
Name:
url-filter
Comment:
Color:
Host:
kyle
Service:
FW1_ufp
OK
Cancel
Help

Figure 8-6 UFP Server Definition, General tab

The options listed on this screen are described as follows:

Name: The name of the resource (must be unique).

Color: Select whichever color you would like.

Host: This is the workstation object on which the UFP server is running.

Service: The service used to communicate with this server. Normally, this should be FW1_UFP (TCP 18182).

You can select the Dictionary tab (as shown in Figure 8-7) to validate your connection with the UFP server. Click the Get Dictionary button.

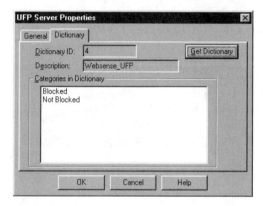

Figure 8-7   UFP Server Definition, Dictionary tab

In this example, the categories returned are "blocked" and "not blocked," which is what a Websense 4.x server returns.[1] Other versions of Websense and other UFP applications return a more detailed category list. The categories, which you actually select in the URI definition, allow you to choose the kind of Web sites you want to filter. InWebsense 4.x, this is controlled in the Websense application, not within FireWall-1.

You can then create your URI resource as shown in Figure 8-8. For this example, call the resource websense and make it of type UFP.

Next, go to the Match tab, select the UFP Server url-filter, and select the "Blocked" category, as shown in Figure 8-9. Note that the actual URLs that will be blocked are configured in the Websense server.

If you wanted to, you could go to the Action tab and specify other filtering options, but let's not do that for this example. You can then create the rules to block Web sites that Websense has been configured to block. See Figure 8-10.

---

1.   Websense 4.x has a detailed category list. Which URLs are allowed under what conditions are controlled through a Websense management interface separate from FireWall-1.

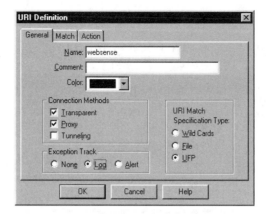

Figure 8-8   URI Definition for Websense, General tab

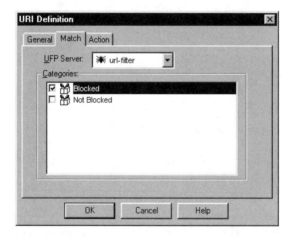

Figure 8-9   URI Definition for Websense, Match tab

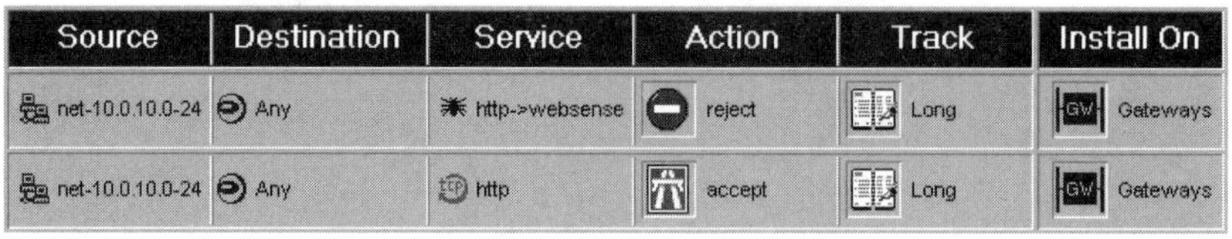

Source	Destination	Service	Action	Track	Install On
net-10.0.10.0-24	Any	http->websense	reject	Long	Gateways
net-10.0.10.0-24	Any	http	accept	Long	Gateways

Figure 8-10   Sample Rule with URI filtering

The first rule is created by using the "Add with Resource" option for the service column, selecting http, and then selecting websense. This rule catches all websense-filtered URLs. The second rule permits URLs that are not filtered by Websense. This second rule is necessary to allow access to all URLs except for those prohibited by Websense.

CVP with the HTTP Security Server

The CVP server is a third-party application that should be run on a different platform from the firewall. There are a variety of CVP servers available for FireWall-1 that run on Windows NT or Solaris. I will not attempt to cover their setup in this book. It is sufficient to say that once they are set up correctly, FireWall-1 will then be able to communicate with them on TCP port 18181.

To configure CVP to work with FireWall-1 and the HTTP Security Server, the following steps need to be performed:

1. Define the workstation object that the CVP server is running on (if necessary).
2. Define the server object that represents the CVP server.
3. Define a resource that uses the CVP server (or modify an existing one).
4. Use the rule with the resource, install policy.

Let's assume you have created a workstation object named "queeg" where the CVP server is installed. Select Manage, and then choose Servers from the Policy Editor. Create a new CVP called cvp-filter, as shown in Figure 8-11.

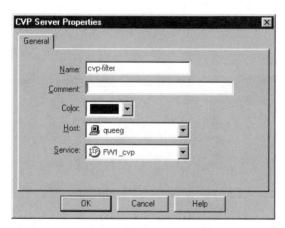

Figure 8-11   CVP Server Properties

The options on this screen are described as follows:

Name: The name of the CVP server object (must be unique).

Comment: Description of the resource in more detail.

Color: Select whichever color you would like.

Host: This is the workstation object on which the CVP server is running.

Service: The service used to communicate with this server. Normally, this should be FW1_CVP (TCP 18181).

You then need to create a resource that performs CVP. Create a new resource called virusscan as shown in Figure 8-12, which matches all URIs but performs virus scanning.

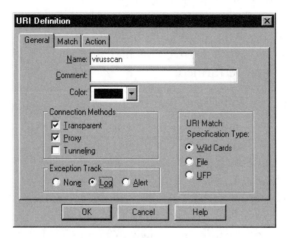

Figure 8-12 URI Definition Virusscan, General tab

The Match tab, shown in Figure 8-13, will match all URLs.

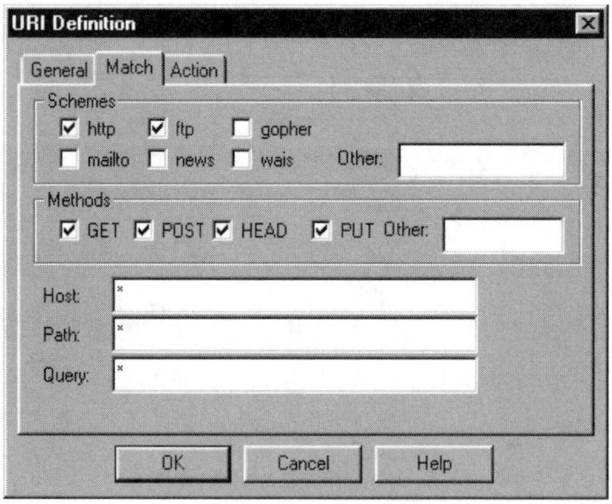

Figure 8-13 URI Definition Virusscan, Match tab

The Action tab, shown in Figure 8-14, is where you define which CVP resource to apply.

You then need to add this resource to a rule. You can combine it with the UFP example so that both URLs and content are filtered. See Figure 8-15.

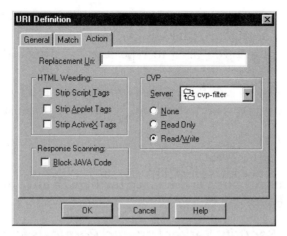

Figure 8-14   URI Definition Virusscan, Action tab

Source	Destination	Service	Action	Track	Install On
net-10-0-10-0-24	Any	http->websense	reject	Long	Gateways
net-10-0-10-0-24	Any	http->virusscan	accept	Long	Gateways

Figure 8-15   HTTP virus scanning with URI filtering rules

Frequently Asked Questions about the HTTP Security Server

In the interest of keeping all the information about a particular Security Server together, I will provide corresponding FAQ sections at the end of each of the Security Server sections.

8.1: Can I Filter HTTP on Other Ports (e.g., port 81)?

There are five steps necessary to enable filtering on other ports:

1. Create a TCP service for the port in question (e.g., http81), and make it of type URI.
2. Add a rule with resource using the new service.
3. Install the security policy.
4. Reconfigure $FWDIR/conf/fwauthd.conf to support the Security Server on that port.
5. Bounce the firewall (fwstop; fwstart).

Creating the services is straightforward. Create a new service of type TCP. Set the Protocol Type to URI and the port as necessary (e.g., port 81). If you do an "add with resource" in the services section of a rule, you will be able to associate a resource with the new service you created (e.g., http81). If you do filtering with wildcard resources, you need to enter the host part of the URL as "`host:port.`" For example, to match "all," instead of entering *, you need to type it as *:*. If you do not do this, your resource will fail.

To reconfigure $FWDIR/conf/fwauthd.conf, you need to add a line to this file for each "unusual" port you want to filter on. For port 81, for instance, the line would read as follows:

```
    81  in.ahttpd    wait    0
```

Reinstall the security policy, and bounce the firewall after making these changes (e.g., fwstop; fwstart).

8.2: Can the HTTP Security Server Forward Requests to a Caching Proxy Server?

Yes, but only if your clients are configured to use the firewall as their proxy server. Set the "HTTP Next Proxy" setting in the Policy Properties Security Servers tab.

8.3: When Trying to Filter Traffic Going to a Proxy Server, Why Do I Get the Error "Request to Proxy Other Than Next Proxy Resource http://proxy.foo.com"?

Set the "HTTP Next Proxy" setting in the Policy Properties Security Servers tab to point at the proxy server. This setting only allows you to filter traffic to one HTTP Proxy Server.

8.4: How Do I Redirect People Who Try to Access Sites I Do Not Want Users Accessing to a Page That Gives Our Usage Policy?

You can take one of two approaches:

- Create a resource that matches the sites you do not want to allow access to. Use this resource in a rule as shown earlier in the chapter, setting the replacement URL accordingly in this resource.
- Create a resource that matches the sites you *want* to allow access to. If you want to then redirect them to a policy page if they access a page they are not allowed to, use the "matchall" resource, and set the replacement URL accordingly. Should you want to allow them access to only the sites matched by the resource "allowedsites" and deny access to everything else (via a "matchall" resource), the rules would look like those shown in Figure 8-16.

Source	Destination	Service	Action	Track	Install On
internal-network	Any	http->allowed-sites	accept	Long	Gateways
internal-network	Any	http->matchall	reject	Long	Gateways

Figure 8-16   Rules to allow access to certain sites only

NOTE!   If you use the replacement URL in conjunction with User Authentication and a user is redirected to a policy page, the user will get FireWall-1's Authentication Failed page with a link to the redirected page.

8.5: How Do I Prevent People from Downloading Files or Accessing Streaming Media via HTTP?

You can use the HTTP Security Server to deal with both of these issues. If you have CVP, you may be able to use the CVP server to screen out those MIME types. If you are not using a CVP server, you can do this with a wildcard URI. In the Path section of the Match tab, you can specify all file extensions that you do not want people to download.

- *For Real Audio/Real Video:* *.{ra,ram,rm,rv}
- *Most Internet downloads:* *.{exe,zip,com,bat,sit,tar,tgz,tar.gz,lha,rar,r0+}

You would then create a rule that uses this resource and denies access to anything matching this resource. This rule would appear before your other rules that permit HTTP.

NOTE!   Attempting to filter based on extension or even MIME type is futile. There are plenty of ways to get around these filters, either by using different extensions or different MIME types, which are merely suggestions for how the file should be treated. In order to filter out all the files you don't want, you will likely filter files that you *do* want (throwing the baby out with the bath water).

8.6: Can I Allow Certain Users to Download Files Provided They Authenticate?

In order for this to work correctly, all users need to authenticate, even to use normal HTTP. The rules to do this are shown in Figure 8-17.

Figure 8-17   Rules to allow file downloads with authentication

Once a packet potentially matches a User Auth rule—i.e., the source, destination, and service match what is specified in the rule—the rule in the rulebase that is least restrictive is the rule that will actually apply. Therefore, it is important that the rule that denies access to downloads appears before the rule that allows everyone to use HTTP.

8.7: How Can I Set up FireWall-1 to Support Content Security for Outbound HTTPS?

Due to the nature of HTTPS, it is only possible to authenticate or provide Content Security for HTTPS when the client specifies the firewall as the proxy for HTTPS (called "Security" in recent versions of Netscape). Some other steps must be performed as well.

First, ensure the following line exists in `$FWDIR/conf/fwauthd.conf`:

```
443 in.ahttpd wait 0
```

If this line does not exist or it is commented out, add/uncomment it, and bounce FireWall-1. Second, modify the predefined service HTTPS. Change the protocol type from "None" to "URI." You can then use HTTPS for authentication or Content Security as appropriate provided the client is configured to use the firewall as a proxy for HTTPS requests.

Performance Tuning the HTTP Security Server

One of the most-common complaints about performing Content Security is performance. Generally speaking, most people complain about the HTTP Security Server. Some of the performance issues can be overcome by tuning the platform the HTTP Security Server is running on. However, there are some inherent limitations in the Security Servers in terms of the number of users who can go through a single system, because Content Security overall requires significantly more resources than simply passing traffic. Personally, I would not use the HTTP Security Server for more than 1,000 users. It is possible that future versions of FireWall-1 will improve upon this number.

In this section, I talk about what you need to do to improve performance of the Security Servers, which will increase the efficiency of the HTTP Security Servers. You should also apply the general performance tuning suggestions in Appendix I.

Increase the Number of Allowed Entries in proxied_conns

By default, the number of entries in proxied_conns (a table that stores connections via the Security Servers) is 25,000. For best performance, you should modify this number to twice the number of connections you actually expect to handle. In `$FWDIR/lib/table.def` on the management console, modify the following line:

```
proxied_conns = dynamic keep;
```

To modify the line to support 50,000 connections, for example, make it read:

```
proxied_conns = dynamic keep limit 50000;
```

Increase the HTTP Buffer Size

A new feature in FireWall-1 4.1 increases the size of the buffer Check Point uses for each connection. The default size is 4096 bytes. It can be increased to a maximum of 32768. A larger buffer size means fewer system calls; however, each connection will take up that much more memory, so there is a trade-off.

To make this change, edit `$FWDIR/conf/objects.C` on the management console (see Chapter 4, FAQ 4.2 for guidelines on editing `objects.C`). In the `:props (` section, add or modify the following line:

```
:http_buffer_size (xxxxx)
```

The xxxxx variable should be a number less than or equal to 32768.

Increase the Number of Instances of the Security Servers

Increasing the number of instances of the Security Servers is usually necessary with the HTTP Security Server, but can be done for any Security Server. If you have multiple processors on your firewall, increasing the number of instances allows you to take advantage of these processors. You can use this trick if you are using a single processor system, too. To increase the number of instances for any Security Server, you need to modify its line in the `$FWDIR/conf/fwauthd.conf` file:

```
<listen-port><daemon-name>wait -<instances>
```

For example, if you want to run four instances of in.ahttpd, which will all listen on port 80, the corresponding line should look like this:

```
80 in.ahttpd wait -4
```

Connections from the same HTTP client will always be directed to the same daemon within the authenticated session timeout. Connections begin to use alternate daemons only after the previous daemon fills up. All connections from a client will always be handled by the same daemon.

Utilize the URL Performance Enhancements Present in 4.1 SP2 and Later

FireWall-1 version 4.1 SP2 offers two enhancements related to the HTTP Security Server:

- URL Logging can now be done in the kernel. If the only reason you use the HTTP Security Server is to log URLs, this improvement will increase performance tremendously, as it can be done in a way that does not require the HTTP Security Server.
- URL Filtering can cache requests to the UFP server in the kernel. Although this still requires the HTTP Security Server, it can reduce the amount of time it takes to process requests, because it does not have to perform a time-consuming lookup on every URL.

UFP Caching

When an HTTP request is made, the IP address of the destination is checked against the cache. If the IP address is in the cache, the category associated with that IP address is used. If it is not in the cache, the HTTP Security Server sends the request to the UFP server, which returns the appropriate category information and is then cached. Caching can be controlled by FireWall-1 or by the UFP server. Check Point recommends the latter method, which is thought to be more accurate.

If FireWall-1 controls the caching, there are two methods FireWall-1 uses to update the cache:

- *One-request method:* FireWall-1 takes the information returned by the UFP server and writes it to the cache.
- *Two-request method:* Firewall-1 makes a second request to the UFP server to determine if the IP address of the site could match multiple categories. Only if the entire site uses the same category is the data written to the cache.

The one-request method is more aggressive in caching at the expense of cache integrity. The second method is slower, but the cache integrity is significantly improved.

Where the UFP server controls the caching, information necessary to update the cache is returned with each request that is looked up.

To enable UFP caching, create a URI resource, or edit an existing one. Go to the Match tab and enable the caching accordingly, as shown in Figure 8-18.

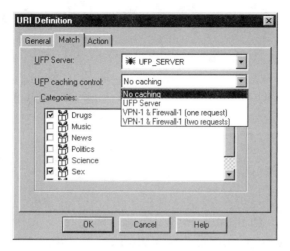

Figure 8-18   URI Definition, Match tab, UFP caching

To make sure you log all URLs accessed, both allowed and not allowed, use rules similar to those shown in Figure 8-19.

The Kernel URL Logging is a service you will create in the next section.

Source	Destination	Service	Action	Track	Install On
net-10.0.10.0-24	Any	http->bad-urls	reject	Long	Gateways
net-10.0.10.0-24	Any	Kernel-URL-Logging	accept		Gateways
net-10.0.10.0-24	Any	http	accept	Long	Gateways

Figure 8-19   Rules for UFP caching

Kernel URL Logging

Kernel URL Logging allows you to log URLs without having to divert the connection to the HTTP Security Server. This improves overall performance in these situations. It can also be used with Kernel UFP caching as shown earlier.

This feature can do some additional inspection of HTTP traffic using a mechanism called TCP Streaming, which has two modes:

- *Passive mode:* FireWall-1 passively listens to network traffic and saves all relevant connection information to memory. Packets can then be reordered if necessary, and all retransmissions can be validated. If FireWall-1 determines there are any violations, the connection is rejected.

- *Active mode:* The checks of passive mode are not done. FireWall-1 may reject packets in certain out-of-sequence circumstances.

Passive mode is the default and recommended setting. However, it does require more kernel memory than Active mode.

To enable Kernel URL Logging, create a service of type Other. In the Match tab, specify the following:

```
URL_LOG_SVC(rule-no, port-no, log-method)
```

If the service requires authentication, use

```
URL_LOG_AUTH_SVC(rule-no, port-no, log-method)
```

where the following is true:

- `rule_no` is the rule number under which URLs are logged.
- `port_no` is the port number to watch for HTTP traffic (usually 80).
- `log-method` is one of the log methods listed in Table 8-2.

Table 8-2   Log methods for Kernel URL Logging

Method	Description
URLOG_NO_LOG	No logging, but Passive TCP Streaming provides additional security.
URLOG_LOG_ALL	All URLs accessed (i.e., each page element) is logged. Meaningful with HTTP/1.1.
URLOG_LOG_FIRST	Only the first URL in a session is logged and is subject to TCP Streaming. In most cases, subsequent requests in a session are for graphical elements (gif, jpg).
URLOG_LOG_FIRST_SECURE	Same as the previous method except TCP Streaming continues for the entire session, providing additional security.
URLOG_USE_ACTIVE_STREAMING	Can be added to URLOG_LOG_ALL and URLOG_LOG_FIRST to enable Active TCP Streaming. URLOG_NO_LOG and URLOG_LOG_FIRST_SECURE rely on Passive TCP Streaming and would effectively nullify these settings.

Once you have created this service, you create two rules, as shown in Figure 8-20. The first rule does the Kernel URL Logging; the second rule actually accepts the HTTP connection.

Source	Destination	Service	Action	Track	Install On
🖳 net-10.0.10.0-24	➤ Any	⚓ Kernel-URL-Logging	🔨 accept		🖥 Gateways
🖳 net-10.0.10.0-24	➤ Any	🌐 http	🔨 accept	📖 Long	🖥 Gateways

Figure 8-20 Kernel URL Logging rules

More Memory, Physical and Virtual

The HTTP Security Server requires lots of memory, especially when it is busy. A busy in.ahttpd process on a Nokia platform handling just 1,024 concurrent connections can reach as high as 87MB! Memory usage for in.ahttpd has proven to be similar on other platforms. The more physical memory you have, the better. Also, your swap size should be a fixed size (preferably on a dedicated device) and should be twice the size of the amount of physical memory you have.

File Descriptors Globally and Per Process

On a UNIX platform, there is a limit to the number of file descriptors available both to a specific process and globally. When started, in.ahttpd attempts to reserve the maximum number of file descriptors allowed by the OS. On Solaris, this is 1,024. On IPSO, this is 2,048. Windows NT does not have this issue.

An HTTP connection going through the Security Server requires two sockets: one for the connection from the client and one for the client to the server. Each socket requires a file descriptor. A limit of 2,048 file descriptors means that less than 1,024 concurrent active connections can go through each instance of the in.ahttpd daemon. Other things like logging require file descriptors as well. When the maximum number of file descriptors has been reached, a "Too many open files" error is entered in $FWDIR/log/ahttpd.log.

Allowing each in.ahttpd to handle more than 1,024 concurrent connections is *not* recommended. Another factor to consider is the amount of memory that each process requires. Using the previous IPSO example, limiting the file descriptors to 1,024 (thus 512 connections per process) reduces the memory utilization to 47MB. The more concurrent connections each process can handle, the larger the process will get. In some cases, it might actually be better to decrease the number of file descriptors and increase the number of processes running.

On IPSO, the number of file descriptors allowed are limited by two kernel variables: kern:maxfiles (global limit) and kern:maxfilesperproc (per process limit). The limits are 8,096 and 2,048, respectively. To modify these values, use the ipsctl command:

```
ipsctl -w kern:maxfiles 4X
ipsctl -w kern:maxfilesperproc X
```

where X is a number you want to modify these values to; 4X means four times the value you choose for X. Because these values are set to their defaults at boot time, you need to add these commands to `/var/etc/rc.local` so they are changed at each startup.

On Solaris, add the following line to `/etc/system` and reboot:

```
set rlim_fd_max = X
```

On Linux, you need to do two things. In `/etc/security/limits.conf`, add the following lines:

```
* soft nofile 1024
* hard nofile X
```

These lines allow users to set their own file descriptor limits on login. You also need to change the systemwide limits by executing the following commands (add to a startup script to be done on each reboot):

```
echo X >/proc/sys/fs/file-max
echo 3X >/proc/sys/fs/inode-max
```

The variable 3X means three times the value you choose for X.

In HP/UX or AIX, these defaults can be changed in "sam" or "smit" accordingly.

Troubleshooting Issues with the HTTP Security Server

Many of the following issues also apply to authentication because Security Servers are also used for authentication. In this section, I talk about how to resolve common problems with the HTTP Security Server. A separate section on gathering debug information from Security Servers appears in the "Debugging the Security Server" section in this chapter.

8.8: Why Won't the HTTP Security Server Work?

One or more objects using the same address as an interface of the firewall (such as a workstation object of the firewall's registered address) is probably defined in the `$FWDIR/conf/objects.C` file before the firewall object itself. You should either delete these objects or manually move the appropriate object to the top of your `objects.C` file.

A Security Server cannot share the same port as another application. For example, if you are using the HTTP Security Server bound to a specific port (say port 80) and you have something else bound to that port (such as Voyager on a Nokia platform), one of the services must be moved.

8.9: My Users See the Error Message "Fw-1 at Kyle: Unknown WWW Server." What Does This Error Mean and Can I Change the Text of This Error Message?

This message could mean a few different things:

- The URL typed was incorrect.
- The firewall is not configured to use DNS for name resolution. The HTTP Security Server requires that the firewall be configured to use DNS.
- When FireWall-1 attempted to look up the name for the site, it timed out.

The message itself cannot be changed. One thing that has been problematic on some OSs (particularly on Solaris 2.5.1) is the presence of the name service caching daemon (nscd). Kill the process and make sure it does not start up on reboot (on Solaris 2.5.1, it is started from `/etc/rc2.d/S76nscd`).

8.10: My Users See the Error Message "Failed to Connect to WWW Server." What Does This Error Mean and Can I Change the Text of This Error Message?

There are two possible reasons for this message:

- Connection to the site timed out or was refused at the remote end. In this case, you can usually do a refresh and the page will load correctly.
- The remote site either has a missing or inconsistent "reverse DNS" entry for its IP address.

Check Point considers the latter a security risk and does not allow these sites to be contacted through the HTTP Security Server. Check Point also does not allow you to turn this feature off. Your options for a workaround are:

- Contact the administrators of the remote site in question to ask them to fix the site's reverse DNS entry.
- Add an entry in your firewall's local host file, and have the system resolve against the host file first.
- Exclude the site in question from going through the Security Server by adding a rule above your Security Server rule that permits normal HTTP to the site.

8.11: Why Do I Have Issues Whenever I Try to Use MSIE through FireWall-1 or Any Other Browser That Supports HTTP/1.1?

FireWall-1 3.0's HTTP Security Server does not support HTTP/1.1. FireWall-1 4.0 SP5 and 4.1 SP1 resolves several issues with MSIE and the HTTP Security Server. If you are running an earlier version of FireWall-1, I suggest upgrading. Some additional changes are necessary to support HTTP/1.1 in FireWall-1. Edit `$FWDIR/conf/objects.C` and add the following lines:

```
:http_cvp_allow_chunked (true)
:http_weeding_allow_chunked (true)
:http_block_java_allow_chunked (true)
:http_allow_ranges (true)
:http_force_down_to_10 (true)
:http_sup_continue (true)
:http_avoid_keep_alive (true)
```

8.12: Why Can I Not Access Certain Web Sites through the HTTP Security Server?

As of FireWall-1 4.1 SP4, there are three known issues involving certain sites with the HTTP Security Server:

- Sites hosted with particular versions of IIS (Microsoft's Web Server) are inaccessible.
- Some sites that send a "302 Redirect" to the same URL as a form of load balancing (e.g., www.boston.com) are inaccessible.
- Any part of a Web site that employs QuickTime streaming will be inaccessible (e.g., www.cnn.com).

As of August 2001, the only workaround is to not use the HTTP Security Server for these sites. This can be accomplished by placing a rule that permits access to these sites above any rule that uses the HTTP Security Server.

8.13: Why Does the Memory Usage of in.ahttpd Grow and Grow?

In just about every version of the HTTP Security Server that I've seen, heavy use of the HTTP Security Server seems to cause the process to grow without bounds until the system crashes. This and the performance issues are the reasons I hesitate to recommend that large sites use the HTTP Security Server. Some memory leaks in in.ahttpd are supposed to be addressed in FireWall-1 4.1 SP4. However, you may have to write a script to monitor in.ahttpd's memory usage and kill this process when it grows beyond a certain limit (25MB is the limit several of my customers use).

FTP Security Server

The FTP Security Server is used to restrict people from uploading or downloading files as well as virus scan all FTP file transfers. The FTP Security Server is enabled when the following situations are true:

- There is a line that permits in.aftpd to start up in `$FWDIR/conf/fwauthd.conf`.

- A valid resource is defined in your security policy or a User Authentication rule involving FTP.

The proper line for the FTP Security Server in `$FWDIR/conf/fwauthd.conf` looks like this (without a comment "#" at the beginning of the line):

```
21              in.aftpd      wait    0
```

If this line is not present or commented out, the FTP Security Server will not run, and any process that relies on it will fail.

To filter FTP, you need to create a resource of type FTP and use it in the rulebase. Let's create a resource called FTP_downloads to allow FTP downloads through the HTTP Security Server. Go to the Manage menu, and select Resources. Then create a new resource of type FTP, as shown in Figure 8-21.

This dialog is fairly self-explanatory, so let's look at the Match tab shown in Figure 8-22.

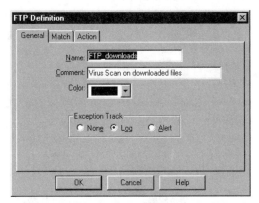

Figure 8-21   FTP Resource Definition, General tab

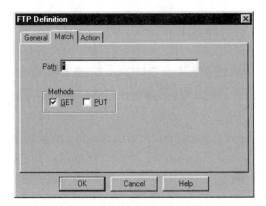

Figure 8-22   FTP Resource Definition, Match tab

Path refers to a specific location on the FTP server. For instance, you could allow people to upload to a specific directory, but deny it to others. An example of this is shown in the "Sample Configurations" section of this chapter.

You can match two types of methods: GET and PUT. Aside from matching the GET command, allowing GET commands also allows RETR, RNFR, and XMD5. Aside from matching the PUT command, allowing PUT commands also allows STOR, STOU, APPE, RNFR, RNTO, DELE, MKD, and RMD. Most other commands are passed to the FTP server for execution.[2]

The Action tab, shown in Figure 8-23, is where you specify the CVP server to use, if any.

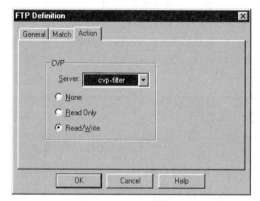

Figure 8-23   FTP Resource Definition, Action tab

You can then add a rule with this resource to the rulebase, as shown in Figure 8-24.

Figure 8-24   FTP with CVP rule

Frequently Asked Questions about the FTP Security Server
8.14: Why Won't the FTP Security Server Let Me Use Certain FTP Commands?

The FTP Security Server restricts certain commands by default. The following commands are enabled by default:

---

2.   For details on what these and other FTP commands are, see RFC 959, which can be obtained from www.rfc-editor.org, among other places.

```
ABOR DELE LIST NLST REST RNFR RNTO MODE PORT RETR STOR SITE MLFL
MAIL MSND MSOM MSAM MRSQ STOU APPE ALLO PASS ACCT REIN USER MRSQ
MRCP CWD PWD RMD MKD HELP BYE QUIT BYTE SIZE MACB FW1C SOCK NOOP
CDUP SYST  XMKD XCWD XRMD XPWD PASV TYPE STRU XCUP XMD5 MDTM
```

To override these defaults, add the following line to the `:props (` section in `$FWDIR/conf/objects.C` on the management console:

```
ftp_allowed_cmds (PORT PASV STAT ...)
```

Note that this solution only works on version 4.0 SP6, 4.1 SP2, and later installations. See Chapter 4, FAQ 4.2 for guidelines on how to edit `objects.C`.

Similar changes can also be made on the firewall module itself. Create the file `$FWDIR/conf/aftpd.conf` with the following lines:

- To allow MACB, add "macb=1" to the file.
- To allow MAIL, MLFL, MRCP, MRSQ, MSAM, MSND and MSOM, add "mail_cmd=1" to the file.
- To allow PORT command to known TCP ports, or to IP addresses different from the client's, add "port_spoof=1" to the file.
- To allow REST, add "restart=1" to the file.
- To allow SOCK, add "sock_cmd=1" to the file.
- To allow SITE, add "site_cmd=1" to the file.
- To allow all other FTP commands, add "optimist=1" to the file.
- To allow PWD reply with no quotes around the directory name, add "pwd_unquoted=1" to the file (only in FireWall-1 4.0 SP6, 4.1 SP1, and later).

8.15: Why Do I Always Have Problems with Certain Sites When Using the FTP Security Server?

When the user issues a `get`, `put`, `delete`, `mkdir`, or `rename`, the FTP Security Server issues a PWD command in order to get the full path. The FTP server must respond to the PWD command with a 257 message, which, according to RFC 959, must contain the absolute path in quotes. If the PWD command is disabled on the remote server or the PWD does not respond in the correct manner, the FTP Security Server will deny the request. See the previous question for how to allow PWD replies without quotes.

8.16: Why Do I Have a Problem FTPing to Any Site with the FTP Security Server?

There appears to be an issue with the nscd on Solaris 2.5.1 (and possibly other UNIX type of OSs). nscd is used to cache name service information. Disabling nscd should solve the problem, although it may take an hour or two for the changes to take effect (unless you reboot).

SMTP Security Server

The SMTP Security Server is used to prevent certain types of mail from passing your gateway. The SMTP Security Server is enabled when the following situations are true:

- There is a line that permits in.asmtpd to start up in `$FWDIR/conf/ fwauthd.conf`.
- A valid resource is defined in your security policy.

The proper line for the SMTP Security Server in `$FWDIR/conf/ fwauthd.conf` looks like this (without a comment "#" at the beginning of the line):

```
25              in.asmtpd      wait    0
```

If this line is not present or commented out, the SMTP Security Server will not run, and any process that relies on it will fail.

The SMTP Security Server acts a bit differently from the other Security Servers. There are actually two separate processes involved: in.asmtpd and mdq. in.asmtpd intercepts SMTP connections and spools the messages to disk. That is all they do. The mdq process periodically scans the spool directory and delivers the messages to their final destination, performing the necessary filtering, header rewriting, and content rewriting. This is more secure than attempting to do everything in one process. A diagram of this is shown in Figure 8-25.

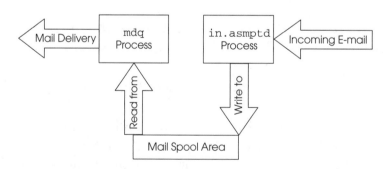

Figure 8-25 How in.asmtpd and mdq interact

$FWDIR/conf/smtp.conf

Aside from using resources, the SMTP Security Server has parameters that are configured in `$FWDIR/conf/smtp.conf`. Descriptions of these parameters and their default settings follow:

timeout: Amount of time in seconds FireWall-1 will spend on CVP scanning a message and delivering it to the Mail Transfer Agent (MTA). It is recommended that this value be at least 900 seconds (the default setting), if not longer. If you change this parameter, it is recommended that you reboot in order for it to take effect. Versions of FireWall-1 prior to 4.0 SP5 have a bug whereby the connection to the CVP server will not properly terminate if this timeout is reached. In this case, you can either increase the timeout value or upgrade.

scan_period: Amount of time (in seconds) for mdq to check the spool directory for e-mail to be delivered. By default, mdq checks for mail every two seconds. Mail found during this scan are delivered. mdq will take a number of e-mails based on the max_load parameter. Once max_load is reached, mdq stops taking mail messages from the spool directory.

resend_period: Amount of time (in seconds) that a message that failed to be delivered will be resent from the SMTP Security Server. The default is 600 seconds (10 minutes).

rundir: Location where FireWall-1 will spool incoming e-mail. The default is $FWDIR/spool. If you expect to process lots of e-mail, consider moving this to a separate partition. Specify a path to the new spool directory (this must exist).

abandon_time: Amount of time (in seconds) that a message is allowed to live in the spool directory before FireWall-1 returns the message to sender. The default is 432,000 seconds (or five days). The error server defined in error_server or the specific resource matched by the rule the message was accepted under is used to deliver the message.

detailed_err_mail: If this parameter is set to a value other than 0 (default is 0), an error mail will be generated when the SMTP Security Server cannot deliver the e-mail to some of the recipients. The error mail includes information regarding which users could not receive the original mail and a reason for each recipient. This mail message will only get sent when the "Notify Sender on Error" flag is enabled in the resource that matches the incoming message. Note that this parameter is only available in version 4.0 SP3 and later.

detailed_security_err_mail: When this parameter is set to a value other than 0 (default is 0), and a mail fails a Content Security check, the generated error mail will include a notification of the failure as well as the explanation message received from the Content Security server. Note that in case of a malicious attempt to insert a virus into an organization, it may be preferable not to use this flag because it allows the generator of the mail containing the virus to receive feedback on the malicious attempt. This error mail is only sent when the "Notify Sender on Error" flag is enabled in the resource that matches the incoming message. Note that this parameter is only available in version 4.0 SP3 and later.

max_load: This value is an abstract measure for the load generated by the mail dequeuer while emptying the mail spool. It corresponds to the number of messages mdq will attempt to deliver at one time using the following formula:

$$\text{max\_load} = 2x + 4y$$

where x is the number of connections that do not involve CVP, and y is the number of connections that do involve CVP.

The default for this parameter is 40. The parameter can be set as high as 60. On Solaris and HP, it can be set to 100. If the value exceeds this limit, the mail dequeuer will not run. This option should be used to adjust the load that the mail dequeuer generates to the load that can be handled by the peer mail server. When the mail dequeuer generates more load than the peer mail server can handle, the peer mail server might refuse the mail dequeuer's connection attempts, possibly causing mails to accumulate in the mail dequeuer's spool, and delaying delivery. This parameter's value should be set according to the load capacity of the main peer mail server.

default_server: Indicates the SMTP server that FireWall-1 will always use to relay e-mail. Resources in the rulebase can override this setting. If this value is not set, FireWall-1 will attempt to use the SMTP server the original SMTP connection attempted to use.

error_server: Indicates the SMTP server that FireWall-1 will always use to send error notifications. Resources in the rulebase can override this setting. If this value is not set, FireWall-1 will attempt to use the SMTP server the original SMTP connection attempted to use.

postmaster: Specifies the e-mail address of the postmaster. This e-mail address is sent nondelivery messages.

SMTP Resources

To filter SMTP, you need to create a resource of type SMTP. Go to the Manage menu, and select Resources in the Policy Editor. Choose New, and select SMTP. The dialog box shown in Figure 8-26 appears.

The options on this tab are described as follows:

Name: The name of the SMTP resource object (must be unique).

Comment: Description of the resource in more detail.

Color: Select whichever color you would like.

Mail Server: If this server is specified and this resource is matched, the e-mail will be forwarded to this server. If nothing is specified, the e-mail will be forwarded to

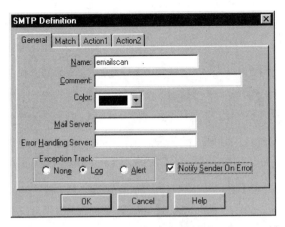

Figure 8-26 SMTP Resource Definition, General tab

the server specified in the *default_server* variable in $FWDIR/conf/smtp.conf. If neither of these are specified, the e-mail will be forwarded to the server the message was originally being sent to. To specify multiple mail servers to attempt, use the form {mailserver1, mailserver2, ...} .

Error Handling Server: If the SMTP Security Server is not able to deliver the message within the abandon time and "Notify Sender on Error" is selected, the message will be sent through this e-mail server. If nothing is specified, the e-mail will be forwarded to the server specified in the *error_server* variable in $FWDIR/conf/smtp.conf. If neither of these are specified, the e-mail will be forwarded to the server the message was originally being sent to. To specify multiple mail servers to attempt, use the form {mailserver1, mailserver2, ...} .

The Match tab is shown in Figure 8-27.

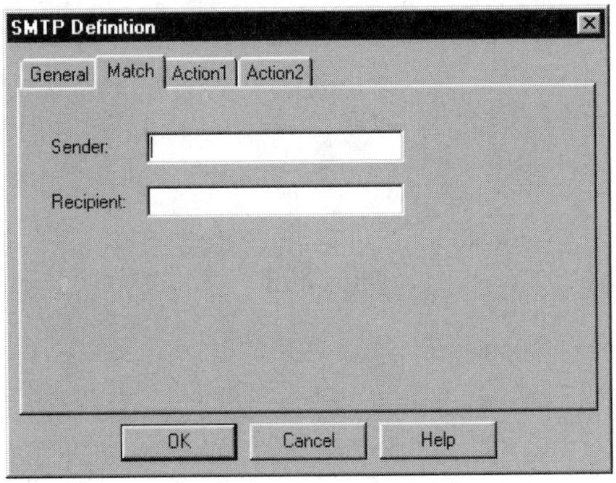

Figure 8-27 SMTP Resource Definition, Match tab

The Sender or Recipient tag can be matched with any of the wildcards previously listed. The Action1 tab is shown in Figure 8-28.

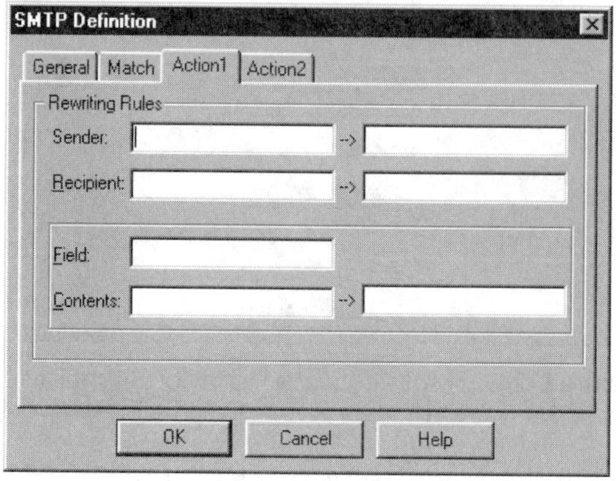

Figure 8-28   SMTP Resource Definition, Action1 tab

The Action1 tab allows you to rewrite the e-mail headers. The left part of each line (the original) is what is matched; the right (what you are changing it to) is its replacement. On the original side, you can use normal wildcards. If you want to make what you matched part of what you translate it to, use the "&" to signify that. For example, if you want to rewrite all addresses of the form user@smtp.weirdal.com to user@ weirdal.com, on the left side, you would specify *@smtp.weirdal.com and on the right, you would specify &@weirdal.com.

You can do this for a custom field as well. If you want to eliminate a field (say the "Received:" lines) on the left, enter "*" and leave the right side blank.

The Action2 tab is shown in Figure 8-29.

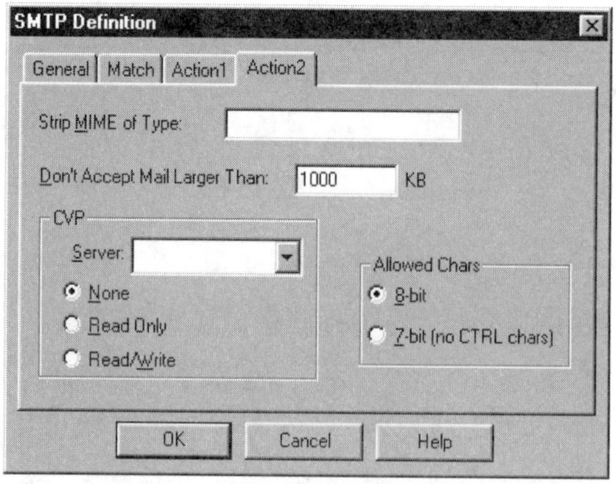

Figure 8-29   SMTP Resource Definition, Action2 tab

If you do not want to allow certain MIME types, you can specify them on the Action2 tab. You can specify multiple MIME types using {,} and *. Filtering on MIME types is an inexact science at best because the e-mail client can use any MIME type it wants and different e-mail clients use different MIME types for the same type of document. For instance, application/msword can be used for Microsoft Word documents. UNIX machines often send these kinds of documents as application/octet-stream, which can also be used for applications or any binary file.

You can also restrict the size of an e-mail on this tab (including attachments) and determine whether or not to perform CVP on these messages.

Some examples of how to use the SMTP Security Server are described in the next section.

Frequently Asked Questions about the SMTP Security Server

The following FAQ are provided for events that may occur with SMTP Security Server.

8.17: When I Use the SMTP Security Server, What Should the MX for My Domain Point To?

Your MX records should point to your normal SMTP server. Provided your rules are set up correctly, FireWall-1 will intercept this traffic automatically. You do not have to change anything with respect to your MX records for your domain.

8.18: Can I Have the Firewall Be the MX for My Domain?

Usually, the SMTP Security Server intercepts communications destined for an internal SMTP server. There are cases where it may be desirable to have the firewall be the mail exchanger. You can do this with the proper SMTP Resource, making sure the following fields are defined:

- *Mail Server* (on the General tab): Enter the IP address of your inbound server in this field. If you have more than one SMTP Server, enter each in the format {ip-address-1,ip-address-2,...}.
- *Notify Sender on Error* (on the General tab): Select this option if you want to notify the sender that his message has been rejected or in case of some other problem.
- *Don't Accept Mail Larger Than* (on the Action2 tab): This option should be set appropriately. The default is 1000KB (or roughly 1MB).

Once you have defined the resource, add a rule similar to the one shown in Figure 8-30, and reinstall the security policy.

Note that your SMTP Server should be responsible for delivering outbound messages. See the next question for more details.

Source	Destination	Service	Action	Track	Install On
Any	firewall	smtp->store_and_forward	accept	Long	Gateways

Figure 8-30   SMTP Security Server rule

8.19: Why Won't the SMTP Security Server Deliver to Lower-Priority MXs?

This is probably the number-one reason most people do *not* use the SMTP Security Server. Users have asked this to be fixed since FireWall-1 3.0, when the Security Server first made its debut in FireWall-1. Check Point claims that it has fixed this problem in the NG release of FireWall-1 (the next major release after version 4.1).

Meanwhile, a workaround is to use a "smart" SMTP Server—that is, a conventional SMTP server that knows how to properly handle MX records. This SMTP Server should probably be in your DMZ. You have to make sure that SMTP traffic from this host to the Internet does not get processed by any SMTP resources. To ensure that this does not happen and to have the most secure setup, use the rules shown in Figure 8-31.

Source	Destination	Service	Action	Track	Install On
Any	Smart-SMTP-Server	smtp	accept	Long	Gateways
Smart-SMTP-Server	internal-network	smtp->smtp_inbound_from_dmz	accept	Long	Gateways
Smart-SMTP-Server	Any	smtp	accept	Long	Gateways
Internal-SMTP-Server	Any	smtp->smtp_outbound	accept	Long	Gateways

Figure 8-31   Rules for Smart SMTP Security Server setup

The first rule matches all SMTP traffic from the Internet to the Smart SMTP Server (which is the MX for your domain). The second rule forces all SMTP traffic from the Smart SMTP Server to the internal network through the SMTP Security Server using the smtp_inbound_from_dmz resource. This resource should have the mail server configured to point to the internal SMTP server(s) and perform any necessary checking. The third rule allows the Smart SMTP Server to communicate to any SMTP server without going through the SMTP Security Server. The fourth rule forces your Internal SMTP Server to communicate through the SMTP Security Server. This last rule is optional, but you should use it if you want to perform virus scanning on any outbound e-mail.

8.20: Can I Use the SMTP Security Server to Help Fight Incoming Spam?

Spam is a notoriously difficult nuisance to filter properly. Many individuals and companies have written various programs to attempt to filter spam. Although not specifically designed to handle this task, FireWall-1 does have some features that can be used to help, namely the SMTP Security Server.

Your inbound SMTP server is likely to be a better tool to stop spam. Most SMTP servers (with the notable exception of Microsoft Exchange 5.0 and earlier) have the capability to turn off unauthorized relaying and/or implement some checks to prevent unauthorized use. You can even subscribe to the Mail Abuse Prevention System (MAPS) or a similar system that maintains a blacklist of known bad sites.

If you are going to use the SMTP Security Server to filter spam, your SMTP Resources should have the recipient and the sender defined. The recipient should be *@yourdomain.com. If you have multiple domains, it should read *@{yourdomain.com,yourotherdomain.com,...} . The send should be configured with a * to match all incoming mail.

8.21: Can the SMTP Security Server Accept E-mails of Any Size?

You should be able to type a number into the appropriate field. The number 999999 seems to work for some users. A blank works for others. In older versions of FireWall-1, you could set this to zero and it would have the same effect. Another way to do the same thing is to manually hack `$FWDIR/conf/objects.C` on the management console. Look for your resource, find the maxsize parameter, and change it to whatever you would like.

Personally, if a user wants to e-mail a large file, I feel he or she should use FTP or something similar. All e-mailed files are turned into 7 bits for transmission into e-mail, which expands the file size by at least 33 percent.

8.22: When Does CVP Get Performed on E-mails in the SMTP Security Server?

This action is actually done as the SMTP message is being delivered to the remote SMTP server. This means the timeout value specified in `$FWDIR/conf/smtp.conf` needs to be sufficiently high enough to both scan and deliver the message.

Troubleshooting the SMTP Security Server

The following solutions are provided for problems that occur with SMTP Security Server.

8.23: I See the Message "Connection Prematurely Closed in $FWDIR/log/asmtpd.log."

This message is said to be an anomaly. It is fixed in versions 4.0 SP5 and 4.1 SP1.

8.24: Mail Appears to Get Stuck in the SMTP Security Server Spool Directory.

Make sure your rules are ordered in such a way as to not use the SMTP Security Server when not necessary. The following sections contain some other events that will cause messages to back up.

Maximum Concurrent Sent Mails Limit Reached

This is a message you might see in the `mdq.log` file. It means that the number of recipients specified in the mail header has exceeded the limit.

```
[195@firewall] max concurrent sent mails limit reached - spool
scanning stops
```

The number of messages that can be sent at one time is specified in `$FWDIR/conf/smtp.conf` with the max_load parameter, as discussed earlier in the chapter.

Messages Continue to Fail on Delivery Attempts

If sending an e-mail continues to fail (or takes a long time to do so), the whole spool will be held up until the troubled e-mail times out. By decreasing the abandon_time from its default of 432,000 seconds (4 days) to 3,600 (1 hour), the spool would clear out quicker, returning error messages to the sender that the e-mail could not be delivered. How to do this is explained in the "$FWDIR/conf/smtp.conf" section earlier in the chapter.

Forcing the Queue to Empty Out

You can force a queue run by using the command `fw mdq`. However, the only way to fix this (short of letting FireWall-1 attempt to deliver these messages until they expire) is to edit each individual file in $FWDIR/spool (or whatever rundir is set to), so that the destination that it tries to contact is an SMTP server that will deliver the message. Each file in the spool directory is the e-mail message. Its format is X#### , where ### is the e-mail order number given by FireWall-1, and *X* is the prefix. There are three types of prefixes:

- *R:* File is waiting for the mail dequeuer.
- *T:* The file is in process (within the mail dequeuer).
- *E:* Error message, when the mail dequeuer cannot send the e-mail.

In all cases, the beginning of a spool file looks like this:

```
AV_SETTING: none
AV_IPADDR: 0.0.0.0
```

```
AV_PORT: 0
AV_HEADERS: 0
COMPOUND: 1
SRC: 10.1.2.100
SPORT: 4784
DST: 10.226.0.201
DPORT: 25
ERR_SERVER: 10.1.2.7
RULE: 31
RULEACT: 0
ERRMAIL: 0
ACCT: 0
LOG_OK: MDQ_LOG
LOG_BAD: MDQ_LOG
LOG_ERR: MDQ_ALERT
```

The headers are described as follows:

AV_SETTING (none|check|cure): Indicates whether or not this message will be checked for viruses. None means do not scan, check means do not send if it contains a known virus, and cure means clean out any known viruses in the message before sending.

AV_IPADDR (a.b.c.d): IP address of the antivirus scanner. Should list 0.0.0.0 if no virus checking is to be done.

AV_PORT (n): Port used for CVP. Normally 18181 or 0.

AV_HEADERS (?): Unknown, but usually set to 0.

COMPOUND (?): Unknown, but usually set to 0.

SRC (a.b.c.d): Source IP address of the machine that sent the e-mail.

SPORT (n): Source port used for the connection to the SMTP Security Server from the Source IP listed.

DST (a.b.c.d): Destination IP address of the machine to send the e-mail to. This will be the IP address of the mail server that the source IP was originally trying to send to unless the matching resource or the default_server parameter is set to some other value; in which case, this value will reflect that instead. This is the IP address that FireWall-1 will use to deliver this message.

DPORT (n): Destination port that will be used to send the mail to. Normally this is 25.

ERR_SERVER (a.b.c.d): If a message has been in the $FWDIR/spool beyond the abandon_time, this is the SMTP server that will be used to attempt to deliver the failure notice. If no error_server is defined in the appropriate resource or smtp.conf, this will be the same as the DST setting.

RULE (n): This is the rule number this message was originally accepted by. When the message is actually delivered, this is the rule number that will be logged.

RULEACT (n): Unknown. The value of this is usually 0, although it appears to get set to 2 if ACCT is set to 1 (see the ACCT header description).

ERRMAIL (0|1): If the mail errors out, this will determine if an actual error e-mail is sent out. This corresponds to the "Notify Sender on Error" check box in the appropriate resource. The value of this header will be 1 if it will attempt to deliver an error, 0 if not.

ACCT (0|1): If the value is 1, perform accounting tracking on this connection. If the value is 0, do not.

LOG_OK (MDQ_LOG|MDQ_ALERT): If the message is delivered successfully, this option specifies how to log it.

LOG_BAD (MDQ_LOG|MDQ_ALERT): If the message is not delivered successfully (i.e., a transient failure), this option specifies how to log it. This corresponds to Exception Track on the appropriate resource. This line will not exist if Exception Track is set to none.

LOG_ERR (x): If an error mail needs to be sent (because the message has passed the abandon time), the option specifies how to log it. This corresponds to the "Notify Sender on Error" check box in the appropriate resource.

Below these entries, you will find two sets of e-mail headers: the original headers (as they were sent with the message) and the modified headers, which are what FireWall-1 will actually send to the remote SMTP server.

You can move the *R* file with the lowest numerical value of the spool directory, enabling the mdq process to work with the next file. The idea is that you can either modify or relocate the problem files, enabling the forwarding of the rest of the spool directory.

Once you have done this to all the files, you can either type

```
# fw mdq
```

or

```
# fw kill fwd ; fwd `cat $FWDIR/conf/masters`
```

to force the SMTP Security Server to reprocess the mail spool.

TCP Security Server

The TCP Security Server is a new feature in FireWall-1 4.1 SP2 and in later versions. It allows you to perform Content Security on any TCP service by sending the raw data stream to the CVP server. The CVP server inspects the content stream and returns the results to the TCP Security Server, which then takes the specified action in the resource.

To configure the TCP Security Server, perform the following steps:

1. Create a new service of type TCP.
2. Set the service port appropriately.
3. Set the protocol type for this service to FTP. (Yes, I do mean FTP.)
4. Enable the TCP Security Server in `$FWDIR/conf/fwauthd.conf`.
5. On UNIX systems, establish a symbolic link for in.genericd.

You will need to add a line in the following format to `$FWDIR/conf/fwauthd. conf`:

```
port  in.genericd  wait  0
```

Port is the port number of the service you are creating. To establish the symbolic link, enter the following set of commands:

```
# cd $FWDIR/bin
# ln -s fw in.genericd
```

General Questions about the Security Servers

Most of the questions regarding the Security Servers are specific to each Security Server used. However, there are a few questions that are specific to the use of Security Servers in general.

8.25: Why Do All the Connections I Make through the Security Servers Appear to Originate from the Firewall Instead of the Client?

This is how the Security Servers work. The firewall redirects the various services to the appropriate Security Server. The Security Server then makes the request on behalf of the client. It is more or less transparent from the client's perspective.

8.26: Why Is the Security Server Used Even If the Rule Matched Does Not Use a Resource?

A prior rule using the Security Servers needed evaluation by the Security Server in order to determine whether or not the rule applied. Refer to Figure 8-10 earlier in this chapter for an example.

If the connection originates from 10.0.10.0/24 and requires HTTP, the Security Server becomes involved because it must determine whether or not the URL meets the criteria specified in the resource. If it does, the connection is rejected. If not, the

HTTP is allowed by the second rule. However, because the packet required evaluation by the HTTP Security Server to determine that it did not meet the previous rule's criteria, the HTTP Security Server processes the connection even though the second rule does not explicitly use a resource.

If you want to ensure that the Security Server is not used in a particular case, you need to place a rule above any other rules that involve the appropriate Security Server rules.

8.27: Can I Mix User Authentication and Content Security?

For HTTP and FTP, yes. Simply use an action of User Authentication where it is appropriate.

8.28: Can I Mix Session Authentication and Content Security?

No, you cannot. The Security Servers are required for Content Security anyway, so it makes no sense to use the Session Authentication in conjunction with Content Security. You can certainly use Session Authentication for other services, just not the ones where Content Security is required.

Debugging the Security Servers

There are several environment variables that can be set in the operating system. If they are defined when `fwd` starts up, FireWall-1 will enable various sorts of debugging and log the information generated into the various files in `$FWDIR/log`. In version 4.0 and earlier, these files include `ahttpd.log`, `asmtp.log`, `mdq.log`, and `aftpd.log`. In version 4.1, all the files end with .elg, which makes it easier to distinguish them from the log files generated by FireWall-1 for rulebase logging.

The general principle is to set the environment variable(s), and then kill and restart `fwd`. On Windows NT, it is far better to restart FireWall-1 instead of trying to restart `fwd`. On UNIX machines running csh, use the command `setenv VARIABLE value`. On UNIX machines running sh, use the command `VARIABLE= value; export VARIABLE`. On Windows NT, use the command `set VARIABLE= value`. To enable the variable, set it to a value of 1 unless otherwise specified. See Table 8-3 for a list of debug variables used with Security Servers.

Summary

Content Security provides additional control over what can be accessed through your firewalls. The HTTP, FTP, SMTP, and TCP Security Servers provide the means to filter content in FireWall-1. Resources are what tell the Security Servers how to filter content.

Table 8-3 Debug variables for the Security Servers

Variable	Description
FWAHTTPD_DEBUG	Various debug information from `in.ahttpd`
HTTP_DEBUG	Various other debug information from `in.ahttpd`
FUNCCHAIN_DEBUG	Debug information from external authentication servers like SecurID and name resolution
FW_RESOLVE_DEBUG	Debug information from name resolution
FWT_DEBUG	Various debugging from fwd. Set to one of the following: all (all debug messages), tevent, async, http, ftp, smtp, cvp, ufp, ra (Remote Auth), 1.1 (HTTP 1.1), ps (proxy), ac (Authentication Client), as (Authentication Server)
FWMDQ_DEBUG	Records all major actions to log file
SMTP_DEBUG	Takes the values 1, 2, or 3, which sets the verbosity of information reported by `in.asmtpd` to the log file
OPSEC_DEBUG_LEVEL	Takes the values 1, 2, or 3, which sets the verbosity of OPSEC related debug information
FWACLIENTD_DEBUG	Prints debugging information from `in.aclientd`
FWAFTPD_DEBUG	Prints debugging information from `in.aftpd`
FWARLOGIND_DEBUG	Prints debugging information from `in.arlogind`
FWATELNETD_DEBUG	Prints debugging information from `in.atelnetd`

CVP is a feature in all of the Security Servers that provides a mechanism for third-party products to scan content for viruses and Trojan horses. UFP is a feature in the HTTP Security Server that provides a way for third-party applications to filter Web site users' attempts to access.

Sample Configurations

The following sections present three situations that build on each other as the network and the needs of the enterprise change.

SMTP Content Security

The Situation

Your company wants to gradually roll in Content Security throughout its enterprise. One of the most-prevalent sources of viruses has been in incoming e-mail, so it is decided to start with e-mail. Both incoming and outgoing e-mail will be scanned.

HTTP and FTP traffic will eventually be scanned, but this functionality will be added in the next two situations. The CVP and UFP servers are sitting in the DMZ. Figure 8-32 shows the network diagram for this company.

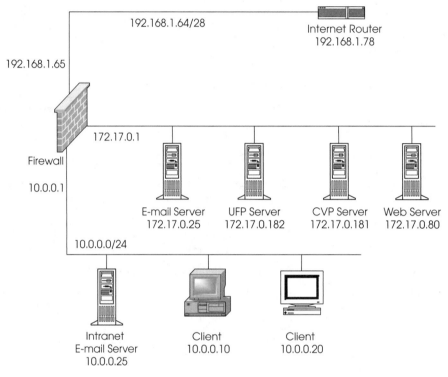

Figure 8-32   Network diagram for sample configuration

The Goals

- The Web server in the DMZ will be accessible via HTTP from anywhere.
- The e-mail server in the DMZ will be accessible via SMTP from anywhere and can send e-mail to anywhere on the Internet.
- The e-mail server in the DMZ can talk to the internal e-mail server via SMTP and vice versa. In either case, all traffic will be scanned for viruses.
- Clients on the internal network can talk to any host via HTTP and FTP.
- The UFP and CVP server will need to download access to their respective vendor's Web site via HTTP to download updates (www.cvp-vendor.com and www.ufp-vendor.com).
- All other traffic should be denied.

Checklist

- Create the necessary network objects.
- Ensure that the SMTP Security Server is enabled in `$FWDIR/conf/fwauthd.conf`.
- Create two SMTP resources to handle inbound and outbound e-mail between the internal and the DMZ e-mail servers and scan viruses.
- Create the appropriate rule(s) in the rulebase.
- Verify and install the policy.

Implementation

The proper line for the SMTP Security Server in `$FWDIR/conf/fwauthd.conf` looks like this (without a comment "#" at the beginning of the line):

```
25              in.asmtpd       wait    0
```

On most systems, this line will be enabled by default, but it never hurts to check to see if this line exists and is not commented out.

The two resources then need to be created. The first resource is for e-mail coming from the DMZ-based e-mail server that forwards it to the internal e-mail server. All incoming e-mail should be forwarded to the internal SMTP server. Any errors that are generated should be sent to the DMZ-based e-mail server so they can be sent to the sender. Figure 8-33 shows what this resource looks like.

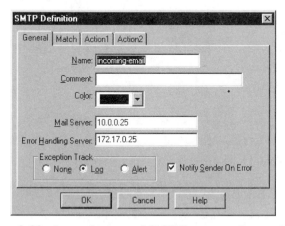

Figure 8-33   Incoming e-mail SMTP Resource, General tab

Note that you *can* leave the Match tab blank if you would like, because the internal and DMZ-based e-mail servers can do address checking on their own. Let's leave the Action1 tab alone as well because there is no need to do any address rewriting. The Action2 tab is where a few changes need to be made, as shown in Figure 8-34.

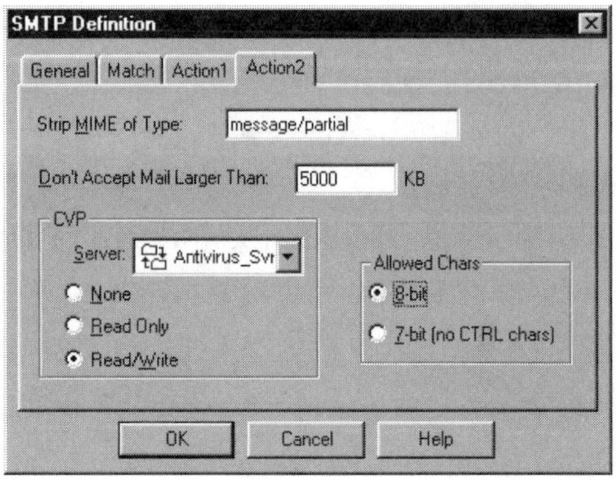

Figure 8-34   Incoming e-mail SMTP Resource, Action2 tab

When doing virus scanning, it is highly recommended to strip out all messages of MIME type message/partial, because it is used for sending a file across more than one message. This makes it difficult, if not impossible, to scan the file for viruses. The GUI makes this suggestion whenever you choose to implement CVP, and it's a good suggestion to follow. The default message size should also be increased from 1,000 KB to 5,000 KB just as a courtesy to users. However, I generally do not recommend sending large files by e-mail, because e-mailed files are actually *bigger* than if the file were downloaded from an FTP or HTTP server. In order for binary files to be e-mailed, they must be turned into a nonbinary format, which increases the overall file size.

Next, create the outbound resource, as shown in Figure 8-35.

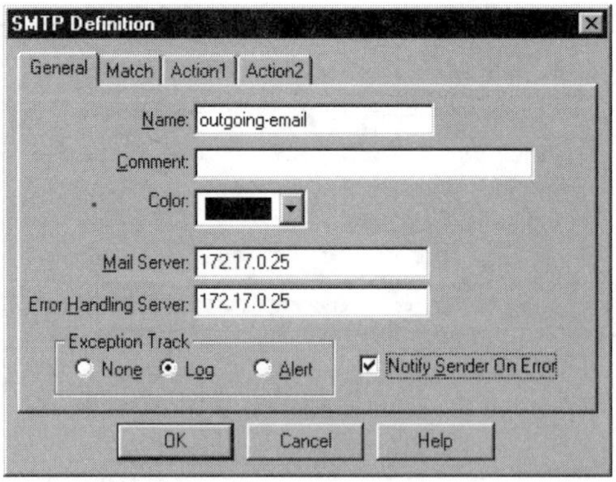

Figure 8-35   Outgoing e-mail SMTP Resource, General tab

It might also be nice to strip out the "received" lines of messages being sent from the inside to the outside. This is done on the Action1 tab, as shown in Figure 8-36.

The Action2 tab should look identical to what was used for the inbound resource. In the end, the rulebase should look similar to the one shown in Figure 8-37.

Once this configuration is set up, verify and install the security policy.

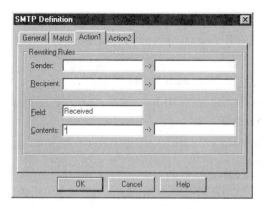

Figure 8-36   Outgoing e-mail SMTP Resource, Action1 tab

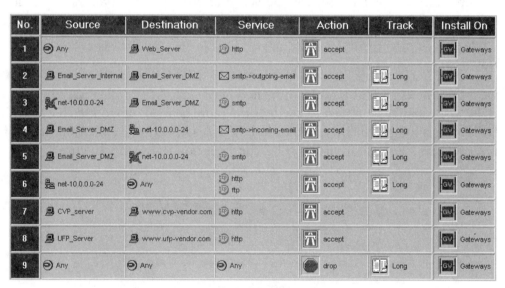

Figure 8-37   Rulebase for SMTP Security Server sample configuration

FTP Content Security

The Situation

The next step in the company's Content Security plan is to turn on Content Security for FTP. Additionally, the company wants to use the FTP Security Server to only allow people to upload files to a specific directory on the Web server.

The Goal

- Create and implement resources to perform the necessary Content Security for FTP.

Checklist

- Ensure that the FTP Security Server is enabled in `$FWDIR/conf/fwauthd.conf`.
- Create an FTP resource to scan for viruses.
- Create an FTP resource to scan for viruses and restrict access to a specific directory on the Web server.
- Create an FTP resource to allow people to download files from the Web server.
- Modify the rulebase to utilize these FTP resources.
- Verify and install the policy.

Implementation

The proper line for the FTP Security Server in `$FWDIR/conf/fwauthd.conf` looks like this (without a comment # at the beginning of the line):

```
21              in.aftpd        wait    0
```

On most systems, this line will be enabled by default, but it never hurts to check to see if this line exists and is not commented out.

The first resource you need to create is the more general one to match everything and allow users to upload and download as they please, with the exception that all file transfers will be scanned for viruses. This configuration is shown in Figure 8-38.

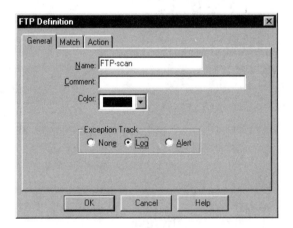

Figure 8-38 FTP Scan Resource, General tab

The Match tab should match all actions and paths, as shown in Figure 8-39.

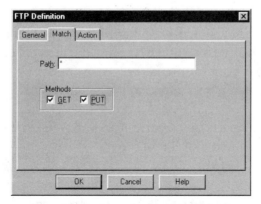

Figure 8-39 FTP Scan Resource, Match tab

The Action tab, of course, should scan for viruses, as shown in Figure 8-40.

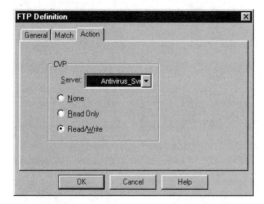

Figure 8-40 FTP Scan Resource, Action tab

The Web Server Upload Resource needs to match a specific path, as shown in Figure 8-41.

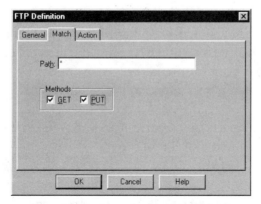

Figure 8-41 FTP Web Server Upload Resource, Match tab

You are going to virus scan anything uploaded to make sure you do not pass any viruses to the outside world. The Action tab for this configuration is shown in Figure 8-40.

Finally, you need to create a resource to allow the internal users to download from the Web server. Because you are not terribly concerned where on that server users download from, the Match tab should match any path for GET commands, as shown in Figure 8-42.

Once the resources are created, you can modify the existing policy to use these resources. The rulebase should look similar to the one shown in Figure 8-43.

Verify and install the security policy.

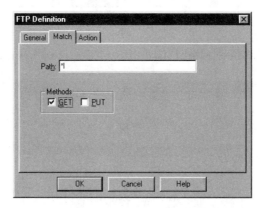

Figure 8-42 FTP Web Server Download Resource, Match tab

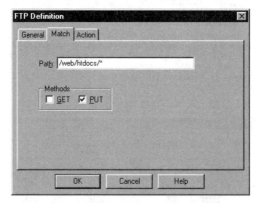

Figure 8-43 Rulebase with SMTP and FTP Security Server sample configuration

HTTP Content Security

The Situation

The final step in implementing your company's Content Security plan is to implement both virus scanning and URL filtering for HTTP traffic.

The Goals

- Create and implement a resource for URL filtering and Content Security for HTTP.
- Make sure Content Security is *not* performed for internal users accessing the DMZ.

Checklist

- Ensure that the HTTP Security Server is enabled in `$FWDIR/conf/fwauthd.conf`.
- Create a resource of type URI for URL filtering for HTTP.
- Create a resource of type URI that matches all URLs and does virus scanning.
- Modify the rulebase to utilize the HTTP resources.
- Verify and install the policy.

Implementation

The proper line for the HTTP Security Server in `$FWDIR/conf/fwauthd.conf` looks like this (without a comment "#" at the beginning of the line):

```
80              in.ahttpd      wait    0
```

On most systems, this line will be enabled by default, but it never hurts to check to see if this line exists and is not commented out.

You first need to create a resource to filter URLs, as shown in Figure 8-44.

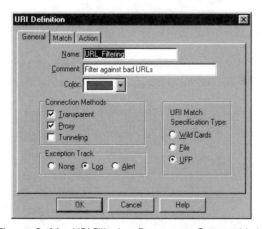

Figure 8-44   URI Filtering Resource, General tab

The Match tab should match the categories of Web sites you do not want the employees to look at, as shown in Figure 8-45.

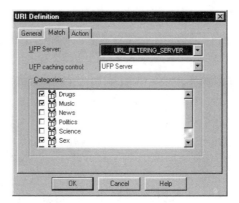

Figure 8-45 URI Filtering Resource, Match tab

The Action tab will redirect rejected URLs to a policy page, as shown in Figure 8-46.

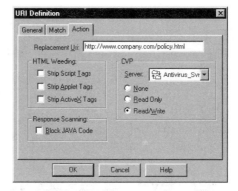

Figure 8-46 URI Filtering Resource, Action tab

This completes the URL Filtering Resource. You then need to do virus scanning on any URL that is accepted. A second resource must be created, as shown in Figure 8-47.

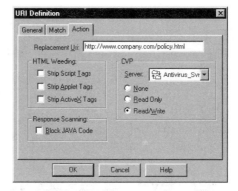

Figure 8-47 URI Virus Scanning Resource, General tab

The Match tab should match all URLs, as shown in Figure 8-48.

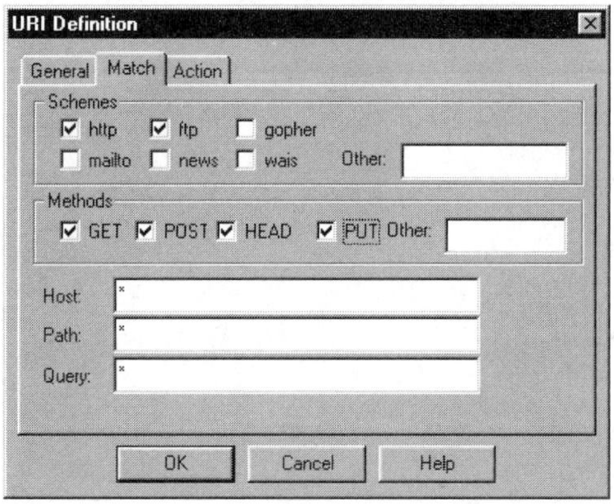

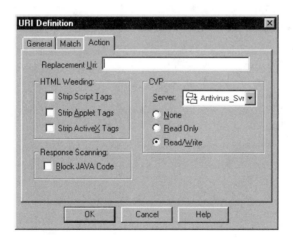

Figure 8-48   URI Virus Scanning Resource, Match tab

The Action tab should filter viruses, as shown in Figure 8-49.

Figure 8-49   URI Virus Scanning Resource, Action tab

You then implement these resources in the rulebase, as shown in Figure 8-50. Verify and install the policy.

Notes

Rule 1 will also match internal users' attempts to access the Web server on the DMZ.

No.	Source	Destination	Service	Action	Track	Install On
1	Any	Web_Server	http	accept		Gateways
2	Email_Server_Internal	Email_Server_DMZ	smtp->outgoing-email	accept	Long	Gateways
3	net-10.0.0.0-24	Email_Server_DMZ	smtp	accept	Long	Gateways
4	Email_Server_DMZ	net-10.0.0.0-24	smtp->incoming-email	accept	Long	Gateways
5	Email_Server_DMZ	net-10.0.0.0-24	smtp	accept	Long	Gateways
6	net-10.0.0.0-24	Web_Server	ftp->web-server-upload	accept	Long	Gateways
7	net-10.0.0.0-24	Web_Server	ftp->web-server-download	accept	Long	Gateways
8	net-10.0.0.0-24	Web_Server	ftp->FTP-scan	accept	Long	Gateways
9	net-10.0.0.0-24	Any	http->URL_Filtering	reject	Long	Gateways
10	net-10.0.0.0-24	Any	http->Security_Scan	accept	Long	Gateways
11	CVP_server	www.cvp-vendor.com	http	accept		Gateways
12	UFP_Server	www.ufp-vendor.com	http	accept		Gateways
13	Any	Any	Any	drop	Long	Gateways

Figure 8-50 Rulebase with SMTP, FTP, and HTTP Security Server sample configuration

Chapter

9

Network Address Translation

This chapter discusses the topic of Network Address Translation (NAT): what it is, why it was created, and how you can implement it in FireWall-1. I first discuss the reasons NAT was created and how NAT is implemented in FireWall-1. Next, I show a step-by-step example of how to implement NAT in a network. I then talk about some of the inherent limitations of NAT and discuss a couple of ways to work around these limitations. Finally, I talk about troubleshooting NAT with a packet sniffer.

By the end of this chapter, you should be able to:

- Understand why NAT is necessary
- Identify what NAT actually does
- Identify why NAT does not always work
- Effectively troubleshoot NAT problems with a packet sniffer
- Implement a NAT Configuration

Introduction

Back in the old days of the Internet, the TCP/IP address space (as defined by IPv4, the version of IP used today) was thought to be more than enough. Organizations could reserve their own address space through the Internet Assigned Numbers Authority (IANA, now called the Internet Corporation for Assigned Names and Numbers [ICANN]), and anyone who wanted a block of IP addresses generally got them.

Since the early 1990s, various people have been predicting that the IPv4 address space will simply run out of available addresses. This is partially due to the explosive growth of the Internet, but it is also due to how the IPv4 address space is divided. Many organizations that were allocated address space early on simply have more address space allocated to them than they are using on the Internet. There are also parts of the IPv4 address space that are not legal for hosts to be assigned to on the Internet, namely the multicast (224.0.0.0/240.0.0.0 mask) and the Class E (240.0.0.0/240.0.0.0) address spaces.

As organizations are connecting to the Internet, some are discovering that their internal network does not connect well to the Internet. The main reason for this is usually a conflict in addressing. Long before the Internet was a household word, some corporations set up their internal networks using made-up addresses. However, you cannot simply make up addresses and use them on the Internet. You must use IP addresses assigned by IANA or an ISP. Renumbering a large, internal network would be a daunting task, not to mention that your ISP or IANA is not likely to give you enough addresses to cover all your hosts. Then again, does every host on your internal network really need to be uniquely addressable on the Internet?

IPv6 (the next version of IP) has far more address space—128 bits of address space versus the 32 provided by IPv4—which will solve this problem. However, most of today's Internet is still running IPv4 and probably will be for some time to come. A solution is needed that will help extend the IPv4 address space that is used today.

Network Address Translation does exactly this. It is a technology that allows hosts to transparently talk to one another with addresses that are agreeable to each other. To put it another way, it allows hosts with illegal or private address space to talk with hosts on a public network and vice versa. It is a godsend for network managers who have limited address space or want to make better use of the address space they have without having to subnet, thus reducing the number of IPs that can be used. NAT can also be perceived as a security enhancement because a firewall is required for communication between the hosts. NAT, as it is commonly implemented today, is described in RFC3022.[1]

NAT is implemented as part of the FireWall-1 Kernel Module that sits between the data link and network layers. As such, NAT can be provided transparently without the client's or the server's knowledge. Application proxies, by their nature, can also provide this functionality, as they originate all connections coming from the internal network. However, proxies usually are not transparent and do not usually give you the level of control you have over FireWall-1's NAT functionality. You can modify the source, destination, and service port of any connection going through FireWall-1.

Consider the following example (see Figure 9-1). Let's say your ISP gives you a /29 block of addresses (net mask 255.255.255.248). If you were to use this address space between your Internet router and your firewall, the address space would break down into the host numbers listed in Table 9-1.[2]

---

1. You can get a copy of RFCs from www.rfc-editor.org, among other places.

2. If you are unfamiliar with subnetting and how it affects address space, you might want to read *LAN Technologies Explained* by Philip Miller and Michael Cummins (ISBN#1555582346), *TCP/IP Illustrated* by W. Richard Stevens (ISBN#0201633469), or any other appropriate TCP/IP book.

Table 9-1   Breakdown of 192.168.0.0/29 address space

Host Number	Description
.0	Network identifier (cannot be used by hosts)
.1	Internet router
.2	Firewall
.3	Available
.4	Available
.5	Available
.6	Available
.7	Broadcast address (cannot be used by hosts)

Between the broadcast address, the network address, your firewall, and your Internet router, you have a grand total of four usable IP addresses. With NAT, you can:

- Give your e-mail, intranet Web server, and Web server externally reachable IP addresses
- Allow all your clients to access the Internet using the firewall's external IP address
- Have all of your computers protected by your firewall
- Change ISPs without having to renumber your internal network

Figure 9-1 illustrates a sample network.

Although NAT does add an extra layer of protection and gives you flexibility, there are some downsides to NAT:

- Using NAT is like using proxies in that NAT must be updated to handle new applications. As a result, it is not compatible with every application that exists today or in the future.
- NAT requires additional work to maintain. This is discussed in more detail in the "Implementing NAT, a Step-by-Step Example" section later in this chapter.
- Only so many connections can be hidden behind a single IP address.
- NAT requires extra memory and CPU on the gateway. In most cases, this is negligible, but it starts becoming noticeable when over 20,000 connections through a single gateway are subject to NAT.

More information about the disadvantages of using NAT is documented in RFC3027.

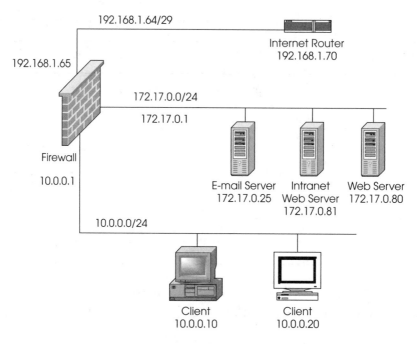

Figure 9-1   Sample network diagram

RFC-1918 and Link Local Addresses

RFC-1918 (which was originally described in RFC-1597) sets aside specific ranges of IP addresses that cannot be used on the Internet. Instead, these addresses are to be used internally within an organization or network. If hosts with RFC-1918 addresses want to communicate with a network like the Internet, they must go through some form of NAT, as no host on the Internet will know how to route RFC-1918 addresses. The addresses assigned by RFC-1918 are as follows:

- 10.0.0.0/8 (net mask 255.0.0.0)
- 172.16.0.0/12 (net mask 255.240.0.0, which covers 172.16.0.0– 172.31.255.255)
- 192.168.0.0/16 (net mask 255.255.0.0)

Another set of address space that can be used for NAT is 169.254/16 (net mask 255.255.0.0). This address space is specified in an Internet Draft called "Dynamic Configuration of IPv4 link-local addresses," which is available at www.ietf.org/internet-drafts/draft-ietf-zeroconf-ipv4-linklocal-02.txt. Essentially, Microsoft Dynamic Host Configuration Protocol (DHCP) clients use this method to assign an address when they are unable to communicate with a DHCP server. This address space is reserved specifically for this purpose, so it will not be in use anywhere on the Internet and is thus safe to use for NAT.

If your situation requires the use of NAT, it is highly recommended that you use address space within the recommended ranges. If you are using someone else's address space within your internal network and you need to communicate with an Internet host that happens to use the same address range, you may find yourself not being able to do so, as the network traffic may never leave your internal network.

How NAT Works in FireWall-1

NAT is configured via the Address Translation tab in the Security Policy Editor. The rules are processed in the order in which they are listed. Once a rule matches a packet, the packet is translated, and no further processing occurs. If a packet does not match a rule in the address translation rules, the packet is not translated.

Four types of NAT are available in FireWall-1, and they can be mixed and matched as necessary: Source Static, Destination Static, Destination Port Static, and Source Hide:

Source Static: Translates the source IP address in an IP packet to a specific IP address. This is a one-to-one address translation. Return traffic, as necessary, is allowed back through without additional NAT rules. However, if you need to initiate connectivity from either side of the firewall, a corresponding Destination Static NAT rule is needed.

Source Hide: Makes more than one host appear as a single host (i.e., a many-to-one translation). In the text, I will refer to this simply as *hide mode*. This is perfect for hosts that require access to the Internet, but should not be accessed *from* the Internet. In order to accomplish this, FireWall-1 changes the source TCP or UDP port of the packet so that it can keep track of which host the connection belongs to (and, consequently, know where to send reply packets). For ICMP packets, the data portion of the packet is munged (the data portion of an ICMP packet usually isn't used). For other IP protocols, hide mode does not work, because there are no ports or data that can be modified. Most standard applications (e.g., Telnet, HTTP, FTP, HTTPS) work fine, but any application that requires a connection initiated from the outside or requires that a connection happen on a specific source port will not work in hide mode. An example of such is Internet Key Exchange (IKE) as used with IPSec implementations.

Destination Static: Translates the destination IP address in an IP packet to a specified IP address. This is a one-to-one address translation for connections. Return traffic, as necessary, is allowed back through without additional NAT rules. However, if you need to initiate connectivity from either side of the firewall, a corresponding Source Static NAT rule is needed.

Destination Port Static: Translates only the destination (or service) port number to a different port. This, for example, allows you to transparently request going from port 8080 to port 80. However, it does *not* allow you to make services running on machines other than the firewall accessible with the firewall's IP address; that is, if you want to make services accessible through the firewall, a different routable IP address is needed.[3]

NAT rules apply to all interfaces and cannot be applied on a per-interface basis. Usually, rules can be crafted in such a way that per-interface rules are not necessary. You can *hide* connections behind the IP 0.0.0.0, which is a special IP that tells Fire-Wall-1 to use the interface the packet has routed out as opposed to a fixed IP address.[4]

Even though NAT can be configured in the Security Policy Editor, you need to configure the host OS, as described in the next section, in order to support NAT.

The Order of Operations

In order to understand how to implement NAT, it is best to review the order of operations as it relates to FireWall-1 and passing traffic in general. Consider the following case, where Client A wants to communicate with Client B (see Figure 9-2).

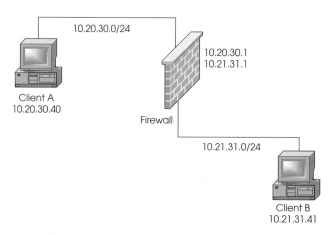

10.20.30.0/24

10.20.30.1
10.21.31.1

Client A
10.20.30.40

Firewall

10.21.31.0/24

Client B
10.21.31.41

Figure 9-2 Client A communicating with Client B

---

3. In order to make services accessible via the firewall's IP address, you need to use a third-party application commonly called a *plug proxy.* Plug proxy simply accepts TCP or UDP packets and forwards them to a configurable host and port.
4. Nokia platforms running Virtual Router Redundancy Protocol (VRRP) with FireWall-1 4.1 SP2 or FireWall-1 4.1 SP3 hiding behind the address 0.0.0.0 may instead use the VRRP IP address. Although some would argue this isn't necessarily bad behavior, it is not the intended behavior. FireWall-1 4.1 SP4 and later should resolve this issue.

NOTE!   In this example, NAT is not configured.

Client A determines that in order to communicate with Client B, the packet must be routed through the firewall. Client A needs to know the Media Access Control (MAC) address for the firewall's IP address (10.20.30.1), so it sends out a request via the Address Resolution Protocol (ARP) requesting the address. The firewall responds with its MAC address. Client A is then able to forward the packet to the firewall for processing.

Note that all of these events happen without any aid from FireWall-1. It is important to be aware of this exchange because when you do address translation, you must be sure that all of the translated IP addresses you set up through FireWall-1 get routed back to the firewall for processing. If the translated IP address is on the same subnet as the firewall, you need to set up a proxy-ARP or static host route for that address. Otherwise, routes to those addresses will be necessary.

Once the packet is received at the firewall, FireWall-1 processes the packet according to the following steps:

1. Checks to see if the packet is part of an established connection. Because this is a new connection, there is no record of the packet in the connections table, so the connection must be checked against the security policy.

2. Checks IP Options. If the packet is denied because of this check, you will see a drop on Rule 0 in the Log Viewer, assuming that IP Options logging is enabled.

3. Performs an anti-spoofing check on the 10.20.30.1 interface. The source of the packet (10.20.30.40) is compared against the valid address setting. If the packet is denied because of this check, you will see a drop on Rule 0 in the Log Viewer, assuming that anti-spoof logging is enabled on that interface. The remote end of the connection will see a "connection timed out" message.

4. Checks properties and the rulebase.

5. The OS routes the packet. The OS determines that in order to communicate with Client B, it needs to route the packet out the 10.21.31.1 interface.

6. Performs IP Options and anti-spoofing checking on the 10.21.31.1 interface. The destination of the packet (10.21.31.41) is compared against the valid address setting. If the packet is denied because of this check, you will see a reject on Rule 0 in the Log Viewer, assuming that anti-spoofing logging is enabled on that interface. The remote end of the connection will receive a reset, which means a client application will see a "connection refused" message.

7. Checks properties and the rulebase. Properties are always checked outbound as well as inbound. A rule's check depends on how you have installed it and how you are enforcing gateway rules.

8. The packet proceeds through the address translation rules. If there was a matching NAT rule, this is where NAT would take place. In this example, NAT is not occurring, so translation is not performed.

9. The packet is sent directly to Client B.

The important detail to note in this process is that NAT is not done until near the very end—that is, after the packet has been routed and has gone through the security policy, but before the packet leaves the gateway. When you do NAT, it means you must make sure that the untranslated packet can pass through your anti-spoofing checks and your rulebase.

Implementing NAT: A Step-by-Step Example

The following sample configuration involves NAT. You are shown what you need to do step-by-step to configure FireWall-1 to support this configuration. (See Figure 9-3.)

The security policy is defined as follows:

- Allow the External Mail and Web server to be reached from anywhere via SMTP and HTTP respectively.
- Allow the External Mail Server to send e-mail to anywhere on the Internet and to the Internal Mail Server.
- Allow a second Web instance of a Web server (running on port 81) to be accessible via a separate IP address on port 80.
- Allow clients on Segment A and Segment B to browse the Internet via HTTP or HTTPS hiding behind a single IP address.
- Allow an Intranet Web server to be accessible on the Internet via HTTP. The Web server will provide its own authentication, so no authentication is necessary by FireWall-1.
- Except for the former requirements, deny all other traffic.

The preceding policy is specially crafted for demonstration purposes only. Generally speaking, it is not wise to permit traffic from the Internet all the way into the internal network without some sort of encryption. Let's take the following steps to set this up:

- Determine which IP addresses will be used for translation.
- Set up the necessary proxy-ARPs.
- Set up the necessary static host routes.

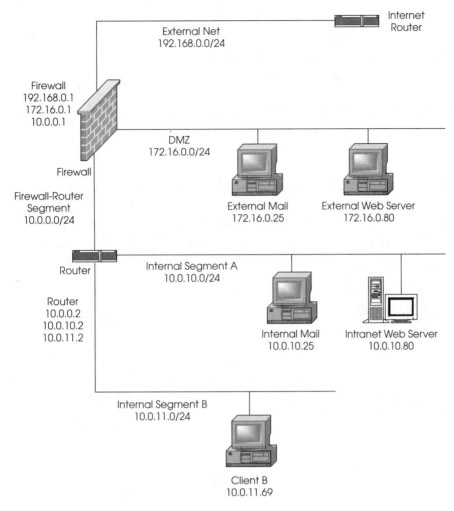

Figure 9-3   Implementing NAT sample network

- Create the necessary network objects.
- Make the necessary modifications to anti-spoofing.
- Create the necessary rulebase rules to permit the desired traffic.
- Create the NAT rules.
- Install the security policy, and verify that everything works as planned.

Determining Which IP Addresses Will Be Used

The legal addresses include everything in 192.168.0.0/24 except for the firewall (.1) and the router (.2). You can choose any other IP address in the range. The following hosts will use the following static mappings:

- *External Mail Server:* 192.168.0.10
- *Web Server:* 192.168.0.11
- *Web Server (instance on port 81):* 192.168.0.12
- *Intranet Web Server:* 192.168.0.13

For the browsing that Segment A and Segment B hosts will need, use the firewall's external IP address of 192.168.0.2.

Proxy-ARPs

Before you begin, you need to determine which MAC address you are going to use to ARP for the translated IP addresses. You know that all of the translated addresses are on the same subnet as the external interface of the firewall. You simply need to determine what the MAC (or physical) address of the external interface is and use that address. To do this, use the following command:

UNIX and Nokia platform: `ifconfig -a`
Windows NT/2000: `ipconfig /all`

On a UNIX platform, you will see something like this:[5]

```
lo0: flags=849 <UP,LOOPBACK,RUNNING,MULTICAST> mtu 8232
        inet 127.0.0.1 netmask ff000000
le0: flags=863 <UP,BROADCAST,NOTRAILERS,RUNNING,MULTICAST> mtu
1500
        inet 192.168.0.1 netmask ffffff00 broadcast
        192.168.0.255
        ether 0:11:22:33:44:55
le1: flags=863 <UP,BROADCAST,NOTRAILERS,RUNNING,MULTICAST> mtu
1500
        inet 10.0.0.1 netmask ffffff00 broadcast 10.0.0.255
        ether 0:c0:78:2:0:d6
le2: flags=863 <UP,BROADCAST,NOTRAILERS,RUNNING,MULTICAST> mtu
1500
        inet 172.16.0.1 netmask ffffff00 broadcast 172.16.0.255
        ether 0:c0:78:20:0:6d
```

On a Nokia platform, the output is slightly different:

```
loop0c0:  flags=57<UP,PHYS_AVAIL,LINK_AVAIL,LOOPBACK,MULTICAST>
        inet mtu 63000 127.0.0.1 –> 127.0.0.1
        phys loop0 flags=10b<UP,LINK,LOOPBACK,PRESENT>
```

---

5. On a Solaris platform, it is likely that you will see the same MAC address on all Ethernet interfaces. The default behavior is to use a hostid-based MAC address and not the hardware MAC. So long as two or more interfaces are not on the same physical network, this should not be a problem. You can change the MAC address on a per-interface basis with the `ifconfig` command.

```
tun0c0:  lname tun0c0
flags=cf<UP,PHYS_AVAIL,LINK_AVAIL,POINTOPOINT,MULTICAST> encaps
vpn
        phys tun0 flags=107<UP,LINK,POINTOPOINT,PRESENT>
eth-s1p1c0:  lname eth-s1p1c0
flags=e7<UP,PHYS_AVAIL,LINK_AVAIL,BROADCAST,MULTICAST>
        inet mtu 1500 192.168.0.1/24 broadcast
        192.168.0.255
        phys eth-s1p1 flags=133<UP,LINK,BROADCAST,
        MULTICAST,PRESENT>
       ether 0:11:22:33:44:55 speed 100M full duplex
eth-s2p1c0:  lname eth-s2p1c0
flags=e7<UP,PHYS_AVAIL,LINK_AVAIL,BROADCAST,MULTICAST>
        inet mtu 1500 10.0.0.1/24 broadcast 10.0.0.255
        phys eth-s2p1 flags=133<UP,LINK,BROADCAST,
        MULTICAST,PRESENT> ether 0:c0:78:2:0:d6 speed 100M full
        duplex
eth-s3p1c0:  lname eth-s3p1c0
flags=e7<UP,PHYS_AVAIL,LINK_AVAIL,BROADCAST,MULTICAST>
        inet mtu 1500 172.16.0.1/24 broadcast
        172.16.0.255
        phys eth-s3p1 flags=133<UP,LINK,BROADCAST,MULTICAST,
        PRESENT> ether 0:c0:78:20:0:6d speed 100M full duplex
```

On a Windows NT or 2000 platform, you will see this:

```
Ethernet adapter 3C5x91:
        Description . . . . . . . . : 3Com 3C5x9 Ethernet
                                      Adapter
        Physical Address. . . . . . : 00-11-22-33-44-55
        DHCP Enabled. . . . . . . . : No
        IP Address. . . . . . . . . : 192.168.0.1
        Subnet Mask . . . . . . . . : 255.255.255.0
        Default Gateway . . . . . . : 192.168.0.254

Ethernet adapter 3C5x92:
        Description . . . . . . . . : 3Com 3C5x9 Ethernet
                                      Adapter
        Physical Address. . . . . . : 00-C0-78-20-00-6D
        DHCP Enabled. . . . . . . . : No
        IP Address. . . . . . . . . : 10.0.0.1
        Subnet Mask . . . . . . . . : 255.255.255.0
        Default Gateway . . . . . . :

Ethernet adapter 3C5x93:
        Description . . . . . . . . : 3Com 3C5x9 Ethernet
                                      Adapter
        Physical Address. . . . . . : 00-0C-87-02-00-D6
        DHCP Enabled. . . . . . . . : No
        IP Address. . . . . . . . . : 172.16.0.1
```

```
Subnet Mask . . . . . . . . : 255.255.255.0
Default Gateway . . . . . . :
```

Use the ether or physical address of the system's external interface. In this case, you will use 00:11:22:33:44:55. Now that you know what that MAC address is, you can set up the ARPs. On UNIX systems, this is done as follows:

```
arp -s 192.168.0.10 00:11:22:33:44:55 pub
arp -s 192.168.0.11 00:11:22:33:44:55 pub
arp -s 192.168.0.12 00:11:22:33:44:55 pub
arp -s 192.168.0.13 00:11:22:33:44:55 pub
```

In order for these ARPs to be available on reboot, you need to add them to a file that executes on startup. Do not add them to the `/etc/rc3.d/S95firewall1` script, which gets overwritten during an upgrade. Create a new startup script like `/etc/rc3.d/S94nat`.

Windows NT does not have a proxy-ARP facility, so Check Point has included it as part of the software. Create the file `%FWDIR%\state\local.arp`, and enter the following information:

```
192.168.0.10    00-11-22-33-44-55
192.168.0.11    00-11-22-33-44-55
192.168.0.12    00-11-22-33-44-55
192.168.0.13    00-11-22-33-44-55
```

These ARPs will not become active until a policy reload is performed. In some cases, it may be necessary to stop and start FireWall-1.

NOTE! The Windows 2000 version of FireWall-1 does not support local.arp prior to version 4.1 SP4. Refer to article ID sk699 in Check Point's Knowledge Base for a workaround.

NOTE! FireWall-1's proxy-ARP function will not work in Windows 2000 if you are running Microsoft's Routing and Remote Access Service. Microsoft has produced a hot fix to this issue. To obtain this hot fix, refer to article ID Q82312 in Microsoft's Knowledge Base.

On the Nokia platform running IPSO 3.1 and later, add these ARPs via the Voyager interface as "Proxy-Only" type. In a VRRP configuration, configure both firewalls and use the VRRP MAC address instead of the network card's MAC. You may also configure the NAT IPs as VRRP backup IPs, thus eliminating the need for proxy-ARPs.

NOTE! Do not configure the NAT IPs as VRRP backup IPs in FireWall-1 4.1 SP2, because there are some bugs with the anti-spoofing code.

NOTE! In IPSO 3.3 or later, there is an option to allow connections to VRRP IP addresses. Make sure this option is disabled if you plan on configuring the NAT IPs as VRRP IPs.

NOTE! There is a bug with proxy-ARP when used with VRRP MAC addresses that causes some switches to become confused. IPSO 3.3 FCS8, IPSO 3.3.1 FCS7, and IPSO 3.4 and later resolve this problem. Refer to Resolution 3324 in the Nokia Knowledge Base for more details.

Static Host Routes

The only translations for which you need to set up static host routes are those that involve a destination static translation (i.e., where the destination IP address needs to be translated). In this case, you need to set up static host routes for all of them because they will all be connected by their translated IP address.

You need to determine where the real hosts for the virtual IPs are in relation to the firewall. This is so you can determine the next hop for the static host routes you will set up. Using Figure 9-3, you know the following information:

- The external mail and external Web servers are on the same subnet as the firewall. In this case, you simply use the real host's IP address as the next hop.

- The intranet Web server is not on the same subnet as the firewall. In this case, you want to use the next hop IP address, which is the router that is connected to Segment A—the segment on which the intranet Web server is connected. This is 10.0.0.2.

On UNIX platforms (not IPSO), you would add the static routes like this:[6]

```
route add 192.168.0.10 172.16.0.25 1
route add 192.168.0.11 172.16.0.80 1
route add 192.168.0.12 172.16.0.80 1
route add 192.168.0.13 10.0.0.2 1
```

---

6. There is a way to add static routes on IPSO using the command line. However, you do not use the route command; you issue three separate `dbset` commands. Resolution 1783 in Nokia's Knowledge Base contains a program called addstatic that makes use of these commands.

Like the previous ARPs, these lines need to go into a startup file so that they are available after a reboot. On Windows NT platforms, the static routes are similar:

```
route add 192.168.0.10 172.16.0.25 -p
route add 192.168.0.11 172.16.0.80 -p
route add 192.168.0.12 172.16.0.80 -p
route add 192.168.0.13 10.0.0.2 -p
```

Note that on Windows NT/2000, if you use the -p flag, the routes are persistent; that is, they are stored in the Registry and will stay there until they are deleted, even after a reboot.

On a Nokia platform, you add these static routes via Voyager.

Network Objects

You must create network objects for both translated and untranslated objects as well per Table 9-2.

Anti-Spoofing

When configuring your firewall object, set your Valid Address settings according to the settings shown in Table 9-3.

These settings are configured on the Interfaces tab. Also, make sure that each interface has the Spoof Tracking set to "Log" to catch any errors in the anti-spoofing configuration.

Security Policy Rules

The rules created are based on the security policy defined earlier in the "Implementing NAT, a Step-by-Step Example" section. (See Figure 9-4.)

Address Translation Rules

Once the security policy is defined, NAT rules must be defined. Before you begin, make sure you define a service for port 81. It will be a service of type TCP. In Figure 9-5, it will be referred to as "http81," so you can do the port translation that the security policy requires. Note that the "s" refers to "static" rules, and the "h" refers to "hide" rules. (See Figure 9-5.)

Install the Security Policy and Test

Initiate a connection to exercise each rule to ensure that each rule is functioning as you expect. Test access from inside and outside the network.

Limitations of NAT

NAT does not work in all cases. The following sections document some of the instances where NAT will not work as expected.

Table 9-2   Network objects to create

Name	Object Type	IP/Mask/Group Objects	Description
net-dmz	Network	172.16.0.0/255.255.255.0	Your DMZ
smtp-dmz	Workstation	172.16.0.25	Mail Server in the DMZ
smtp-dmz-ext	Workstation	192.168.0.10	Translated version of smtp-dmz
web-server	Workstation	172.16.0.80	Web Server in the DMZ
web-server-ext	Workstation	192.168.0.11	Translated version of web-server (for port 80)
web-server-ext2	Workstation	192.168.0.12	Translated version of web-server (for port 81)
net-router-segment	Network	10.0.0.0/255.255.255.0	Segment shared by firewall and internal router
net-segment-a	Network	10.0.10.0/255.255.255.0	Segment A
web-intranet	Workstation	10.0.10.80	Intranet Web Server
web-intranet-ext	Workstation	192.168.0.13	Translated version of web-intranet
smtp-internal	Workstation	10.0.10.25	Internal SMTP Server
net-segment-b	Network	10.0.11.0/255.255.255.0	Segment B
valid-dmz	Group	net-dmz + web-server-ext + web-server-ext2 + smtp-server-ext	Represents your DMZ interface's valid addresses for anti-spoofing
valid-internal	Group	net-segment-a + net-segment-b + web-intranet-ext + net-router-segment	Represents your internal interface's valid addresses for anti-spoofing
Firewall	Workstation	192.168.0.1	Your firewall

Table 9-3   Valid address settings for firewall

Interface	Valid Address Setting
DMZ	Specific: valid-dmz
Internal	Specific: valid-internal
External	Others

No.	Source	Destination	Service	Action	Track	Install On
1	Any	Web-Server-Ext Web-Server-Ext2 web-ntranet-ext	http	accept	Short	Gateways
2	valid-internal	smtp-dmz-ext	smtp	accept	Short	Gateways
3	smtp-dmz-ext smtp-internal	smtp-internal smtp-dmz-ext	smtp	accept	Short	Gateways
4	smtp-dmz-ext	valid-nternal	smtp	accept	Short	Gateways
5	net-segment-a net-segment-b	Any	http https	accept	Long	Gateways
6	Any	Any	Any	drop	Long	Gateways

Figure 9-4 Security policy for sample NAT configuration

No.	Original Packet			Translated Packet			Install On
	Source	Destination	Service	Source	Destination	Service	
1	Any	Web-Server-Ext	Any	Original	Web-Server	Original	Gateways
2	Any	Web-Server-Ext2	http	Original	Web-Server	http81	Gateways
3	Any	web-intranet-ext	Any	Original	web-intranet	Original	Gateways
4	Any	smtp-dmz-ext	Any	Original	smtp-dmz	Original	Gateways
5	smtp-dmz	Any	Any	smtp-dmz-ext	Original	Original	Gateways
6	net-segment-a	Any	Any	Firewall	Original	Original	Gateways
7	net-segment-b	Any	Any	Firewall	Original	Original	Gateways

Figure 9-5 NAT policy for sample NAT configuration

The main components that NAT changes are the IP addresses in the TCP/IP headers, and possibly the TCP or UDP ports. This works for some applications, but many applications embed IP addresses in the data portion of the packet (e.g., Microsoft Networking[7]) or expect packets to come from a particular source port (e.g., IKE negotiations for IPSec). In these cases, NAT has to act somewhat like an application proxy in that it must understand the underlying protocol and make intelligent changes to the packets so that the protocol will work despite undergoing NAT.

---

7. Microsoft used to say that Microsoft Networking was incompatible with NAT and that NAT, if present in your network, should be removed. It would not surprise me if they still stood by this claim.

FireWall-1 understands certain protocols like FTP, RealAudio, and Microsoft Networking (if support is specifically enabled in FireWall-1 4.1 SP1 and later). There are plenty of applications that do not work correctly with FireWall-1's NAT, not necessarily because they are impossible to make work with NAT, but because Check Point has not added support for them. However, there are some protocols that are simply impossible to make work with NAT. Any protocol that uses IP datagram types other than TCP or UDP often fail when NAT is applied. Protocols that validate the IP packet headers between source and destination (such as the Authentication Header mechanism of IPSec) will not work with NAT. To a protocol that protects network traffic from man-in-the-middle attacks—attacks where the headers or payload changes in transit—NAT looks like a hacker. The bottom line: NAT breaks end-to-end connectivity and should only be employed in instances where you can live with the limitations.

NAT will be problematic in situations where the firewall is not between both the source and the destination. Using the example in the previous step-by-step configuration (see Figure 9-3), consider the situation where a host on Segment B (10.0.11.69) tries to access the intranet Web server via the translated IP address (192.168.0.13). The host 10.0.11.69 tries to initiate a connection to 192.168.0.13. Routing will eventually take this packet to the firewall. The packet is accepted by the firewall's security policy and is then processed by NAT. The first rule that matches the packet is Rule 3, which translates the destination of the packet from 192.168.0.13 to 10.0.10.80. The "source" of the packet is not changed (the rule says not to touch it). The packet will then be routed back to 10.0.10.80 via 10.0.0.2.

When 10.0.10.80 sends its reply, it is sent to 10.0.11.69 (the "source" of the connection attempt). The reply is routed to 10.0.10.2 and then directly to 10.0.11.69. The host 10.0.11.69 expects replies from 192.168.0.13 (which it tries to connect to), not 10.0.10.80, so the reply packets are ignored.

What would happen if the rule hides 10.0.11.0/24 behind the firewall's external IP address? When 10.0.11.69 tries to access 10.0.10.80, the packet gets routed to the firewall and passes through the rulebase. NAT then would rewrite the source of the packet to be 192.168.0.2. The destination of the packet would still be 192.168.0.13 (i.e., it does not get translated) but gets routed out the internal interface. The Internet router sees this packet and routes it back to the firewall (it is an external address, after all). The packet would ping-pong back and forth until the packet's Time To Live (TTL) value expired.

One reason you might connect to the translated IP address is because your internal client's DNS server resolves the host's name to the external address. You can resolve this problem by implementing *split-horizon DNS*, that is, maintaining an internal version of your DNS and an external version of your DNS, typically on separate servers. The external DNS would be accessible from the Internet and contain only a subset of names and addresses contained in the internal DNS server. An internal DNS contains all the names used internally and reflects the internal IP address for a host. The external DNS server reflects the externally resolvable IP addresses for the host.

Other than implementing split-horizon DNS, can you get around this problem? Yes, there are two tricks you can use, which are documented in the following sections. However, it is highly recommended you not place yourself in a position where you have to use these tricks.

Dual NAT (Translating Both Source and Destination)

FireWall-1 allows you to translate both the source and destination IP address at once. It is simply a matter of crafting the correct rules and placing them in the right order. In the preceding case, if you want to allow your internal network to access the internal host via its translated IP address, modify your NAT rules so they read as shown in Figure 9-6.

No.	Original Packet			Translated Packet			Install On
	Source	Destination	Service	Source	Destination	Service	
1	Any	Web-Server-Ext	Any	Original	Web-Server	Original	Gateways
2	Any	Web-Server-Ext2	http	Original	Web-Server	http81	Gateways
3	net-segment-a	web-intranet-ext	Any	Firewall	web-intranet	Original	Gateways
4	net-segment-b	web-intranet-ext	Any	Firewall	web-intranet	Original	Gateways
5	Any	web-intranet-ext	Any	Original	web-intranet	Original	Gateways
6	Any	smtp-dmz-ext	Any	Original	smtp-dmz	Original	Gateways
7	smtp-dmz	Any	Any	smtp-dmz-ext	Original	Original	Gateways
8	net-segment-a	Any	Any	Firewall	Original	Original	Gateways
9	net-segment-b	Any	Any	Firewall	Original	Original	Gateways

Figure 9-6   NAT policy with dual NAT rules

The two rules that were added are shown in Figure 9-7.

3	net-segment-a	web-intranet-ext	Any	Firewall	web-intranet	Original	Gateways
4	net-segment-b	web-intranet-ext	Any	Firewall	web-intranet	Original	Gateways

Figure 9-7   Dual NAT rules added to Figure 9–6

These rules will hide the source address behind the firewall's IP address and modify the destination IP to be the web-intranet address.

In this particular case, there is another issue to contend with: ICMP Redirects. Because the firewall will be routing a packet out the same interface from which it was received, the system sends the client an ICMP Redirect, giving it a more direct route to the host. Depending on the exact circumstances, the ICMP Redirect will either cause the connection to never take place or take a long time to establish as the client will be trying to communicate directly to a host using an IP address it knows nothing about. There are a couple of ways around this situation:

- Bind the translated IP address to the server's loopback interface. See the next section for details.
- Block ICMP Redirects. You can block outgoing ICMP Redirects in FireWall-1 with the FireWall-1 rule shown in Figure 9-8.

Figure 9-8   Rule to block ICMP Redirects

- On some operating systems, there is an option to disable sending ICMP Redirects. On Solaris, you do this by typing:

```
/usr/sbin/ndd -set /dev/ip ip_send_redirects 0
```

On a Nokia platform, this can be done on a per-interface basis by typing

```
ipsctl -w interface:<physical-
interface>:family:inet:flags:icmp_no_rdir 1
```

where you replace `<physical-interface>` with the physical interface name (e.g., eth-s1p1).

NOTE!   By default, ICMP Redirects are not enabled on any interface running VRRP. This is highly recommended in a VRRP configuration, as it limits the possibility that your machine's physical address is propagated.

Assuming this trick works, a side effect can occur, which makes traffic traverse your network twice: once to the firewall and once to the server. This could add to an already congested network.

Binding the NAT IP Address to the Loopback Interface

The basic idea is to bind the translated IP address to the loopback interface of the server. On Windows NT, you need to add the MS Loopback interface (a software-only network adaptor) and add the IP address to this interface with a net mask of 255.255.255.255. In IPSO, you can simply add an IP address to the loop0c0 interface via Voyager. On UNIX machines, use a command such as the following:

```
ifconfig lo0:0 204.32.38.25 up
```

If packets come into the system for the translated IP address (because, for instance, they did not come to the firewall), the system will respond to packets for this IP address. This method does require slightly more administration because you must also maintain the NAT on the individual servers.

Troubleshooting NAT

To troubleshoot NAT, you should first verify that each necessary step has been performed. This means:

- Validate that an ARP entry exists for the translated IP (or that the translated IP is somehow being routed to the firewall).
- Validate that a static host route exists on the firewall to route the translated IP address to either the untranslated address or the next hop address if the real system is more than one hop away from the firewall.
- Validate anti-spoofing. Make sure that the destination IP address is being translated, and verify that the translated IP address will pass anti-spoofing checks.
- Validate that the rules are set up correctly. Set any security policy rule that applies to a NAT host to track long, and ensure that address translation is happening as you expect.

Wherever a verification of the configuration fails, a packet sniffer can be your friend. The remainder of this section shows you what you should see in a packet sniffer, what you shouldn't, and how to fix it.

Although there are plenty of external packet-sniffing devices, they can be expensive and inconvenient to use. Fortunately, some operating systems come with their own. Solaris comes with a tool called `snoop`. IPSO, Linux, and AIX come with `tcpdump`. Both of these tools will be discussed briefly in this chapter. Windows NT/2000 machines come with a limited packet sniffer in Network Monitor, but you can obtain a free copy of Ethereal from www.ethereal.com, which works far better.

Since version 4.0, FireWall-1 has also come with its own packet-sniffing utility called `fw monitor`. Because it works at the same level as FireWall-1 (i.e., just after the

MAC layer and before the network layer), its use in troubleshooting NAT issues is limited. `fw monitor` relies on INSPECT code and is discussed in Chapter 13.

Consider the network and configuration that was used in the earlier step-by-step example (see Figure 9-3). Let's assume that host 192.168.42.69 is attempting to connect to 192.168.0.13, the Intranet Web Server, which really resides at 10.0.10.80.

With a successful connection, a `tcpdump` of the external interface should show you the following (`-i` is what you use to specify an interface to listen to):

```
# tcpdump -i eth-s1p1
tcpdump: listening on eth-s1p1
18:51:20.806020 arp who-has 192.168.0.13 tell 192.168.0.2
18:51:20.806020 arp reply 192.168.0.13 is-at 0:11:22:33:44:55
18:51:54.135062 192.168.42.69.1777 > 192.168.0.13.80: S
1184222758:1184222758(0) win 16384 <mss 1460,nop,wscale
0,nop,nop,timestamp[|tcp]> (DF) [tos 0x10]
18:51:54.135062 192.168.0.13.80 > 192.168.42.69.1777: S
1332216451:1332216451(0) ack 1184222759 win 32120 <mss
1460,nop,nop,timestamp 2739310[|tcp]> (DF)
18:51:54.415021 192.168.42.69.1777 > 192.168.0.13.80: . ack 1 win
17376 <nop,nop,timestamp 11362405 2739310> (DF) [tos 0x10]
```

If you were to use `snoop`, you would see the following (`-d` on `snoop` allows you to specify an interface to listen to):

```
# snoop -d hme0
Using device /dev/hme (promiscuous mode)
192.168.0.2 -> (broadcast)   ARP C Who is 192.168.0.13 ?
192.168.0.1 -> 192.168.0.2 ARP R 192.168.0.13 is 0:11:22:33:44:55
192.168.42.69 -> 192.168.0.13 HTTP C port=1777
192.168.0.13 -> 192.168.42.69 HTTP R port=1777
192.168.42.69 -> 192.168.0.13 HTTP C port=1777
```

Note that you may not necessarily see the ARP packets, especially if the originator of the packet already has the MAC address in its ARP cache. If you see SYN, SYN/ACK, and ACK packets, the connection should be established.

ARPs

The first part of the communication you should see is the request for MAC addresses via an ARP packet. When everything is working correctly, you will see an exchange like the following on the external interface with `tcpdump`:

```
18:13:20.806020 arp who-has 192.168.0.13 tell 192.168.0.2
18:13:20.806020 arp reply 192.168.0.13 is-at 0:11:22:33:44:55
```

With `snoop`, it looks like this:

```
192.168.0.2 -> (broadcast)  ARP C Who is 192.168.0.13 ?
192.168.0.1 -> 192.168.0.2 ARP R 192.168.0.13 is 0:11:22:33:44:55
```

If you do only see the first packet over and over again (e.g., the ARP who is), this means that nobody owns or is proving a proxy-ARP for the translated address. Add a proxy-ARP as described previously. In some cases (especially when Windows NT is the firewall), you may need to add a static host route on the external router.

SYN Packets with No Response

You should then see the SYN packet, which looks something like this with `tcpdump`:

```
18:13:22.040132 192.168.42.69.1777 > 192.168.0.13.80: S
3911298019:3911298019(0) win 16384 <mss 1460,nop,wscale
0,nop,nop,timestamp[|tcp]> (DF) [tos 0x10]
```

With `snoop`, it looks like this:

```
192.168.42.69 -> 192.168.0.13 HTTP C port=1777
```

If this packet repeats over and over again, one of four things may be wrong:

- The security policy is dropping the packet. Check your logs for drops.
- The packet is being sent to the wrong MAC address.
- The packet is not being routed properly.
- The packet isn't actually getting translated, thus it is getting ignored.

Verify that the MAC address it is being sent to is correct (in this case, it should be 0:11:22:33:44:55). In `tcpdump`, you do this with the –e flag, which adds the MAC address to the output. In `snoop`, the only way to do this is with the –v flag, which unfortunately is extremely verbose.

Also in this example, you are only going to show packets coming from host 192.168.0.13 by means of adding `host 192.168.0.13` to the end of your `tcpdump` or `snoop` command line. This will only show packets going to or from 192.168.0.13.

```
# tcpdump -e -i eth-s1p1 host 192.168.0.13
tcpdump: listening on eth-s1p1
18:21:49.201680 0:aa:bb:cc:dd:ee 0:55:44:33:22:11 ip 82:
192.168.42.69.2000 > 192.168.0.13.80: S 90360382:90360382(0) win
16384 <mss 1460,nop,wscale 0,nop,nop,timestamp[|tcp]> (DF) [tos
0x10]
18:21:54.240965 0:aa:bb:cc:dd:ee 0:55:44:33:22:11 ip 82:
192.168.42.69.2000 > 192.168.0.13.80: S 90360382:90360382(0) win
16384 <mss 1460,nop,wscale 0,nop,nop,timestamp[|tcp]> (DF) [tos
0x10]
```

```
18:22:07.209125 0:aa:bb:cc:dd:ee 0:55:44:33:22:11 ip 82:
192.168.42.69.2000 > 192.168.0.13.80: S 90360382:90360382(0) win
16384 <mss 1460,nop,wscale 0,nop,nop,timestamp[|tcp]> (DF) [tos
0x10]

# snoop -v -d hme0 host 192.168.0.13
Using device /dev/hme (promiscuous mode)
ETHER:  —- Ether Header —-
ETHER:
ETHER:  Packet 27 arrived at 16:47:50.83
ETHER:  Packet size = 58 bytes
ETHER:  Destination = 0:55:44:33:22:11,
ETHER:  Source      = 0:aa:bb:cc:dd:ee,
ETHER:  Ethertype = 0800 (IP)
ETHER:
IP:     —- IP Header —-
IP:
IP:     Version = 4
IP:     Header length = 20 bytes
IP:     Type of service = 0x00
IP:           xxx. .... = 0 (precedence)
IP:           ...0 .... = normal delay
IP:           .... 0... = normal throughput
IP:           .... .0.. = normal reliability
IP:     Total length = 44 bytes
IP:     Identification = 47535
IP:     Flags = 0x4
IP:           .1.. .... = do not fragment
IP:           ..0. .... = last fragment
IP:     Fragment offset = 0 bytes
IP:     Time to live = 245 seconds/hops
IP:     Protocol = 6 (TCP)
IP:     Header checksum = f23f
IP:     Source address = 192.168.42.69
IP:     Destination address = 192.168.0.13
IP:     No options
IP:
TCP:    —- TCP Header —-
TCP:
TCP:    Source port = 2000
TCP:    Destination port = 80 (HTTP)
TCP:    Sequence number = 90360382
TCP:    Acknowledgement number = 0
TCP:    Data offset = 24 bytes
TCP:    Flags = 0x02
TCP:           ..0. .... = No urgent pointer
TCP:           ...0 .... = No acknowledgement
TCP:           .... 0... = No push
TCP:           .... .0.. = No reset
```

```
TCP:          .... ..1. = Syn
TCP:          .... ...0 = No Fin
TCP:  Window = 8760
TCP:  Checksum = 0xda2b
TCP:  Urgent pointer = 0
TCP:  Options: (4 bytes)
TCP:    - Maximum segment size = 1460 bytes
TCP:
```

In the preceding case, MAC 0:aa:bb:cc:dd:ee (which is the MAC of the external router) is trying to send to MAC 0:55:44:33:22:11, which is not the correct MAC. This problem can usually be resolved by flushing the ARP cache on the external router and retrying the test.

If the packet is not being routed properly, you could see a reset (RST) packet (see the section "SYN Followed by RST"), or you could see an ICMP Destination Unreachable packet. Verify that the static host route for 192.168.0.13 is pointing to the next hop address (10.0.0.2 as show in Figure 9-3).

If the packet is not actually being translated, you will see it very clearly in a tcpdump or snoop on the internal interface:

```
# tcpdump -i eth-s1p2 host 192.168.42.69
tcpdump: listening on eth-s1p2
18:13:22.040132 192.168.42.69.1777 > 192.168.0.13.80: S
3911298019:3911298019(0) win 16384 <mss 1460,nop,wscale
0,nop,nop,timestamp[|tcp]> (DF) [tos 0x10]
18:18:25.040168 192.168.42.69.1777 > 192.168.0.13.80: S
3911298019:3911298019(0) win 16384 <mss 1460,nop,wscale
0,nop,nop,timestamp[|tcp]> (DF) [tos 0x10]
18:40:30.040342 192.168.42.69.1777 > 192.168.0.13.80: S
3911298019:3911298019(0) win 16384 <mss 1460,nop,wscale
0,nop,nop,timestamp[|tcp]> (DF) [tos 0x10]
```

```
# snoop -d hme0
Using device /dev/hme (promiscuous mode)
192.168.42.69 -> 192.168.0.13 HTTP C port=1777
192.168.42.69 -> 192.168.0.13 HTTP C port=1777
192.168.42.69 -> 192.168.0.13 HTTP C port=1777
```

Normally, you should see the translated IP address on the internal interface. If you do not see translated packets, check your NAT rules.

SYN Followed by RST

If the packet that follows the SYN is an RST packet (with snoop, you need -v to see the TCP flags):

```
# tcpdump -i eth-s1p1 host 192.168.0.13
tcpdump: listening on le0
18:13:22.040132 192.168.42.69.1777 > 192.168.0.13.80: S
3911298019:3911298019(0) win 16384 <mss1460,nop,wscale
0,nop,nop,timestamp[|tcp]> (DF) [tos 0x10]
18:13:22.040132 192.168.0.13.80 > 192.168.42.69.1777: R 0:0(0)
ack 3911298020 win 0 [tos 0x10]

# snoop -V -d hme0
Using device /dev/hme (promiscuous mode)
```

```
192.168.42.69 -> 192.168.0.13 ETHER Type=0800 (IP), size = 58
bytes
192.168.42.69 -> 192.168.0.13 IP  D=192.168.0.13 S=192.168.42.69
LEN=44, ID=47247
192.168.42.69 -> 192.168.0.13 TCP D=80 S=1777 Syn Seq=3052932309
Len=0 Win=8760 Options=<mss 1460>
192.168.42.69 -> 192.168.0.13 HTTP C port=1777
```

```
192.168.0.13 -> 192.168.42.69 ETHER Type=0800 (IP), size = 60
bytes
192.168.0.13 -> 192.168.42.69 IP  D=192.168.42.69 S=192.168.0.13
LEN=40, ID=61295
192.168.0.13 -> 192.168.42.69 TCP D=64836 S=80 Rst Ack=3052932310
Win=0
192.168.0.13 -> 192.168.42.69 HTTP R port=1777
```

then one of three things is wrong:

- The firewall is rejecting the packet on anti-spoofing. Verify that 192.168.0.13 is permitted by your anti-spoofing configuration on the internal interface.
- The remote server is not running the service specified (in this case, port 80, HTTP).
- The packet is being routed incorrectly.

If the remote server isn't actually running the service, you will see the following in a tcpdump and snoop on the internal interface:

```
# tcpdump -i eth-s1p1 host 10.0.10.80
tcpdump: listening on le0
18:13:22.040132 192.168.42.69.1777 > 10.0.10.80.80: S
3911298019:3911298019(0) win 16384 <mss 1460,nop,wscale
0,nop,nop,timestamp[|tcp]> (DF) [tos 0x10]
18:13:22.040132 10.0.10.80.80 > 192.168.42.69.1777: R 0:0(0) ack
3911298020 win 0 [tos 0x10]

# snoop -V -d hme0
Using device /dev/hme (promiscuous mode)
```

```
192.168.42.69 -> 10.0.10.80 ETHER Type=0800 (IP), size = 58 bytes
192.168.42.69 -> 10.0.10.80 IP D=10.0.10.80 S=192.168.42.69
LEN=44, ID=47247
192.168.42.69 -> 10.0.10.80 TCP D=80 S=1777 Syn Seq=3052932309
Len=0 Win=8760 Options=<mss 1460>
192.168.42.69 -> 10.0.10.80 HTTP C port=1777
```

```
192.168.0.13 -> 192.168.42.69 ETHER Type=0800 (IP), size = 60
bytes
192.168.0.13 -> 192.168.42.69 IP  D=192.168.42.69 S=10.0.10.80
LEN=40, ID=61295
192.168.0.13 -> 192.168.42.69 TCP D=64836 S=80 Rst Ack=3052932310
Win=0
192.168.0.13 -> 192.168.42.69 HTTP R port=1777
```

The internal interface should see the untranslated packets (10.0.10.80 is the system's real IP). If the packet is being routed to the wrong interface, you will also see the same behavior as in the preceding output, but you will see a reject on Rule 0 in the Log Viewer as well. Verify that the static host route is set up correctly.

Useful `tcpdump` Flags

Table 9-4 contains a list of some useful flags for `tcpdump`, which takes commands in the following format:

```
tcpdump -i interface-name [other-flags] [expression]
```

Table 9-4 `tcpdump` Flags

Flag	Description
`-e`	Displays MAC addresses with each packet.
`-i interface`	Required. Specify an interface to listen on.
`-l`	Buffer stdout, which is useful for piping `tcpdump` output to other programs.
`-n`	Disables name resolution on packets shown.
`-p`	Do not put interface in promiscuous mode (i.e., only show packets destined for the host).
`-r filename`	Read `tcpdump` capture from specified file.
`-s N`	Capture N number of bytes for each packet. The default is 68. (Useful with –x or –X.)
`-S`	Print absolute TCP sequence numbers instead of relative ones.
`-w filename`	Write captured packets to specified file.
`-x`	Hex dump of received packets.
`-X`	Hex and ASCII dump of received packets (IPSO only).

`tcpdump` *Expressions*

All `tcpdump` commands can be followed by an expression that filters the displayed (or saved) packets so that only the packets that are interesting are shown. Some useful expressions are shown in Table 9-5.

Table 9-5   `tcpdump` Expressions

Expression	Description
port 80	Show all packets with source or destination port 80 (TCP or UDP).
host 192.168.0.3	Show all packets coming from or going to host 192.168.0.3.
host 192.168.0.3 and tcp port 80	Show all packets coming from or going to host 192.168.0.3 and that are TCP packets with a source or destination port of 80.
proto vrrp	Show all VRRP packets. On non-IPSO platforms, use "ip proto 112."
icmp	Show all ICMP packets.
\(src host 192.168.0.1 or src host 192.168.0.2\) and proto vrrp	Show all VRRP packets that originate from 192.168.0.1 and 192.168.0.2 (the \ before the parenthesis is to escape it for the shell).
ether host aa:bb: cc:dd:ee:ff	Show all packets that come from or go to the specified MAC address.
ip proto 50	Show all packets of IP Proto 50 (IPSec AH in this example).
ip[2:2] > 576	Show IP packets that are longer than 576 bytes ([2:2] refers to the specific byte location in the TCP header and its length).
tcp[13] & 0x12 != 0	Show only TCP SYN/ACK packets. tcp[13] refers to the 13th byte in the TCP header of the packet.
icmp[0]	Show ICMP type 0 packets (i.e., echo reply). Icmp[0] refers to the 0th byte in the ICMP header.
icmp[0] = 3 and icmp[1] = 4	Show ICMP type 3, code 4 packets. These happen to be a response to receiving a packet that is too large to process and has the Don't Fragment bit set.

Useful `snoop` Flags

Table 9-6 contains a list of some useful flags for `snoop`, which takes commands in the following format:

```
snoop [flags] [expression]
```

`snoop` *Expressions*

All `snoop` commands can be followed by an expression that filters the displayed (or saved) packets so that only the packets that are interesting are shown. Some useful

Table 9-6 snoop Flags

Flag	Description
`-d interface`	Specify an interface to listen on.
`-v`	Verbose mode. All packet data is displayed for each packet.
`-V`	A less-verbose verbose mode. A summary line is displayed for each layer in the ISO model.
`-n`	Disables name resolution on packets shown.
`-P`	Do not put interface in promiscuous mode, which means only show packets actually destined for this host (not useful on a switched segment).
`-i filename`	Read packets previously captured from file filename.
`-o filename`	Write packets to capture file named filename.
`-s numbytes`	Capture numbytes bytes for each packet. Normally, all bytes in the packet are captured.
`-p x,y`	Show packets numbered between x and y. The first packet captured is 1.
`-t [a|d|r]`	Timestamp format: a (absolute, i.e., wall clock time), d (delta, since capture was started), and r (relative time).

expressions are shown in Table 9-7. Note that many of the expressions are similar to `tcpdump`.

Table 9-7 snoop Expressions

Expression	Description
port 80	Show all packets with source or destination port 80 (TCP or UDP).
host 192.168.0.3	Show all packets coming from or going to host 192.168.0.3. You can also omit the "host" qualifier as well.
host 192.168.0.3 and tcp port 80	Show all packets coming from or going to host 192.168.0.3 and that are TCP packets with a source or destination port of 80.
Icmp	Show all ICMP packets.
from 192.168.0.1 or to 192.168.0.2	Show all packets that originate from 192.168.0.1 or are destined for 192.168.0.2.
ether aa:bb: cc:dd:ee:ff	Show all packets that come from or go to the specified MAC address.
ip proto 50	Show all packets of IP Proto 50 (IPSec AH in this example).
greater 576	Show packets longer than 576 bytes. You can use the word "less" instead of "greater" to show packets smaller than 576 bytes.
tcp[13] & 0x12 != 0	Show only TCP SYN/ACK packets. tcp[13] refers to the 13th byte in the TCP header of the packet.

Summary

NAT is necessary because organizations and individuals need the ability to allow more hosts to communicate with the Internet than their address space allows. Specific blocks of IP addresses have been set aside to accommodate NAT.

NAT also provides a way to more efficiently use address space without the overhead imposed by subnetting. However, NAT imposes restrictions of its own, and it may not be appropriate for every situation.

Sample Configurations

The following three situations presented are representative of situations I have come across in the real world. Each is designed to demonstrate what people typically do with NAT and how the situations would be implemented on the chosen platform.

A Simple Network with NAT

The Situation

You work for a small company with a few hosts on a flat network segment. Your firewall runs on a Windows NT platform. The ISP has only given you a /29 net block, which effectively gives you six hosts you can use on the outside segment. Because the firewall and Internet router each need a unique IP address, this leaves a total of four addresses that can be used for other hosts. (See Figure 9-9.)

The Goals

- Allow Internet users access to the Mail and Web Servers via SMTP and HTTP, respectively. In the future, these services will be provided on separate systems, so setting up each service with a unique IP is desirable to make future migration easier.

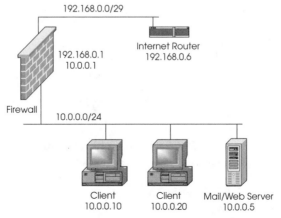

Figure 9-9   Sample configuration network #1

- Allow internal users to access anything on the Internet. All outbound users will be hidden behind a single IP address; however, this IP address should be different from the firewall.

Checklist

- Determine which IP addresses will be used for translation.
- Set up the necessary proxy-ARPs.
- Set up the necessary static host routes.
- Create the necessary network objects.
- Make the necessary modifications to anti-spoofing.
- Create the necessary rulebase rules to permit the desired traffic.
- Create the NAT rules.
- Install the security policy.

Implementation

You must first determine which IPs you will use. Your usable IPs are 192.168.0.2–192.168.0.5. Let's make 192.168.0.2 the IP you use for your external clients to hide behind, 192.168.0.3 for the SMTP server, and 192.168.0.4 for the HTTP server.

Next, set up the static ARPs for the translated addresses. In order to do this, you need to determine the MAC address of your external interface. Use the command `ipconfig /all` to determine this address:

```
Ethernet adapter 3C5x91 :
        Description . . . . . . . . . : 3Com 3C5x9 Ethernet Adapter
        Physical Address. . . . . . : 00-22-44-66-88-AA
        DHCP Enabled. . . . . . . . : No
        IP Address. . . . . . . . . : 192.168.0.1
        Subnet Mask . . . . . . . . : 255.255.255.248
        Default Gateway . . . . . . : 192.168.0.6
Ethernet adapter 3C5x92:
        Description . . . . . . . . . : 3Com 3C5x9 Ethernet Adapter
        Physical Address. . . . . . : 00-00-87-20-66-69
        DHCP Enabled. . . . . . . . : No
        IP Address. . . . . . . . . : 10.0.0.1
        Subnet Mask . . . . . . . . : 255.255.255.0
        Default Gateway . . . . . . :
```

The external MAC is `00-22-44-66-88-AA`, which you will enter along with the IP addresses in the `%FWDIR%\state\local.arp`:

```
192.168.0.2 00-22-44-66-88-AA
192.168.0.3 00-22-44-66-88-AA
192.168.0.4 00-22-44-66-88-AA
```

Both 192.168.0.3 and 192.168.0.4 each need a static host route. The 192.168.0.2 address does not need one, as users should never be directly connecting to 192.168.0.2. Because the real host is on the same subnet as the firewall, the static route should be directed at the host itself:

```
route -p add 192.168.0.3 10.0.0.5
route -p add 192.168.0.4 10.0.0.5
```

Because you are using the -p option, these routes will be available after a reboot; they will be stored in the Registry.

Table 9-8 lists the network objects you will create.

Table 9-8 Network objects for sample configuration #1

Name	Object Type	IP/Net Mask/Group Objects	Description
Net-internal	Network	10.0.0.0/255.255.255.0	The network that represents the Internal Network
mail-web-server	Workstation	10.0.0.5	Mail/Web Server on the Internal Network
mail-ext	Workstation	192.168.0.3	Translated IP for Mail Server
web-ext	Workstation	192.168.0.4	Translated IP for Web Server
external-hide	Workstation	192.168.0.2	IP that users will hide behind when going out
valid-internal	Group	net-internal + mail-ext + web-ext	Represents your internal interface's valid addresses for anti-spoofing
firewall	Workstation	192.168.0.1	Your firewall

When configuring your firewall object, set your valid address settings according to the settings shown in Table 9-9.

Table 9-9 Valid address settings for firewall

Interface	Valid Address Setting
Internal	Specific: valid-internal
External	Others

The valid address settings are set on the Interfaces tab. Also, make sure that each interface has the Spoof Tracking set to "Log" to catch any errors in the anti-spoofing configuration.

The rulebase should look similar to the rules shown in Figure 9-10.

The NAT rules should look like the rules shown in Figure 9-11.

Save and install the policy.

No.	Source	Destination	Service	Action	Track	Install On
1	Any	web-ext	http	accept	Short	Gateways
2	Any	mail-ext	smtp	accept	Short	Gateways
3	net-internal	Any	Any	accept	Long	Gateways
4	Any	Any	Any	drop	Long	Gateways

Figure 9-10   Security policy for sample configuration #1

No.	Original Packet			Translated Packet			Install On
	Source	Destination	Service	Source	Destination	Service	
1	Any	web-ext	Any	Original	mail-web-server	Original	Gateways
2	Any	mail-ext	Any	Original	mail-web-server	Original	Gateways
3	net-internal	Any	Any	external-hide	Original	Original	Gateways

Figure 9-11   NAT policy for sample configuration #1

Notes

It is not a wise idea to have your internal hosts on the same LAN segment as hosts that are accessible from an untrusted network like the Internet. However, this is a situation that, for various reasons, all too many security administrators find themselves in. From a security standpoint, you are much better off trying to move externally accessible servers to a DMZ. It will cost a couple hundred dollars to purchase an extra LAN adaptor, an extra switch or hub, and a few extra cables, but the extra security gained will be well worth it.

You will not be able to access the Mail/Web server from the internal segment via its translated addresses without some additional configuration.

Migrating to a Larger Net with NAT

The Situation

The company you work for has grown. Your ISP has given you an external segment with a few more addresses (192.168.1.64/28), and you have a separate LAN segment for your DMZ, which now also has a few more hosts in it. Your firewall platform has also changed from Windows NT to Solaris.

A certain amount of "backward compatibility" needs to be maintained with the old setup; that is, certain hosts need to be reachable by their old addresses. For the external addresses, the ISP is continuing to route the 192.168.0.0/29 segment to you until such time as the address space is no longer needed. (See Figure 9-12.)

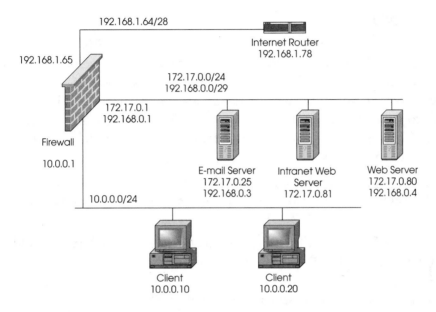

Figure 9-12   Sample configuration network #2

The Goals

- Allow Internet users access to the Mail and Web Servers via SMTP and HTTP, respectively. Note that the servers will have to be accessible by their old, historical IPs as well as their new IPs.
- Allow internal users to access anything on the Internet. All outbound users will be hidden behind a single IP address; however, this IP address should be different from the firewall.
- Allow internal users to access the Intranet Web server by its old IP address (10.0.0.5). This server will not be accessible from the Internet.

Checklist

- Determine which IP addresses will be used for translation.
- Set up the necessary proxy-ARPs.

- Set up the necessary static host routes.
- Create the necessary network objects.
- Make the necessary modifications to anti-spoofing.
- Create the necessary rulebase rules to permit the desired traffic.
- Create the NAT rules.
- Install the security policy.

Implementation

To simplify your NAT configuration a bit, assign the 192.168.0.0/29 network to the DMZ. Make sure the external router is configured to route all requests for this network to the firewall. You also need to give the firewall an IP address of 192.168.0.1 on the DMZ interface. In Solaris, you add an `/etc/hostname.qe3:1` file with this IP address. You also have to modify `/etc/netmasks` so that 192.168.0.0 has the correct net mask (255.255.255.248). So that you don't have to reboot for this to take effect, execute the following set of commands:

```
# ifconfig qe3:1 plumb
# ifconfig qe3:1 inet 192.168.0.1 netmask 255.255.255.248
broadcast 192.168.0.7 up
```

The SMTP and HTTP servers need to have secondary IP addresses of 192.168.0.3 and 192.168.0.4, respectively. Similar steps need to be taken on these servers.

You must then determine which IPs you will use for translation. Your new usable address range is 192.168.1.66-192.168.1.77. Let's make 192.168.1.66 the IP you use for your external clients to hide behind, 192.168.1.67 the new IP for your SMTP server, and 192.168.1.68 for your HTTP server. You are also translating 10.0.0.5 to 172.17.0.81.

Next, set up the static ARPs for the translated addresses. Because you are translating both internal and external addresses to the DMZ, you need both the external and internal interfaces' MAC address. An `ifconfig -a` shows you the following:

```
lo0: flags=849 <UP,LOOPBACK,RUNNING,MULTICAST> mtu 8232
        inet 127.0.0.1 netmask ff000000
le0: flags=863 <UP,BROADCAST,NOTRAILERS,RUNNING, MULTICAST> mtu
1500
        inet 192.168.1.65 netmask ffffff0 broadcast
        192.168.1.79
        ether 0:12:34:56:78:9a
qe0: flags=863 <UP,BROADCAST,NOTRAILERS,RUNNING, MULTICAST> mtu
1500
```

```
          inet 10.0.0.1 netmask ffffff00 broadcast 10.0.0.255
          ether 8:0:20:6d:0:20

qe3: flags=863 <UP,BROADCAST,NOTRAILERS,RUNNING,MULTICAST> mtu
1500
          inet 172.17.0.1 netmask ffffff00 broadcast 172.17.0.255
          ether 8:0:20:20:0:6d
qe3:1 flags=863 <UP,BROADCAST,NOTRAILERS,RUNNING, MULTICAST> mtu
1500
          inet 192.168.0.1 netmask fffffff8 broadcast 192.168.0.7
```

The external MAC is 00:12:34:56:78:9a, and the internal MAC address is 8:0:20:20:0:6d. The ARPs you would do are as follows:

```
arp -s 192.168.1.66 0:12:34:56:78:9a pub
arp -s 192.168.1.67 0:12:34:56:78:9a pub
arp -s 192.168.1.68 0:12:34:56:78:9a pub
arp -s 10.0.0.5     8:0:20:20:0:6d   pub
```

Static routes are as follows (note that you still need static routes for the "old" addresses, even if you don't need ARPs for them):

```
route add 192.168.1.67 172.17.0.25 1
route add 192.168.1.68 172.17.0.80 1
route add 10.0.0.5     172.17.0.81 1
```

Because this is a UNIX platform, these ARPs and routes will disappear after a reboot. You need to add these routes and ARPs to a startup file. It is recommended that you create a new script for this purpose (such as /etc/rc3.d/S94addroutes), and add the preceding commands to this file.

Table 9-10 shows the network objects that will be created.

When configuring your firewall object, set your valid address settings according to the settings shown in Table 9-11.

These settings are configured on the Interfaces tab. Also, make sure that each interface has the Spoof Tracking set to "Log" to catch any errors in the anti-spoofing configuration.

The rulebase should look similar to the rules shown in Figure 9-13.

The NAT rules should look like the rules shown in Figure 9-14.

Save and install the policy.

Notes

Sites on the DMZ should be accessible by their translated IP addresses, even from the internal network. This is because the communication is now mediated by the firewall. In the previous example, this was not the case.

Table 9-10 Network objects for sample configuration

Name	Object Type	IP/Net Mask/Group Objects	Description
net-internal	Network	10.0.0.0/255.255.255.0	The network that represents the Internal Network
net-dmz	Network	172.17.0.0/255.255.255.0	The network that represents the DMZ
net-external-old	Network	192.168.0.0/255.255.255.248	The old external network now on the DMZ
mail-server	Workstation	172.17.0.25	The Mail Server
mail-server-ext	Workstation	192.168.1.67	Translated IP for the Mail Server
mail-server-ext-old	Workstation	192.168.0.3	Translated IP for the Mail Server (historical)
web-server	Workstation	172.17.0.80	The Web Server
web-server-ext	Workstation	192.168.1.68	Translated IP for the Web Server
web-server-ext-old	Workstation	192.168.0.4	Translated IP for the Web Server (historical)
intranet-web-server	Workstation	172.17.0.81	The Intranet Web Server
intranet-web-server-int	Workstation	10.0.0.5	Translated IP for the Intranet Web Server
external-hide	Workstation	192.168.1.66	IP that users will hide behind when going out
valid-dmz	Group	net-dmz + intranet-web-server-int + mail-server-ext + web-server-ext + net-external-old	Represents your DMZ interface's valid addresses for anti-spoofing
valid-internal	Group	net-internal	Represents your internal interface's valid addresses for anti-spoofing
firewall	Workstation	192.168.1.65	Your firewall

Table 9-11 Valid address settings for firewall

Interface	Valid Address Setting
DMZ	Specific: valid-dmz
Internal	Specific: valid-internal
External	Others

No.	Source	Destination	Service	Action	Track	Install On
1	Any	web-server-ext / web-server-ext-old	http	accept	Short	Gateways
2	Any	mail-server-ext / mail-server-ext-old	smtp	accept	Short	Gateways
3	net-internal	net-dmz / net-external-old	Any	accept	Long	Gateways
4	net-internal	intranet-web-server-int	http	accept	Short	Gateways
5	Any	Any	Any	drop	Long	Gateways

Figure 9-13 Security policy for sample configuration #2

No.	Original Packet			Translated Packet		
	Source	Destination	Service	Source	Destination	Service
1	Any	web-server-ext	Any	Original	mail-web-server	Original
2	Any	web-server-ext	Any	Original	mail-web-server	Original
3	net-internal	intranet-web-server-int	Any	Original	intranet-web-server	Original
4	net-internal	Any	Any	external-hide	Original	Original

Figure 9-14 NAT policy for sample configuration #2

Double-Blind Network Configuration

The Situation

There is a device within your network that has a faulty IP implementation and can only talk to hosts on the same subnet as it is on (i.e., it has no concept of routing).[8] Because it is also not desirable to allow everyone to access this host, a firewall is necessary to restrict access to this host. The host is using nonroutable addresses and cannot

---

8. Don't laugh; I've actually run into this situation with an IP-enabled PBX system.

be seen by the rest of the network. It must be given a routable address so that it can be accessed. Because neither side of the connection can know the true IP address of its peer, this is referred to as a *double-blind* network configuration.

A Nokia IP330 will be used to protect this device, which will be directly connected to the device via a crossover cable. The rest of the network (the entire 10.0.0.0/8) is used internally. Figure 9-15 only shows the relevant parts of the network.

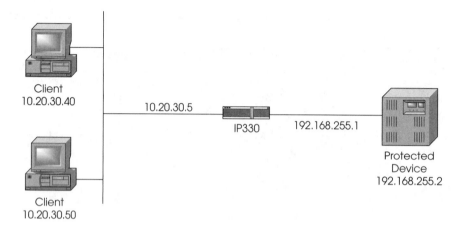

Figure 9-15 Sample configuration network #3

The Goals

- Allow FTP and Telnet access to 10.20.30.6 (the translated IP address for this device).
- Allow HTTP access to the IP330 for management purposes from a specific management console (10.250.0.5, not pictured here).
- Allow SSH access to the IP330 for management purposes from anywhere.

Checklist

- Determine which IP addresses will be used for translation.
- Set up the necessary proxy-ARPs.
- Set up the necessary static host routes.
- Create the necessary network objects.
- Make the necessary modifications to anti-spoofing.
- Create the necessary rulebase rules to permit the desired traffic.
- Create the NAT rules.
- Install the security policy.

Implementation

From the preceding goals, you know that you will be translating 10.20.30.6 to 192.168.255.2. You also know that all access to this protected device must appear to be coming from a device on the same subnet. The firewall is appropriate in this case.

You need to create an ARP for 10.20.30.6 using the MAC address of the external interface of the IP330. You can easily do this in Voyager. Figure 9-16 shows the interface ARP entries, which are on the ARP configuration page.

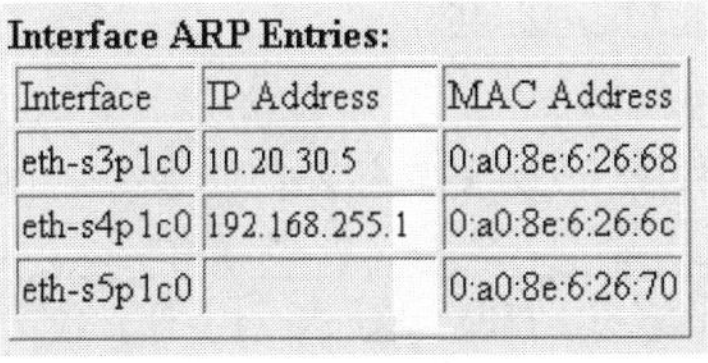

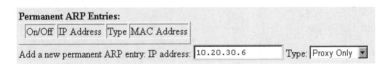

Figure 9-16 Interface ARP entries in Voyager

You can see the two interfaces and their MAC addresses. For 10.20.30.6, you will use 0:a0:8e:6:26:68. Right above the Interface ARP entries on the Voyager page is where you create this ARP entry (see Figure 9-17).

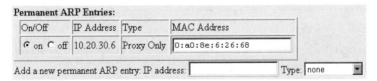

Figure 9-17 Create ARP entries in Voyager.

Click the Apply button at the bottom of the page. You then need to set the MAC address for this entry (see Figure 9-18).

Permanent ARP Entries:

On/Off	IP Address	Type	MAC Address
⊙ on ○ off	10.20.30.6	Proxy Only	0:a0:8e:6:26:68

Add a new permanent ARP entry: IP address: _____ Type: none ▼

Figure 9-18 Add MAC to ARP entries in Voyager.

Click Apply again. Go to the bottom of the static route page in Voyager, and add a static route to route 10.20.30.6 to 192.168.255.2 (see Figure 9-19).

Figure 9-19 Add static route in Voyager.

Click Apply, and then click Save. This configuration is now active across reboots. The network objects you will create are shown in Table 9-12.

Table 9-12 Network objects for sample configuration

Name	Object Type	IP/Net Mask/Group Objects	Description
net-protected-device	Network	192.168.255.0/255.255.255.0	The network that the protected device is on
net-internal	Network	10.0.0.0/255.0.0.0	The internal network
protected-device	Workstation	192.168.255.2	The protected device's internal IP
protected-device-xlate	Workstation	10.20.30.6	Translated IP for the protected device
management-device	Workstation	10.250.0.5	Host allowed to connect to IP330 via HTTP
firewall-eth-s4p1	Workstation	192.168.255.1	A workstation object (defined without Fire-Wall-1 installed) that represents the system's interface facing the protected device. You will need this later.
valid-eth-s4p1	Group	net-protected-device + protected-device-xlate	Represents the valid address setting for eth-s4p1, the interface that the protected device is hooked to
Firewall	Workstation	10.20.30.5	Your firewall

When configuring your firewall object, set your valid address settings according to the settings shown in Table 9-13.

Table 9-13 Valid address setting for firewall

Interface	Valid Address Setting
eth-s4p1c0	Specific: valid-eth-s4p1
eth-s3p1c0	Others

These settings are configured on the Interfaces tab. Also, make sure that each interface has the Spoof Tracking set to "Log" to catch any errors in the anti-spoofing configuration.

The rulebase should look similar to the rules shown in Figure 9-20.

No.	Source	Destination	Service	Action	Track	Install On
1	Any	protected-device-xlate	telnet / ftp	accept	Short	Gateways
2	management-device	firewall	http	accept	Short	Gateways
3	Any	firewall	ssh	accept	Long	Gateways
4	Any	Any	Any	drop	Long	Gateways

Figure 9-20 Security policy for sample configuration #3

The NAT rules should look like the rule shown in Figure 9-21.
Save and install the policy.

No.	Original Packet			Translated Packet			Install On
	Source	Destination	Service	Source	Destination	Service	
1	net-internal	protected-device-xlate	Any	firewall-eth-s4p1	protected-device	Original	Gateways

Figure 9-21 NAT policy for sample configuration #3

Notes

You could do this in the reverse direction as well (i.e., have the protected device access hosts on the other side of the firewall as if they were on the same subnet), but this sample configuration only shows the connections occurring in one direction.

Chapter

10

Site-to-Site VPNs

This chapter is designed to be a practical guide to planning and configuring site-to-site Virtual Private Networks (VPNs) with FireWall-1. I briefly cover a few key terms and concepts and jump right into what can be done in FireWall-1 and how to do it. This chapter is not meant to comprehensively cover encryption or encryption technologies.

By the end of this chapter, you should be able to do the following:

- Plan for a VPN
- Determine which key exchange and encryption schemes FireWall-1 uses
- Set up a VPN with FireWall-1 step-by-step
- Understand what a Gateway Cluster is and what functions it provides
- Troubleshoot VPN problems

Introduction to a VPN

A VPN is a technology that allows two or more locations to communicate securely over a public network while maintaining the security and privacy of a private network. Encryption, authentication, and packet integrity checks are key enablers of VPNs, as they ensure that the data is private and the integrity of the data is maintained. The main reason for using VPNs is that private networks are expensive to acquire and maintain. Companies are finding VPNs a cost-effective way to connect sites to one another.

Given that firewalls are designed to be the gatekeeper between public and private networks, it makes sense to integrate VPN capabilities into a firewall. Not only can you filter traffic but also subject VPN usage to a security policy that is integrated with your existing one. In FireWall-1, there is no separate place to create a VPN rulebase; it is simply part of your existing security policy. This makes it really easy to implement a VPN in FireWall-1.

Concepts

Many generic concepts are used throughout in this chapter and are briefly defined in the following sections. Because this chapter is not meant to comprehensively cover encryption, these descriptions may seem inadequate.[1]

Encryption

Encryption is one of the main technologies that make a VPN possible. It is the transformation of data into a nearly random form that can only be reversed in specific circumstances. Encryption ensures privacy by keeping information hidden from anyone for whom it is not intended, even those who have access to the encrypted data.

Encryption Key

An encryption key is used to either encrypt data, decrypt data, or both. The kind of key used depends on the type of encryption algorithm being used. The number of bits in this key plays a role in determining how strong the encryption is. The fewer the bits, the easier it is to guess the encryption key by brute force (i.e., simply trying each possible key).

Symmetric Encryption

Symmetric encryption uses the same key for encrypting and decrypting data. However, the encryption key needs to be kept secret and should be exchanged via some sort of secure mechanism. Symmetric encryption is generally used for bulk data encryption because it is faster than other methods. Examples of symmetric encryption include the Data Encryption Standard (DES), Blowfish, the recently approved Advanced Encryption Standard (AES), and FWZ.

Asymmetric Encryption

Asymmetric encryption uses different keys for encrypting and decrypting data. Asymmetric encryption schemes are approximately 1,000 times slower than symmetric encryption on similar hardware and are only used to exchange small amounts of data (for example, encryption keys for a symmetric algorithm).

All public-key cryptography systems, such as RSA, are asymmetric algorithms. In these systems, each node has a public key (which is widely distributed) and a private key (which is kept secret). A node's public and private key have a peculiar property in that they effectively cancel the effects of each other out, thus allowing you to encrypt and decrypt them in combination with another person's keys.

---

1. For a more detailed description of these concepts, refer to the Web site at www.garykessler.net/library/crypto.html.

Consider the following example: The source node can encrypt a message using the destination node's public key and only the destination node can encrypt it. More importantly, a source node can encrypt the message with its private key *and* the destination node's public key. The destination node can decrypt it using its own private key and the source node's public key. Aside from encrypting the message, the process provides verification that the source node was the correct node, another important function.

Hash Function

A hash function is a one-way function. One-way functions have the unique property of being irreversible, meaning given the function and its output, it is impossible to determine what value(s) was originally plugged into the function to give that output. Although they do not encrypt data, per se, the functions themselves are based in cryptography and provide a very important purpose in the encryption process: validation. When data is placed through a hash function, the result is sort of a "checksum." Hash functions are designed in such a way that it is highly unlikely that any two inputs will give the same result, which means you can be assured, with a high level of confidence, that the data has not been tampered with. Examples of hash functions include MD5 and SHA-1.

Certificate Authority (CA)

A CA is a trusted third party that is used to certify public keys. The CA has its own public and private keys. The CA takes prudent steps to verify the authenticity of the public key. The CA then signs the node's public key by encrypting it with its private key, which is then widely distributed. A node can verify it has the correct public key by decrypting using the CA's public key.

A firewall management console is the CA for FWZ and Simple Key-Management for IP (SKIP) encryption. FireWall-1 does support third-party CAs.

Diffie-Hellman (DH) Keys

FWZ and SKIP use DH keys, which are essentially public- and private-key pairs used in an asymmetric encryption algorithm. To verify that the keys have not been tampered with, they are typically signed by a CA key.

Encryption Domain

Encryption domain is a concept that is not entirely unique to FireWall-1, but the term is. Generally speaking, it contains everything on the private side of the network (i.e., all hosts behind the gateway in question). Note that this does not mean that every host in the encryption domain is allowed to communicate through a VPN. This is controlled by the defined security policy. It just defines the potential for encryption. You must include all translated IP addresses for internal hosts. In general, the firewall is not part of the encryption domain but can be. It should be if the firewall is being used as the *hide* address for internal hosts.

A Word about Licensing

The VPN features of FireWall-1 require binaries that support encryption and a license that enables it. This option costs money above and beyond the base functionality of FireWall-1. You can only use this functionality if you have purchased the proper license and have the correct binaries.

To ensure that you have binaries capable of supporting the appropriate level of encryption, check the contents of Table 10-1 against the output of `fw ver` on your system.

In FireWall-1 4.1, the license string includes the product SKU as listed on Check Point's price lists. This will tell you what level of encryption you have purchased, if any. See Table 10-2.

In FireWall-1 4.0 and earlier, your license string will contain one of the features listed in Table 10-3.

Table 10-1   Encryption strength and `fw ver` output

`Fw ver` **Output**	**Encryption Strength**
VPN + DES + STRONG	Strongest encryption available
VPN + DES	56-bit encryption and lower
VPN	40-bit encryption only
None of the above	No encryption capabilities

Table 10-2   FireWall-1 4.1 SKUs and encryption strength

SKU	**Encryption Strength**
3DES	Strongest encryption available
DES	56-bit encryption and lower
FWZ1	48-bit encryption and lower
40bit	40-bit encryption only

Table 10-3   FireWall-1 4.0 and earlier licenses and encryption strength

SKU	Encryption Strength
vpnstrong	Strongest encryption available
vpndes	56-bit encryption and lower
fwz	48-bit encryption and lower
vpn	40-bit encryption only

Supported Key-Management and Encryption Schemes

FireWall-1 supports four encryption-key-management schemes. These key-management schemes support different encryption schemes that are used for data encryption and integrity checking.

FWZ

FWZ is Check Point's proprietary key-management system and has been available since Check Point made VPN technology part of FireWall-1 in version 2.0. FWZ incorporates the following:

- A CA (a FireWall-1 management console).
- Asymmetric encryption for the exchange of CA, DH, and per-session encryption keys.
- Symmetric encryption for actual data encryption using FWZ1, a proprietary Check Point algorithm that encrypts at 48 bits or DES, and the U.S. government's data encryption standard at 56 bits.
- Optional data integrity checking with an MD5 hash.
- Out-of-band management of encryption keys with the RDP protocol (which runs on UDP port 259).

Unlike most encryption methods, which encrypt the entire packet (data and headers) and encapsulate it in a new packet, FWZ encrypts only the data portion of the packet, leaving the original IP headers intact. This means that little additional transmission overhead is incurred. However, it also means that if you want other hosts to access nonroutable address space behind your firewall, you must also perform NAT in order to participate in a VPN.

Most people no longer use FWZ in favor of the other protocols FireWall-1 supports, mainly because they support stronger encryption algorithms.

IPSec

The rest of the key-management systems supported by FireWall-1 are IPSec key-management systems. IPSec is a set of standards designed by the Internet Engineering Task Force (IETF), which define how hosts communicate to one another in a secure manner. In tunnel mode (which is what FireWall-1 uses), all communication between any two hosts is completely encapsulated (both IP headers and data) in new packets, which adds up to 100 bytes per packet.

IPSec has two main protocols: an Authentication Header (AH), which is designed to provide integrity and authentication without confidentiality to IP datagrams, and the Encapsulating Security Payload (ESP), which is designed to provide integrity, authentication, and confidentiality to IP datagrams. AH and ESP can be used together or separately, but AH is rarely used in IPSec, because ESP provides everything that AH provides plus encryption.

There are many different encryption algorithms used in IPSec for both encryption and data integrity checking. Some of them include:

- 3DES (168-bit)[2]
- DES (56-bit and 40-bit versions)
- AES (128-bit and 256-bit)[3]
- CAST (40-bit and 128-bit versions)
- RC2 (40-bit)
- RC4 (40-bit)

NOTE! Not all of these encryption algorithms are part of the IPSec standard. Extra care should be taken when setting up a VPN with third-party products.

For data integrity purposes, FireWall-1 uses:

- SHA-1 (192-bit)
- MD5 (128-bit)
- RSA (1024-bit)
- CBC-DES (64-bit)

---

2. 3DES is essentially the DES algorithm run at 56 bits with three separate passes using three different encryption keys. Although many people claim this is 168-bit encryption (3*56 = 168), cryptanalysis done on the 3DES algorithm shows it is no more effective than encryption done with a secret key of 112 bits.

3. AES support (also called *Rijndael*) was added by Check Point in FireWall-1 4.1 SP4.

Note that the exact versions you have available will vary depending on the version of FireWall-1, the key-management scheme you are attempting to use, and the encryption level of the software you have.

The main differences between the types of IPSec keys are:

- How the AH and ESP are handled
- How the encryption keys are managed between gateways
- Which algorithms can be used (although these restrictions are less of an issue in version 4.0 SP5, 4.1 SP1, and later)

Manual IPSec

Manual IPSec, as its name implies, is a manual implementation of IPSec key management. Encryption keys are defined and updated manually by an administrator. A Security Parameters Index (SPI) must be defined at each end of the VPN. The SPI defines the encryption schemes and data integrity methods used. The definition must match on both ends. However, this means that a fixed SPI is used for both ends of the connection, which a hacker could potentially guess using brute force. Manual IPSec is therefore not recommended, except perhaps in initial testing and configuration. Manual IPSec is relatively easy to get working, particularly when testing a VPN with a non-Check Point endpoint.

Manual IPSec has been in FireWall-1 since version 3.0. Sources within Check Point have told me that Check Point is planning to remove Manual IPSec support in the NG release of FireWall-1. I would therefore consider using a different key-management system, such as Internet Key Exchange (IKE).

SKIP

SKIP defines a way in which two parties can agree on encryption and authentication keys and change these keys frequently. SKIP is stateless, as each packet contains (almost) all the information needed for its decryption and authentication. All a party needs to know beforehand is the IP address of the peer party and its public DH keys.

Attempts were made to make SKIP part of the IPSec support in IPv6 (the next version of IP) but have been supplanted by IKE. However, SKIP is still in use today.

SKIP has been in FireWall-1 since version 3.0.

IKE

IKE is the new name for ISAKMP/OAKLEY, which is the standard IPSec key-management scheme in IPv6. Like SKIP, it supports automated key exchange. However, IKE also supports Public Key Infrastructure (PKI), which allows encryption keys to be managed by a separate, central server. A "pre-shared secret" (effectively a password) can also be established between two nodes.

IKE has been in FireWall-1 since version 4.0. Unlike Manual IPSec and SKIP, it can also be used with SecuRemote clients. SecuRemote is covered in Chapter 11.

How to Configure Encryption

As you will find, the steps in configuring encryption are very similar regardless of which encryption scheme you use. Throughout this section, I will refer to the proposed VPN setup in Figure 10-1 while walking through the various ways that a VPN can be established between these two sites.

Planning Your Deployment

You will need the following four items when planning a FireWall-1-based VPN:

- Which hosts and/or networks the remote site will be able to access through the VPN (your encryption domain)
- Which hosts and/or networks will be accessible at the remote site (the partner's encryption domain)
- Which key-management scheme you will use (IKE should be used in the vast majority of cases)
- Which host at the remote site is the CA (only needed if you use SKIP or FWZ)

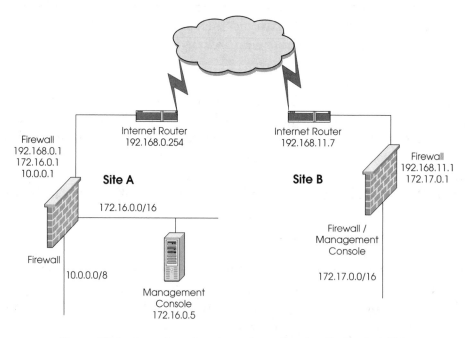

Figure 10-1   Sample network configuration for site-to-site VPN

Site A has networks 10.0.0.0/8 and 172.16.0.0/16 behind its gateway. The encryption domain for Site A should include these networks along with any translated IP addresses for hosts on these networks. Likewise, Site B has the network 172.17.0.0/16 behind its gateway. The encryption domain for Site B should include these networks along with any translated IP addresses for hosts on this network.

Note that it may not be desirable for every host within the various networks to be accessible. This is okay. It is possible to restrict which hosts are accessible via the security policy. The encryption domain simply contains every network and host that could potentially be accessed through the VPN.

Which key-management scheme should you use? Generally speaking, it is your choice as to which one you would like to use, although your choice will depend on the version of FireWall-1 you are using and which firewall (and version) is being used at the remote end. IKE is recommended because it is a widely recognized standard and gives you the most flexibility. SKIP or Manual IPSec should be used in cases where IKE cannot be (e.g., trying to establish a VPN with a FireWall-1 3.x box or with another vendor's VPN product). FWZ is rarely used in site-to-site VPNs these days. The other encryption methods support better encryption schemes and are more standards compliant than the proprietary FWZ.

If you are using FWZ or SKIP for an encryption scheme and are setting up a VPN with a firewall that uses a different management console (i.e., one of a business partner), both ends will need to ensure that their management consoles have valid routable addresses (can be provided with static NAT if necessary) and that the remote firewall is permitted to talk to the local management station using the FW1 service (TCP port 256). This is so they can exchange CA and DH keys, which is necessary to establish the VPN between the sites. If the same management console manages all the firewalls in the VPN, you do not need to define the management console separately.

In this example, Site A's management console is 172.16.0.5. Site B's management console is the same as the firewall: 192.168.1.1. In the case where the remote firewall's management console is on a separate host and it uses a different management console, you must define it in the Rulebase Editor so encryption keys can be fetched correctly. Using the existing example, this means Site B would need to define an object for Site A's management console. On a FireWall-1 3.x or 4.0 system, you would define it as a workstation object that is external, has a host, and has FireWall-1 installed. On a FireWall-1 4.1 system, define it as a workstation object that is an external host and is a management station. Also, make sure "FireWall-1 Installed" is *not* selected. Note that if NAT is involved, use the IP address provided by NAT, not the system's real IP address.

Now that you know the information you need to about the different sides of the VPN, let's talk about how to set this up under the various encryption methods.

Using IKE

It is probably best to start out with the encryption scheme that most people will want to use: IKE. In general, the steps to set up IKE are similar to those that you use for other encryption schemes. The other schemes that are discussed in this chapter will refer back to this section from time to time.

You first need to define the encryption domain for Site A and Site B on both gateways. Site A's encryption domain includes:

- 10.0.0.0/255.0.0.0 (or 10.0.0.0/8)
- 172.16.0.0/255.255.0.0 (or 172.16.0.0/16)

Define network objects for both of these networks. Put them into a group called SiteA-encdomain. Similarly, for Site B, the encryption domain contains 172.17.0.0/255.255.0.0 (or 172.17.0.0/16).

Define a network object for this network. Even though it is only one object, place it into a group called SiteB-encdomain. This makes it easier to expand later.

Once you have done this, you must configure Site A and Site B's local firewall workstation object so that it has both the correct encryption domain and defined encryption keys. Go to Site A's management console, and bring up the workstation object for Site A's firewall. Click the Encryption tab (in version 4.0 and earlier) or the VPN tab (version 4.1 and later). See Figure 10-2.

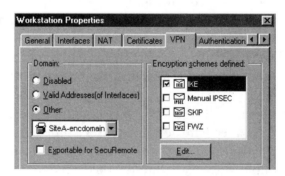

Figure 10-2 Workstation object, VPN tab

On this tab, you define both the encryption domain and the schemes that are defined for encryption. The options for the encryption domain are described as follows:

Disabled: This option means encryption is disabled on this gateway. All of the encryption schemes' check boxes need to be unchecked if this is to remain disabled.

Valid Addresses: This option uses the anti-spoofing defined on this firewall object as the encryption domain. If you think about it, this makes a lot of sense, as the encryption domain is supposed to contain everything behind the gateway, and the anti-spoofing is an accurate reflection of that. Note that "Others" is not considered part of the encryption domain (your external interface is usually defined this way). You can only use this option if you have defined anti-spoofing on your firewall workstation object.

Other: Select the relevant network object or group to reflect your encryption domain.

On Site A's firewall, select Site A's encryption domain. Site B's firewall will have Site B's encryption domain.

Because you are configuring IKE (it will appear as ISAKMP/OAKLEY in 4.0), select IKE under the Encryption Schemes Defined, and click Edit. You are then presented with the dialog shown in Figure 10-3.

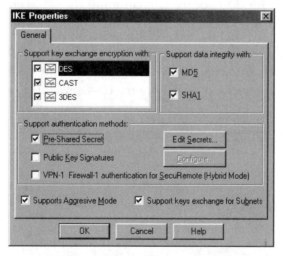

Figure 10-3   Workstation object, VPN tab, IKE Properties

On this tab, you choose the appropriate encryption and data integrity methods this firewall will support. There are also several authentication methods listed on this screen, which include:

Pre-Shared Secrets: If both ends of the VPN lack access to a compatible certificate server, then pre-shared secrets should be used. Once you have defined all of the endpoints of your VPN, you can come back to this dialog, click Edit, and establish a password that is used to authenticate the other end of the connection (both ends of the connection must be configured with the same password).

Public Key Signatures: You can only use this method if you have configured a compatible certificate server and have configured this workstation object to use that certificate server via the Certificates tab in the workstation properties. You can then choose which certificate you would like to use for this host.

VPN-1 FireWall-1 Authentication for SecuRemote (Hybrid Mode): You will only see this method in version 4.1 SP1 and later; it is only relevant for Secu-Remote. This option is discussed in Chapter 11. It is not relevant to a site-to-site VPN configuration.

Supports Aggressive Mode: Instead of doing a standard six-packet IKE Phase 1 key exchange, a three-packet key exchange is used instead. Only use this option if the other endpoints of your VPN are configured to use this.

Support Keys Exchange for Subnets: Versions of FireWall-1 earlier than version 4.1 only supported key exchanges for individual hosts. Version 4.1 supports key exchanges for entire subnets, which significantly reduces the number of key exchanges that are necessary. Use this option if the other endpoints of your VPN are configured for this. Do not use this option if the other endpoint of the VPN is running FireWall-1 4.0. (Note that this screen option does not exist in version 4.0.)

Once you have chosen the various options for Site A's firewall on Site A's management console, you can exit the object. Next, create Site B's firewall's workstation object on Site A's management console. Figure 10-4 shows the workstation properties

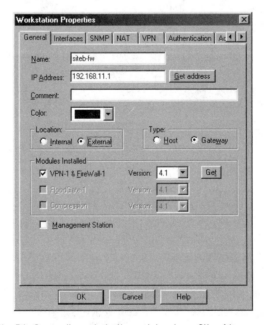

Figure 10-4 Site B's firewall workstation object on Site A's management console

for this object. Note that if the remote end is using a non-Check Point system for encryption, uncheck VPN-1 and FireWall-1 Installed.

Define the encryption domain and IKE parameters accordingly. On Site B's management console, configure Site B's firewall workstation object as Internal and Site A's firewall as External. Otherwise, configure them the same as they are configured on Site A's management console. Once both firewalls are configured, you can then go into the IKE properties on either firewall and configure the pre-shared secret (if necessary). Note that this must be done on both management consoles.

Once you have configured the encryption domains and the firewall objects for encryption, you can then create rules in your rulebase for encryption. The rules, which need to be added to the rulebase at both sites, look like the rules shown in Figure 10-5.

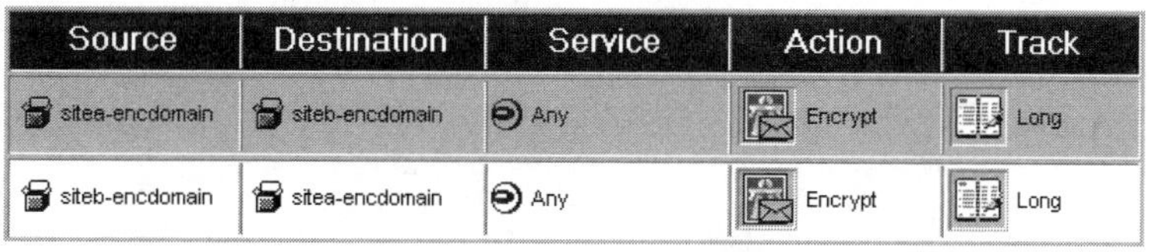

Source	Destination	Service	Action	Track
sitea-encdomain	siteb-encdomain	Any	Encrypt	Long
siteb-encdomain	sitea-encdomain	Any	Encrypt	Long

Figure 10-5 Encryption rules

Note that there are two rules listed: one to permit the traffic from Site A to Site B and one to permit the traffic from Site B to Site A. Although you can certainly combine the two rules into one, I do it this way to suppress the error message "Encryption Failed: gateway connected to both endpoints," which is described in FAQ 10.11 later in this chapter.

The two rules permit everything between the encryption domains. You can make these rules more restrictive by adding a specific service, specific hosts, or both, or even eliminate one of the rules to restrict this to a one way VPN. There is nothing that says you have to allow access to all hosts in the encryption domain; I just do it here for simplicity.

Once these rules are established, you need to configure the Encrypt action for both rules. This configuration specifies the actual encryption methods that will be used. Right-click the Encrypt action on the appropriate rule, and then click Edit Properties. A screen that looks like Figure 10-6 appears.

Select IKE, and click Edit. The screen shown in Figure 10-7 appears.

On this screen, you specify which encryption method (if any) will be used for this rule along with which Peer Gateways are allowed to use these rules (generally this is set to Any). Perfect Forward Secrecy ensures that an eavesdropper who uncovers a long-term encryption key cannot use it to decrypt traffic he or she may have captured in the past. This option is recommended. The defaults for everything else generally suffice,

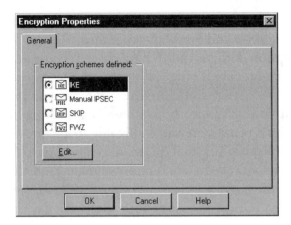

Figure 10-6 Encryption Rule Properties, IKE

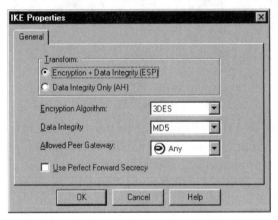

Figure 10-7 Encryption Rule Properties, IKE Properties

but you should verify that the other end of the VPN has the same settings, or you will have problems establishing the VPN.

Check the Rulebase Properties, Encryption tab (see Figure 10-8) for IKE-specific parameters.

These parameters control how often the encryption keys are changed. These values should match on both ends of the VPN.

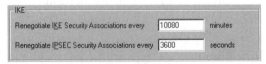

Figure 10-8 Rulebase Properties, Encryption tab, IKE

Once you have set up the properties for both rules and the IKE parameters, install the security policy on both sides, and then test the VPN by trying to communicate through it.

Using Manual IPSec

Although similar in set up to IKE, Manual IPSec is actually a little easier to configure, as there are fewer options you need to configure.

You first need to configure the encryption domain into the firewall workstation objects. Next, make sure Manual IPSec is selected on the VPN or Encryption tab of the firewall workstation object for both Site A and Site B's firewall. There are no options to configure on this screen (if you click the Edit button, you will be told so). Figure 10-9 shows Site B's firewall Workstation Properties VPN tab.

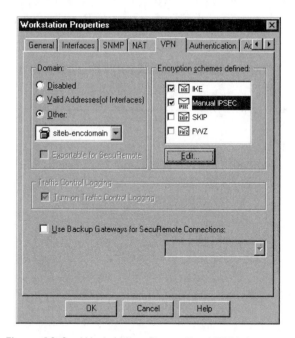

Figure 10-9   Workstation Properties, VPN tab

NOTE!   It is acceptable to have multiple encryption types defined in a workstation object. The encryption rules actually determine which key exchange and encryption method will be used.

You then need to define the SPI that will be used between the two sites. Before doing this, verify what the acceptable range is set to in the Rulebase Properties Encryption tab, as shown in Figure 10-10.

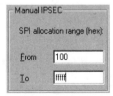

Figure 10-10 Rulebase Properties, Encryption tab, Manual IPSec

The default is from 0x100 to 0xffff (4*f*s). Note that in this example, it has been changed to 0xfffff (5*f*s). Once you have done this, select Keys from the Manage menu. You are then given the option of creating a new SPI value, as shown in Figure 10-11.

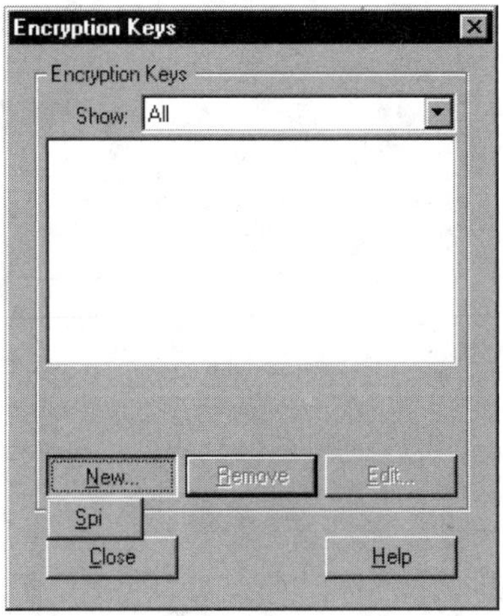

Figure 10-11 Manage Keys

The window shown in Figure 10-12 will then appear.

Enter the SPI you want to use (it must be entered in hex beginning with "0x" and greater than "0x100") and a comment. Then select the appropriate IPSec options, and define the actual encryption keys. If both ends are FireWall-1, you can choose the encryption keys by simply choosing the same seed value on both ends. Both ends of the VPN must agree on what the SPI is and how that SPI is configured.

You can then create your encryption rules as shown earlier. You will need to change the encryption properties for the rules so they use Manual IPSec. Set the Protocol

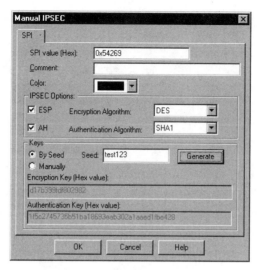

Figure 10-12   Manual IPSec SPI Properties

Diagnostic to Log (if there are problems establishing the VPN, this will give you some hint as to what went wrong). These settings are shown in Figure 10-13.

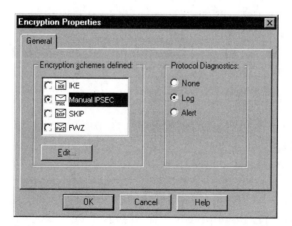

Figure 10-13   Encryption Rule Properties, Manual IPSEC

You need to tell FireWall-1 which SPI you would like to use, so click Edit. You are then presented with a dialog where you specify this SPI, as shown in Figure 10-14.

Once you have set up the properties for both rules, install the security policy on both sides, and test the VPN by trying to communicate through it.

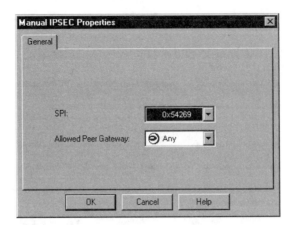

Figure 10-14 Encryption Rule Properties, Manual IPSEC Properties

SKIP and FWZ

SKIP and FWZ involve generating encryption keys locally and then allowing your VPN partner to fetch those keys. This means a couple of extra steps in comparison to the other methods. The steps required to configure SKIP and FWZ are nearly identical, so they are described in the same section. Most of the screen shots provided in this section are from SKIP; however, the screens are nearly identical in FWZ. Any FWZ-specific screen shots are also shown.

SKIP has a dependency on the local system time. Make sure that all related firewalls and management consoles are set with the correct time for the local time (i.e., they should be identical with respect to GMT). If you do not do this, you may have problems establishing a VPN with SKIP.

As with the other encryption schemes, you configure encryption domains into the firewall workstation objects. Next, make sure SKIP or FWZ (as appropriate) is selected in the VPN or Encryption tab of the firewall workstation object for both Site A and Site B's firewall. You then need to define the local firewall's encryption keys. Select SKIP or FWZ as appropriate, and click Edit. A screen that looks like Figure 10-15 appears.

The different key-manager options, which define which CA you are using, include:

None: This option is only used in SKIP when the remote end of the connection does not use a FireWall-1 management console (i.e., a third-party SKIP implementation). FireWall-1 can import Unsigned DH keys, which FireWall-1 is capable of generating as well.

Local: If this particular management console is the management console used for this firewall, select Local. For example, on Site A's management console, you would select Local on the workstation object for Site A's firewall. Note that if all of

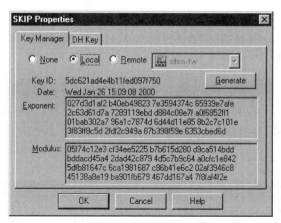

Figure 10-15   Workstation Properties, VPN tab, SKIP Properties, Key Manager tab

the other fields (Key ID, Date, etc.) are blank, you need to click Generate to generate a new CA key.

Remote: If this management station is not used to manage this firewall object, select Remote. You will either select the remote firewall object itself (if the firewall and management are on the same host) or the management console for that host (if the firewall and management are on different hosts). For example, on Site A's management console, when defining Site B's firewall workstation object, you would select Site B's firewall workstation object. On Site B's management console, when defining Site A's firewall workstation object, you would set the object that represents Site A's management console.

Once you have selected the appropriate CA, select the DH Key tab, which is shown in Figure 10-16.

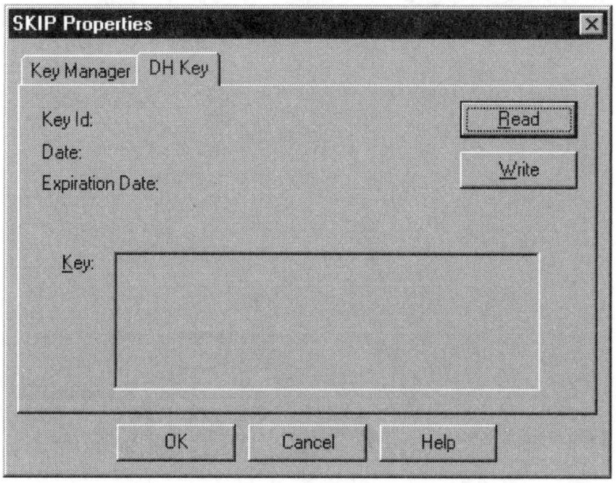

Figure 10-16   Workstation Properties, VPN tab, SKIP Properties, DH Key tab

Click Generate to generate a new encryption key. The Key ID, Date, and Expiration Date should populate with information. If you have to interact with a third-party SKIP implementation, you can save the key generated as an unsigned DH key by clicking Write.

Once both sites have generated their CA and DH keys, you need to create a rule to permit the two management consoles to fetch the CA and DH keys. For Site A and Site B, the rules should be placed above any stealth rules and look like the rule shown in Figure 10-17. Remember that Site B uses the firewall as its management console.

Source	Destination	Service	Action	Track
sitea-mgmt siteb-fw	siteb-fw sitea-mgmt	FW1	accept	Long

Figure 10-17   Rule to permit CA and DH key exchange

Install the security policy on both sides. This will make this rule take effect and save the encryption-key information so the remote site can fetch it.

You then need to set up the remote firewall on each management console. Let's walk through setting up Site A's firewall on Site B's management console. The steps are identical on Site A's management console except you are configuring the information for Site B. Go to the workstation object for Site A's firewall, go to the VPN tab, configure the correct encryption domain, select FWZ or SKIP as appropriate, and click Edit. You then want to set the Key Manager to Remote and select Site A's management console, as shown in Figure 10-18.

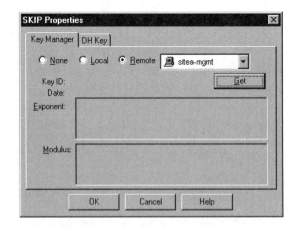

Figure 10-18   Workstation Properties, VPN tab, SKIP Properties, Key Manager tab, Remote Manager

Click Get. You will be given a warning about having fetched the public key *without authentication*. Normally, any keys fetched are signed, so you know if they have been tampered with. Because this is the first time these two firewalls have exchanged information, they have no information on each other. The dialog asks you to manually verify the information received. An easy way to do this is to read the Key ID to your partner over a secure channel to see if the IDs match.

Once you have done this, go to the DH Key tab, and click Fetch to get the DH key for the remote firewall. The information will populate the various fields. Because you are done fetching the encryption keys, you can define the encryption rules, which are the same as the ones for the other encryption methods except for the Encryption Properties. Select FWZ or SKIP as your encryption type, and then click Edit. If you choose SKIP, the screen will look like Figure 10-19.

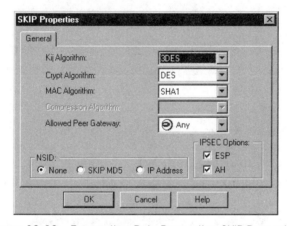

Figure 10-19 Encryption Rule Properties, SKIP Properties

The SKIP Properties on this screen are described as follows:

Kij Algorithm: Kij refers to the encryption keys in SKIP and how they are encrypted for both authentication and encryption.

Crypt Algorithm: Encryption method used for data encryption.

MAC Algorithm: Method used for data integrity checking.

Allowed Peer Gateway: Controls which firewalls this rule will allow you to talk to. Generally, this can be left as "Any."

NSID: Name Space ID, which controls how the encryption keys are stored in the SKIP headers. None means that they are stored directly in the packet, SKIP MD5 means they are an MD5 hash based on the Diffie-Hellman public keys, and IP Address means they are an MD5 hash based on the system's IP address.

IPSec Options: ESP means encryption, and AH means authentication. Typically, both of these options are selected. If only AH is checked, no encryption will be performed.

If you choose FWZ, the screen looks like Figure 10-20.

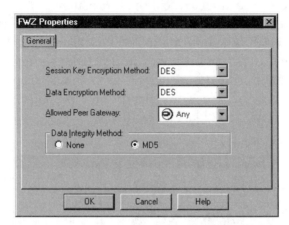

Figure 10-20 Encryption Rule Properties, FWZ Properties

The FWZ Properties on this screen are described as follows:

Session Key Encryption Method: When an encryption key is established, it is encrypted with this method. Clear means it is sent in the clear (not recommended). Any means use any of the supported schemes, autonegotiating the best choice.

Data Encryption Method: When data is encrypted, it is done with this method. Clear means it is sent in the clear (not recommended). Any means use any supported scheme.

Allowed Peer Gateway: Controls which firewalls this rule will allow you to talk to. Generally, this can be left as "Any."

Data Integrity Method: Provides a check to ensure that the encrypted data has not been tampered with. This setting can either be None or MD5.

You also need to configure how frequently SKIP will change the encryption keys and whether or not to use Exportable (i.e., 40-bit) Encryption methods. You do this on the Rulebase Properties Encryption tab, as shown in Figure 10-21.

Configure the Exportable SKIP option as necessary. Generally speaking, the defaults for how often SKIP changes encryption keys are sufficient, but verify that the other end of the VPN uses the same parameters.

Once you have set up the properties for both rules, install the security policy on both sides, and test the VPN by trying to communicate through it.

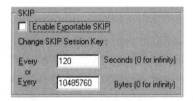

Figure 10-21   Rulebase Properties, Encryption tab, SKIP

Gateway Clusters for High-Availability VPNs

Gateway Clusters are a new feature incorporated into FireWall-1 4.1 that allow for High-Availability (HA) VPNs in combination with third-party HA products, which includes the Nokia-based VPN-1 Appliance. It, along with FireWall-1's State Synchronization Mechanism, allows for a secondary gateway to be able to process encrypted traffic in the event the primary firewall fails. The Gateway Cluster object can only be utilized if an underlying HA solution is present. This could be Stonesoft's Stonebeat Full Cluster, IPSO's VRRP, Rainfinity's Rainwall, or Check Point's own HA Module. You also need to have your management console on a separate platform from the systems that you intend to configure into a Gateway Cluster.

A Gateway Cluster is nothing more than a virtual firewall. It takes two or more firewalls in an HA configuration and makes them appear as a single entity for the purposes of installing a security policy and encryption. Setting up a VPN involving Gateway Clusters is not very different from setting up a VPN involving a single gateway. The moment you make a firewall workstation object part of a Gateway Cluster, many of the tabs in the workstation properties simply disappear. This configuration needs to be done from the Gateway Cluster object. When you configure the VPN-related parameters for the firewall, you configure them on the Gateway Cluster object, not on the workstation object for the firewalls that are members of the Gateway Cluster.

To enable Gateway Clusters, you need to select the option on the Rulebase Properties High Availability tab, as shown in Figure 10-22.

You must have the "Enable Gateway Clusters" check box selected. Optionally, you can also select the "Install Security Policy on Gateway Cluster" check box if you want to ensure that you have the same policy installed on all members of the Gateway Cluster. This is highly recommended.

You can then create a Gateway Cluster object, which is shown in Figure 10-23.

The IP address you use for this object should be an IP address that addresses the "virtual" firewall. All of the HA schemes have some sort of concept of a virtual IP address. This IP address points to whichever firewall is active. When a failover occurs, it points to a different firewall. This is the IP address you should use for your Gateway Cluster object.

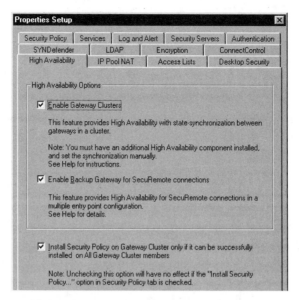

Figure 10-22   Rulebase Properties, High Availability tab

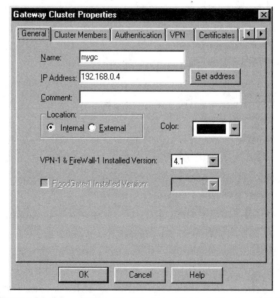

Figure 10-23   Gateway Cluster object, General tab

NOTE!   If you are using an IPSO-based box with Gateway Clusters, make sure you are running version 4.1 SP1 or later. It is not possible to directly use the VRRP IP address as a Gateway Cluster address with version 4.1 Base Release.

Notice that Gateway Cluster Properties has many of the same tabs as a normal workstation object. In this object, you define the shared properties, such as encryption keys, certificates, and allowed encryption types. You must go into each of the firewall workstation objects and make them part of the Gateway Cluster object. Once you have done this, various tabs from the workstation object will disappear, as shown in Figure 10-24.

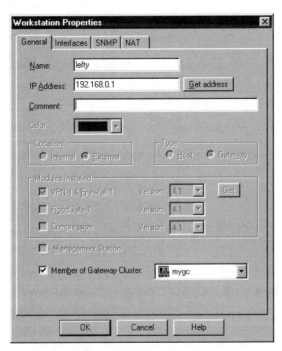

Figure 10-24   Workstation Properties, Member of Gateway Cluster, General tab

When you are defining the remote end of the VPN and it is a Gateway Cluster, you simply treat it as if it were a single-firewall object. You can simply refer to a remote Gateway Cluster with a single-workstation object. However, you need to define the Interfaces tab. Include all of the IP addresses on all gateways in the Gateway Cluster including the Gateway Cluster IP address. An example of this is shown in Figure 10-25.

The interfaces' names and the net masks are not important, because you are not using this as a basis for enforcing anti-spoofing. What is important is that you enter all of the IPs.

The Gateway Cluster feature was only designed to work with IKE and FWZ. Even though it might work with other encryption methods, Check Point only supports IKE and FWZ in a Gateway Cluster configuration.

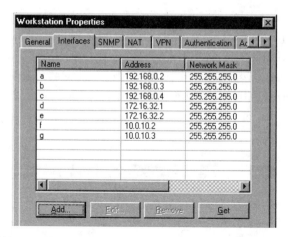

Figure 10-25 Workstation Properties, Member of Gateway Cluster, Interfaces tab

Due to how Gateway Clusters work, there are some interoperability issues with Gateway Clusters and third-party VPN products. These issues, along with solutions, are documented in the next section.

Frequently Asked Questions about VPNs in FireWall-1

Some questions that are frequently asked about VPNs in FireWall-1 are as follows.

10.1: Does FireWall-1 Interoperate with Third-Party VPN Products?

Generally, yes. Usually it is a matter of making sure the settings match on both ends. This is made somewhat difficult because each vendor refers to a setting with a slightly different name.

10.2: Does the Gateway Clusters Feature Interoperate with Third-Party VPN Products?

Versions prior to 4.1 SP3 had a problem interoperating with non-Check Point firewalls. This is because encrypted packets would originate from the system's real IP address, not the Gateway Cluster address.

A new feature present in FireWall-1 4.1 SP3 and later allows FireWall-1 to interoperate with other VPN products when using Gateway Clusters. Effectively, these features NAT the packets to the appropriate address. Both the firewalls and management console must be running FireWall-1 4.1 SP3 or later. Add the following properties to the `:props (` section in `$FWDIR/conf/objects.C` on the management module:

```
:IPSec_main_if_nat (true)
:IPSec_cluster_nat (true)
```

For more information about editing `objects.C`, see Chapter 4, FAQ 4.2.

NOTE! On IPSO, there are problems with failovers with Gateway Clusters and third-party VPN products when the ifwd process is disabled. Ensure that the ifwd process is enabled in Voyager.

10.3: Can I Run Microsoft Networking Protocols through a VPN?

If you use the IPSec-based protocols, yes, you can, because these protocols encapsulate the traffic in new packets. If you use FWZ and you have a nonroutable address, you cannot easily do this, because you must employ some nonstandard NAT rules and routing to make this work. It's not impossible, but it's not pretty either and will not be covered in this text.

10.4: Can I Set up a VPN with a Site without Giving It Access to All My Machines?

Yes. Even though your encryption domain typically contains everything behind your gateway, you can set up the rules in such a way so the other site can only access certain machines. Note that this does not prevent the site from using the allowed services and destination to access other machines inside your network.

10.5: Can I Set up More Than One VPN with Different Sites Each Using Different Encryption Schemes?

Yes, you can. The "Sample Configuration" section of this chapter provides an example where this is done.

10.6: Can I Set up More Than One VPN with Different Sites and Use a Different Source IP Address for Each Site?

Unfortunately, no. FireWall-1 uses the node name IP address as the source IP address for IPSec packets. This means that for each site with which you set up a VPN, the node name IP address of your firewall must be routable. Note that if each site is reachable from a different interface, you can add the `:IPSec_main_if_nat` property to `objects.C` in FireWall-1 4.1 SP3 or later, as documented in FAQ 10.2. This property will NAT the IPSec packet with the interface's main IP address.

10.7: Does FireWall-1 Support a "Hub and Spoke" Model Like Some VPN Hardware Devices Support?

A "hub and spoke" model means that all remote sites only know about the main hub site. When a remote site (a spoke) wants to communicate with another site, including the main site or even the Internet, the data is encrypted and sent to the main site. The main site knows how to get to everyone. The data is then decrypted, re-encrypted if necessary, and sent on to the appropriate site. This makes configuration of the spoke sites very easy, although it adds additional overhead because the data must traverse two sites.

FireWall-1 does not support this kind of configuration. Sites that want to talk to one another do so directly over the Internet via the VPN. If a particular site wants to communicate to a host over the Internet, that site must be able to communicate to the Internet directly. This is referred to as a *mesh* model.

10.8: How Does NAT Interact with Encryption?

NAT is applied before a packet is encrypted or applied after decryption. You can utilize both NAT and encryption if you need to, but unless you are using FWZ, it is generally not necessary to use both NAT and encryption. I usually suggest creating rules in your NAT rulebase that do not NAT any traffic between the encryption domains. Figure 10-26 shows an example of a rule you would use on Site A's security policy.

Original Packet			Translated Packet			Install On
Source	Destination	Service	Source	Destination	Service	
sitea-encdomain	siteb-encdomain	Any	Original	Original	Original	GW Gateways

Figure 10-26 Rules for disabling NAT between encryption domains

If you do decide to use NAT, make sure you include any translated addresses in the encryption domain.

10.9: Can I Require User Authentication in Addition to Encryption?

Yes, you can. There is an example of how to do this in the "Sample Configurations" section of this chapter.

Troubleshooting VPN Problems

The following is a list of common problems and resolutions that relate to establishing a VPN. Note that any error messages you see in the Log Viewer are documented in the Check Point manuals. Some of the more-common error messages follow.

10.10: General Troubleshooting Guidelines for VPN Problems

Ensure that the appropriate kinds of traffic are being permitted between the two endpoints. If there are any filtering routers along the way, make sure they permit the following protocols:

- IP Protocols 50 and 51 (for any IPSec-related scheme)
- UDP Port 500 (for IKE)
- UDP Port 259 (for RDP for FWZ)

Also, you should make sure that there is no NAT being performed on any of these packets.

There are times when you may need to put explicit rules in the firewall permitting this traffic. In most cases, this isn't necessary, but it may be necessary from time to time. The rules are shown in Figure 10-27.

Source	Destination	Service	Action	Track	Install On
siteb-fw sitea-fw	sitea-fw siteb-fw	IPSEC IKE RDP SKIP	accept	Long	Gateways

Figure 10-27 Rules permitting encryption traffic between firewalls

Note that this rule contains all the protocols. Include only the protocols you need depending on which encryption scheme you use (IKE and IPSec for IKE, IPSec for Manual IPSec, SKIP for SKIP, and RDP for FWZ).

You may also want to use a packet sniffer (`tcpdump`, `snoop`, `fw monitor`) to verify that packets are reaching the gateway. If the packets are not reaching the gateway, FireWall-1 cannot encrypt or decrypt them.

10.11: Crypt Rule X Not Found

This error message appears on your console when you have defined multiple objects with the same IP address, and one of them is your gateway. Perhaps you defined one as a host for address translation purposes and one with all the encryption keys. This confuses FireWall-1. Only one object should be defined per IP address.

10.12: Encryption Failed: Gateway Connected to Both Endpoints

This is not a fatal error message but will crop up if you decide to combine the encryption rules into one, such as in Figure 10-28.

This means that the gateway is seeing traffic originating from the same encryption domain it is destined for (usually broadcast traffic). This is the main reason I suggest using two rules for encryption.

Source	Destination	Service	Action	Track	Install On
sitea-encdomain siteb-encdomain	siteb-encdomain sitea-encdomain	Any	Encrypt	Long	Gateways

Figure 10-28 Combined encryption rule

10.13: Encryption Failure: One of the Keys Is Not Yet A Valid Scheme: SKIP

This error message means that the clocks on one of the two firewalls are not synchronized. SKIP relies on the date and time being the same (or within a few minutes) on all the machines in the VPN. Set the machines to the same time relative to GMT (each machine can be in a different time zone, thus have a different "local" time), completely regenerate the CA and DH keys for SKIP, refetch all the keys, reinstall the security policy, and it should work fine. You can also use Network Time Protocol (NTP) to keep the firewalls in sync as well.

10.14: Peer Failed to Reply

This error usually means one of the following:

- The encryption domains are not correct. The encryption domain for firewall A should contain all the hosts behind A and any translated IP addresses (including hides). The firewall should be included if it is used as the hide address. The same is true for firewall B—all the hosts behind B, any translated IPs, and B itself if it is used as a hide address.

- The remote end does not currently have a rule that will decrypt the packet.

- If FWZ or SKIP is used, the encryption keys are not defined (correctly) on both firewall objects. Regenerate the DH keys and reinstall the security policy on both firewalls. If the firewalls are managed by separate management consoles, refetch the encryption keys, and reinstall the security policy a second time.

- The remote firewall is not set up with encryption at all.

- The remote firewall is set up with the wrong protocol (one side is FWZ; the other is SKIP).

- Something is blocking communication between the VPN endpoints. Check to make sure the remote firewall is properly receiving the IP packets by using a packet sniffer. For FWZ, look for UDP port 259 packets. For Manual IPSec or SKIP, look for IP Protocol 57 packets, IP Protocol 50, or IP Protocol 51 packets. For ISAKMP, look for UDP port 500 packets.

- If FWZ is used and you are communicating from and/or to nonroutable addresses, it will not work, because FWZ does not change the IP headers. You must either employ static NAT (include the static NAT IPs in the encryption domain) or use an IPSec-based protocol.

- If you are using FireWall-1 4.1 SP2 build 15 on IPSO 3.2.1, the problem may result from packets coming from the wrong IP address (i.e., a VRRP address instead of the real one). You can verify that this is the case by using `tcpdump` on the external interface and viewing the source IP address of the packets. This would cause IPSec negotiations to fail. This problem is addressed in IPSO 3.3 and FireWall-1 4.1 SP2 build 24.

10.15: GUI Crashes When Editing Encryption Keys

The file that stores these keys, $FWDIR/conf/fwauth.NDB, has become corrupt. Unfortunately, this is also the user database file, so you must export and reimport the user database into a brand-new fwauth.NDB file, not to mention regenerate the encryption keys. The necessary steps to resolve this are:

1. Make a list of the user groups you have created for your users. This list will be used in the export and import of the user database later on.

2. Quit any GUIs that are running. Run the following command, which will export your users to $FWDIR/conf/users.export:

   # **fw dbexport -f users.export**

3. Make backup copies of your user database and rulebase files:

   # **cd $FWDIR/conf**
   # **cp fwauth.NDB fwauth.NDB.bak**
   # **cp rulebases.fws rulebases.fws.bak**
   # **mkdir bak**
   # **cp *.W bak**

4. Remove your user database file:

   # **rm fwauth.NDB**

5. Go back into the GUI, and re-create all the user groups. Quit the GUI when you are done.

6. Check to see which rulebase files (*.W, rulebases.fws) have recently been modified. Restore these files from the backups you made previously. Most likely, rulebases.fws will have been modified:

   # **cp rulebases.fws.bak rulebases.fws**

7. Reimport your users database as follows:

   # **fw dbimport -r -v -f users.export**

8. If any errors pop up, you will need to manually massage users.export in a text editor. Keep trying to import and massage users.export until the import succeeds.

9. Regenerate your FWZ CA and DH keys, which is necessary if you are using FWZ encryption. If your firewall object was called *tinderbox,* the commands would look like this:

```
# fw keygen -manage
# fw keygen tinderbox
```

10. If you manage other firewalls, you should also regenerate their DH keys. For instance, if you manage bricks and thewall, you would type:

```
# fw keygen bricks
# fw keygen thewall
```

11. Regenerate your SKIP CA and DH keys, which is necessary if you are using SKIP encryption. If your firewall object was called *tinderbox,* the commands would look like this:

```
# fw keygen -s skip -manage
# fw keygen -s skip tinderbox
```

12. If you manage other firewalls, you should also regenerate their DH keys. For instance, if you manage bricks and thewall, you would type:

```
# fw keygen -s skip bricks
# fw keygen -s skip thewall
```

13. Reload the GUI, and install your security policy and user database on any firewalls you manage.

If you have VPN partners that you work with, they will have to refetch your CA and DH keys. SecuRemote users may have to delete and re-add the site in order to be functional again.

10.16: ISAKMP AddNegotiation: Try to Handle Too Many Negotiations

FireWall-1 4.0 and 4.1 can handle roughly 100 ISAKMP key negotiations at once. As this is an architectural limit in the Check Point code, it cannot be increased. Check Point will supposedly allow for more negotiations in its next major release, FireWall-1 NG (Next Generation).

A key negotiation occurs when a connection is first established from one host to another. If you see this message, it means that FireWall-1 is handling more than 100 key negotiations at once. Connections that have this message associated with them in the log will fail. FireWall-1 4.0 does not support subnet key negotiation, which means a key has to be exchanged for each host that communicates rather than for the entire subnet. This means FireWall-1 has to do far more key negotiations in version 4.0 than in 4.1, which supports this. If you cannot upgrade to version 4.1 (which is highly recommended if you use IKE), consider changing your encryption scheme to Manual IPSec or SKIP.

10.17: Debugging Interoperability Issues with IKE

Everyone has a different interpretation about how to follow standards. As a result, when third-party products talk to one another, communication doesn't always work. The good news is that FireWall-1 4.1 has a more compliant IKE implementation than previous versions of FireWall-1. It is highly recommended that you upgrade to FireWall-1 4.1 if you need to talk to third-party IKE implementations.

If you are having problems with a third-party IKE implementation, you can gather more information by turning on the IKE debugging flags. Set the environment value `FWIKE_DEBUG=1` in FireWall-1 4.1 (`FWISAKMP_DEBUG=1` in FireWall-1 4.0), and rerun the FireWall-1 daemon (do: `fwstop; fwstart`). All subsequent IKE negotiations will be dumped in `$FWDIR/log/IKE.elg` in FireWall-1 4.1or `$FWDIR/log/ISAKMP.log` in FireWall-1 4.0. This file should be sent to Check Point Support regarding IKE issues whenever you contact technical support.

10.18: Traceroute Does Not Appear to Work through a VPN

Check Point currently does not support traceroute through an IPSec VPN. A request for enhancement has been filed with Check Point on this issue.

Traceroute works by sending out packets with successively larger Time To Live (TTL) values. It is explained in more depth in Chapter 1. Each hop along the way generally returns an ICMP Time Exceeded, an ICMP Destination Unreachable message, or an ICMP Echo Reply.

In an IPSec VPN, all communication between the sites is encapsulated. When FireWall-1 encapsulates a traceroute packet, the new packet inherits the TTL value of the packet being encapsulated. As a result, each hop between the firewalls sends an ICMP Time Exceeded packet back to the firewall. These packets are ignored by the firewall. The user will see these messages in their traceroute as "request timed out."

10.19: VPN Fails When Transferring Large Packets

Some applications set the Don't Fragment bit on certain packets. When the IPSec headers are added onto the already large packet, the packet will require fragmentation in order to pass through the firewall. When Check Point creates the IPSec packet, the Don't Fragment bit from the original packet is maintained. FireWall-1 creates a fragmented packet that has the Don't Fragment bit set, so it cannot be fragmented and thus will get dropped at the next router.

You can force FireWall-1 to clear the Don't Fragment bit by setting the `fw_ipsec_dont_fragment` kernel variable to zero. See Appendix I for details on how to do this.

Summary

VPNs are an increasingly important technology as companies expand, merge, acquire, and partner with others. Having a basic understanding of the terminology is important. There are many different ways you can establish a VPN with FireWall-1, and some ways you cannot. You now know how to establish a site-to-site VPN in FireWall-1 and troubleshoot when things go wrong.

Sample Configurations

The following three situations presented are representative of situations I have come across in the real world. Each is designed to demonstrate what people typically do with site-to-site VPNs and how the situations would be implemented on the chosen platform.

A Three-Site VPN

The Situation

You are the firewall administrator with a company that has several sites. The main sites are in Spokane (where corporate headquarters are), Sacramento, and London. Until recently, a private WAN was used to connect the various sites to one another. It is now desirable to use an IPSec VPN based on Check Point FireWall-1 4.1 to connect these sites, as it is more cost-efficient. IKE with pre-shared secrets is the desired method. The main management console in Spokane manages the firewalls at the remote sites. No NAT is involved. Assume that all IPs are routable. Figure 10-29 shows a simplified network diagram.

The Goals

- Allow all hosts behind each of the three networks to communicate with each other unencumbered.
- Allow the remote firewalls to be remotely managed over the Internet.
- All sites are allowed to access sites on the Internet via FTP, HTTP, or HTTPS.
- SMTP can originate from predefined SMTP servers inside the Spokane network to the Internet (they are in a group called SMTP-Servers).
- SMTP can go to the external-smtp server from anywhere (external-smtp-server is already defined).
- Deny all other traffic.

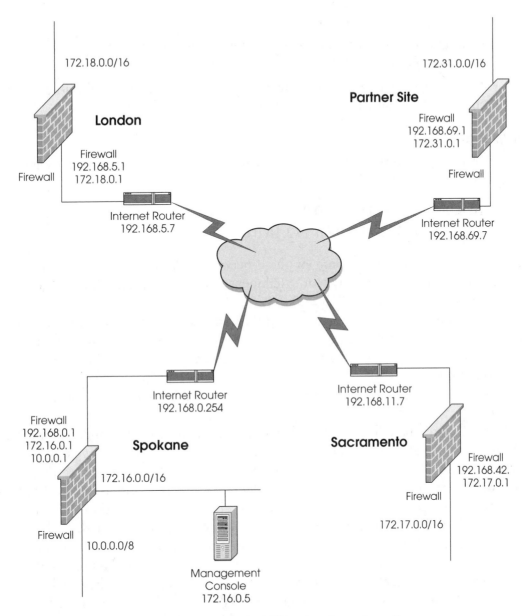

Figure 10-29 A three-site VPN network configuration

Checklist

- Define the encryption domains for each site.
- Define the firewall workstation objects for each site.
- Configure the firewall workstation objects for the correct encryption domain, and use IKE with pre-shared secrets.

- Create the necessary encryption rules.
- Configure the encryption properties for each encryption rule.
- Install the security policy.
- Make the appropriate changes to the internal routing to allow traffic to flow through the firewalls across the VPN.

Implementation

You first need to define the encryption domain for the three sites. Spokane's encryption domain is:

- 10.0.0.0/255.0.0.0 (or 10.0.0.0/8)
- 172.16.0.0/255.255.0.0 (or 172.16.0.0/16)

Define network objects for both of these networks. Place them in a group called spokane-encdomain. Similarly, for Sacramento, the encryption domain contains 172.17.0.0/255.255.0.0 (or 172.17.0.0/16).

Define a network object for this network. Even though it is only one object, place it into a group called sacramento-encdomain. This makes it easier to expand later. Similarly, for London, the encryption domain contains 172.18.0.0/255.255.0.0 (or 172.18.0.0/16).

Define a network object for this network. Place it into a group called london-encdomain.

Chances are, these firewalls have been remotely managed, so you do not need to create the workstation objects for the firewalls. They should all be defined as Internal Gateway with FireWall-1 installed. However, you need to modify them so they have the correct encryption domains and are configured to use IKE. Go to the Workstation Properties for each of the firewalls, select the appropriate encryption domain, and enable IKE and pre-shared secrets (the other options can be left at their defaults). When you get to the last firewall, edit the shared secrets. You will see all of the other firewalls. The pre-shared secrets on London's firewall are shown in Figure 10-30.

Click a firewall, click Edit, type in the desired shared secret, and then click Set. Do this for each firewall listed. The shared secret will be established for all the firewalls. You do not need to go to each workstation object individually and set these passwords—this will set it globally.

FireWall-1 management functions employ their own encryption, which uses an encryption scheme called fwa1 with a key size of 192 bits. For remote management to continue to work correctly, you must make sure this traffic is excluded from the VPN and that this traffic is allowed. These rules should appear before the VPN rules. If you enable FireWall-1 Control Connections in the Rulebase Properties, you do not need these rules.

Figure 10-30 Workstation object, VPN tab, IKE Properties, Pre-Shared Secrets

You can then create all the necessary rules, which are shown in Figure 10-31.

No.	Source	Destination	Service	Action	Track	Install On
1	spokane-mgmt	sacramento-fw, london-fw, spokane-fw	FW1	accept		Gateways
2	sacramento-fw, london-fw, spokane-fw	spokane-mgmt	FW1, FW1_log	accept		Gateways
3	sacramento-fw, spokane-fw, london-fw	sacramento-fw, spokane-fw, london-fw	IKE	accept	Long	Gateways
4	sacramento-encdomain	spokane-encdomain, london-encdomain	Any	Encrypt	Long	Gateways
5	spokane-encdomain	sacramento-encdomain, london-encdomain	Any	Encrypt	Long	Gateways
6	london-encdomain	sacramento-encdomain, spokane-encdomain	Any	Encrypt	Long	Gateways
7	sacramento-encdomain, spokane-encdomain, london-encdomain	Any	telnet, http, https	accept		Gateways
8	SMTP-Servers	Any	smtp	accept		Gateways
9	Any	external-smtp-server	smtp	accept		Gateways
10	Any	Any	Any	drop	Long	Gateways

Figure 10-31 Rulebase for a three-site VPN

You need to edit the encryption properties for Rules 4, 5, and 6 so that they do IKE. The defaults should suffice except that Perfect Forward Secrecy[4] should be enabled.

---

4. Perfect Forward Secrecy ensures that an eavesdropper who uncovers a long-term encryption key will be unable to use it to decrypt traffic sent in the past.

Notes

This is a somewhat simplified example. Most sites have far more complex security policies. Just make sure your VPN rules are listed before any rules that allow outbound traffic to the Internet.

Adding a Business Partner to the VPN Mesh
The Situation

A business partner would like to be able to come in and update information on a particular UNIX Web server at the Spokane site's DMZ (172.16.0.80). The information would be transferred via Telnet or FTP. Because the information is very confidential in nature, it would be desirable to do this in a secure fashion. Because the business partner also uses FireWall-1 (albeit a single gateway 50-user license of FireWall-1 3.0), it is determined that a SKIP-based VPN would be the best way to go. There is no reason to access the partner site through the VPN, so access is only needed one way. In addition to being encrypted, strong authentication is desired. It is impractical to do the authentication on the UNIX Web server, so the firewall needs to be able to provide this functionality. S/Key is deemed acceptable for an authentication scheme.

In the context of this lab, the local site refers to Spokane, and the remote site refers to the partner site. Figure 10-32 shows the new network map.

The Goals

- Maintain the previous security policy as much as possible (from the previous lab).
- Allow the remote site to access 172.16.0.80 via FTP and Telnet with authentication using S/Key authentication, and encrypt the communication.

Checklist

- Define the encryption domains for each site.
- Define the firewall workstation objects for each site.
- Configure the firewall workstation objects for the correct encryption domain, and use SKIP.
- Create the necessary rules so the CA and DH keys can be fetched.
- Create the necessary encryption rules.
- Configure the encryption properties for each encryption rule.
- Install the security policy.

Implementation

At the local site, you need to create an encryption domain for the remote site's encryption domain, which is 172.31.0.0/16. For this example, call it *partner-encdomain*. At

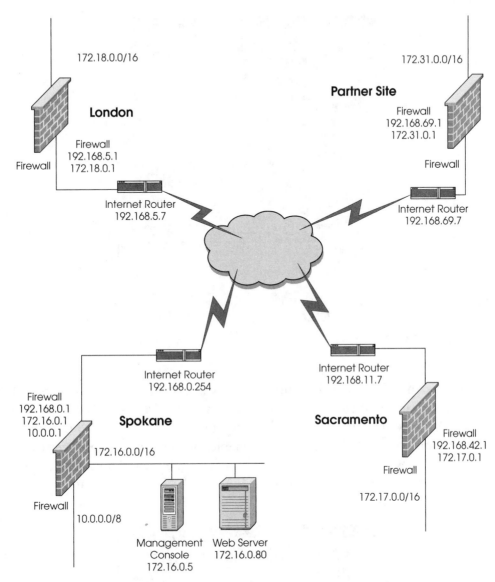

172.18.0.0/16

172.31.0.0/16

Partner Site

London

Firewall
192.168.69.1
172.31.0.1

Firewall
192.168.5.1
172.18.0.1

Firewall

Firewall

Internet Router
192.168.5.7

Internet Router
192.168.69.7

Internet Router
192.168.0.254

Internet Router
192.168.11.7

Firewall
192.168.0.1
172.16.0.1
10.0.0.1

Spokane

Sacramento

172.16.0.0/16

Firewall
192.168.42.1
172.17.0.1

Firewall

Firewall

10.0.0.0/8

172.17.0.0/16

Management
Console
172.16.0.5

Web Server
172.16.0.80

Figure 10-32   The three-site VPN with a business partner

the partner site, you need to create an encryption domain for the remote site (which, in this case, is Spokane). Because the only host that will be accessible will be the Web Server at 172.16.0.80, the encryption domain could simply be this host. Put a work-station object for this host in a group called *spokane-encdomain.*

On Spokane's management console, create a workstation object for the remote firewall. Configure it as shown in Figure 10-33.

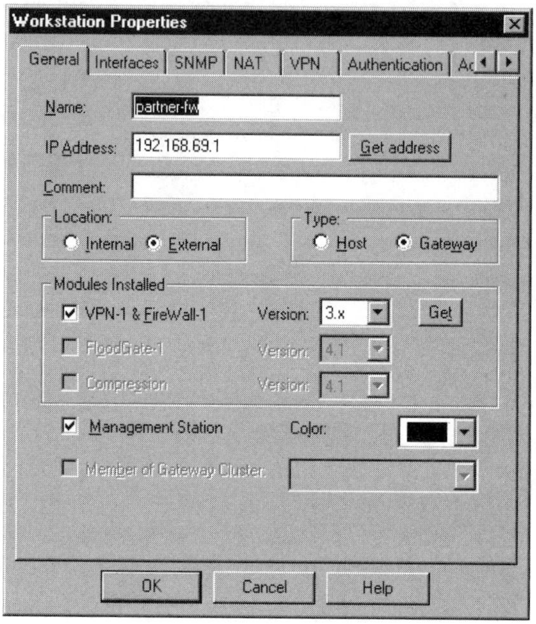

Figure 10-33 Definition of partner's firewall on Spokane's management console

On the partner site's firewall, define two network objects, one for the firewall and one for the management console. Define them as shown in Figures 10-34 and 10-35 (note that these are version 3.x screen shots because the remote firewall is using 3.x).

On Spokane's firewall, SKIP needs to be enabled and encryption keys need to be generated. Go to the Workstation Properties VPN tab for the firewall object. Select SKIP as an encryption type, and click Edit. Generate CA and DH keys as necessary.

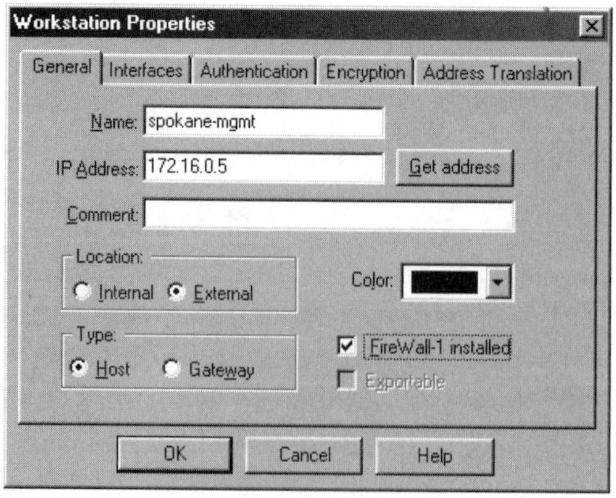

Figure 10-34 Definition of Spokane's management console at partner site

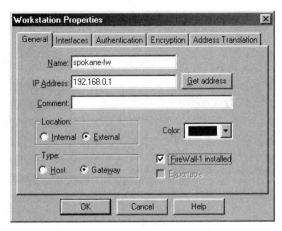

Figure 10-35 Definition of Spokane's firewall at partner site

On the partner site's firewall, administrators for that site will go to the Workstation Properties for its firewall, enable SKIP, and generate CA and DH keys as necessary.

Both sites will then add the rule shown in Figure 10-36 to their rulebase and install the rulebase.

Source	Destination	Service	Action	Track	Install On
spokane-mgmt partner-fw	partner-fw spokane-mgmt	FW1	accept		Gateways

Figure 10-36 Rule permitting key exchange between firewalls

You then need to set up the remote firewall on each management console. On Spokane's firewall, go to the partner's firewall Workstation Properties VPN tab. Select its encryption domain, select SKIP as the supported scheme, and click Edit. Specify your partner's management console as the Key Manager. In this case, it is your partner's firewall, as shown in Figure 10-37.

Click Get. You will be given a warning about having fetched the public key *without authentication*. The dialog will ask you to manually verify the information received. An easy way to do this is to read the Key ID to your partner over a secure channel and see if the Key IDs match. Once you have done this, go to the DH Key tab, and click Fetch to get the DH key for the remote firewall. The information will populate the various fields.

On the partner site's firewall, you need to edit the Spokane firewall's Workstation Properties Encryption tab (remember, the partner site is running FireWall-1 3.0). Set

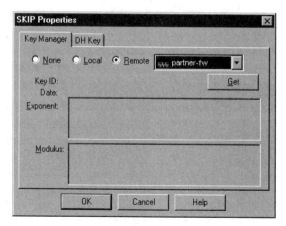

Figure 10-37 Workstation Properties, VPN tab, SKIP Properties for partner on Spokane

the encryption domain, select SKIP as the supported scheme, and then click Edit. Specify the management console for Spokane's firewall as the CA, as shown in Figure 10-38.

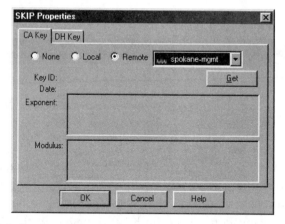

Figure 10-38 Workstation Properties, Encryption tab, SKIP Properties for Spokane on partner

Click Get. You will be given a warning about having fetched the public key *without authentication*. The dialog will ask you to manually verify the information received. An easy way to do this is to read the Key ID to your partner over a secure channel and see if the Key IDs match. Once you have done this, go to the DH Key tab, and click Fetch to get the DH key for the remote firewall. The information will populate the various fields.

At the partner site, the administrator simply needs to create two rules for encryption: one to permit the SKIP traffic, and the other to perform the encryption. These rules are shown in Figure 10-39.

Source	Destination	Service	Action	Track	Install On
spokane-mgmt partner-fw	partner-fw spokane-mgmt	SKIP	accept		Gateways
partner-encdomain	spokane-encdomain	Any	Encrypt	Long	Gateways

Figure 10-39 Rules added to partner firewall rulebase

At the Spokane site, the configuration is a little more complicated. You have to create users for the partner site. Let's say two people are going to be performing the updates, Ren and Stimpy. Create the users with S/Key authentication. Place the two users into a group called partner-users. See Chapter 8 for the details on how to do this. Next, create the appropriate rules. The complete rulebase is shown in Figure 10-40.

No.	Source	Destination	Service	Action	Track	Install On
1	spokane-mgmt	sacramento-fw london-fw spokane-fw	FW1	accept		Gateways
2	sacramento-fw london-fw spokane-fw	spokane-mgmt	FW1 FW1_log	accept		Gateways
3	spokane-fw partner-fw	partner-fw spokane-fw	SKIP	accept		Gateways
4	sacramento-fw spokane-fw london-fw	sacramento-fw spokane-fw london-fw	IKE	accept	Long	Gateways
5	sacramento-encdomain	spokane-encdomain london-encdomain	Any	Encrypt	Long	Gateways
6	spokane-encdomain	sacramento-encdomain london-encdomain	Any	Encrypt	Long	Gateways
7	london-encdomain	sacramento-encdomain spokane-encdomain	Any	Encrypt	Long	Gateways
8	All Users@partner-encdomain	web-server	http telnet	User Auth	Long	spokane-fw
9	sacramento-encdomain spokane-encdomain london-encdomain	Any	telnet http https	accept		Gateways
10	SMTP-Servers	Any	smtp	accept		Gateways
11	Any	external-smtp-server	smtp	accept		Gateways
12	Any	Any	Any	drop	Long	Gateways

Figure 10-40 Rulebase for Spokane site with partner connection

The new rules in this rulebase are Rule 3 and Rule 8. Rule 3 permits SKIP traffic between the two firewalls. Rule 8 performs authentication and encryption (the envelope indicates encryption). How is this rule created? For the action, select User Auth. Right-click again, and select Add Encryption. You can edit the encryption properties from this menu as well. Edit the encryption so that DES is used as the data encryption scheme. Use DES because version 4.1 SP1 and later supports 3DES, but FireWall-1 3.0 only supports DES as an encryption method.

Install the security policy and test.

Notes

There are known problems with IPSec-based protocols when communicating between FireWall-3.0 and FireWall-1 4.0. FireWall-1 3.0 and FireWall-1 4.0 use slightly different methods for dealing with packets that are close to the TCP/IP Maximum Transmit Unit (MTU) size. If connections seem to work with smaller packets, but not bigger packets, this is probably the reason. Upgrade the other side to FireWall-1 4.0 to resolve this problem, or use FWZ.

Switching the Spokane Firewall to a Gateway Cluster Configuration
The Situation

This lab uses the previous configuration except for the following two changes:

1. A pair of Nokia IP440s is replacing the Spokane firewall configured in a Gateway Cluster configuration for High Availability and redundancy.
2. The Partner-FW has been upgraded to version 4.1 and will use IKE with pre-shared secrets as its encryption type because Gateway Clusters do not support SKIP.

All other configurations remain identical. The network map is also identical except that the Spokane-FW site has two firewalls instead of one. The new "virtual" firewall created by the Gateway Cluster will have the same IPs as the old firewall, so only minimal changes will be necessary at the remote sites. Figure 10-41 shows the new network diagram.

The Goals

- Convert the Spokane site into a Gateway Cluster configuration.
- Convert the partner site to IKE with pre-shared secrets.
- Maintain the security policy from the previous lab as much as possible.

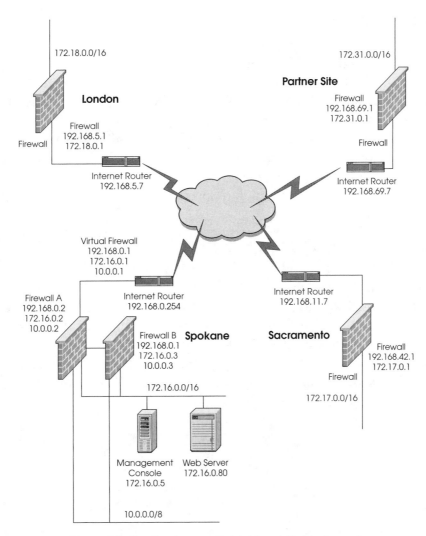

Figure 10-41   Spokane with highly available firewalls

Checklist

- Configure the firewall workstation object for the partner site to use IKE.
- Create a Gateway Cluster object for the Spokane site, defining encryption parameters.
- Define the workstation objects for Firewall A and FireWall B, making them part of Spokane's Gateway Cluster.
- Modify the encryption rules to support IKE instead of SKIP.
- Install the security policy.

Implementation

As part of bringing the Gateway Cluster into existence, you must also configure VRRP on the Nokia Security Platforms. This should be done first. Although not covered in this text, Resolution 1214 in Nokia's Knowledge Base covers this sufficiently well. Both firewalls will be configured with 192.168.0.1, 172.16.0.1, and 10.0.0.1. For the purposes of this exercise, Firewall A is the "primary" firewall, and Firewall B is the "secondary" firewall (i.e., it will take over if Firewall A fails). You also need to configure state synchronization on both of these firewalls. This is covered in Chapter 12. Use a crossover cable between the two platforms, assign IP addresses (172.30.0.2 and 172.30.0.3 for Firewall A and Firewall B, respectively), and run state synchronization across this interface.

Edit the partner site so that it is using a version 4.1 firewall object and supports IKE instead of SKIP. This is shown in Figure 10-42.

Click the VPN tab to modify the encryption properties, disabling SKIP and enabling IKE, as shown in Figure 10-43.

Select IKE, and click Edit. Make sure that Pre-Shared Secrets is correctly enabled, as shown in Figure 10-3 earlier in this chapter. You can then create the Spokane Gateway Cluster object, as shown in Figure 10-44.

You need to verify that S/Key is set on the Authentication tab of this object (remember that the partner site must authenticate with HTTP or Telnet using S/Key

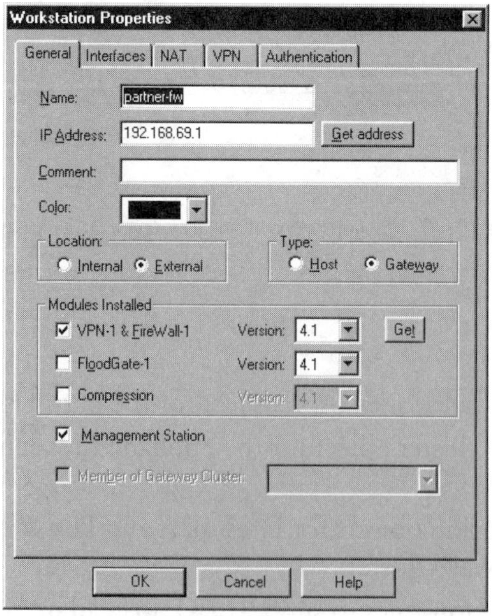

Figure 10-42 Updated partner firewall definition at Spokane site, General tab

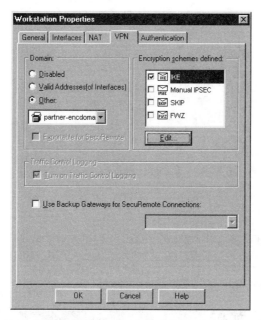

Figure 10-43   Updated partner firewall definition at Spokane site, VPN tab

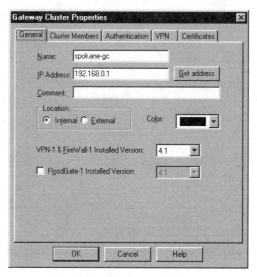

Figure 10-44   Spokane Gateway Cluster object, General tab

authentication). Figure 10-45 shows the Authentication tab of the Gateway Cluster object.

You then need to set up the VPN tab with the encryption domain to use IKE encryption, as shown in Figure 10-46.

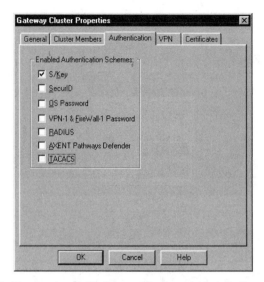

Figure 10-45 Spokane Gateway Cluster object, Authentication tab

Figure 10-46 Spokane Gateway Cluster object, VPN tab

Select IKE, and click Edit. Make sure Pre-Shared Secrets is selected, as shown in Figure 10-3 earlier in the chapter. Click Edit Secrets to make sure that the remote firewalls have a shared secret defined. Partner-fw will not, so you will have to click Edit, enter the shared secret, and click Set, as shown in Figure 10-47.

Figure 10-47   Spokane Gateway Cluster object, VPN tab, IKE Properties, Pre-Shared Secrets

All of the shared secrets have been defined. It is time to define the workstation objects for both Spokane firewalls. Figures 10-48 and 10-49 show how spokane-fwa is defined. These screens will look similar for spokane-fwb.

Note the difference between being part of a Gateway Cluster and not—namely, the number of tabs. Some of the tabs disappear because the shared properties are defined in the Gateway Cluster. The Interfaces tab is very important to define (in fact, the GUI won't allow you to exit from the object until you have). You may not be able

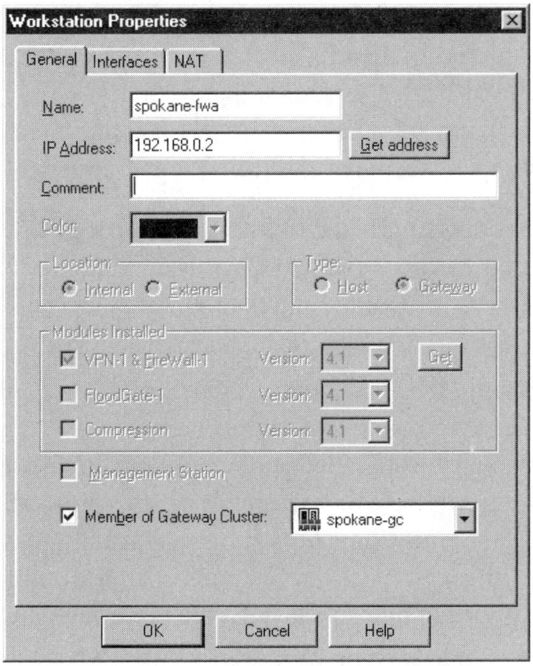

Figure 10-48   Spokane-fwa workstation object, General tab

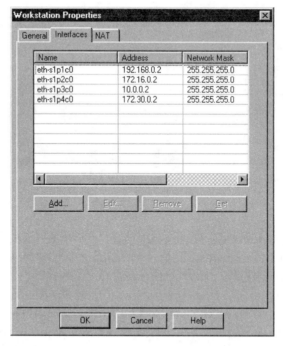

Figure 10-49 Spokane-fwa workstation object, Interfaces tab

to use the Get button to define the interfaces, so you may have to do it manually. Figure 10-49 shows a completed Interfaces tab.

Once you have defined both spokane-fwa and spokane-fwb and have made them part of the spokane-gc Gateway Cluster, you can modify the rulebase. The rulebase essentially remains the same except for the following changes:

- Rule 3 (the rule permitting SKIP between the partner firewall and spokane-fw) is no longer needed, because IKE is being used.
- All rules involving the firewalls must include spokane-fwa and spokane-fwb. This includes Rules 1, 2, and the new Rule 3 (the old Rule 4).
- You must also permit IKE packets to reach the Gateway Cluster address. However, it is not currently possible to add the Gateway Cluster to the rulebase. Create a second workstation object (called spokane-gc-ws) that uses the same IP address as the Gateway Cluster. Note that you will get a warning about having more than one object with the same IP address. This is normally not a good thing, but it is unavoidable in this case. Use this as a permitted destination in the IKE rule. FireWall-1 will not originate packets with the Gateway Cluster address.
- Rule 7 (old Rule 8) needs to be modified to use IKE instead of SKIP. Also, the install-on needs to be changed to spokane-gc.

Although you have made some subtle changes to the rulebase, it is basically the same as in the previous sample configuration. Figure 10-50 shows the updated rulebase.

No.	Source	Destination	Service	Action	Track	Install On
1	spokane-mgmt	sacramento-fw london-fw spokane-fwa spokane-fwb	FW1	accept		Gateways
2	sacramento-fw london-fw spokane-fwa spokane-fwb	spokane-mgmt	FW1 FW1_log	accept		Gateways
3	spokane-fwa spokane-fwb sacramento-fw london-fw	sacramento-fw london-fw spokane-fwa spokane-fwb spokane-gc-ws	IKE	accept	Long	Gateways
4	sacramento-encdomain	spokane-encdomain london-encdomain	Any	Encrypt	Long	Gateways
5	spokane-encdomain	sacramento-encdomain london-encdomain	Any	Encrypt	Long	Gateways
6	london-encdomain	sacramento-encdomain spokane-encdomain	Any	Encrypt	Long	Gateways
7	All Users@partner-encdomain	web-server	http telnet	User Auth	Long	spokane-gc
8	sacramento-encdomain spokane-encdomain london-encdomain	Any	telnet http https	accept		Gateways
9	SMTP-Servers	Any	smtp	accept		Gateways
10	Any	external-smtp-server	smtp	accept		Gateways
11	Any	Any	Any	drop	Long	Gateways

Figure 10-50   Upgraded rulebase for Spokane site with partner connection

I have not discussed the changes that need to be made on the partner end of the VPN. Surprisingly, there are not that many.

1. Change the encryption properties to IKE on both workstation objects.
2. Define the Interfaces tab on the spokane-fw workstation object.
3. Change the properties on the Encryption rules to use IKE instead of SKIP.

You should know how to do the first and third steps already. However, it is not clear what you need to do to define the spokane-fw interfaces on the partner side of the VPN. Basically, you must make sure all IPs of both firewalls and the Gateway Cluster IP are listed on the Interfaces tab. The interfaces' names and net masks are not important, because you are not setting up anti-spoofing (that is a bit difficult to do on a firewall you do not control anyway!). The Interfaces tab should look something like Figure 10-51 when you are done.

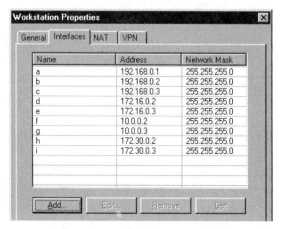

Figure 10-51 Spokane firewall definition, Interfaces tab on partner firewall

Once both sets of changes are made, you can install the security policy and test.

Notes

You may notice that not all of the VRRP IP addresses are defined on the Interfaces tab. That is okay. IPSO never originates a packet using the VRRP IP address (except when FireWall-1 tells it to). FireWall-1 will use an interface IP address (usually the external one) unless the modifications discussed in FAQ 10.2 are made. You may also notice that you did not define the spokane-fw as a Gateway Cluster object on the partner side of the VPN. Provided you have defined the interfaces on the Workstation tab correctly, this will work without having to do so.

Chapter

11

SecuRemote and Secure Client

This chapter is designed to be a practical guide to planning and configuring site-to-site VPNs in FireWall-1. A few key terms and concepts are discussed throughout the chapter. It is not meant to comprehensively cover encryption or encryption technologies.

By the end of this chapter, you should be able to:

- Identify the differences between SecuRemote and Secure Client
- Configure your firewall to support SecuRemote and Secure Client
- Install SecuRemote and Secure Client
- Identify a Multiple Entry Point configuration and its features
- Identify a Hybrid Authentication mode and the reasons you would want to use it
- Determine where SecuRemote and Secure Client can and cannot be used
- Troubleshoot SecuRemote problems

Introduction

SecuRemote and Secure Client are really just two different names for the same piece of software: Check Point's VPN client software for Windows 95, NT, and 2000. This software is designed to allow a single Windows client to transparently initiate a client-to-site VPN with a Check Point firewall. This chapter builds on the concepts discussed in Chapter 10. It is a separate chapter because the setup and troubleshooting for SecuRemote are different from those for site-to-site VPNs.

References to SecuRemote also include Secure Client, which has some additional features that allow network administrators to enforce a security policy on the client. If the client has a policy that does not match the one prescribed, the client can be denied access to the VPN. This extra functionality requires FireWall-1 4.1. Secure Client can be used with a FireWall-1 4.0 installation, albeit without the ability to use the advanced features.

Much like FireWall-1 on Windows NT, SecuRemote binds to the Windows TCP/IP stack. This allows it to intercept connections destined for a remote encryption domain and encrypt them. Likewise, it can decrypt incoming packets that are encrypted. There is also a user-level process that allows you to fetch the remote encryption domain, be authenticated, and otherwise control SecuRemote. This manifests itself on the client as a little envelope in the Windows taskbar.

Much of the planning that goes into using SecuRemote is pretty much the same as planning for site-to-site encryption; that is, you still have to define an encryption domain and configure network objects. However, you can do things on a user-by-user basis; for example, you can have some users using FWZ and others using IKE (also called ISAKMP/OAKLEY). You can restrict some users from going some places, but not others. You get all the flexibility of User Authentication with encryption.

One issue you do have to worry about with SecuRemote is end-user support. Although the client is generally easy to install and use, sometimes it does not go well. Exotic network configurations or hardware can sometimes confuse SecuRemote or cause issues with your TCP/IP stack. Users may also not know what to do when various dialog boxes appear or even fully understand what is going on, especially if they are behind a NAT device. I've also encountered more than my share of destroyed TCP/IP stacks, at least with version 4.0 and earlier builds of SecuRemote.

A Word about Licensing

As with VPN, SecuRemote requires both binaries that support it and licenses to enable it. However, the basic SecuRemote functionality is provided as part of a standard encryption license, although you must specifically request the functionality when requesting your license. The Secure Client functionality comes at an additional charge above and beyond an encryption license.

If you have FireWall-1 4.1 and you have CPVP-VSR as part of your license, you have SecuRemote functionality. If you have CPVP-VSC as part of your license, you have Secure Client functionality. The number that appears after this designation is the number of users your license permits. If you have FireWall-1 4.0, you need to have a license feature that starts with "sr," as shown in Table 11-1.

In FireWall-1 3.0 or FireWall-1 2.1, you must simply have a license that includes encryption. No special license is needed for SecuRemote on these versions.

Table 11-1   FireWall-1 4.0 licenses for SecuRemote

Feature	Number of Users Supported
srulight	50
srlight	100
srmedium	500
srlarge	1,000
srsuper	5,000
srunlimit	Unlimited

Steps to Configure SecuRemote on FireWall-1

The general steps for configuring FireWall-1 to use SecuRemote are:

1. Choose an appropriate encryption scheme.
2. Configure firewall workstation object for SecuRemote.
3. Create SecuRemote users.
4. Install the user database.
5. Create Client Encryption rules.
6. Configure Desktop Security options.
7. Install security policy.

Choosing an Encryption Scheme

SecuRemote can use either FWZ or IKE for encryption. Because there was a need for encapsulation prior to the introduction of IKE in FireWall-1, Check Point has an encapsulated mode for FWZ, which uses IP Protocol 94 (IP-in-IP Encapsulation). Each of the three methods are used in certain situations.

Use unencapsulated FWZ when:

- You are using FireWall-1 3.0 or earlier.
- The IP addresses behind the firewall use routable addresses without NAT.
- The SecuRemote client is not subject to NAT.

Do *not* use unencapsulated FWZ, but instead use encapsulated FWZ when:

- You are using FireWall-1 3.0 or later.
- The SecuRemote client is not subject to NAT.

- NAT is necessary to reach internal machines, and you must use non-NAT-friendly protocols (namely, Microsoft Networking).
- Your clients must access machines behind the firewall via nonroutable addresses.

Use IKE when:

- You are using FireWall-1 4.0 or later.
- You want strong encryption (3DES) support.
- NAT is necessary, and you must use non-NAT-friendly protocols (namely, Microsoft Networking).
- Your clients must access machines behind the firewall via nonroutable addresses.
- Your SecuRemote client systems are subject to NAT (hide or static) before they reach the firewall.

Do *not* use IKE if:

- Your security policy mandates that remote access requires a one-time password like SecurID or S/Key, and you use a version of FireWall-1 prior to 4.1 SP1.
- You are using FireWall-1 4.0 and require a password to be entered every so often. FireWall-1 4.1 has an option that supports this feature.

Generally speaking, IKE is the best encryption scheme to use. It supports stronger encryption and is not subject to the weaknesses discovered in FireWall-1's proprietary protocols.[1]

Configuring Firewall Workstation Object for SecuRemote

Similar to site-to-site encryption, you must configure the firewall object with the appropriate encryption types and encryption domain. A checkbox is also provided for "Exportable for SecuRemote," as shown in Figure 11-1.

"Exportable for SecuRemote" is somewhat of a misnomer because it actually means that when a SecuRemote client connects to the management console to request topology (i.e., the encryption domain), this firewall's encryption domain will be provided to the SecuRemote client. If this checkbox is not enabled, a SecuRemote client will not be able to download the encryption domain.

---

1.   I would avoid using encapsulated FWZ entirely, because it is quite possible for unauthorized individuals to use this scheme to tunnel through your firewall. For more details, see the Black Hat 2000 presentation on FireWall-1 at www.dataprotect.com/bh2000/ or www.phoneboy.com/docs/bh2000/.

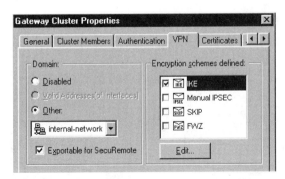

Figure 11-1   Workstation Properties, VPN tab

 **NOTE!**   In version 4.0 and earlier, the "Exportable for SecuRemote" checkbox is located on the General tab of the workstation object.

In IKE, you need only enable the appropriate type of authentication (Pre-Shared Secret or Public Key). The actual parameters specific to each user are defined in each user's definition. For FWZ, you need to generate CA and DH keys, much like those generated for site-to-site VPNs. However, there is a third option that needs to be configured depending on whether or not you use encapsulated FWZ. On the screen where CA and DH keys are defined, an Encapsulation tab also appears, as shown in Figure 11-2.

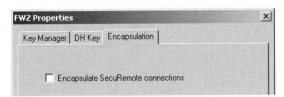

Figure 11-2   Workstation Properties, VPN tab, FWZ Properties, Encapsulation tab

If you want to use FWZ with encapsulation, select the "Encapsulate SecuRemote connections" check box.

Creating Users for Use with SecuRemote

The same users you use for User Authentication for outbound access can be used to authenticate SecuRemote users for inbound access. For more information on how to create users, see Chapter 7.

The Encryption tab in the user definition is where you can specify which encryption schemes are defined for this particular user. See Figure 11-3.

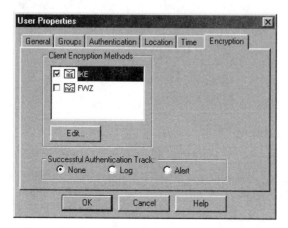

Figure 11-3 User Properties, Encryption tab

On this tab, you can also specify whether to log or alert when this user logs in via SecuRemote. Select the appropriate key-management schemes you want to define for this user, and click Edit. For FWZ, you have the options shown in Figure 11-4.

Figure 11-4 User Properties, FWZ Properties

The properties are very similar to those you might see in the properties for an encryption rule for FWZ. You can specify the Session Key and Data Encryption methods as well as whether or not to use MD5. You can also specify how long a user's password is valid. Note that unlike User Authentication, this applies to all password types, static or one-time password schemes.

Figure 11-5 shows the options presented for the authentication of IKE sessions.

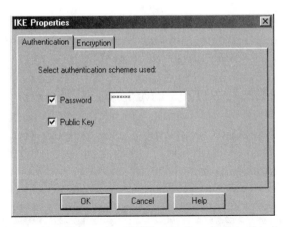

Figure 11-5   User Properties, IKE Properties, Authentication tab

On the Authentication tab, you specify which authentication methods are supported: Shared Secret (which you must enter) or a Public Key, where authentication is based on certificates. You would only select Shared Secret if you want to use a fixed password. If you want to use an external authentication server, like SecurID or RADIUS, leave this box unchecked and follow the instructions in the "Hybrid Authentication Mode for IKE" section.

On the IKE Properties Encryption tab, shown in Figure 11-6, you get the same options as when setting up a site-to-site VPN with IKE.

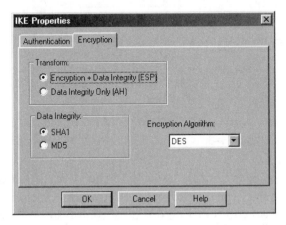

Figure 11-6   User Properties, IKE Properties, Encryption tab

Client Encryption Rules

The rules defined for client encryption are very similar to the rules you created for combining authentication and encryption in Chapter 10 except the action used for the rule is Client Encrypt.

The first rule shown in Figure 11-7 permits your SecuRemote clients to fetch the topology from the management console. Versions of Secure Client 4.1 and later together with FireWall-1 4.1 and later use the FW1_topo service (TCP port 264). All other versions or combinations thereof use the FW1 service (TCP port 256). The second rule allows either IKE or RDP (for FWZ) packets to your firewall. This is necessary if the "Enable FireWall-1 Control Connections" property is unchecked. The third rule actually permits the SecuRemote users to enter your encryption domain. The Client Encrypt action (see Figure 11-8) has properties that look very similar to those used for User Authentication.

Source	Destination	Service	Action
Any	Management-Console	FW1 FW1_topo	accept
Any	yourfirewall	IKE RDP	accept
authors@Any	encryption-domain	Any	Client Encrypt

Figure 11-7 Rules for secure client access

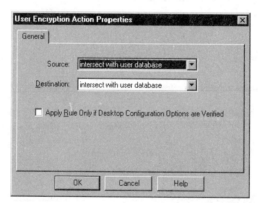

Figure 11-8 Client Encrypt Action Properties

The only difference between this screen and the User Authentication screen is the check box, which requires the Desktop Configuration Options be set correctly on Secure Client. So how do you set those options? You do so on the Rulebase Properties Desktop Security tab.

NOTE! If you select the Apply Rule Only if Desktop Configurations Options are Verified check box, be aware that you will be preventing versions of SecuRemote prior to build 4115 from connecting to your firewall. These versions of SecuRemote do not contain the Desktop Security Options. See also the licensing notes mentioned earlier in the "A Word about Licensing" section.

Desktop Security

Desktop Security requires FireWall-1 4.1 and later as well as Secure Client 4.1 and later. To use the Desktop Security options, you must create a server object of type policy servers and permit the FW1_pslogon service (TCP port 18207) to access the policy server. Because a policy server must reside on a firewall, you must permit this service as shown in Figure 11-9.

Figure 11-9 Rules for Desktop Security

Figure 11-10 shows the dialog used to create a policy server.

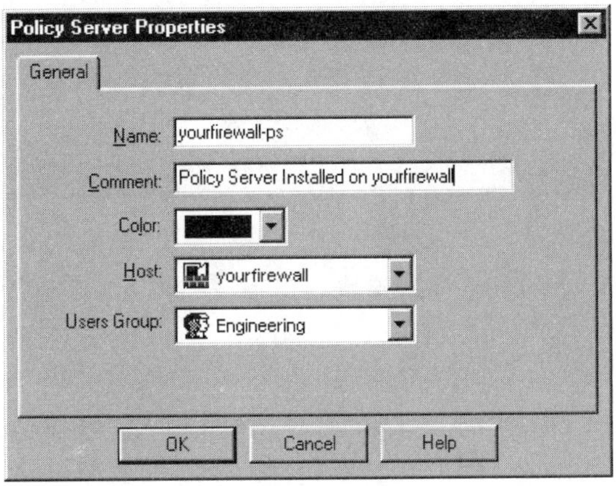

Figure 11-10 Policy Server Properties

The Policy Server Properties are defined as follows:

Name: The name used to represent this policy server.

Comment: Description of this object.

Color: Select whichever color you would like.

Host: Only firewalls are listed because a policy server can only reside on a firewall module. Gateway Clusters are not listed. Check Point plans on correcting this in a future version. For now, you can simply create a policy server object for each member of the Gateway Cluster.

Users Group: Specifies a certain users group that will use this policy server. You cannot simply select "All Users." An actual group must be specified.

The policy enforced by this policy server is defined on the Policy Properties Desktop Security tab, shown in Figure 11-11.

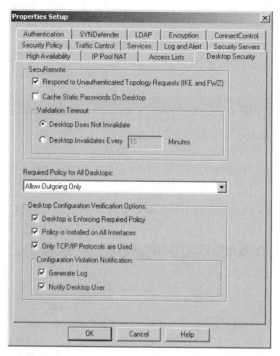

Figure 11-11   Rulebase Properties, Desktop Security tab

The options on the Desktop Security tab are defined as follows:

Respond to Unauthenticated Cleartext Topology Requests: As part of setting up a SecuRemote client, the user must connect to the FireWall-1 management console and download the encryption domain. In the past, this was done in the clear, so someone sniffing the wire could find out the topology of the internal network. Many people found this a breach of security. In version 4.0, Check Point modified this feature so that users could require authentication when downloading the topology. Unfortunately, this only works with SecuRemote version 4.0 clients *and* only when IKE is used as the encryption type. To allow older SecuRemote clients and/or the use of FWZ, this box should be selected. If you are only using the latest version of the SecuRemote or Secure Client client and using IKE, you can uncheck this box.

NOTE!   The Respond to Unauthenticated Cleartext Topology Requests option exists in the Encryption tab in FireWall-1 version 4.0.

Cache Static FWZ Passwords on Desktop: If a static password scheme is used along with FWZ, this option controls whether or not the SecuRemote client will cache this information so that the user does not have to reauthenticate. Generally, this option is disabled and the user must reauthenticate every so often.

Validation Timeout: IKE does not have the ability to time out and requires the user to reauthenticate after a certain period of time. FireWall-1 can force users to reauthenticate after a certain period of time if desired. "Desktop Does Not Invalidate" means that the user remains authenticated until the user kills the SecuRemote client (either manually or via a reboot). "Desktop Invalidates After X Minutes" means that after X minutes, SecuRemote will ask the client to provide his or her password again.

Required Policy for All Desktops: One of four options can be chosen:

- *Allow All:* Enforce no specific policy.
- *Allow Outgoing and Encrypted:* User can initiate communication to the Internet (unencrypted) or the VPN.
- *Allow Outgoing Only:* User can initiate a connection to the Internet, but not the VPN.
- *Allow Encrypted Only:* User can initiate a connection to the VPN, but not the Internet.

In the NG release of FireWall-1, you will be able to define a more granular policy for each client.

Desktop Is Enforcing Required Policy: The user will not be allowed into the network if this box is selected and the SecuRemote client is configured with a different policy from what is specified in this option. The client receives an error to this effect when he authenticates.

Policy Is Installed on All Interfaces: All TCP/IP interfaces must have this interface enforced on them. If they do not, it is possible that other hosts could compromise the Secure Client client. If this option is selected and the user does not have Secure Client installed on all active interfaces, the user will not be allowed into the network.

Only TCP/IP Protocols Are Used: If the user has a non-TCP/IP protocol installed on the network adapter, the client will be denied. Secure Client can only protect TCP/IP.

Configuration Violation Notification: If a user attempts to connect but has an incorrect policy, this information is logged to the regular FireWall-1 log, and/or the user is informed that his policy does not match.

Installing Secure Client

Users must install SecuRemote before they can use it. There are different versions of SecuRemote for Windows 95/98/ME, Windows NT, and Windows 2000 because the TCP/IP stack is very different in these three versions of Windows. Make sure the correct version for your particular operating system is installed. Before running the enclosed setup.exe, read the README file to make sure you are about to install the correct version.

During the installation process, you will be asked if you would like to install only on the dial-up adapters or on all adapters. FireWall-1 only recognizes standard Microsoft Dial-up Adapters (or RAS in Windows NT/2000) as dial-up adapters, so if you need to use a special adapter (for AOL, for instance), install on All Adapters. During the installation process, your only choices are all, or nothing; that is, you cannot choose to only install interfaces on specific adapters. In Windows 9x and 2000, you can easily change the interfaces SecuRemote is bound to by modifying the Network Properties after Secure Client has been installed. Windows NT does not provide a way to change interfaces which Secure Client is bound to.

What does it mean if SecuRemote is bound to a particular interface or not? Simply put, if SecuRemote is bound to the interface, it can send encrypted traffic through it. This may have unintended consequences in some circumstances. Generally, only binding SecuRemote to those interfaces you intend to use to communicate to a remote encryption domain is the right thing to do. Binding SecuRemote to an interface does not preclude you from using that interface for nonencrypted traffic. However, an administrator can change this behavior with the Desktop Security features.

On Secure Client installations, you are given the option of whether or not to include the Desktop Security options (i.e., the Secure Client functionality). There is no reason not to include support for this even if you do not plan on using it right away. You must reboot in order for SecuRemote to be usable. In some cases, you will not be able to reboot correctly after installing SecuRemote. These problems are discussed in the "Troubleshooting" section.

Once Windows comes up, you will see an icon in your taskbar. It lets you know that SecuRemote is active. The icon will animate when encrypted data is being sent to a remote site. Click on this icon to see a screen similar to the one shown in Figure 11-12.

Any sites that are defined are shown in this window. However, because this is a fresh install, no sites are listed. Let's add a new site. Click the Add New Site button at the top of the Secure Client window. A dialog similar to the one shown in Figure 11-13 appears.

Enter the fully qualified domain name or IP address of the site, which is either the management console or, if you are running FireWall-1 4.1 or later, the firewall module.

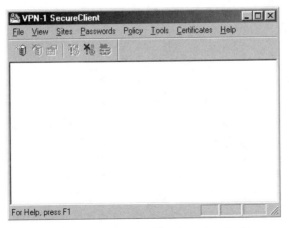

Figure 11-12 Secure Client main window

Figure 11-13 Add a new site to Secure Client.

In the latter case, you must have SecuRemote licenses installed on the firewall module. You can also choose a nickname for the site (i.e., just a user-friendly name). Click OK. Depending on whether or not you require authentication for downloading the network topology, you may be prompted for a login and password. If you authenticate successfully (or do not require authentication), you will then see new information appear, as shown in Figure 11-14.

Note that if FWZ is not defined, you will not see a Key ID or Key ID Date, because IKE generates keys on the fly.

Click OK to save this data to the client. After this point, anytime the client initiates a communication to a host inside the encryption domain, SecuRemote will prompt you for authentication, as shown in Figure 11-15.

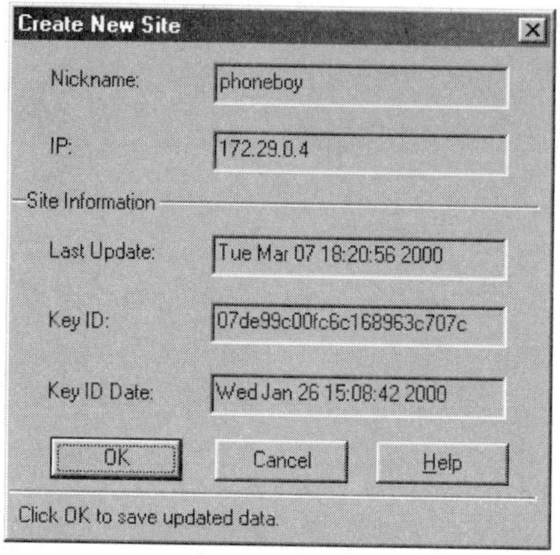

Figure 11-14 Add a new site to Secure Client #2.

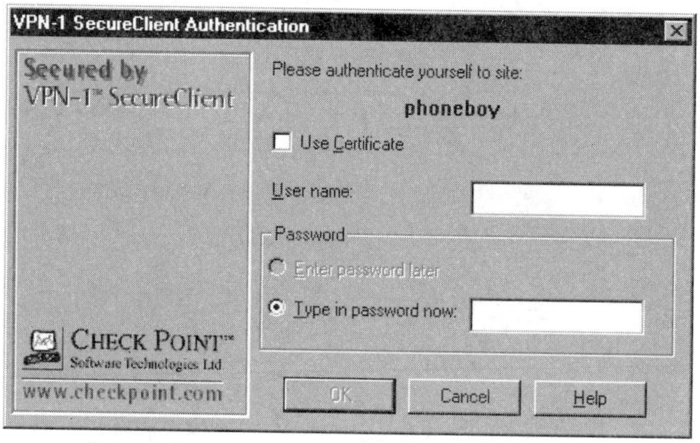

Figure 11-15 Secure Client Authentication

Type in the appropriate name and password. If all goes well, you should see an authentication-successful message, as shown in Figure 11-16.

If you do not see this message (or something similar), it means you have typed in the incorrect authentication information, there is a misconfiguration, or there is some other issue. See the "Troubleshooting" section later in this chapter.

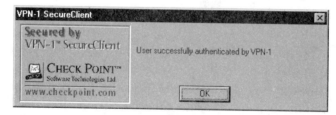

Figure 11-16 Secure Client Authentication successful

NOTE! Some versions of Secure Client do not display a message on successful authentication. This should be fixed in build 4185 or later of Secure Client.

High-Availability and Multiple Entry Point Configurations

In order to take advantage of the features discussed in this section, FireWall-1 4.1 SP1 or later and SecuRemote build 4115 or later are required.

If your firewall is configured into an HA (High-Availability) configuration, it is possible to use the Gateway Cluster feature to provide seamless failover of SecuRemote connections. Simply configure your workstation objects for each member of the cluster, and then add them to the Gateway Cluster object. You configure all of your encryption schemes and keys within this object. When the SecuRemote client fetches the encryption domain, all of the physical IPs plus the virtual IP of the Gateway Cluster will be included as part of the gateway definition. This allows any system in the cluster to be used to process a SecuRemote connection.

In addition, it is now possible to have multiple firewalls responsible for the same encryption domain. This allows you to have different firewalls in different physical locations provide access to the same encryption domain. This is useful for large companies that have multiple ways to reach the Internet through different firewalls at (possibly) physically different locations.

Gateway Clusters also provides a level of High Availability. Although it does not provide for transparent failover (i.e., if the primary gateway fails, connections will not fail over), it does allow you to automatically use a secondary gateway in the event of a failure.

The biggest challenge to overcome in High-Availability environments is to make sure that the same firewall is used for both incoming traffic and outgoing traffic for the client. IP Pool NAT, a new feature in FireWall-1 4.1 designed explicitly for SecuRemote is a "reverse NAT" for incoming SecuRemote connections. As SecuRemote users authenticate and connect into the encryption domain, the client is allocated an IP address from a pool of addresses on a first-come, first-served basis. All packets coming from that SecuRemote client are then statically "NATted" to that IP address. The pool of addresses chosen must be unique for each firewall. If the pool of IP addresses is on the same subnet as the firewall's internal interface, proxy-ARPs must be present for each IP in the pool to ensure that packets are forwarded to the firewall. The preferred method would be to use one or more subnets of nonroutable address space and ensure that internal routing routes these subnets to the correct firewall.

It may be desirable to allow SecuRemote users to access certain resources where you only want to allow access from within the internal network (e.g. the access is restricted by other firewalls or router access control lists). IP Pool NAT is designed to work in these environments. Each incoming SecuRemote user will be allocated his own IP address on the internal network, "masking" his external IP address from internal firewalls or router access control lists.

To configure IP Pool NAT, go to the Rulebase Properties High Availability tab, shown in Figure 11-17.

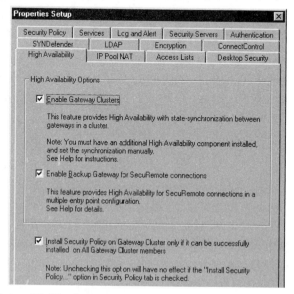

Figure 11-17   Rulebase Properties, High Availability tab

In this dialog, make sure the "Enable Backup Gateway for SecuRemote connections" check box is selected. You can then configure the IP Pool NAT tab, which is shown in Figure 11-18.

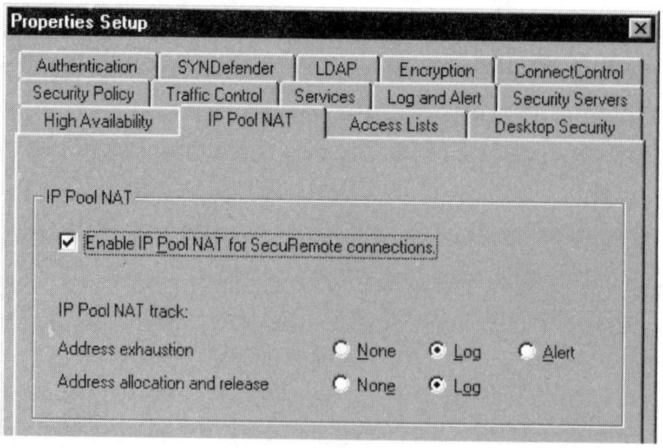

Figure 11-18   Rulebase Properties, IP Pool NAT tab

Enable IP Pool NAT and configure the logging for various events. You must then go into the firewall workstation object and specify both the backup firewalls and the IP Pool to be used. Start by going to the VPN tab and selecting the check box "Use Backup Gateways for SecuRemote Connections," shown in Figure 11-19.

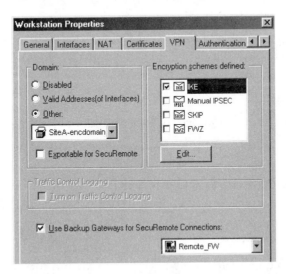

Figure 11-19   Workstation Properties, VPN tab, Backup Gateways

Select the workstation, Gateway Cluster, or group object that will be the backup for this encryption domain (note that the backup gateways will not have a Backup Gateway specified). Next, go to the NAT tab and specify the IP Pool to use, as shown in Figure 11-20.

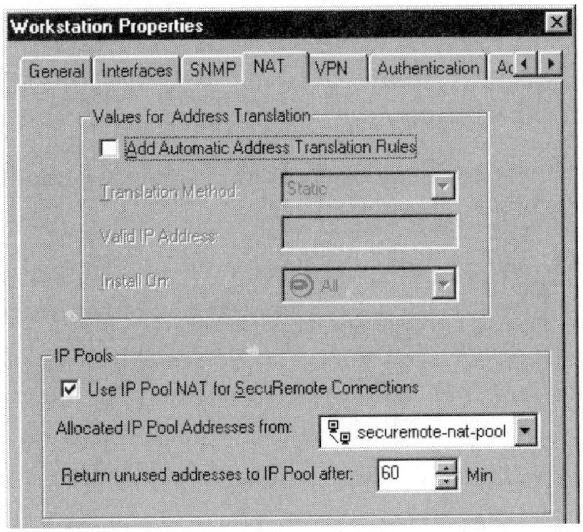

Figure 11-20   Workstation Properties, NAT tab, IP Pools

You can specify a network object, an address range, or a group. Install the security policy, and have your SecuRemote clients update the site.

The following caveats apply to Multiple Entry Point configurations:

- All gateways must belong to the same management console.
- Partial overlapping of encryption domains is not allowed.
- When a failover occurs, all existing connections will fail and need to be restarted.
- Gateway to gateway configurations are not supported—this feature was designed only for SecuRemote.
- All gateways must be running FireWall-1 4.1 or later.
- All clients must be running SecuRemote build 4115 or later.
- Only IKE encryption is supported.

Hybrid Authentication Mode for IKE

The newer versions of the IKE standard have a provision for using something other than a fixed password for IKE encryption. As a result, FireWall-1 4.1 SP1 and later and SecuRemote build 4153 and later have support for a feature called Hybrid Authentication for IKE. This feature simply allows you to use your existing authentication servers (like RADIUS or SecurID) as shared secrets for IKE. From a security perspective, this allows you to use much more secure one-time password schemes. From an administration perspective, the user's password and authentication scheme are defined on the Password tab of the user definition, which makes administration a little easier.

There are several steps you need to take on the management console to configure Hybrid Authentication. First, you need to perform an `fwstop` on the management console. This allows you to make some of the changes you will need to make. Second, you need to create your own Internal CA key for use in the Hybrid Authentication process. An example of this command is as follows:

```
mrhat[admin]# fw internalca create -dn "o=phoneboy, c=us"
Internal CA created successfully
```

Note that the **o=phoneboy, c=us** is your own Distinguished Name, which will look familiar to anyone who has used Lightweight Directory Access Protocol (LDAP). Two parts are needed: an organization (in this case, phoneboy) and a country (in this case, the United States). You may specify other parts if you'd like.

You then need to create a certificate for your firewall module. If your firewall's name were "mrtwig," you would generate the key as follows:

```
mrhat[admin]# fw internalca certify -o mrtwig "o=phoneboy, c=us"
Certificate created successfully
```

Next, restart the management console by typing **fwstart**. The certificate you just generated will be visible on the firewall workstation object's Certificates tab. You then need to enable Hybrid Authentication mode. Go to the firewall's workstation object VPN tab, and edit the IKE properties, as shown in Figure 11-21.

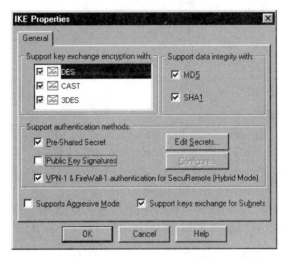

Figure 11-21 Workstation Properties, VPN tab, IKE Properties

"VPN-1 FireWall-1 authentication mode for SecuRemote (Hybrid Mode)" needs to be selected, and "Supports Aggressive Mode"[2] needs to be unchecked. Reinstall the security policy for this to take effect.

You need to make sure your users are configured properly. In the user definition, make sure that on the Encryption tab IKE is set up so that the user does *not* have a shared secret defined. You can do this by simply unchecking the "Shared Secret" check box on the Authentication tab of the IKE Properties.

On the client side, the user then needs to update the site. The user must double-click the envelope on his taskbar, double-click the appropriate site, and then click Update. You can verify that this information is correct by opening `userc.C` on the client. The following is a truncated version of what you should see in `userc.C` (the bolded parts are of interest):

```
:managers (
 : (mrhat
  :obj (
   :type (node)
   : (192.168.43.44)
```

---

2. Aggressive mode uses a three-packet IKE exchange instead of the standard six-packet one. Not all IKE implementations support this, and it does not work correctly with Hybrid Authentication mode.

```
  )
  :dnsinfo ()
  :MgmtInternalCA (
   :public (
    :value (010001)
   )
   :modulus (
    :value (b4f5f0...432bd5)
   )
   :cert (8d2786...0018230)
   :dn ("O=phoneboy,C=us")
   :date (392f6c6d)
  )
```

You should see the Internal CA key you created in the previous steps. The modulus and cert number should match those shown in the GUI. You should also see the `:ISAKMP_hybrid_support (true)` property on the site object with the `userc.C` file (note that this is not shown in the preceding output).

Your user should then be able to use whatever password scheme you have defined for him, including SecurID and RADIUS.

Microsoft Networking and Secure Client

A common configuration involving Secure Client includes the ability to access Microsoft Windows Networking services, such as Network Neighborhood, and authenticate to a Windows NT domain. Getting this configuration working with Secure Client is covered in this section.

This is not a Secure Client problem per se, but rather a general problem with how Microsoft Windows resolves names. To ensure that NetBIOS name resolution happens correctly, you need a WINS server that resides somewhere in the encryption domain, and it should know how to resolve all of your machines capable of speaking NetBIOS. Alternatively, you can use a well-populated `lmhosts` file containing names of all your NetBIOS-capable systems. However, without a WINS server, you will likely not be able to see all of these systems in Network Neighborhood.

If you have a WINS server, your SecuRemote client needs to be configured to use it. If the user accesses the encryption domain via a dial-up connection, configure it in the Dial-up Networking profile he uses to access the network. If the user uses a LAN card, configure the WINS server IPs on the LAN card profile. With FireWall-1 4.1 SP1 and later along with Secure Client SP2 and later, `lmhosts` and WINS information can be propagated with Secure Client. See FAQ 11.7 later in this chapter for more details. Note that if your internal network uses illegal or private network addresses, you will need to use FWZ with Encapsulation or IKE for WINS resolution to work correctly.

Another problem is that SecuRemote typically does not start up until after you have logged into Windows. Current versions of Secure Client (4.1 SP1 and later, build 4153) have a feature called Secure Domain Logon (SDL), which configures Secure Client so that it starts up in such a way that you can perform Windows NT Domain Authentication. It also tweaks a Registry value that increases the Windows NT Domain Authentication timeout so that SecuRemote has a chance to bring up the VPN tunnel. However, this feature does not always work. When prompted for Windows NT Domain Authentication when using SDL, do not attempt to log on to the domain right away. Instead give Secure Client enough time to start up. Depending on your configuration, it can take two to three minutes to fully start up.

SDL works for all Windows NT and 2000 platforms, although enabling the function requires local administrative privileges. It will also work on Windows 9x platforms that connect to the Internet via a LAN adapter. It will not work for Windows 9x users that connect to the Internet via a Dial-up Adapter.

If you are not using an SDL-enabled version of SecuRemote (i.e., a version earlier than build 4153), you can apply the following workarounds instead. However, it is highly recommended that you use the latest version of Secure Client instead of applying these workarounds. If you are using Windows 9x and accessing the Internet via a LAN adapter, you can accomplish almost the same thing as SDL by reconfiguring SecuRemote to start up as a service. Move the Registry entry at `HKEY_LOCAL_MACHINE\Software\icrosoft\Windows\CurrentVersion\Run\fwenc.exe` to `HKEY_LOCAL_MACHINE\Software\Microsoft\Windows\CurrentVersion\RunServices\fwenc.exe`. After you are prompted for your Windows password at startup, wait a minute so that `fwenc.exe` has a chance to start up.

When prompted for your domain password, type in your login and password, click OK, and wait for the SecuRemote pop-up window (you may have to click the window to bring it into focus). Log in with your SecuRemote password and, provided your Windows NT domain password is correct, you should be logged into the Windows NT domain. Note that you may receive a "No Domain Server is Available" message; in which case, click Cancel, and then click OK.

If you are using Windows NT, you can only log into the domain if you are accessing the network via a LAN card (i.e., not Dial-up Networking), and you have a fixed password (i.e., it is not a one-time password like S/Key or SecurID). The reason a fixed password is required is that it is currently not possible to get SecuRemote to prompt you until after your desktop comes up, even though part of the following procedure forces SecuRemote to run as a service. SecuRemote must be configured to run with the login and password directly, which can only be done when the password does not change.

Aside from configuring WINS and/or `lmhosts`, you must have `fwenc.exe` running as a service. Running it as a service on Windows NT is a bit tricky. By itself, you are not able to make it run as a service. Therefore, a third-party application is needed as sort of a "wrapper" to run the application for you. The application I have tested this with is called AppToService from Basta Computing and is available at www.basta.com/ProdAppToService.htm. However, in all likelihood, any similar sort of application may be used as well. To use AppToService, follow these steps:

1. Download AppToService from Basta Computing's Web site. Unzip to a directory where the executable will not be deleted.

2. Open a command prompt to that directory, and run the AppToService application as follows (the following command must be typed on one line):

```
apptoservice /install /dependon:"fw1" /show:2 /startup:a
    c:.exe /arguments:"-n user -p password"
```

The /arguments should only be included if you want to cache your SecuRemote login and password. If you need to remove the service, use the following command:

```
apptoservice /remove c:\winnt\fw\bin\fwenc.exe
```

For more options, run:

```
apptoservice /?
```

3. Open `regedit`, and remove the Registry entry at `HKEY_LOCAL_MACHINE\ SOFTWARE\Microsoft\Windows\CurrentVersion\Run\fwenc.exe`.

4. Reboot.

Frequently Asked Questions

Some questions that are frequently asked about SecuRemote are as follows.

11.1: Can I Use SecuRemote If My Client Is Subject to NAT?

If your SecuRemote client is behind a device that does any form of address translation (including another FireWall-1 firewall) and you are using a version of FireWall-1 earlier than 4.0, SecuRemote will not work. FireWall-1 4.0 and later will support clients that are subject to NAT with the following restrictions:

- The SecuRemote client must be version 4.0 or later (build 4003 or later).
- You cannot use encapsulation with the FWZ key-management scheme. (You can use IKE or unencapsulated FWZ, however.)
- If the client is subject to static NAT (i.e., one-to-one translation), it will work provided you follow the appropriate steps outlined within this section.
- If the client is subject to Pool NAT (i.e., a many-to-many translation done by Cisco PIX firewalls and other similar devices), it will work so long as each client

is given a unique IP address, and you follow the appropriate steps outlined within this section.

- If the client is subject to Hide NAT (i.e., a many-to-one translation), only one user at a time can use SecuRemote unless you use UDP Encapsulation mode (more on this in a bit). This should work well for users that use a device that performs NAT for their home-office network (e.g., users with cable modems or those with UNIX or Windows machines performing NAT).

Hide NAT will only work correctly with IKE (it does not work with FWZ), provided the following is true:

- Make sure that UDP port 500 on your NAT gateway is mapped to the SecuRemote client. FireWall-1 tries to communicate via this port.

- Make sure your NAT gateway can pass IPSec traffic (IP Protocol 50) if UDP Encapsulation is not used.

- If UDP Encapsulation mode is used, make sure the NAT gateway can pass UDP port 2746.

- If Gateway Clusters are used with UDP Encapsulation, you need to upgrade to FireWall-1 4.1 SP3 or later for this to work correctly

- Make sure that each Hide NAT client is using a different IP address. If two clients attempt to use SecuRemote and have the same nonroutable address, neither client will be able to access the internal network correctly. This commonly occurs if two or more clients use the same type of NAT router with the default configuration.

If your Hide NAT gateway is a Linux machine, go to the Web site at www.phoneboy.com/faq/0372.html for more information.

If your Hide NAT is being done by a Linksys DSL router, make sure you are using at least version 1.34 of the firmware if you are not using UDP Encapsulation.

You will also need to modify `$FWDIR/conf/objects.C` on the management console. For guidelines on editing `objects.C`, see Chapter 4, FAQ 4.2. After the `:props (` line, add or modify the following lines to read:

```
:userc_NAT (true)
:userc_IKE_NAT (true)
```

FireWall-1 4.1 SP2 and Secure Client 4.1 SP2 and later have a UDP Encapsulation feature that uses UDP to encapsulate the encrypted data when IKE is used. This should be far more compatible with NAT devices as all communication will occur over UDP instead of using IP datagrams, which are about as unreliable as UDP packets are anyway (meaning, there is no built-in retransmission mechanism as in TCP). Both FireWall-1 4.1 SP2 and Secure Client 4.1 SP2 (and later) are required to make use of this feature.

To enable UDP Encapsulation, look for the section in your `$FWDIR/conf/objects.C` that has your firewall or Gateway Cluster object. It looks something like this (my object is `phoneboy-gc`):

```
: (phoneboy-gc
        :color (black)
        :type (gateway_cluster)
        :host_schemes_val (121)
        :host_schemes_names (
                : ("S/Key")
                : ("Internal Password")
                : (RADIUS)
                : (Defender)
                : (TACACS)
        )
    ...
    )
```

Note that the object definition can actually go on for several screens. It is important to look for your firewall or Gateway Cluster object's name in `objects.C`. Right before the ")" (which closes off the definition of phoneboy-gc), add the following:

```
:isakmp.udpencapsulation (
        :resource (
                :type (refobj)
                :refname
            ("#_VPN1_IPSEC_encapsulation")
        )
        :active (true)
    )
```

The object definition should then look like this:

```
: (phoneboy-gc
        :color (black)
        :type (gateway_cluster)
        :host_schemes_val (121)
        :host_schemes_names (
                : ("S/Key")
                : ("Internal Password")
                : (RADIUS)
                : (Defender)
                : (TACACS)
        )
```

```
                        . . .
                                :isakmp.udpencapsulation (
                                    :resource (
                                            :type (refobj)
                                            :refname
                                ("#_VPN1_IPSEC_encapsulation")
                                        )
                                    :active (true)
                                )

                        )
```

You also need to create a service called VPN1_IPSEC_encapsulation, if it does not exist. It is a UDP service on port 2746.

By default, FireWall-1 versions 4.1 SP2 and later, which have had these changes made, will invoke this mode if the UDP port 500 packet coming from the SecuRemote client has a source port that is not port 500. This mode can be forced on the client by going into `userc.C` on the Secure Client and adding the following under the Options section:

```
    :force_udp_encapsulation (true)
```

It can also be disabled entirely on the firewall by changing active to false instead of true in the preceding `objects.C` modification. You cannot force UDP Encapsulation on the server side, however.

UDP Encapsulation is known to have an issue with Gateway Cluster: It selects the wrong IP address to source UDP Encapsulation packets. This causes problems when the client is behind a NAT gateway. To resolve this issue, upgrade to FireWall-1 4.1 SP3 or later, and add the following two lines to the `:props (` section of `objects.C`:

```
    :IPSec_main_if_nat (true)
    :IPSec_cluster_nat (true)
```

This tells FireWall-1 to always send the packets out with the Gateway Cluster IP address, which it does not do by default.

11.2: How Do I Initiate an Encrypted Session to a SecuRemote Client?

SecuRemote was only designed to handle encrypted connections initiated from the client side. To handle the possibility of connections back to the client, FireWall-1 keeps track of IPs that are SecuRemote clients in a table called userc_rules. So long as the SecuRemote client has initiated a connection to the encryption domain within the previous 15 minutes, its IP address will be listed in this table. Any outgoing connection that is accepted by FireWall-1 is checked against this table. If the connection is going to an IP in this table, it is automatically encrypted. Note that this occurs despite the fact that the action of the rule is "accept" versus "Encrypt" or "Client Encrypt."

If you want to allow certain services out, but only to those machines that have authenticated with SecuRemote (i.e., you wouldn't want to permit these services outbound in an unencrypted fashion), you can make this work. You need to create the service srMyApp of type Other with the following information in the Match field (assuming for a moment that "myApp" is a TCP service on port 5555):

```
tcp,dport=5555,<dst,0>in userc_rules
```

Then simply put this service in an accept rule. This rule only matches if it is going to the correct port and to an IP address that has recently initiated an encrypted session through the gateway.

A more detailed explanation of what this code does is provided in Chapter 13.

11.3: What If My SecuRemote Client Must Pass through a FireWall-1 Gateway?

There may be circumstances where you need to run SecuRemote to access an encryption domain where the client is behind a Check Point FireWall-1 gateway. Assuming you are not doing address translation or can work around it, as was explained in FAQ 11.1, part of what needs to be done will depend on whether or not the remote FireWall-1 is configured to use encapsulation for SecuRemote connections.

General Configuration

In all cases, you need to permit the following traffic through your local firewall. See Figure 11-22.

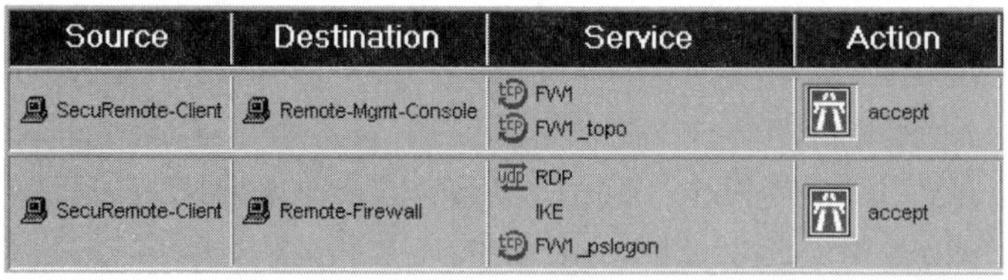

Source	Destination	Service	Action
SecuRemote-Client	Remote-Mgmt-Console	FW1 FW1_topo	accept
SecuRemote-Client	Remote-Firewall	RDP IKE FW1_pslogon	accept

Figure 11-22   Rules to allow SecuRemote through FireWall-1

The services are needed for the following reasons (do not use the ones that are not needed):

- FW1 (TCP port 256) is needed if either using SecuRemote build 4005 or earlier or any version of SecuRemote talking to a version 4.0 or earlier management console.

- FW1_topo (TCP port 261) is needed if you are using SecuRemote build 4115 and later and talking to a version 4.1 or later management console.
- RDP (UDP port 259) is needed if the SecuRemote client uses FWZ.
- IKE (UDP port 500) is needed if the SecuRemote client uses IKE.
- FW1_pslogon (TCP port 18207) is needed if Secure Client is used and a policy needs to be downloaded.

Remote Site Uses FWZ Encapsulation

If the remote site uses encapsulation for SecuRemote clients, the additional rule shown in Figure 11-23 needs to be added.

Source	Destination	Service	Action
SecuRemote-Client Remote-Firewall	Remote-Firewall SecuRemote-Client	FW1_Encapsulation	accept

Figure 11-23   Rule to allow FWZ Encapsulation through the firewall

FW1_encapsulation is predefined on most current FireWall-1 boxes. If it is not predefined on yours, create it as a service of type Other using "ip_p=94" in the Match field.

Remote Site Uses IKE

If the remote site uses encapsulation for SecuRemote clients, the additional rule shown in Figure 11-24 needs to be added.

Source	Destination	Service	Action
SecuRemote-Client Remote-Firewall	SecuRemote-Client Remote-Firewall	IPSEC VPN1_IPSEC_encapsulation	accept

Figure 11-24   Rule to allow IKE through the firewall

IPSec is predefined on most current FireWall-1 boxes. If it is not predefined on yours, create it as a service of type Other using "ip_p=50" in the Match field. VPN1_IPSEC_encapsulation uses UDP port 2746 and is only used when Secure Client 4.1 SP2 is used with FireWall-1 4.1 SP2 and later.

WARNING! A problem occurs if the local firewall is a Gateway Cluster and has been modified with `IPSec_main_if_nat (true)`, and `IPSec_cluster_nat (true)` as discussed in FAQ 10.2 and FAQ 11.1. The local firewall will translate IKE packets (whether or not UDP Encapsulation is used). This should be fixed in FireWall-1 4.1 SP4 and later.

Remote Site Uses FWZ without Encapsulation

If the remote site does not use encapsulation, you need to permit the necessary traffic to and from the remote site by your local firewall's rulebase. You need to make sure that none of the traffic is processed through the Security Servers or an intermediary proxy, or you might get unreliable or unpredictable results. You should also disable the Rulebase Property "enable decryption on accept." The rule near the top of your rulebase should suffice. See Figure 11-25.

Source	Destination	Service	Action	Track
🖳 SecuRemote-Client	🖴 Remote-Servers	➲ Any	🏛 accept	

Figure 11-25   Rule to allow unencapsulated FWZ through the firewall

The "any" in Figure 11-25 can be replaced with the specific services the SecuRemote client needs to use.

 **WARNING!** It has been reported that using FWZ encryption with SecuRemote can break an IKE VPN between two sites when the client on one side of the VPN tries to use SecuRemote to access a resource on the other end of the VPN. In other words, the client is at a site that has a VPN established with a partner site, and the client tries to use SecuRemote with FWZ to connect to the partner site instead of trying in the clear. This problem has been resolved in FireWall-1 4.1.

11.4: How Can I Use SecuRemote When I Am behind a Proxy?

SecuRemote uses protocols that proxy servers are not designed to process: generic IP datagrams. Secure Client 4.1 SP2 when used with FireWall-1 4.1 SP2 and later have an option to encapsulate over UDP port 2746. It remains to be seen whether or not this can go through a UDP proxy.

Even when FWZ without encapsulation is used, the proxy server is not likely to process the encrypted traffic. If you can only access the Internet through a proxy server, you cannot use SecuRemote through it.

11.5: How Do I Disable SecuRemote at Boot?

Remove `HKEY_LOCAL_MACHINE\Software\Microsoft\Windows\CurrentVersion\Run\fwenc.exe` from the Registry, and SecuRemote will not start at boot time.

11.6: How Do I Automate SecuRemote Configurations?

Most configuration settings are in `userc.C` or `userc.set` on the SecuRemote client, including encryption domain. Manually configure the client to your liking, copy the `userc.C` and/or `userc.set` file from this system, and replace the `userc.C` or `userc.set` file that is part of the normal SecuRemote installation files. Package this file, and distribute it to the users. When they install SecuRemote, their client will automatically be configured with your encryption domains, encryption keys, and most of your preferred settings.

You can also modify the product.ini that is included in the installation files. The information needed in this file includes:

- *Edition=3DES:* This is DES for a DES version.
- *MaxKeyLength=168:* 56 for a DES version.
- *Encryption=1:* 1 is currently the only valid setting; this may change in the future.
- *DesktopSecurityDefault=1:* Desktop Security enabled by default, 0 if not.
- *DesktopSecurityAskUser=1:* Use with previous setting to silently set this setting.
- *IncludeEntrustCertUtil=1:* If not using Entrust, you can set this to 0.
- *IncludeBrandingFiles=0:* Include `logo.bmp` with installation to replace Check Point logo.
- *SupportFWZ=1:* If set to 0, FWZ is not supported.
- *Support3rdPartyGina=0:* If you are using a third-party GINA.DLL[3], set to 1.
- *OvewriteEntINI=0:* If you have an existing `entrust.ini` file, overwrite if set to 1.

11.7: How Can I Configure Secure Client to Access DNS or WINS Servers Inside My Encryption Domain without Manually Configuring the Clients?

In FireWall-1 4.1, a new file called `$FWDIR/conf/dnsinfo.C` was created. This file exists on your management console and allows you to send information about internal DNS and `lmhosts` entries to Secure Client clients as part of the network topology. The following is a sample `dnsinfo.C` file:

```
(
:dns_servers (
   : (spock
   :obj (
```

---

3. GINA.DLL is used on Microsoft Windows systems to control the interactive logon procedure. To alter the interactive logon procedure, you can replace Microsoft's GINA.DLL file (which gets renamed MSGINA.DLL) with a custom GINA.DLL. Secure Client expects to find Microsoft's GINA.DLL. If another vendor's or a custom-developed GINA.DLL is present, Check Point needs to know about it so it can tie into Microsoft's GINA.DLL.

```
            : (10.10.1.100)
        )
    :topology (
        : (
            :ipaddr (10.10.1.0)
            :ipmask (255.255.255.0)
        )
    )
    :domain (
        : (
            :dns_label_count (5)
            :domain (.trek.com)
          )
        )
      )
    )
:encrypt_dns (true)
:LMdata (
    : (
            :ipaddr (10.10.1.10)
            :name (PDC-KIRK)
            :domain (DOM-NCC1701)
        )
    : (
            :ipaddr (10.10.1.10)
            :name (PDC-KIRK)
        )
    : (
            :ipaddr (10.10.1.20)
            :name (PDC-SPOCK)
            :domain (DOM-NCC1701)
        )
    )
    )
```

 **WARNING!**   The `dnsinfo.C` file is extremely sensitive to spacing and capitalization. Use spaces where indicated in the preceding sample.

In the preceding example:

- The DNS domain is trek.com.
- The DNS names xxx.trek.com, xxx.yyy.trek.com, and xxx.yyy.zzz.trek.com are passed to the internal DNS server.

- The DNS server runs on 10.10.1.100. The workstation object for this host is spock. These settings need to be replaced with the appropriate values for your situation.
- There are appropriate entries for 10.10.1.10 and 10.10.1.20. The second entry for PDC-KIRK is used explicitly for Windows 98, which requires it in order to browse the domain correctly.

To use the encrypted DNS functionality, you also need to make some additional changes to the management console. Modify `$FWDIR/lib/crypt.def` to support encrypted DNS. Above the line that reads

```
define USERC_DECRYPT_SRC
```

add the following line:

```
#define ENCDNS
```

Disable the various "Accept DNS" properties, creating explicit rules to allow DNS as shown in Chapter 4. You also need to add some lines to the `userc.C` file on the SecuRemote client. For SecuRemote build 41xx, make sure the following lines exist in `userc.C` in the `:options (` stanza:

```
:active_resolver (true)
```

For SecuRemote build 400x, make sure the following lines exist in `userc.C` in the `:options (` stanza:

```
:dns_xlate (true)
:dns_encrypt (true)
```

If SecuRemote is running in either case, kill and restart the client. Also, reinstall the security policy, and have the clients add the site again. If this is done correctly, you should see the information in the client's `userc.C` file and in his `lmhosts` file.

NOTE: Only one DNS server can be specified in the `userc.c` file

11.8: Can I Share an Internet Connection and Use SecuRemote?

It is common to want to run SecuRemote and some sort of NAT program on the same system, like SyGate, WinRoute, or Windows Internet Connection Sharing. The only NAT program I've heard of that works with SecuRemote is a program called AllAboard, which can be obtained at www.internetshare.com. Another approach that will work is using a real proxy server. From SecuRemote's perspective, all the connections would originate from the client itself, which means SecuRemote would encrypt them.

 WARNING!   Although there is nothing to prevent you from using a proxy server on a SecuRemote client, this configuration could potentially create a hole through which a hacker could access your internal network using a "trusted source" (i.e., the SecuRemote client).

Troubleshooting

Troubleshooting SecuRemote can be somewhat tricky. Many problems with SecuRemote are a result of bad interactions with Windows, although there are also plenty of ways to misconfigure settings.

11.9: SecuRemote Client Needs NAT or a Proxy

There are conditions where you can make SecuRemote work with NAT, as described in FAQ 11.1. However, NAT on the whole can cause problems. Many times, it is simply understanding that NAT is taking place.

As stated in FAQ 11.4, proxy servers cannot deal with the protocols necessary. However, with the new UDP Encapsulation mode, it may be possible to utilize a transparent proxy.

11.10: SecuRemote Communication Ports Are Blocked

SecuRemote requires that the following ports and protocols be allowed by any intermediary device (routers, firewalls):

- *TCP port 264 or 256* between the client and management console. This is only needed to fetch and update the site information and will always originate from the SecuRemote client. These are the services FW1_topo and FW1, respectively.
- *UDP port 259* to negotiate encryption and authentication information when FWZ is used. This is the service RDP.
- *UDP port 500* to negotiate encryption keys when IKE is used. This is the service IKE.
- *UDP port 2746* between the client and the firewall when UDP Encapsulation mode is used.
- *IP Protocol 94* bidirectionally when FWZ encapsulation is used. This service is called FW1_encapsulation.
- *IP Protocol 50* bidirectionally when IKE is used. This service is represented by the IPSec group of services.

11.11: ISP Uses a Custom Adapter to Connect

This situation applies to anyone who uses anything other than a standard Ethernet NIC or Microsoft's Dial-up Adaptor to connect to the Internet.

It is becoming increasingly common, particularly with cable or DSL providers, to require PPP over Ethernet (PPPoE) to connect. PPPoE effectively treats your connection to the Internet like a dial-up connection. However, it adds additional protocols and virtual adapters to the TCP/IP stack, not to mention additional overhead due to the PPP encapsulation. This means that SecuRemote will either not bind to the PPPoE stack properly or experience performance problems due to encapsulation (see FAQ 11.13).

The bindings for PPPoE and SecuRemote look something like this:

```
Ethernet Adaptor -> PPPoE Adaptor -> FW1 Adaptor -> FW1 Protocol -> TCP/IP
```

You should not have TCP/IP bound to your Ethernet adapter or your PPPoE adapter.

11.12: Problems Adding the New Site

When you are adding a new site, you need to enter the IP address of the management console, *not the firewall itself* (unless, of course, the firewall *is* the management console). FireWall-1 4.1 also supports adding the IP address of the firewall provided a SecuRemote license is installed on the firewall module and the proper ports are allowed to the firewall. If you get the error message "connection to site x.y.z.w has failed," ensure that your SecuRemote client can communicate to that IP via TCP port 264 or TCP port 256.

When you create a new site, information about the encryption domain will be downloaded to the system and stored in a file called userc.c on the client. Check the userc.c file to ensure that your internal network(s) are listed. If they are not, the firewall administrator needs to make sure that the "Exportable" flag is checked in the firewall's network object under the Encryption tab. Once that change has been made and the security policy has been reinstalled, a site update should update userc.c with the correct information. You can either update the site by double-clicking the site icon in Secure Client or by removing and adding the site again in Secure Client.

11.13: Encapsulation and Packet Sizes

If you plan on using any Microsoft Networking services or any service that does not perform address translation very well through SecuRemote, the use of IKE or encapsulated FWZ is necessary.

Encapsulation creates a problem with fragmentation. FWZ encapsulation adds 4 bytes to the size of the packet. IKE probably adds approximately 100 bytes (depending on the options used). A packet with a size close to the TCP/IP stack's Maximum Transmit/Receive Unit (MTU/MRU) will become greater than the supported MTU/MRU and will have problems in transit. Most of the problems that happen with fragmentation seem to occur with FWZ encapsulation, not IKE.

A problem similar to the one mentioned in the previous paragraph: if there are large packets with the don't fragment bit set, SecuRemote and FireWall-1 will have problems. See FAQ 10.18 for details on how to resolve this issue.

Secure Client build 4157 does some automatic adjusting of the MTU size. If you are not using this version, you can adjust the MTU/MRU sizes. In Windows NT 4.0 SP3 or later (with the appropriate hot fixes), you can also modify the MTU size the OS uses by modifying the Registry entries under `HKEY_Local_Machine\ystem\ Current ControlSet\Services\NdisWan\Parameters`. Add or modify the following entries:

```
Value name:    IPMTU
Data Type:     REG_DWORD
DATA           576 decimal

Value name:    TunnelMTU
Data Type:     REG_DWORD
DATA           576 decimal
```

On Windows 2000, the appropriate settings are:

```
HKEY_LOCAL_MACHINE\SYSTEM\
CurrentControlSet\Services\Tcpip\
Parameters\Interfaces\<adapter ID>\MTU
(REG_DWORD)

HKEY_LOCAL_MACHINE\SYSTEM\
CurrentControlSet\Services\Tcpip\
Parameters\Enable PMTU Discovery=0
(REG_DWORD)
```

On Windows 98 (or 95 with Dial-up Networking 1.3 installed), you can modify the parameters on the Dial-up Adapter. Set the Packet Size parameter to "Small." For NICs, modify the Registry keys under `HKEY_LOCAL_MACHINE\System\ CurrentControlSet\Services\Class\netTrans\00n` where *n* is the TCP/IP binding associated with your NIC. You will easily be able to tell which *n* is correct for your interface, as the IP address will be listed in this hive. Note that Maximum Segment Size (MaxMSS) should be 40 less than the MaxMTU value.

```
Value Name:    MaxMTU
Data Type:     String
DATA           576
```

```
Value Name:      MaxMSS
Data Type:       String
DATA             536
```

11.14: Windows NT and File Permissions

As a nonprivileged user, you receive the SecuRemote authentication dialog and then the successful-authentication message, but you cannot connect to the internal network. No incoming packets from the SecuRemote client can be seen at the firewall. If SecuRemote is restarted and authenticated again, everything works splendidly.

To resolve this issue, change the rights to the directory `%SystemRoot%\system32\drivers\etc` to RWX:RWX. As such, you can only do this if Windows is installed on an NTFS partition under Windows NT.

11.15: Mixing NICs and Dial-up Adapters

If you have a NIC configured with an IP address inside the encryption domain, SecuRemote will not work correctly. This happens most often with laptops used on the road as well as in the office. The following sections contain a list of potential configurations, the problems associated with them, and workarounds.

NIC Uses Static IP, Has IP in the Encryption Domain

This particular problem occurs whether or not your NIC is using DHCP. If your NIC has an IP address in the encryption domain and you either dial up to the Internet or use the local LAN, SecuRemote will not attempt to talk to your internal network in an encrypted fashion as it will attempt to use the NIC directly. This is not a SecuRemote-specific issue.

You can remove the route associated with the network on which the NIC is configured. For instance, if your IP address is 172.17.55.10 and your net mask is 255.255.255.0, you can remove the route by typing the command **route delete 172.17.55.0 mask 255.255.255.0 172.17.55.10**. If SecuRemote is installed on all NICs and the NIC in question is not physically installed at the time, this command will fail. See the "SecuRemote Bound to All Adapters" section later in this chapter.

NIC Uses DHCP, Has IP in the Encryption Domain

SecuRemote can have problems with DHCP, either in obtaining an IP address or because the IP address (previously) obtained is part of the encryption domain. Secure Client build 4153 seems to address many issues, but you may still run into a problem. SecuRemote has to bind to the network interface before TCP/IP is usable. On Windows NT, the SecuRemote service and the DHCP Client service can conflict with each other. If you use Secure Domain Logon with Windows NT, Secure Client may "eat" the DHCP packet, preventing the system from ever receiving an IP address. On

Windows 9x, the initial DHCP request never gets sent out, because SecuRemote was not bound to the interface at that time, thus no IP address is obtained from the DHCP server.

The following three sections document some workarounds.

Windows 9x

Invoke DHCP Renew manually. Run the winipcfg program, and click Renew. Alternatively, you could add it to a batch job that runs from the startup group as in `winipcfg /renew_all /batch`.

Windows 98 (not Windows 95) has some peculiar behavior with DHCP in that the leased IP is retained across a reboot. This can cause a problem if your DHCP IP address is in the encryption domain. This IP address can be released on reboot with the help of a couple of Registry hacks documented in Microsoft's Knowledge Base article 217035:

```
Key: HKEY_LOCAL_MACHINE\System\CurrentControlSet\
Services\VxD\DHCP
Value name: ReleaseLeaseOnShutdown
Type: DWORD
Value data: 0x00000001 (1)

Key: HKEY_LOCAL_MACHINE\System\CurrentControlSet\
Control\Shutdown
Value name: FastReboot
Type: STRING
Value data: 0
```

Note that you must disable FastReboot in order for "ReleaseLeaseOnShutdown" to actually work. You should also disable IPAutoconfiguration via the following Registry entry (you will need to create this one), which will prevent Windows from assigning an IP address in the 169.254.x.x address space:

```
Key: HKEY_LOCAL_MACHINE\System\CurrentControlSet\
Services\VxD\DHCP
Value name: IPAutoconfigurationEnabled
Type: DWORD
Value data: 0x00000000 (0)
```

Windows NT

When in an office using DHCP on Windows NT, disable the DHCP client service before leaving the office. This seems to work well, and users won't get the DHCP timeout when they turn on their computer and connect to their ISP. When you are ready to come back into the office, simply connect the LAN connection again, boot up the system, and log in. Kill SecuRemote in the taskbar, start up DHCP Client in manual mode, and then start the service. Do not reboot.

Windows NT Registry Hack

The purpose of the Registry hack is to make DHCP dependent on the startup of SecuRemote. This means that DHCP will not try to obtain an IP address until after SecuRemote has bound to the interface, which should cause DHCP to function as expected.

To make this change, go into `regedit` and look at the value:

```
HKEY_LOCAL_MACHINE\SYSTEM\CurrentControlSet\
Services\DHCP\DependOnService.
```

The value will appear in a window displaying both hexadecimal and ASCII. The ASCII will look something like this:

```
Tcpip.Afd.NetBT..
```

You need to change this to:

```
Tcpip.Afd.NetBT.FW0.FW1..
```

Note that the "." symbols used are actually null characters (which you need to enter as 00 on the hexadecimal side of the window). You also need two nulls at the end of the string.

Once you have made the Registry change, reboot.

SecuRemote Bound to All Adapters

You only need to bind SecuRemote to all adapters in the following cases:

- When a NIC is used to access the Internet (i.e., for DSL, cable modems)
- If you use Windows NT (you do not have a choice)

Binding SecuRemote to all adapters can cause additional problems in the previously mentioned cases (i.e., the NIC has an IP address inside the encryption domain). If you bind SecuRemote to all adapters, it is advisable to keep your NIC cards plugged in at all times. Sometimes, removing and reinstalling a NIC will hose the TCP/IP stack entirely. A reboot is the only way to recover. For the physically uninstalled but configured NICs (e.g., a laptop's unplugged PCMCIA card), the routing table will show the uninstalled NICs routing information. Without SecuRemote installed on all interfaces, the information related to the removed NIC card will not be shown in the routing table (i.e., when you type **route print**).

If the NIC is plugged in and if the NIC has an IP address in the encryption domain, you can expect problems. However, if the NIC is *not* plugged in, you really don't have an IP address in the encryption domain, so it should work. However, the uninstalled NIC's routing information is in the routing table (as if it were installed), so it does not work. Trying to remove the bogus routing information with `route delete` commands does not work, because the NIC is not really installed. Check Point has confirmed that this is a bug. Secure Client build 4153 and later do not appear to have this problem.

Summary

The organizational security policy can be extended to remote desktops while enabling access to the organizational network thanks to Secure Client. It is an extension of site-to-site VPNs, but Secure Client has several unique issues to overcome, including having to potentially support the machines and networks of users at home. This chapter covered many of the major issues you are likely to face and provided strategies for dealing with them.

Sample Configurations

The following three situations presented are representative of situations I have come across in the real world. Each is designed to demonstrate what people typically do with SecuRemote and Secure Client and how the situations would be implemented on the chosen platform.

A Simple Client-to-Site VPN

The Situation

You are the firewall administrator with a company that has one site employing several telecommuters. The clients need to be able to fully access the internal network. Clients also require protection, so Secure Client will be used. IKE with pre-shared secrets will be used to authenticate the users. An existing security policy exists for outgoing traffic (listed in the "Goals" section). The management console and the firewall are on separate hosts. See Figure 11-26.

The Goals

- Allow SecuRemote clients to access all hosts on the internal network with any service.
- Internal hosts are allowed to access sites on the Internet via FTP, HTTP, or HTTPS.
- SMTP can originate from predefined SMTP servers inside the network to the Internet. (They are in a group called SMTP Servers.)

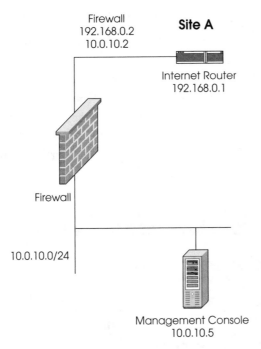

Firewall
192.168.0.2
10.0.10.2

Site A

Internet Router
192.168.0.1

Firewall

10.0.10.0/24

Management Console
10.0.10.5

Figure 11-26 Simple client-to-site VPN network diagram

- SMTP can go to the external-smtp server from anywhere (external-smtp-server is already defined).
- Deny all other traffic.

Checklist

- Define the necessary users, put them into a group (if necessary), and install the user database.
- Define the encryption domains for the local site.
- Configure the firewall workstation objects for the correct encryption domain, and use IKE with pre-shared secrets.
- Create the necessary encryption rules.
- Configure the encryption properties for the encryption rule.
- Configure the rule to permit FW1_Topo service to the management console.
- Install the security policy.

Implementation

For this example, let's use the names beavis, butthead, stewart, and daria. Users are placed into a group called telecommuters. Create users as shown in Chapter 7. To configure pre-shared secrets, you can do either of the following:

- Configure the Pre-Shared Secret option on the Encryption tab.
- Use Hybrid Authentication mode, and configure the password per the Password tab.

Let's assume standard pre-shared secrets are used for each user (i.e., without Hybrid Authentication). Edit each user's IKE Encryption Properties on the User's Encryption tab, select the "Password" check box, and enter a password as shown in Figure 11-6.

Next, you need to define the encryption domain. The internal network is a single logical segment. You can simply create a network object that covers this segment, as shown in Figure 11-27.

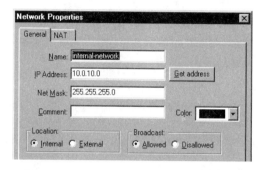

Figure 11-27   Internal network segment

Assign this object as the encryption domain for the firewall, as shown in Figure 11-28.

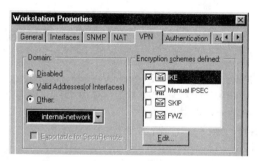

Figure 11-28   Workstation Properties, VPN tab

Edit the IKE properties, and make sure "Pre-Shared Secrets" is selected, as shown in Figure 11-29.

Your rulebase needs to look like Figure 11-30.

Rule 1 is the rule that permits the telecommuters to access the internal network via SecuRemote.

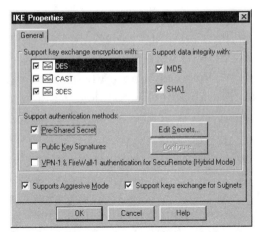

Figure 11-29 Workstation Properties, VPN tab, IKE Properties

No.	Source	Destination	Service	Action	Track	Install On
1	telecommuters@Any	internal-network	Any	Client Encrypt	Long	Gateways
2	Any	management-console	FW1_topo	accept	Long	Gateways
3	Any	firewall	IKE	accept	Long	Gateways
4	internal-network	Any	ftp http https	accept		Gateways
5	SMTP-Servers	Any	smtp	accept		Gateways
6	Any	external-smtp-server	Any	accept	Long	Gateways
7	Any	Any	Any	drop	Long	Gateways

Figure 11-30 Rulebase for sample configuration

Rule 2 is the rule that permits SecuRemote users to fetch the network topology. Without this rule, users cannot establish the site in the SecuRemote client. You can restrict this to authorized users only by unchecking the "Respond to Unauthenticated Topology Requests" check box on the Desktop Security tab of the Rulebase Properties. Note that if you have clients using SecuRemote 4.0 and earlier, you also need to permit the "FW1" service.

Rule 3 is the rule that permits UDP port 500 packets necessary for IKE to hit the firewall. Without this rule, these packets would be dropped by the firewall.

Rules 4 through 7 are necessary to establish the security policy defined in the "Goals" section.

Install the security policy and test.

Notes

This is a somewhat simplified example. Most sites have far more complex security policies or will want to use Hybrid Authentication. Just make sure your VPN rules are listed before any rules that allow outbound traffic to the Internet, that you have the necessary rules to permit IKE, and that the topology requests are listed before any firewall stealth rules.

Secure Client with Gateway Clusters

The Situation

The previous firewall has been replaced with a pair of Nokia IP440s in an HA configuration using VRRP Monitored Circuits. All other aspects of the network and the security policy are the same except for those conditions necessary to implement VRRP Monitored Circuits. See Figure 11-31.

The Goals

- Maintain the security policy as much as possible (from the previous lab).
- Add rules to support the use of the VRRP protocol (necessary for Monitored Circuits).
- Add rules to permit specific management clients the ability to FTP, SSH, and HTTP to the firewalls to perform management functions.

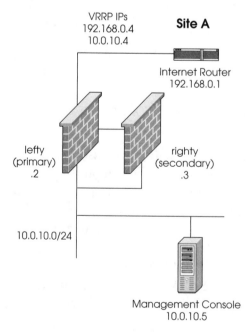

Figure 11-31 Simple client-to-site VPN network diagram with Gateway Clusters

Checklist

- Define the firewall workstation objects for each firewall.
- Define the Gateway Cluster object.
- Configure the firewall workstation objects to be part of the Gateway Cluster.
- Configure the Gateway Cluster object for IKE with pre-shared secrets.
- Configure the rulebase to support VRRP and allow the client management stations access to the firewalls.
- Install the security policy.
- Secure Client users must update the site definition.

Implementation

A workstation object for each firewall needs to be created. Each needs to be defined as Internal Gateways with FireWall-1 installed. You also need to make sure the Interfaces tabs have all of the physical interfaces properly defined. Next, create the Gateway Cluster object. Define it with the VRRP IP address used in your Monitored Circuit configuration (use the external IP, of course). Then, go back to each of your workstation objects and make them part of the Gateway Cluster object, as shown in Figure 11-32.

Go back to the Gateway Cluster object, define the encryption domain, and select IKE as the encryption scheme, as shown in Figure 11-1. Click IKE, and select Edit. Make sure Pre-Shared Secrets is selected, as shown in Figure 11-21.

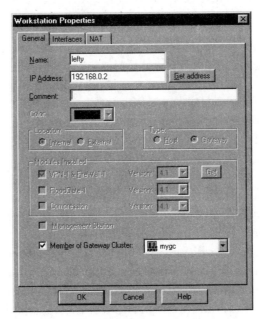

Figure 11-32 Workstation object for lefty as part of a Gateway Cluster

You have now defined your Gateway Cluster correctly. The next step is to define the VRRP service. It is a service of type Other defined as shown in Figure 11-33.

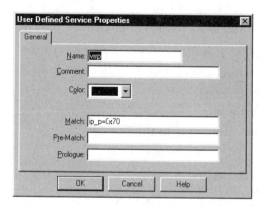

Figure 11-33 VRRP service definition

In order to enable VRRP to work, the rulebase and/or anti-spoofing must allow for the following:

- VRRP packets can originate from either firewall.
- VRRP packets can go to the VRRP Multicast Address (vrrp.mcast.net, 224.0.0.18) on any interface where VRRP is configured.
- VRRP packets can also go to a specific firewall interface for a triggered VRRP update.

You need to ensure that your firewall workstation objects have the Interfaces tab correctly defined with all of the IP addresses of the firewall. Also, put them into a group called "firewalls." In addition, you need to create vrrp.mcast.net, which is a workstation object with the IP address 224.0.0.18.

Next, create the rules to allow the workstations that manage the firewalls to access the firewalls via FTP, SSH, and HTTP. Create a group, add the various workstation objects to this group, and then use this group in a rule.

Other than these two rules, the rulebase looks the same as it did in the previous lab. Figure 11-34 shows what the rulebase looks like.

The object named *firewall* needs to have its IP address changed to that of the Gateway Cluster object. It is not possible to add a Gateway Cluster object directly in the rulebase, so a separate workstation object needs to be used.

Once you install the security policy, users will have to update their sites to take full advantage of the Gateway Cluster configuration. The client's `userc.c` will, after a site update, contain the IP addresses of the real firewalls and the virtual firewall's IP address.

No.	Source	Destination	Service	Action	Track	Install On
1	firewalls	firewalls vrrp.mcast.net	vrrp	accept		Gateways
2	firewall-managers	firewalls	ftp ssh http	accept	Long	Gateways
3	telecommuters@Any	internal-network	Any	Client Encrypt	Long	Gateways
4	Any	management-console	FW1_topo	accept	Long	Gateways
5	Any	firewall	IKE	accept	Long	Gateways
6	internal-network	Any	ftp http https	accept		Gateways
7	SMTP-Servers	Any	smtp	accept		Gateways
8	Any	external-smtp-server	Any	accept	Long	Gateways
9	Any	Any	Any	drop	Long	Gateways

Figure 11-34   Rulebase of sample configuration with Gateway Clusters

Notes

In order for connections to fail over, state synchronization must be established between the two gateways. How to establish state synchronization is covered in Chapter 12.

This is an overly simplistic configuration, but it demonstrates how to use Gateway Clusters. It also shows that, once implemented, the configuration does not change all that much.

Multiple Entry Point Secure Client

The Situation

The network used in these sample configurations has been merged into a larger network via a WAN link. Other parts of this WAN have their own Internet access protected by Check Point FireWall-1. It is desirable to use these other connections and firewalls as backup gateways for SecuRemote users. Because of this configuration, IP Pool NAT is required. Each firewall needs to be allocated a unique, nonroutable subnet so that incoming SecuRemote clients can be NATted to a specific firewall. Also, the original site needs to be reorganized somewhat to account for the WAN link. A WAN router has been added between the Nokia IP440s and the internal network with a new subnet. This is to keep the routing configuration a bit simpler.

Note that most of your attention should be focused on the original site (Site A in Figure 11-35). I will discuss the changes that need to occur on Site B (they are similar), but will leave the actual steps as an exercise for the reader.

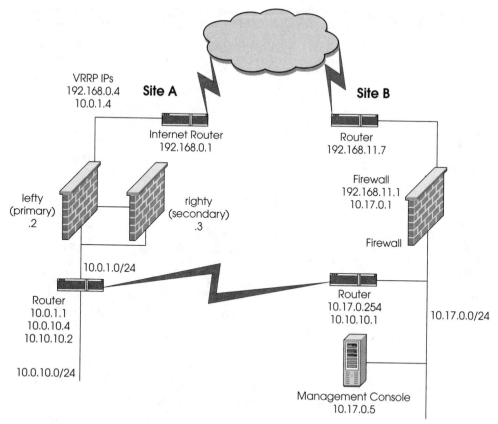

Figure 11-35   A multiple entry point configuration with Gateway Clusters

The Goal

- Maintain the security policy as much as possible (from previous lab).

Checklist

- Modify the encryption domains on all firewalls to include the same set of network objects, including all the firewalls.
- Configure Rulebase Properties to enable Backup Gateways for SecuRemote Clients and IP Pool NAT logging options.
- Choose appropriate address ranges for each gateway to use for IP Pool NAT.
- Configure each workstation and/or Gateway Cluster so that the other firewalls are backup gateways.
- Configure each local gateway's workstation or Gateway Cluster object so NAT is performed for SecuRemote connections.
- Install the security policy.

Implementation

The other site (Site B in Figure 11-35) has an encryption domain of 172.17.0.0/16. Both sites need to have an encryption domain that contains the following:

- All three firewalls at both sites
- 10.0.10.0/24
- 10.17.0.0

Note that because there are no hosts in 10.0.1.0/24 except for the firewalls, you do not need to include it in the encryption domain. You may, in fact, use some of these IP addresses for IP Pool NAT, which is discussed in a moment.

To enable Backup Gateways for SecuRemote Clients, you must go to the Rulebase Properties High Availability tab and make sure the appropriate check box has been selected. See Figure 11-36.

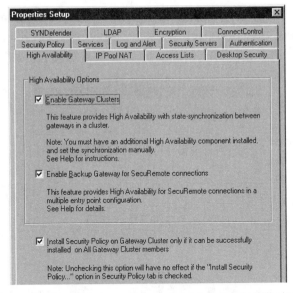

Figure 11-36   Rulebase Properties, High Availability tab

You should also enable IP Pool NAT for SecuRemote Connections by going to the IP Pool NAT tab and selecting the appropriate box, as well as setting the appropriate level of logging, as shown in Figure 11-18.

Next, define an address range for use by the IP Pool NAT function. You should choose IP addresses that will route back to the firewall. In this case, let's use unused addresses on the LAN segment 10.0.1.0/24. You can use 10.0.1.5 through 10.0.1.254 (the others are in use). To make sure these packets route back to the firewall, you have to establish a proxy-ARP for each of these IP addresses or establish static routes on the WAN router to point these addresses to the firewall's VRRP address. More details on why this is necessary are provided in Chapter 9.

Let's create an address range object to represent this address range. See Figure 11-37. You will create a similar address range object for the backup gateway.

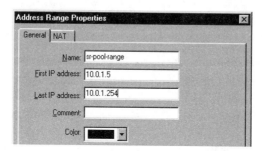

Figure 11-37   Address Range object

Next, go to the Gateway Cluster's VPN tab, and select the remote gateway as the backup gateway for SecuRemote connections. See Figure 11-38. Note, do *not* do this on maingw's object.

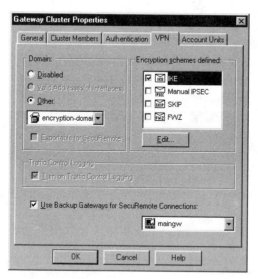

Figure 11-38   Gateway Cluster object, VPN tab, enable backup gateway

In a Gateway Cluster configuration, configure the NAT tab on the individual members of the Gateway Cluster. On each of the NAT tabs, enable IP Pool NAT, and select the address range created previously, as shown in Figure 11-39. On maingw, you will make a similar configuration change.

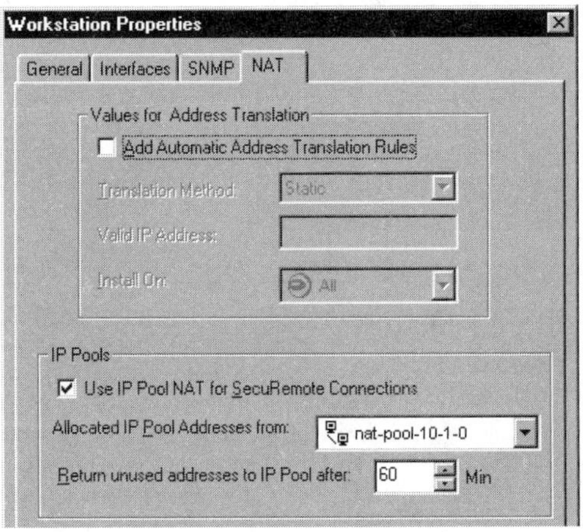

Figure 11-39 Gateway Cluster object, NAT tab, enable IP Pool NAT

To accommodate the new encryption domain, you have to change Rule 3 in your rulebase so that the rule includes "encryption-domain" instead of "internal-network." Other than that, the rulebase is identical to the one in the previous lab. See Figure 11-40.

Notes

Despite the fact that Gateway Clusters are being used, a failover of the primary firewall will cause any active connections to terminate. If both members of the cluster fail, only then will the backup gateway be utilized.

No.	Source	Destination	Service	Action	Track	Install On
1	firewalls	firewalls vrrp.mcast.net	vrrp	accept		Gateways
2	firewall-managers	firewalls	ftp ssh http	accept	Long	Gateways
3	telecommuters@Any	encryption-domain	Any	Client Encrypt	Long	Gateways
4	Any	management-console	FW1_topo	accept	Long	Gateways
5	Any	firewalls	IKE	accept	Long	Gateways
6	net-10-0-10-0-24	Any	ftp http https	accept		Gateways
7	SMTP-Servers	Any	smtp	accept		Gateways
8	Any	external-smtp-server	Any	accept	Long	Gateways
9	Any	Any	Any	drop	Long	Gateways

Figure 11-40 Rulebase for multiple entry point configuration

Chapter

12

High Availability

In today's business environment, downtime anywhere in the network is simply not an option. This includes your network security enforcement points. The focus of this chapter is on making firewalls highly available. I will touch on the issues that arise when you have more than one firewall in parallel and outline a strategy for load balancing traffic across multiple firewalls.

By the end of this chapter, you should be able to:

- Configure FireWall-1 state synchronization
- Identify vendors that provide High-Availability and load-balancing solutions
- Understand asymmetric routing and why it is bad for firewalls
- Establish a method for load balancing across multiple firewalls

State Synchronization's Role in High Availability

An application is said to be highly available when you have taken steps to minimize single points of failure. In the mid-1990s, several companies introduced High-Availability (HA) software that provided an infrastructure allowing applications to be monitored on the primary system and "failed over" to a secondary system when a failure was detected. The applications were stored on a shared medium (usually a mirrored disk connected to both systems), and state for the applications had to be stored on the shared disk drive. This allowed the secondary system to pick up where the primary left off.

Although this was a boon for many companies, it had some drawbacks:

- Only one system at a time was active. The secondary system was usually idle.

- Some state was always lost. Placing state on disk had its limits and was not possible with many applications, including FireWall-1.

A more ideal way of handling HA is to have both systems active at a time, actively sharing information. In FireWall-1, this can be done with a feature called *state synchronization*.

State synchronization is a mechanism in FireWall-1 that allows two firewalls to share information contained within their respective state tables. This allows a firewall to more readily take over in the event of a failure. Although state synchronization preserves most connections, any connections involving the Security Servers will not fail over properly. This is because all Security Server-related connections actually terminate at a single firewall. It is difficult to fail over connections that terminate at a specific firewall.

State synchronization occurs via one of two mechanisms:

- Using TCP port 256
- Using UDP port 8116

All systems support the TCP port 256 method (sometimes called *old sync*). Only systems that support the Check Point HA Module can sync over UDP. Even where UDP sync is used, TCP-based sync is used when full table synchronization is needed (e.g., at startup, after a policy install).

Two steps must be taken to set up state synchronization:

- Create $FWDIR/conf/sync.conf on each firewall module. This file contains IP addresses or resolvable hostnames that tell the firewall module which machines they synchronize with.
- Establish an authenticated control connection between the firewall modules. This is done via the fw putkey command.

For example, let's say you want to establish synchronization between two firewalls named "beavis" (192.168.5.42) and "butthead" (192.168.5.69). Before you can do this, two things need to happen:

- A dedicated interface between the two firewalls should exist for the sole purpose of transferring state table information. This is not strictly required, but it is highly recommended.
- The time on both firewalls must be synchronized (within a minute or two). It is highly recommended that you use something like Network Time Protocol (NTP) to either synchronize each firewall or use a third-party time server.

The IP addresses given next to each host are the IP addresses on the sync interface. On beavis, you would add the following entry to $FWDIR/conf/sync.conf:

```
192.168.5.69
```

Conversely, on butthead, you would add the following entry to `$FWDIR/conf/sync.conf`:

```
192.168.5.42
```

You would then perform an `fw putkey` to establish an authenticated control connection between the two.[1] On beavis, you would execute the following command:

```
fw putkey -p abc123 192.168.5.69
```

On butthead, the command is:

```
fw putkey -p abc123 192.168.5.42
```

After you have done this, a restart of FireWall-1 is required on both platforms. The `fw putkey` command is explained in more detail in Chapter 6.

UDP State Synchronization

If you want to use UDP state synchronization, enter the following statement on the first line of `$FWDIR/conf/sync.conf`:

```
SyncMode=CPHAP
```

The preceding statement assumes UNIX. For Windows NT, you have to set the following Registry entry to 1:

```
HKEY_LOCAL_MACHINE\System\CurrentControlSet\Services\CPHA\HAMode
```

Whether or not you are using the Check Point HA Module, you will have to enable Check Point HA options and configure synchronization interfaces and machine IDs per the *Check Point 2000 Getting Started Guide*. If you are not using the Check Point HA Module, you will also need to edit the file `$FWDIR/conf/cpha.conf` as follows: Replace the line `mode N`, where *N* is either "primary-up" or "active-up," with the line `mode service`. Make sure that no other word appears in the `mode service` line.

NOTE! `fw putkey` **needs to be executed in addition to the Check Point HA Module configuration, as UDP sync also relies on TCP sync for times when full synchronization is needed.**

---

1. An alternative approach would be to edit `$FWDIR/lib/control.map` and set the command `sync` to "none" authentication.

How Do I Know State Synchronization Is Working?

Two methods (neither guaranteed nor foolproof) are used to check sync on a pair of FireWall-1 firewalls.

Run `netstat -na` on each machine, and look for a pair of connections with the firewall module you are synchronizing with. The output should include something like the following:

```
tcp   0   0   192.168.5.42.256    192.168.5.69.1056   ESTABLISHED
tcp   0   0   192.168.5.42.1054   192.168.5.69.256    ESTABLISHED
```

The important numbers in the netstat output are the IP addresses of each of the two firewalls (on the "sync" ports) and the port "256." Notice in the preceding example that port 256 is open on firewall 1 in the first line and firewall 2 in the second line.

The other method to check proper sync between two FireWall-1 firewalls is to compare the size of the connections table on each firewall. Use the command `fw tab -t connections -s`. Each firewall will display a table similar to the following:

```
HOST            NAME            ID   #VALS
localhost       connections     14   2143
```

The two #VALS numbers should be roughly equivalent on both firewalls. If they are different, run the commands again after waiting a few seconds.

What Are the Limitations of State Synchronization?

You should be aware that state synchronization happens approximately every 100ms. All changes in the state table since the last sync interval are sent to the peer firewalls. It also takes roughly 55ms for these changes to be incorporated into the state tables. This means it takes a minimum of 155ms for the peer firewall to be updated. The actual amount of time varies based on system load.

What does this delay in synchronization mean? The long and the short of it is, if one firewall receives a TCP SYN packet and the other firewall receives a corresponding TCP SYN/ACK before the synchronization actually occurs, you will end up dropping or severely delaying the establishment of the TCP connection. This is a condition known as *asymmetric routing*, which is discussed in its own section later in this chapter.

Some other important restrictions concerning state synchronization include:

• The firewalls must be running on the same type of platform. This means that two Nokia, two Windows NT, or two Solaris platforms may synchronize with one another, but a Nokia and a Windows NT platform cannot. This is due to differences in how each platform internally stores the tables.

- The firewalls must be running the same version of the software. This means that a version 4.1 platform cannot synchronize with a 4.0 or 3.0 platform. All the firewalls should be running the same service pack, but this is not strictly required.
- The firewalls must have the same security policy.
- IKE and FWZ encryption schemes can be synchronized as of FireWall-1 4.1 provided the Gateway Cluster feature is used. Please see Chapter 10 for more details. Note that SKIP or Manual IPSec cannot be synchronized.
- With respect to NAT, careful consideration must be given to routing. Where routing is symmetric, it is usually only necessary to make the needed ARP and routing changes on both firewalls. Where routing is asymmetric, additional configuration on routers on either side may need to be done.
- No connections or information relating to Security Servers are synchronized. This is because they rely on individual processes on the platforms in question and cannot be easily synchronized.
- If accounting logging is used, neither firewall will be able to provide accurate data on how much traffic was transferred, because accounting data is not synchronized.
- State synchronization does not scale well beyond two firewalls, at least when using the TCP method. UDP may be slightly better in this regard, but it is still a difficult task keeping more than two firewalls synced. In some applications (particularly firewalls protecting HTTP farms), state synchronization can be either eliminated or greatly reduced.

Implementing High Availability

State synchronization is a very important component for implementing HA. Without it, other firewalls that may be called in to take over will not know the current status of connections and will cause a break in connectivity. However, it is not the only piece to this equation. Another component must be involved to allow other routers or hosts around the firewall to know which firewall to use at the time. Dynamic routing protocols can certainly be used to achieve this, but this is not always practical and comes with its own problems—namely, they can create asymmetric routing.

All HA solutions for FireWall-1 provide for some sort of virtual IP address, which is shared between the firewalls. The active firewall at any given time possesses a number of these virtual addresses, at least one on each physical interface (exactly how and when are specific to each implementation). This provides a virtual firewall. Clients and routers can simply point to this virtual address where appropriate and always be assured that some machine will respond accordingly.

Asymmetric Routing

Asymmetric routing means that packets on a connection take different paths coming into and going out of a given network—namely, your own network. Any time packets have multiple paths to take through a network, there is always a possibility they will take a different path. If you observe how the Internet as a whole works, it is quite customary for sent packets to take a slightly different path from packets that are received.

Asymmetric routing is not a problem if all that is occurring is packets are being routed and connection state is not tracked. If connection state must be tracked (for instance, when you are trying to perform network security functions), then asymmetric routing causes problems. Any HA solution must ensure that asymmetric routing does not occur or must have some way to deal with it when it does.

Consider the network diagram in Figure 12-1.

For 10.0.10.0/24, there are two possible routes to the Internet: mrhat and mrtwig. There are also two possible routes back to 10.0.10.0/24 from the Internet: mrhat and

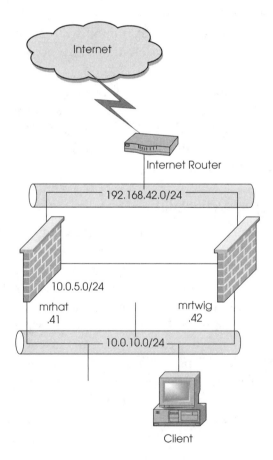

Figure 12-1 Sample network configuration

mrtwig. This means that it is possible to have an asymmetrical routing situation. For illustrative purposes, let's assume that mrhat is the default route for clients on the 10.0.10.0/24 network and that the Internet Router routes all packets destined for 10.0.10.0/24 to mrtwig. This means there is an asymmetric routing condition. Let's also assume that both firewalls in question are synchronizing their state tables via Check Point's state synchronization mechanism.

Connections originating from 10.0.10.0/24 going to the Internet may actually work fairly well. It works better the longer the latency is between sending the first packet through mrhat and receiving its reply through mrtwig. Hosts out on the Internet can easily take more than 155ms to respond.

Connections originating from the Internet and destined for 10.0.10.0/24 will be slow in establishing (if they do at all). This is because the latency between the time the packet is initially received on mrtwig, responded to by the client, and then sent out via mrhat will likely be less than 155ms (in the preceding situation, it would be less than 10ms). This means state synchronization will not have had an opportunity to do its job. If the packet received on mrtwig is a SYN packet and the packet received on mrhat is a SYN/ACK packet (i.e., packets that start a TCP session), mrhat will see that the packet is not part of an established connection and will drop the packet. About three seconds later,[2] the server on the 10.0.10.0/24 network not having received an ACK packet to acknowledge the SYN/ACK will resend the SYN/ACK packet. By that time, synchronization will have occurred, and the packet will be allowed through. Note that with UDP or any IP datagrams, retransmissions only occur if the application using the packets does it, so it is quite possible these packets will simply be dropped.

The good news is that this problem only has the potential to occur within that 155ms or so right when the connection is being established. Once the connection is properly established and synchronized, an asymmetric condition is not a problem.

HA Solution Providers

You have several different choices of HA software. The most common choices include:

- *Stonebeat's FullCluster (www.stonebeat.com):* A software product that runs on the same platform as FireWall-1. It provides both hot standby failover as well as failover with load sharing.
- *Rainfinity RainWall (www.rainfinity.com):* A software product that runs on the same platform as FireWall-1. It provides hot standby failover as well as failover with load sharing.

---

2. This time period is actually dependent on the TCP/IP implementation. However, most TCP/IP stacks are based on BSD's TCP/IP stack, which has this default.

- *Check Point's High Availability Module (www.checkpoint.com):* A software product that is integrated into FireWall-1, although it requires a separate license. It provides a hot standby failover.
- *Nokia (www.nokia.com/securitysolutions/):* Nokia platforms include support for Virtual Router Redundancy Protocol (VRRP, see RFC 2338), which provides failover capabilities to FireWall-1. Load balancing is not part of this solution but can easily be achieved with third-party hardware.
- *Radware's Fireproof (www.radware.com):* A hardware product that provides hot standby failover as well as failover with load sharing.
- *Foundry's ServerIron (www.foundry.com):* A hardware product that provides hot standby failover as well as failover with load sharing.
- *Alteon/Nortel Networks ACEswitch and ACEdirector (www.alteonwebsystems. com):* A hardware product that provides hot standby failover as well as failover with load sharing.

From this list, you can see that there are two schools of thought: hardware-based solutions and software-based solutions. For HA, either solution works well, although software-based solutions do have somewhat of an edge because they can interact with FireWall-1 more directly. When load balancing is factored into the equation, hardware solutions quite simply scale better, although they tend to be somewhat more expensive. You can use both hardware and software HA systems together.

Any HA solution must address the problem of asymmetric routing. HA software vendors claim to be able to handle the asymmetric routing problem. However, I am skeptical of any software product's ability to handle this well. Assuming both firewalls are synchronized, there is simply no way to synchronize fast enough to be able to handle asymmetric connections in all situations. Packets can be held by some other process so that the synchronization process can catch up, or packets can be set up so that all firewalls hear the packets and only the right one responds, which seems to be a waste. Either latency or throughput is compromised in this situation. Specialized hardware can do this much faster than a general purpose platform can and is usually more scalable.

Load Balancing

When you have more than one firewall in parallel, the next logical question is, how can I have each firewall take part in the overall network load to increase throughput? Most people do not like the idea of purchasing extra equipment only to leave it sitting around unused most of the time.

Any effective load-balancing solution for FireWall-1 must handle packets for connections symmetrically (i.e. in and out through the same firewall), or at the very least, be able to do this long enough for state synchronization to catch up. Stonebeat and

Rainfinity have solutions for this problem built into their respective HA software products. Despite what their marketing literature states, their ability to scale is somewhat limited. Although hardware solutions are more expensive, they are more robust and more resilient. You get what you pay for.

Static Load-Balancing Techniques

A cheap way to load balance is to logically group your hosts behind the firewall. This involves the following:

- Hosts behind your gateway need to be configured with a static default route to the proper firewall for their group. Each group should be on different logical networks or at least be grouped on a reasonable subnet boundary.
- The border router(s) needs to be configured with different routes to different firewalls.
- If VRRP (or something similar) is used, there needs to be multiple virtual IP addresses (one for each group) that can be failed over. This will provide resilience in case one of the firewalls fails.

Figure 12-2 illustrates static load balancing in action.

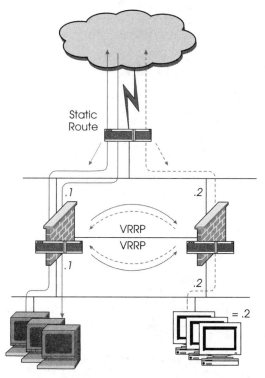

Figure 12-2   Static load balancing

In Figure 12-2, the grey hosts use the .1 firewall as its default route, the white hosts use the .2 firewall, and the border router has static routes for grey hosts and white hosts back to their respective firewalls.

You can also do something similar with multiple site-to-site VPNs, although it requires an internal router capable of doing policy routing based on source addresses to ensure that packets go to the proper firewall. Figure 12-3 illustrates static load balancing with policy routing.

The main issue with static load balancing is that load distribution is not automatic. If one part of your network starts consuming more bandwidth, you will have to manually adjust the load balancing. However, static load balancing is relatively inexpensive and straightforward to set up and maintain.

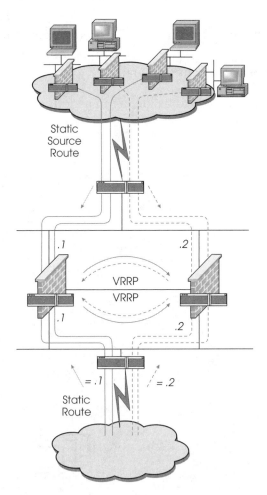

Figure 12-3 Static load balancing with policy routing

N+1 Resilience

Due to the lack of scalability of state synchronization, you can have a firewall that exists for the sole purpose of dealing with failovers. You could have N firewalls that are primary firewalls and a single backup firewall that handles each of the N firewalls. Synchronization would only occur between each firewall and the backup firewall. All failovers would default to the backup firewall. See Figure 12-4. However, it is also quite possible that the backup firewall may fail due to the load of state synchronization.

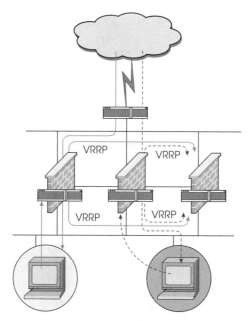

Figure 12-4   N+1 resilience

Load Balancing with Switches

Thus far, I have assumed a single inbound and outbound connection. Although NIC cards and hubs/switches are generally pretty reliable, from time to time these components fail. To provide more throughput and greater resilience, you should double the number of connections and switches, as shown in Figure 12-5.

Each interface must be associated with a logically different subnet, which gives you the ability to use multiple switches. However, this does present two external interfaces to FireWall-1, which means you can only use this method if you have an unlimited firewall module license regardless of how many hosts you are protecting.

One advantage to this method is increased theoretical throughput. You now have two interfaces, which means you can potentially send twice as much data. Unfortunately, only the most-powerful machines will be able to fully utilize both interfaces at

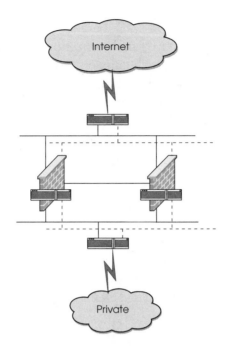

Figure 12-5   Load balancing with switches

maximum capacity. However, some modest performance gains can still be achieved, even without full utilization.

Dynamic Load Balancing

Dynamic load balancing is generally preferable to static load balancing because it usually provides a better load balance and is more accommodating of changes that occur in your network. However, extra care must be taken to ensure symmetry. Most load-balancing techniques use some sort of hash function that is nondeterministic. This creates asymmetric routing. Deterministic forwarding on both sides of the firewall is used to ensure that the same path is taken in both directions. This also provides a nice way to load balance.

Deterministic load balancing can also be done with a hash. Most load balancers perform an XOR of the source and destination IP address. This produces a symmetric result with packets going from host A to host B or host B to host A, as shown in Figure 12-6.

Assuming only two paths (i.e., two parallel firewalls), you simply look at the last bit in the XOR. A zero means pass the packet to one firewall; a one means send it to the other firewall. Using hashing only, you are limited to the number of firewalls that are powers of two (2, 4, 8, 16, etc.). However, most systems enhance the hashing

```
Incoming
SourceIP          172.16.64.1        10101100.00010000.01000000.00000001
DestinationIP     192.168.30.65      11000000.10101000.00011110.01000001
XOR               108 184 94 64      01101100 10111000 01011110 01000000
Outgoing
SourceIP          192.168.30.65      11000000.10101000.00011110.01000001
DestinationIP     172.16.64.1        10101100.00010000.01000000.00000001
XOR               108 184 94 64      01101100 10111000 01011110 01000000
```

Figure 12-6   XOR of incoming and outgoing packets by IP

mechanism to support any number of firewalls and include methods that check the chosen path before using it and require their own sort of state synchronization.

Because of these accessible techniques, you can now build a fully meshed solution with resilient load balancers and firewalls. There are many different products that can perform this function, including products from Nortel Networks, Cisco, Cabletron, F5, Foundry, Radware, and TopLayer. Once the connection is established and state synchronization occurs, a failure can occur in any component, and the connections will continue to flow. See Figure 12-7.

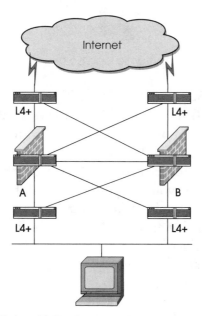

Figure 12-7   Dynamic load balancing

Network Address Translation

NAT makes load balancing much more complex, mainly because packets look different inside and outside the firewall. However, if only the source *or* destination IP address is subject to NAT, you can still use a hash function to accomplish load balancing by hashing against the IP address that does not change.

Consider Figure 12-8.

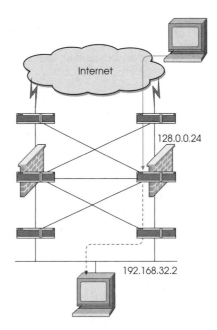

Figure 12-8   Dynamic load balancing with NAT

The machine with IP address 192.168.32.2 is accessed via 128.0.0.24 on the Internet by means of a NAT. If 192.168.32.2 initiates a connection to the Internet, the destination IP address will not change. Conversely, if something initiates a connection to 128.0.0.24, the source address will not change.

Therefore, on the outside routers, you can perform a hash based on the source IP address. On the inside routers, you can perform a hash based on the destination IP address. Both of these hashes should return the same value, thus allowing you to forward all traffic through a particular firewall. This technique will not work with dual NAT (i.e., where source and destination are both translated) or in a VPN. The next section discusses load balancing with VPNs.

Site-to-Site VPNs

The problem you have with a VPN is that, from the outside world, the packets look like they are coming from host A and going to host B, even though inside the packet it may be host X going to host Y. This is because the packets are encapsulated and encrypted. Encrypted packets have zero correlation to their unencrypted counterparts, so none of the hashing techniques that have been discussed thus far will handle them.

A system that will map a particular application or connection to a next hop Ethernet address is required. This can be done with a fairly sophisticated hash table that stores where to forward a packet. An example of this might be:

```
(hash key: [srcIP: ingress if, ingress MAC], [dstIP: egress if,
egress MAC]).
```

When a packet arrives at the load balancer, a symmetric hash is performed, usually on layer 3 and 4 information. You then check to see if there is a match in the table based on the hash value and the source IP address. You check the hash for a match, and you check to see if either the source or destination IP address in the table entry matches the source address of the received packet. If there is a match, you forward it to the appropriate MAC address based on the source IP address of the packet and refresh the table entry. If there is no match, you figure out the ingress and egress interfaces and MAC address, create a new table entry, and forward accordingly. Figure 12-9 shows a flowchart of this process.

For example, assume you have a situation similar to Figure 12-7 except you are using load balancers that implement the technique discussed in this section. Let's follow

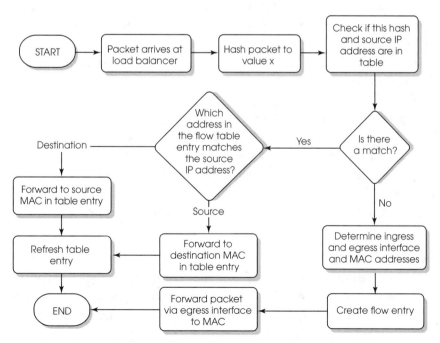

Figure 12-9   Flowchart of dynamic load balancing with VPNs

an IPSec-encrypted TCP SYN packet as it enters the network from the Internet and the SYN/ACK reply as it exits. Let's call the load balancers on the outside of the firewalls elb1 and elb2, the two firewalls A and B, the two firewall's virtual IP address C (which is also the Gateway Cluster address), and the load balancers inside the firewalls ilb1 and ilb2.

The IPSec packet has a source IP address of F and a destination IP address of C. It is received at elb1 via interface elb1-1. The packet it hashed to value x and elb1 determines that no flow entry exists. The next hop for this packet is determined to be firewall A out interface elb1-3. An entry is added to the table that looks like this:

```
(hash x, F [elb1-1, upstream router MAC], C [elb1-3, firewall-A's
external MAC])
```

Firewall A receives the packet, accepts the packet, decrypts it, and forwards it to ilb1. The packet now has a source IP address of P and a destination IP address of Q. ilb1 hashes the packet to value y and determines that no flow entry exists. The next hop for this packet is determined to be an internal router out interface elb1-4. The packet was received on elb1-1. An entry is added to the table, which looks like this:

```
(hash y, P [elb1-1, Firewall-A's internal MAC], Q [elb1-4,
downstream router MAC])
```

When the SYN/ACK packet comes back to elb1, it has a source IP of Q and destination IP of P. ilb1 hashes the packet to value y (remember, the hash function is symmetric). An entry for this hash exists in the table. Q matches the "destination" IP address of this entry (it is a reply, so the source/destination are reversed), so the packet is forwarded out interface elb1-1 to Firewall-A's internal MAC address. Firewall A receives the packet, accepts it, encrypts it, and forwards it out to elb1 where a similar process takes place.

This process is beneficial because it is interface independent. The forwarding is unit independent, thus NAT and VPNs will work. This approach is particularly clever in that it does not matter that the switch does not know of a flow, because the forwarding technique is deterministic. Obviously the hash table has to be aged. It can be viewed as a sophisticated ARP table.

Products by Foundry and F5 support load balancing described in this section.

Summary

This chapter touched on many of the issues that come up in High Availability. It is by no means a complete guide on the subject. The two important issues covered were how to implement state synchronization in FireWall-1 and the dangers of asymmetric routing.

Chapter

13

INSPECT

INSPECT is a feature in Check Point FireWall-1 that is poorly documented but can be *very* useful if people become familiar with it. Certain people within Check Point claim it is poorly documented because the language itself has not stabilized, which Check Point claims will be the case by the time NG comes out.[1] This chapter offers a brief introduction to how INSPECT works, and the information should be useful to those of you who are looking for a more detailed understanding of how FireWall-1 works and to those who want to permit more-advanced services through FireWall-1. It is not meant to cover the INSPECT language comprehensively. Several examples of INSPECT code are included.

By the end of this chapter, you should be able to:

- Understand what INSPECT is
- Determine what you can and cannot do with INSPECT
- Understand how FireWall-1 converts your rulebase into INSPECT
- Write your own INSPECT code

What Is INSPECT?

INSPECT is a programming language for Check Point's Stateful Inspection engine in FireWall-1. When you install your security policy generated in the Policy Editor, your rulebase is converted to an INSPECT script. Most people never need to look at INSPECT code, but if you need to make FireWall-1 support more than just simple services (i.e., where only one connection is opened from the client to the server), you will need to use INSPECT. You may not have to write a full INSPECT script, but you may have to use snippets of INSPECT to accomplish what you need to.

---

1. Various individuals have told me that Check Point has basically been saying "it will have INSPECT better documented in the next version of FireWall-1" for quite some time now.

The primary purpose of INSPECT is to analyze a packet from the network layer down to the application layer and make decisions based on what is found. INSPECT, although a very powerful language, only has a few basic functions:

- Makes comparisons based on any part of a packet
- Adds, modifies, or deletes entries from state tables
- Accepts, rejects, drops, or vanishes a packet
- Calls functions (such as log)

Basic INSPECT Syntax

This section presents a more rudimentary description of how to read and understand INSPECT code by providing simple examples. It should be read in conjunction with the INSPECT chapter of your FireWall-1 documentation, which includes more details about functions available in your specific version.

INSPECT is a fairly simple script-like language containing a series of statements designed to evaluate packets and make decisions about what to do with the packet. Although this is not a complete BNF[2] for the language, it should give you a rough idea as to what to expect:

```
inspect script  ::= { <statement> }

:statement      ::= <scope> <condition> { "," <condition> | "and"
                    <condition> |
                    "xor" <condition> | "or" <condition> }  ";"
scope           ::= <direction> "@" <host>

direction       ::= "<" | ">" | "<>" | ""

condition       ::= <short circuit> |
                    <table command> |
                    <identifier> { <operand> <identifier> }  |
                    <function>

operand         :== + | - | / | * | % | "|" | ^ | "==" | "!=" | ">" | "<"
                    | "<=" | ">="

short circuit   ::= accept | reject | drop | vanish
```

---

2.   BNF is an acronym for Backus Normal Form or Backus Naur Form, which is a standard format used to describe programming languages. And I thought it was just a way to torture unsuspecting computer science students. ☺

```
table command    ::= get <table entry> from <table name> |
                     delete <table entry> from <table name> |
                     modify <table entry> in <table name> |
                     record <table entry> in <table name> |
                     get <table entry> to <register name> |
                     <table entry> in <table name>
```

Each statement is processed in order until the operation either reaches the end of the script (which means INSPECT will drop the packet) or it hits a short circuit as defined earlier (`accept`, `reject`, `deny`, and `vanish`). A description of these short circuits appears in Table 13-1.

Table 13-1   Short circuits in INSPECT

Action	Description
`accept`	Accept the packet (allow it to pass)
`drop`	Drop the packet silently
`reject`	Drop the packet loudly (i.e., send a TCP RST or ICMP Unreachable message)
`vanish`	Drop the packet silently and leave no trace

The difference between `drop` and `vanish` involves how FireWall-1 handles packets received for established TCP packets (i.e., have the ACK flag set, but not the SYN flag set) that FireWall-1 holds no state information for. The `drop` action doesn't really "drop" the packet, but mangles the packet and passes it through the firewall. All the data in the packet is removed, leaving only the IP and TCP headers. This effectively makes the packet harmless. The TCP sequence numbers of the packet are also changed. When the destination host receives the mangled packet, it should immediately respond due to the mangled sequence number. If the TCP connection is still valid, this response will be matched by the security policy and the connection will be re-recorded in the connections table. If the connection has become invalid, the host will send back a TCP reset (packet). FireWall-1 notices that it drops a reply to a mangled TCP packet and therefore does not mangle it again but rather drops it for good.

Prior to FireWall-1 4.1 SP2, you could send unsolicited ACK packets through FireWall-1 and cause a denial of service against hosts behind the firewall (the "ACK DoS" attack). This was because FireWall-1 used `drop` when processing unestablished TCP packets. In FireWall-1 4.1 SP2 and later, `vanish` is used on these packets. This does not do the packet mangling that `drop` performs; it simply causes the packet to disappear without a trace. For earlier versions of FireWall-1, there is an "ACK DoS" fix you can apply that resolves this issue.

Basically, statements are a series of conditions separated by ANDs (signified by a comma or the keyword "AND") and ORs (using the word "OR"). There is very limited ability for indirection with functions. There are no loops or recursion in INSPECT. What you see is pretty much what you get with INSPECT.

Consider the following statement (note that a and b are generic conditions):

```
a, b, accept;
```

This line means accept the packet if condition a and b are both true. You can also write the statement as:

```
accept a, b;
```

It means the same thing (accept if a and b are true). Note that drop, reject, and vanish can also be used in this manner.

In both statements, if a is found to be false, b is never evaluated. This is a very important concept to understand. In a long, complex statement, you can essentially "skip the rest" if part of the statement is false. For example, if a is false in the following statement, none of the other statements are evaluated:

```
a, b, c, d, e, f, accept;
```

You can also combine ANDs and ORs. The following statement:

```
a, b or c, d or e, f, accept;
```

is evaluated as if it were (logically, in pseudocode in C):

```
if ( a AND ( b OR c ) AND ( d OR e ) AND f ) { accept ; }
```

Note that you can force operator precedence with parentheses. You can also do something like this:

```
a, b or reject, accept;
```

If a and b are true, accept the packet (reject is skipped in this case). If a is false, simply go to the next statement. If a is true and b is false, reject the packet. Note that this is different from:

```
(a, b) or reject, accept;
```

which would reject the packet if either a or b were false.

Conditions

In the previous example, a single letter (like a, b, and c) was used to represent generic conditions. An actual condition looks more like this:

```
x = y
x != y
x > y
x < y
```

This script evaluates true if x equals y, x does not equal y, x is greater than y, and x is less than y. You can also see if something is in a table (tables are discussed in the "Manipulating Table Entries" section):

```
<ip_src, ip_dst, sport> in http_table
```

Note that you can negate a particular statement by using not and parentheses. For example:

```
not (<ip_src, ip_dst, sport> in http_table)
```

You can also AND (&), OR (|), or XOR (^) two values together in a bitwise fashion to determine their value or use arithmetic functions (+, -, *, and /). In addition, you can bitshift values left and right with << or >>.

You can see some of the parts of a packet by looking at the predefined parts of a packet in $FWDIR/lib/tcpip.def, which includes information from IP, TCP, and UDP headers. There are also several identifiers that INSPECT has defined, which you can use as well. Some of these identifiers are documented in Table 13-2.

Table 13-2 Predefined identifiers

Identifier	Description
src	Source IP address
sport	Source TCP/UDP port
dst	Destination IP address
dport	Destination TCP/UDP port
ip_p	IP Protocol number
tcp	True if current packet is TCP (same as ip_p = 6)
udp	True if current packet is UDP (same as ip_p = 17)
icmp	True if current packet is ICMP (same as ip_p = 1)
tod	Time of day (in 24-hour hh:mm:ss format)
date	Current system date (in dd mmm format)
day	Day of the week (using standard three-letter abbreviation)

You can also look at other parts of the packet by specifying which parts of the packet you would like to look at up to four bytes at a time. For example, if you would like to see if the 50th through the 53rd byte of the packet contain the command GET (with the space), you would do the comparison like this:

```
[50, b] = 0x47455420 // ASCII for "GET "
```

The ", b" means to read the data in big endian format and is generally needed if you want to look at TCP/IP packets more than one byte at a time. Four bytes are captured by default. If you only want to look at the 50th byte of the packet, you would look at it like this:

```
[50:1, b] = 0x47 // ASCII for "G"
```

Constants

FireWall-1 interprets numbers in octal, hexadecimal, and decimal. A number beginning with a 0 is always evaluated as an octal value. Hexadecimal numbers begin with a "0x." All other numbers are treated as decimal.

Time periods can be represented in hh:mm:ss format. For example, for 11:59 P.M. and 30 seconds, the format would be 23:59:30. Dates are represented by dd mmm format. For example, June 20 would be represented by 20 Jun. The standard three-letter abbreviations for days of the week (i.e., sun, mon, tue, wed, thu, fri, sat) are constants that refer to the specific day of the week.

INSPECT also handles IP addresses entered in their dotted-quad notation (e.g., 192.168.42.69) as well as their physical interface name (e.g., eth-s1p1c0, le0, el59x1) and domain names (e.g., .phoneboy.com, .awl.com). Note the leading "dot" on domain names.

Registers

Registers are the closest elements INSPECT has to variables. Check Point actually uses registers to modify certain internal functions, but you can use them for variables in your own code as well. They are of the format srN, where N is a number between 0 and 15. You set their value as follows:

```
set sr1 15;
```

You can use this to accept a particular packet if the 60h byte is equal to 15:

```
accept sr1 = [60:1];
```

You can also use a register to specify an offset to a specific place in a packet. For example, you could do something like this:

```
sr1.[4:2, b]
```

which would give you bytes 19 and 20 in big endian format (15 + 4 = 19).

Manipulating Table Entries

Tables allow FireWall-1 to remember various details about connections. Each entry in a table is of the following format:

```
< KEY ; VALUE @ TIMEOUT >
```

where KEY and VALUE are one or more comma-separated items. TIMEOUT is an integer value that determines how long (in seconds) a particular entry will last in the table before expiring. For tables defined with the `refresh` tag (more on this in the next section), any "read" or "write" to a particular table entry will reset this timeout. Note that only a KEY is required, the other parameters are optional. The TIMEOUT, if not specified, is taken from the default specified by the table. For example:

```
<42,69;5@50>
```

The KEYs in this table are 42 and 69, the value is 5, and the entry has a timeout value of 50 seconds. If the entry is not accessed again within 50 seconds (if the table is defined with the `refresh` tag), the entry will expire and be removed from the table. If you want to add this to a table called `foobar`, you would use the command:

```
record <42,69;5@50> in foobar;
```

If you want to verify whether <42,69> is in the table foobar, you would use the command:

```
<42,69> in foobar
```

which returns true if it is in the table, false if not. If you want to read the value stored in this table entry, you would use the command:

```
foobar [42,69]
```

You can also read the values into registers directly, which you must do if the value is a tuple. In this case, use the command `get`. For the following table entry in foobar:

```
<5,42,69;7,9,73>
```

use this command:

```
get <5,42,69> from foobar to sr1
```

This puts the values in successive registers (i.e., sr1 = 7, sr2 = 9, and sr3=73). Note that if this entry does not exist in table `foobar`, the command returns false, and the registers maintain their previous values.

You can also simply verify that an entry exists in a table by checking to see if a particular key exists in the table. For instance:

```
<src,sport,dst,dport,ip_p> in connections
```

If the entry exists, the command returns true.

You can remove a particular entry from `foobar` by using the `delete` command:

```
delete <5,42,69> from foobar
```

You can also modify a particular table entry without resetting the timeout counter by using the `modify` command:

```
modify <5,42,69;5,20,71> in foobar
```

Creating Your Own Tables

Before you can start adding your own entries to tables, the tables must first be created. There are several predefined tables in `$FWDIR/lib/table.def`. Note that this does not define all the tables used in FireWall-1, but it does define tables that can be modified by the user's INSPECT code (such as the connections table).

There are actually two kinds of tables in FireWall-1: static and dynamic. Static tables are defined as follows:

```
table name = static {} ;
```

In a static table, you can use your own name. This table, once defined, cannot be changed. A comma separates each entry in the table. For example:

```
table authors = static { 10.0.0.1, 10.68.0.1, 10.31.0.1 } ;
```

If each entry in the table has more than one value, the group of entries is enclosed in angle brackets:

```
table authors = static { <1, 10.0.0.1>, <2, 10.68.0.1>, <3,
10.31.0.1> } ;
```

Dynamic tables are defined as follows:

```
table name = dynamic {}  attributes;
```

The `name` variable represents the name of the table, `dynamic` tells FireWall-1 that this is a dynamic table, and `attributes` refers to one or more of the items listed in Table 13-3.

How Your Rulebase Is Converted to INSPECT

Your security policy is stored as a .W file on the management console as well as inside the `rulebases.fws` file. Your rulebase file contains all of the rules you have defined in the Security Policy Editor referencing network objects. Your `objects.C` file contains the definitions for the network objects referenced in your rulebase file as well as properties that further define your rulebase (the "implicit rules"). When you load a policy, the .W file is put through a compiler that takes the .W file along with your

Table 13-3   Table attributes

Attribute	Description
`expires N`	When entries are added to the table without an explicit timeout, the entries will be given a default timeout of *N* seconds.
`refresh`	Reset the timeout value for an entry in the table when the entry is accessed.
`hashsize N`	This should be set to a power of two roughly equal to the table size.
`keep`	All tables are flushed on a policy install except for those defined with a `keep` attribute.
`kbuf N`	The `Nth` argument in the value section is a pointer to an encryption key (used internally by FireWall-1 for encryption).
`implies table_name`	If an entry is removed from this table, also remove it from table_name.
`limit N`	Limit the number of entries in the table to *N*. The default is 25,000.
`sync`	Synchronize this table with the state synchronization mechanism.

`objects.C` file (and other files) and creates a .pf (packet filter) file. This .pf file contains INSPECT code that represents your security policy as well as some familiar-looking compiler directives: #include and #define. These directives work pretty much the same way as they do in a normal C compiler.

As each packet enters the Stateful Inspection engine, they are processed according to your security policy as defined by the .pf file. The packet goes through, line-by-line, statement-by-statement, until it is accepted, rejected, dropped, or vanished. Let's use the rulebase shown in Figure 13-1.

No.	Source	Destination	Service	Action	Track	Install On
1	firewalls	firewalls ospf-all.mcast.net ospf-dsig.mcast.net vrrp.mcast.net	vrrp ospf	accept		Gateways
2	firewall-managers	firewalls	ftp http-8080 ssh https	accept	Long	Gateways
3	firewalls-priv	firewalls-priv	Any	accept		Gateways
4	Any	Any	NBT	drop		Gateways
5	Any	Any	ident	reject		Gateways
6	Any	Any	Any	drop	Long	Gateways

Figure 13-1   Sample rulebase

At the very top of the .pf file, you should see something like the following:

```
// INSPECT Security Policy Script Generated by dwelch@kenny at
15May2000 18:22:09
// from Rulebase template.W by FireWall-1 Version 4.1 Code
Generation
// Running under WindowsNT 4.0
```

This tells you who generated the INSPECT code on what platform. The next section is denoted by the following:

```
/////////////////////////////
// Exported Rules Database //
/////////////////////////////
```

This shows you what the rulebase looks like. It looks very similar to what `rulebases.fws` would show you for this rulebase. There are also some tables that get defined as a result of the rulebase and `objects.C` in this section (listed after the rulebase). The next section is indicated by the following in the .pf file:

```
/////////////////////////////
// Beginning of Prologue //
/////////////////////////////
```

What follows is based on several things:

• Constants based on settings in the Policy Properties
• Defined services

Generally, actual INSPECT code is not in this section. However, if you were to put in some code in the prologue section of a service of type Other and that service were used in the rulebase, you would see that code listed in this section. The next section is denoted by the following in the .pf file:

```
////////////////////////////////////////
// Beginning of Security Policy Code //
////////////////////////////////////////
```

This section contains definitions for all of your network objects. These definitions were defined in the Security Policy Editor, although the names will be different (more generic). For example:

```
service_list4 = { <21, 22>, <443, 443>, <8080, 8080> } ;
ip_list2 = { <172.16.32.1, 172.16.32.120>, <172.29.0.41, 172.29.0.42>,
<10.0.43.41, 10.0.43.42> } ;
ip_list3 = { <172.16.32.1, 172.16.32.120>, <172.29.0.41, 172.29.0.42>,
<207.225.43.41, 10.0.43.42>, <224.0.0.5, 224.0.0.6>, <224.0.0.18,
224.0.0.18> } ;
ip_list5 = { <172.29.0.4, 172.29.0.4>, <10.0.43.45, 10.0.43.46> } ;
```

The table service_list4 is basically the representation for the four services used in Rule 2, which includes FTP, HTTPS, HTTP port 8080, and SSH. The table ip_list2 is a representation for the group "firewalls." Note that these are listed as ranges, which cover all IPs (or ports) in between. For example, in the table ip_list2, the entry

```
<172.16.32.1, 172.16.32.120>
```

includes all IP addresses from 172.16.32.1 through 172.16.32.120, including the endpoints.

Note that only the objects actually used in your policy will be listed in this section.

Next are your address translation rules. The format should look very similar to the rules shown in the Security Policy Editor. The next interesting section is denoted by the following in the .pf file:

```
// User defined init code and global init code
```

In this section, various parts of FireWall-1's lib directory are included as well as your user-defined file, user.def. Next is the section:

```
// Code for First-Bounded Properties
```

Notice that a call to include the file code.def is listed below this line. The main purpose of this file is to accept established connections and make sure the IPs that are trying to access the system are not blocked by suspicious activity monitoring (SAM). This section would also include any anti-spoofing checking that is defined in the firewall's network object. You then have the following section:

```
// Service other pre-match code
```

All pre-match code and some rulebase property code is listed in this section. Next, you have:

```
// Rule-Base And Before-Last Properties Code
```

In this section, you start getting into the real security policy. Assuming you are using the rulebase shown in Figure 13-1, the first rule in the rulebase is represented by the following INSPECT code:

```
inbound all@target_list1
 accept start_rule_code(1),
   (other, vrrp or ospf),
   (ip_src in ip_list2),
   (ip_dst in ip_list3),
   RECORD_CONN(1);
```

This code is translated into English line-by-line as follows:

- If the packet is being inspected inbound from any interface on a firewall listed in target_list1 (the two firewalls being used)
- Accept the packet if all of the following comparisons are true:
  - start_rule_code (which always returns true)
  - The service is VRRP or OSPF
  - The source IP is in ip_list2 (which corresponds to the firewall IP addresses)
  - The destination IP is in ip_list3 (which corresponds to ip_list2, the VRRP multicast address, and the OSPF multicast addresses)
  - Record the connection under Rule 1 (always returns true)

If you want to put a rule in that generates a log entry, you might use the following rule:

```
inbound all@target_list1
 accept start_rule_code(2),
   (tcp, dport in service_list4),
   (ip_src in ip_list5),
   (ip_dst in ip_list2),
   RECORD_CONN(2),
   LOG(long, LOG_NOALERT, 2);
```

A translation of the preceding code into English follows:

- If the packet is being inspected inbound from any interface on a firewall listed in target_list1
- Accept the packet if the following comparisons are true:
  - start_rule_code(2) (always true)
  - The service is TCP on a port listed in service_list4 (in this case, FTP, SSH, HTTP-8080, and HTTPS)
  - The source IP address is in ip_list5 (which corresponds to the group "firewall-managers")
  - The destination is an IP address in gateway_list2 (which corresponds to the firewall IP addresses)
  - Record the connection under Rule 2 (always returns true)
  - LOG (which should log the packet appropriately and always returns true)

Note that in either of these examples, should one of these statements after accept return false, the rest of the statement is not evaluated. So, for example, if the packet were of type UDP, both of these rules would be bypassed before the destination port was evaluated.

Services of Type Other

A service of type Other contains three parts that must be defined: the Match field, the Prologue field, and the Pre-Match field. The Match field should contain INSPECT code that matches the service. For example, if you want the code to match HTTP, the Match field would contain tcp, `dport=80`. You could also reference your own INSPECT code in this field.

The Prologue field inserts code prior to the prologue in the compiled .pf file. This allows you, for instance, to define tables or constants used by the pre-match code. The Pre-Match field allows you to define code that matches the specific service (like the Match field), but it is designed to catch reply packets. The code referenced in this field gets inserted after the prologue but before any of the rulebase properties. Examples of both of these fields are shown in the following "Sample INSPECT Code" section.

Sample INSPECT Code

Now that I have talked about how INSPECT works and how your rulebase translates to INSPECT code, I can show you some sample INSPECT code. Note that unless stated, none of this code has seen serious testing in a production network, so exercise appropriate caution before implementing any code.

FireWall-1 4.0 and later include a place for user-defined INSPECT scripts: `$FWDIR/lib/user.def`. Check Point will not overwrite this file on an upgrade; therefore, it is the recommended location to place any custom INSPECT code. In earlier versions, you should add the code to the bottom of `$FWDIR/lib/base.def`.

All INSPECT changes should be done on the management console. A policy reinstall is required after any of these types of changes in order for them to take effect.

Allowing Outbound Connections to SecuRemote Clients

Allowing outbound connections to SecuRemote clients was mentioned in Chapter 11, but it is worth bringing up again, simply because it can be used as an example of INSPECT code. Recall that the quandary was how to allow a connection on port TCP 5555 to a particular machine only if it were an authenticated SecuRemote client. Whenever a SecuRemote client successfully authenticates to FireWall-1, an entry is created in the table userc_rules: <ip, 0>. This is so FireWall-1 knows to encrypt all traffic to this IP address. You can also use this table entry as a basis for allowing a service. Create a service of type Other with the following in the Match field:

```
tcp,dport=5555,<dst,0> in userc_rules
```

This service will accept the packet if it is of type TCP. Its destination port (service) is 5555, and the entry <dst,0> appears in the table userc_rules. As you will recall from a previous section, dst means the destination IP address of the current packet. In a .pf file, a rule using this service would look like this:

```
inbound all@target_list1
  accept start_rule_code(3),
  (tcp,dport=5555,<dst,0> in userc_rules),
  (ip_src = kenny),
  (ip_dst in gateway_list3),
  RECORD_CONN(3),
  LOG(long, LOG_NOALERT, 3);
```

Point-to-Point Tunneling Protocol (PPTP)

Another example of INSPECT code is needed for the service PPTP only because it uses a variation of the GRE protocol.[3] Normally, to allow GRE through FireWall-1, you need to create two services:

- TCP port 1723 for a control session
- A variation of the GRE protocol (IP Protocol 47) for data

Create this service as a service of type Other. In the Match field, enter:

```
ip_p = 47, [22:2,b] = 0x880B
```

The first part of the preceding code line identifies the protocol type (47) as GRE. The second part indicates that you are using PPTP embedded in GRE (you look at the 22nd and 23rd bytes together to see if they equal 880b).

You could create two services to do this, but let's create one service that handles both possibilities. Let's call the service PPTP. You want to allow a packet for this service if it is going to destination TCP port 1723 or if it is a PPTP data packet. You could then create a single service of type Other with the following in the Match field:

```
(tcp, dport=1723) or (ip_p=47, [22:2,b] = 0x880b)
```

This new service will match either the PPTP control connection or the PPTP data packets.

 **NOTE!**   PPTP is not supported with Hide NAT, only Static NAT. This is due to the fact that the transport mechanism used does not lend itself to many-to-one IP address translations.

---

3.   PPTP is defined in RFC2637.

Allowing a Connection Based on a Previous Connection

There is a particular application available that uses UDP port 3000, but it performs its communications in a rather unusual manner in that the reply packet uses the same destination port as was used to make the communication (normally on a reply packet, the source and destination ports are reversed). FireWall-1 doesn't normally handle services that communicate in this manner. In order to allow this service, you will need to generate custom INSPECT code.

Because you need to write code to catch certain types of reply packets, you need to write prologue code. You want to accept the packet if and only if the first packet was accepted. So, you can just look in the connections table for that entry. In the Match field for this service of type Other, you need the following:

```
udp, dport=3000, record <src,0,dst,3000,ip_p> in accepted
```

This code line records the connection in a different table called *accepted,* which is typically used for FTP data connections. The 0 argument is a sort of wildcard. In order to use this wildcard, put the following in the Prologue field:

```
accept udp, dport=3000, <dst,0,src,dport,ip_p> in accepted;
```

 **NOTE!** The method that is used to deal with the UDP port 3000 service effectively adds three table entries: two in the connections table (one for the connection in each direction) and one in the accepted table.

HTTP

The HTTP Security Server inspects all HTTP traffic. However, the HTTP Security Server does more than you might need. All you really need is to validate the first few bytes of the first real data packet as a valid HTTP 1.0 request. All requests start with GET, HEAD, or POST. If the first packet with data does not contain this information, or when you connect, your remote server sends back information, you can assume it is not a valid HTTP communication and immediately close it down. You keep track of these connections in your own table, so you know they have been validated, and remove the table entries when the connection is closed.

You need to create a service of type Other because you will need to use code in the prologue packets that appear before the actual rulebase, and the normal mechanism for handling established TCP connections needs to be bypassed to accomplish this. You will have to add your own INSPECT code to a .def file, which will inspect this code. The $FWDIR/lib/user.def file has existed since FireWall-1 4.0 for safe placement of user-defined INSPECT code. This file is not overwritten during upgrades.

You must first figure out how to match a legitimate request. Determining *when* to match this request will be accomplished later. You know that the first data packet coming from the client will have GET, HEAD, or POST as the first few bytes of the data. You need to define these as constants so you can compare the packet against them. You cannot do a string compare, but you can turn the strings into their ASCII equivalents and make them constants. You do this with `#define` statements in INSPECT code:

```
#define HTTP_GET_MAGIC  0x47455420 /* "GET " */
#define HTTP_HEAD_MAGIC 0x48454144 /* "HEAD" */
#define HTTP_POST_MAGIC 0x504f5354 /* "POST" */
```

Notice that a space is added to the end of GET. This is to make the request four bytes for all three constants, which makes coding very easy. You can simply look at the first few bytes of the data portion of the packet to determine whether or not it contains a valid HTTP request. You can then put these statements into a function:

```
define http_match {
  [TCPDATA,b] = HTTP_GET_MAGIC or
  [TCPDATA,b] = HTTP_HEAD_MAGIC or
  [TCPDATA,b] = HTTP_POST_MAGIC
} ;
```

When this function is called in INSPECT script, it will look at the first four bytes of the data portion of the packet. If it matches, the function returns true. If not, it returns false.

You can then focus your attention on the prologue code that you need to create. Because this code will see all packets after the initial SYN packet, you need to make sure it handles the appropriate cases, which include:

- Do nothing with the packet if it is not for one of the HTTP ports.
- Accept the packet if the connection has already been verified (i.e., you have an entry for it in your own table).
- Accept the packet if it has no data in it (this allows the first ACK packet through).
- Accept the packet if it contains an HTTP request, and log it to the HTTP table.
- Accept the packet if it is the end of an HTTP connection you already know about (and remove it from your table).
- Reject the connection if the packet from the client contains data but does not contain a valid HTTP request.
- Reject the connection if the server sends data back before the client. In normal HTTP, this never happens.

- Accept the SYN/ACK packet from the HTTP server.
- If you see a FIN packet from the server, remove the entry from your table.
- If none of these conditions are met, pass the packet through to be handled by FireWall-1 normally.

The following code handles all of the preceding situations:

```
define http_prologue {
 accept (
  tcp, dport in http_port_tab, (
   ( <src,sport,dst> in http_table ) or
   ( established, ip_len = 40 ) or
   ( http_match,
     record <src,sport,dst> in http_table, log long ) or
   ( tcpdone,
     delete <dst,dport,src> from http_table )
  )
 ) or accept (
  tcp, sport in http_port_tab, <dst, dport, src> in http_table
 ) or reject (
  tcp, dport in http_port_tab, not http_match, log long
 ) or reject (
  tcp, not (sport in http_port_tab), ack, ip_len < 40, log long )
 ) or accept (
  tcp, sport in http_port_tab, syn, ack
 ) or accept (
  tcp, sport in http_port_tab, tcpdone,
   delete <dst,dport,src> from http_table
 )
} ;
```

Next, you need some code to call this code and a service to start it. You can create a service of type Other that will call the prologue code. In the Prologue field, use http_prologue. In the Match field, you can simply use tcp, dport in http_port_tab.

You then need to define http_port_tab. Unfortunately, because of the way the INSPECT compiler works, you need to add a definition to one of the files that is over-written during an upgrade: $FWDIR/lib/fwui_head.def. This line should read:

```
http_port_tab = { 80, 8080, 81 }   (or whatever ports you want)
```

It defines the ports you consider valid for HTTP.

An alternative approach to this is to modify $FWDIR/conf/objects.C in Fire-Wall-1 4.1 and later. In the service of type Other you will create, you can add a field called *tabledef* that allows you to define the table. The following example shows what a modified service entry might look like:

```
: (http-pb
        :type (other)
        :tabledef ("http_port_tab = { 80, 8080, 81 } ;")
        :prolog ("http_prologue;")
        :exp (tcp,dport in http_port_tab)
        :inexp ()
        :outexp ()
        :comments ()
        :color (Blue)

)
```

The INSPECT code for Stateful Inspection of HTTP exists in its entirety in Appendix D.

Ping and Traceroute

Bill Burns, a Chief Security Architect at Netscape, has written his own code that performs Stateful Inspection for ping and traceroute. Versions of FireWall-1 earlier than 4.0 did not do this. Check Point added its own code in version 4.0 and later, but many feel that it does not work correctly. The entire program is included in Appendix E.

Because this code is rather lengthy, I will not provide a step-by-step description of it in this section. Bill does an excellent job explaining the code. For his expert commentary, visit http://people.netscape.com/shadow/work/inspect/index.html.

Different Rules for Different Interfaces

Atul Sharma developed INSPECT script that enforces different policies on different interfaces. For example, Telnet is allowed if the connection originates from one interface, but not the other. This is not something the FireWall-1 GUI allows you to define, but it is something the INSPECT language is able to do. The complete sample program is provided in Appendix F.

Changing Your Default Filter

The default filter is the security policy that loads when FireWall-1 starts up before it attempts to load a policy from the management console. If FireWall-1 fails to load a policy, this is the policy that remains active until a new one is manually loaded. FireWall-1 comes with two such policies:

- The boot filter that allows the firewall to originate connections and accept replies to those connections
- The drop filter that only allows the firewall to communicate with itself, dropping all other traffic

Normally, you switch between these default filters with `fwconfig` (FireWall-1 4.0) or `cpconfig` (FireWall-1 4.1 and later). IPSO does not allow you to do this for some reason, and the drop default filter is the default. You can still switch to the boot default filter manually by executing the following commands:

```
# rm $FWDIR/state/default.bin
# cp $FWDIR/lib/defaultfilter.boot $FWDIR/conf/defaultfilter.pf
# fw defaultgen
# cp $FWDIR/state/default.bin $FWDIR/conf/default.bin
```

On a Windows NT platform, the commands would be:

```
C: del %FWDIR%\state\default.bin
C: copy %FWDIR%\lib\defaultfilter.boot %FWDIR%\conf\ defaultfilter.pf
C: fw defaultgen
C: copy %FWDIR%\state\default.bin %FWDIR%\conf\default.bin
```

To switch to the drop default filter, use the following commands:

```
# rm $FWDIR/state/default.bin
# cp $FWDIR/lib/defaultfilter.drop $FWDIR/conf/defaultfilter.pf
# fw defaultgen
# cp $FWDIR/state/default.bin $FWDIR/conf/default.bin
```

On a Windows NT platform, the commands would be:

```
C: del %FWDIR%\state\default.bin
C: copy %FWDIR%\lib\defaultfiilter.boot %FWDIR%\conf\defaultfilter.pf
C: fw defaultgen
C: copy %FWDIR%\state\default.bin %FWDIR%\conf\default.bin
```

The next obvious question might be, can you write your own default filter? Certainly, if you know how to write INSPECT code. The following caveats apply: The INSPECT script in question does not include any of the default .def files from `$FWDIR/lib`. You must define everything you need to use as part of the script. When you are ready to compile the script, it needs to be placed in `$FWDIR/conf/defaultfilter.pf`, which is where `fw defaultgen` expects to find the script.

Keep in mind that this policy is a fail-safe policy, not a policy that will generally be used. IP Forwarding will typically be disabled, so the firewall will not be able to forward packets unless you tell FireWall-1 to not control IP Forwarding (which is not recommended). As a result, this policy is only relevant to packets originating from or going to the firewall.

Appendix G provides a sample default filter policy that accepts packets coming to port 22 (SSH) or port 256 (fw1 management protocol), which permits you to load a policy to the firewall or SSH to the firewall for further management. Remember that

IP Forwarding should be disabled on the platform, so even if a packet destined for another host is permitted by this policy, it will not be forwarded past the firewall.

fw monitor

`fw monitor` is similar to a packet sniffer and is built into FireWall-1. It shows you how packets are entering and exiting the FireWall-1 kernel module. Because FireWall-1 resides just above the MAC layer, `fw monitor` cannot be used to see layer 2 traffic, but it can still be useful as a layer 3 and above packet sniffer, and it can also be used to monitor multiple interfaces simultaneously.

 **NOTE!** On IPSO 3.3 and later, when "flows" is enabled in the IPSO kernel (it is by default), `fw monitor` will only show the initial packet exchange for TCP and UDP. This is because the IPSO kernel handles the inspection and forwarding of packets that have been flowed directly in the kernel, which increases performance and throughput. FireWall-1 never sees the flowed packets.

The reason this command is documented in this chapter instead of the address translation chapter (where it might also be appropriate) is that INSPECT is necessary to make use of `fw monitor`. Usage for the `fw monitor` command is as follows:

```
fw monitor [-d] [-D] -e inspect-filter -f filter-file [-l len] [-
m mask]
   [-x offset[,len]] [-o file]
```

To use this command, you may need an "fwc" license on your firewall module. This is included in a management console license or a temporary license.

There are four inspection points as packets pass through FireWall-1. You choose where you want to see packets with the `-m` option:

- Before FireWall-1 processes the packet in the inbound direction (i or PREIN)
- After FireWall-1 processes the packet in the inbound direction (I or POSTIN)
- Before FireWall-1 processes the packet in the outbound direction (o or PRE-OUT)
- After FireWall-1 processes the packet in the outbound direction (O or POSTOUT)

Because there can be lots of packets, you need some way to determine which packets you are interested in seeing. You do this by means of an INSPECT filter, which can be typed in directly on the command line or provided via an INSPECT filter file. One of the options `-f` or `-e` is required.

Once you execute this command, FireWall-1 compiles the specified INSPECT script (either on the command line or in a file), loads it into the kernel module, and displays the packets in the terminal window or prints them to an output file, which is a Solaris `snoop` format. FireWall-1 continues to do this until an interrupt signal is sent to the program (Ctrl-C) or another security policy is loaded, after which it will unload the filter and exit.

The INSPECT script should return an `accept` in order for packets to be displayed. Any other return code will cause packets not to be displayed. If you want to only catch packets on a certain interface, do not use `le0@all` (for example), but instead use `direction=x, ifid=y` where x=0 for inbound, `1` for outbound, and y is an interface number returned by the `fw ctl iflist` command. Do not use table names that are used by the security policy.

Table 13-4 lists the command-line options for `fw monitor`.

Examples

The following code line displays all TCP packets entering and leaving FireWall-1:

```
fw monitor -e '[9:1]=6, accept;' -l 100 -m iO -x 20
```

Although 100 bytes of data are captured for each packet, up to 80 bytes of TCP header and data will be displayed starting at offset 20 (assuming no IP options are used).

The following code line displays all packets entering and exiting FireWall-1 in the inbound direction (i.e., before the OS routes the packet):

```
fw monitor -e 'accept;' -m iI
```

Table 13-4 Command-line options for `fw monitor`

Flag	Description
-d	Turns on debugging
-D	Turns on debugging
-e script	Specifies an INSPECT script via the command line
-f filename	Specifies an INSPECT script contained in filename
-l numbytes	Specifies the number of bytes to capture in each packet
-m mask	Specifies inspection points mask, any one or more of i, I, o, O as explained previously
-o outfile	Specifies an output file, which will be in Solaris `snoop` format
-x offset,len	Performs a hex dump of received data, starting at specified offset, showing len bytes

The following code line displays all packets entering interface ID 0 that are coming from or going to 10.0.0.1. The value used for `ifid` corresponds to a number given to an interface by FireWall-1. You can determine which interface has which number by using the command `fw ctl iflist`:

```
fw monitor -e 'accept ifid=0,src=10.0.0.1 or dst=10.0.0.1;'
```

The following code line does the same thing as the previous command except that it looks for packets of IP Protocol 47 only:

```
fw monitor -e 'accept ifid=0,src=10.0.0.1 or
dst=10.0.0.1,ip_p=47;'
```

The following code line displays all TCP packets going to or coming from 10.0.0.1 with either a source port of 80 or a destination port of 80:

```
fw monitor -e 'accept tcp,dport=80 or sport=80,src=10.0.0.1 or
dst=10.0.0.1;'
```

Warnings

Some important notes about using `fw monitor`:

- Do not alter tables used in the security policy, or else unexpected behavior may result (including a system crash).
- Packets are defragmented as the packets leave FireWall-1 in both the inbound and outbound directions.
- Anything that causes a fetch, load, or unload of your security policy will cause `fw monitor` to terminate.
- If you are using `fw monitor` on an IPSO platform and you are using a version of FireWall-1 earlier than 4.1 SP2 IPSO build 24, the command will terminate abnormally if certain packets are received and displayed by `fw monitor`. This happens because FireWall-1 attempts to look up an interface to associate with the packet and it is unable to do so. To resolve this issue, filter on interface ID using ifid as shown previously or upgrade to a more current version of FireWall-1 on your IPSO platform.

Summary

This chapter provided an overview of the INSPECT language in a format very different from Check Point's documentation. Several working and documented examples of INSPECT code were provided so you could see for yourself how it works. INSPECT is a very powerful language designed to give you maximum control over your security policy. It is a pity that Check Point does not make more information about this language available to customers.

#

Securing Your Bastion Host

The information provided herein is based on papers written by other security experts, which I am providing for reference. The following sections assume the host in question is either not connected to a network or connected to an isolated network, as this is the best way to make sure no one else compromises your system before you have had a chance to secure it. The appendix covers Solaris 2.6/2.7, Windows NT 4.0,[1] and Linux.

Securing Solaris

Installing only the "Core" packages in Solaris is recommended, as it minimizes the amount of software on the system, which minimizes the potential security holes.[2] If you only install the core packages, you will also have to install a few additional packages. To do this, first mount the installation CD-ROM as follows.

On an Ultra5/10, use this command:

```
# mount -F hsfs -o ro /dev/dsk/c0t2d0s0 /cdrom
```

On most other Sparc systems, use:

```
# mount -F hsfs -o ro /dev/dsk/c0t6d0s0 /cdrom
```

You then type this:

```
# cd /cdrom/Solaris_2.6/Product
# pkgadd -d .
```

---

1. For Windows 2000, I recommend reading *Securing Windows NT/2000 Servers for the Internet* by Stefan Norberg, ISBN: 1565927680.
2. If you need X windows to run the GUI, you should install "End User" instead of "Core." However, I recommend using a Windows-based platform to run the GUI instead.

To remove packages, use this command:

```
# pkgrm [pkg-name]
```

To maintain security once you have installed and removed the appropriate packages, you should install the latest recommended patch cluster from Sun, which you can download from http://sunsolve.sun.com/pub-cgi/show.pl? target=patches/patch-access. Not only should you install the latest patch regularly, you should check this URL monthly to make sure you always have the latest recommended patch cluster installed.

Minimal Packages for Sparc Solaris 2.6

A core installation on Solaris 2.6 installs the following packages:

```
system    SUNWadmr     System & Network Administration Root
system    SUNWatfsr    AutoFS, (Root)
system    SUNWatfsu    AutoFS, (Usr)
system    SUNWcar      Core Architecture, (Root)
system    SUNWcg6      GX (cg6) Device Driver
system    SUNWcsd      Core Solaris Devices
system    SUNWcsr      Core Solaris, (Root)
system    SUNWcsu      Core Solaris, (Usr)
system    SUNWdfb      Dumb Frame Buffer Device Drivers
system    SUNWdtcor    Solaris Desktop /usr/dt filesystem anchor
system    SUNWesu      Extended System Utilities
system    SUNWhmd      SunSwift SBus Adapter Drivers
system    SUNWide      IDE device drivers
system    SUNWkey      Keyboard configuration tables
system    SUNWkvm      Core Architecture, (Kvm)
system    SUNWlibms    Sun WorkShop Bundled shared libm
system    SUNWnisr     Network Information System, (Root)
system    SUNWnisu     Network Information System, (Usr)
system    SUNWos86u    Platform Support, OS Functionality (Usr)
system    SUNWpcelx    3COM EtherLink III PCMCIA Ethernet Driver
system    SUNWpci      PCI Simba device drivers
system    SUNWpcmci    PCMCIA Card Services, (Root)
system    SUNWpcmcu    PCMCIA Card Services, (Usr)
system    SUNWpcmem    PCMCIA memory card driver
system    SUNWpcser    PCMCIA serial card driver
system    SUNWpd       PCI Drivers
system    SUNWploc     Partial Locales
system    SUNWpsdpr    PCMCIA ATA card driver
system    SUNWsolnm    Solaris Naming Enabler
system    SUNWswmt     Patch Utilities
system    SUNWvplr     SMCC sun4u new platform links
system    SUNWvplu     SMCC sun4u new usr/platform links
system    SUNWxwdv     X Windows System Window Drivers
system    SUNWxwmod    OpenWindows kernel modules
```

Of these 34 packages, the following 16 are not needed for FireWall-1 and can be removed using the command pkgrm. Don't worry about errors on dependencies, because you are also removing the dependencies.

```
system    SUNWpcelx    3COM EtherLink III PCMCIA Ethernet Driver
system    SUNWpcmci    PCMCIA Card Services, (Root)
system    SUNWpcmcu    PCMCIA Card Services, (Usr)
system    SUNWpcmem    PCMCIA memory card driver
system    SUNWpcser    PCMCIA serial card driver
system    SUNWpsdpr    PCMCIA ATA card driver
system    SUNWnisr     Network Information System, (Root)
system    SUNWnisu     Network Information System, (Usr)
system    SUNWatfsr    AutoFS, (Root)
system    SUNWatfsu    AutoFS, (Usr)
system    SUNWxwdv     X Windows System Window Drivers
system    SUNWxwmod    OpenWindows kernel modules
system    SUNWsolnm    Solaris Naming Enabler
system    SUNWdtcor    Solaris Desktop /usr/dt filesystem anchor
system    SUNWadmr     System & Network Administration Root
system    SUNWcg6      GX (cg6) Device Driver
```

There are a couple of packages you will need to install if you install a core installation. You may have others you want or need to add based on your requirements. The following packages are needed by FireWall-1:

```
system    SUNWter      Terminal Information -> FW-1 needs /bin/ed
system    SUNWlibC     Sun Workshop Compilers Bundled libC -> used by
                       cpconfig
system    SUNWscpu     Source Compatibility, (Usr) -> /usr/ucb/ln
                       required
```

The last package only needs /usr/ucb/ln, which you can easily obtain without installing the package by executing the following command:

 # /bin/ln -s /bin/ln /usr/ucb/ln

Some other useful packages that are not required but might be useful are as follows:

```
system    SUNWtoo      Programming Tools -> truss, strings, ldd, savecore
system    SUNWdoc      Documentation Tools -> Used by SUNWman
system    SUNWman      On-Line Manual Pages -> man pages
system    SUNWxcu4     XCU4 Utilities -> Includes grep, and showrev(1M)
system    SUNWadmc     System administration core libraries
system    SUNWadmfw    System & Network Administration Framework
```

If you want to add compiling capabilities (not recommended), add these packages:

system	SUNWsprot	Solaris Bundled tools
system	SUNWhea	SunOS Header Files
system	SUNWtoo	Programming Tools
system	SUNWarc	Archive Libraries
system	SUNWbtool	CCS tools bundled with SunOS

Minimal Packages for Solaris 2.7

A core installation on Solaris 2.7 includes the following 39 packages:

system	SUNWadmr	System & Network Administration Root
system	SUNWatfsr	AutoFS, (Root)
system	SUNWatfsu	AutoFS, (Usr)
system	SUNWcar	Core Architecture, (Root)
system	SUNWcg6	GX (cg6) Device Driver
system	SUNWcsd	Core Solaris Devices
system	SUNWcsl	Core Solaris, (Shared Libs)
system	SUNWcsr	Core Solaris, (Root)
system	SUNWcsu	Core Solaris, (Usr)
system	SUNWdfb	Dumb Frame Buffer Device Drivers
system	SUNWdtcor	Solaris Desktop /usr/dt filesystem anchor
system	SUNWesu	Extended System Utilities
system	SUNWftpr	FTP Server, (Root)
system	SUNWftpu	FTP Server, (Usr)
system	SUNWhmd	SunSwift SBus Adapter Drivers
system	SUNWkey	Keyboard configuration tables
system	SUNWkvm	Core Architecture, (Kvm)
system	SUNWlibms	Sun WorkShop Bundled shared libm
system	SUNWloc	System Localization
system	SUNWnisr	Network Information System, (Root)
system	SUNWnisu	Network Information System, (Usr)
system	SUNWos86u	Platform Support, OS Functionality (Usr)
system	SUNWpcelx	3COM EtherLink III PCMCIA Ethernet Driver
system	SUNWpcmci	PCMCIA Card Services, (Root)
system	SUNWpcmcu	PCMCIA Card Services, (Usr)
system	SUNWpcmem	PCMCIA memory card driver
system	SUNWpcser	PCMCIA serial card driver
system	SUNWpd	PCI Drivers
system	SUNWploc	Partial Locales
system	SUNWploc1	Supplementary Partial Locales

```
system      SUNWpsdpr      PCMCIA ATA card driver
system      SUNWqfed       Sun Quad FastEthernet Adapter 32bit Driver
system      SUNWsndmr      Sendmail root
system      SUNWsndmu      Sendmail user
system      SUNWsolnm      Solaris Naming Enabler
system      SUNWswmt       Install and Patch Utilities
system      SUNWudfr       Universal Disk Format 1.50
system      SUNWxwdv       X Windows System Window Drivers
system      SUNWxwmod      OpenWindows kernel modules
```

The following 20 packages are not needed. Don't worry about dependencies, because you are removing them.

```
system      SUNWsndmr      Sendmail root
system      SUNWsndmu      Sendmail user
system      SUNWftpr       FTP Server, (Root)
system      SUNWftpu       FTP Server, (Usr)
system      SUNWpcelx      3COM EtherLink III PCMCIA Ethernet Driver
system      SUNWpcmci      PCMCIA Card Services, (Root)
system      SUNWpcmcu      PCMCIA Card Services, (Usr)
system      SUNWpcmem      PCMCIA memory card driver
system      SUNWpcser      PCMCIA serial card driver
system      SUNWpsdpr      PCMCIA ATA card driver
system      SUNWxwdv       X Windows System Window Drivers
system      SUNWxwmod      OpenWindows kernel modules
system      SUNWnisr       Network Information System, (Root)
system      SUNWnisu       Network Information System, (Usr)
system      SUNWcg6        GX (cg6) Device Driver
system      SUNWadmr       System & Network Administration Root
system      SUNWdtcor      Solaris Desktop /usr/dt filesystem anchor
system      SUNWsolnm      Solaris Naming Enabler
system      SUNWatfsr      AutoFS, (Root)
system      SUNWatfsu      AutoFS, (Usr)
```

There are a couple of packages you will need to install if you install a core installation. You may have others you want or need to add based on your requirements. The following packages are needed by FireWall-1:

```
system      SUNWter        Terminal Information -> FW-1 needs /bin/ed
system      SUNWlibC       Sun Workshop Compilers Bundled libC -> used by
                           cpconfig
```

```
system      SUNWscpu      Source Compatibility, (Usr) -> /usr/ucb/ln
                          required
```

The last package only needs /usr/ucb/ln, which you can easily obtain without installing the package by executing the following command:

```
# /bin/ln -s /bin/ln /usr/ucb/ln
```

Some other useful packages that are not required but might be useful are as follows:

```
system      SUNWadmc      System administration core libraries
system      SUNWadmfw     System & Network Administration Framework
                          includes showrev(1M)
system      SUNWdoc       Documentation Tools
system      SUNWman       On-Line Manual Pages
```

If you want to add compiling capabilities (not recommended), add these packages:

```
system      SUNWhea       SunOS Header Files
system      SUNWtoo       Programming Tools
system      SUNWarc       Archive Libraries
system      SUNWbtool     CCS tools bundled with SunOS
```

Partitioning Your Hard Drive

A recommended partitioning scheme includes:

- / (root filesystem), everything else
- /var (for logging), 400MB
- swap, 256MB (or 2x physical RAM)
- /etc/fw/log (for FireWall-1 3.0, this should be a separate physical disk)
- /var/opt/CKPfw/log (for FireWall-1 4.0, this should be a separate physical disk)
- /var/opt/CKPfw1-41/log (for FireWall-1 4.1, this should be a separate physical disk)

Removing Unnecessary Services

Many unnecessary services originate from inetd, which is configured with the file /etc/inetd.conf. You should comment out every service in this file (i.e., add a pound sign/hash in front of each line) except for the two lines for Telnet and FTP. If you install SSH on your firewall, you can probably eliminate these two as well.

Next, look at /etc/rc2.d and /etc/rc3.d, which also contain many unneeded services. Table A-1 lists the services that can be disabled. You can simply disable these services by renaming the file from S<whatever> to s<whatever>. This will keep the file in the directory in case you want to run it in the future, but will prevent Solaris from starting them.

Table A-1 Startup files you can disable in Solaris

Startup File	Description
`/etc/rc2.d/S73nfs.client`	Used for NFS mounting a system.
`/etc/rc2.d/S74autofs`	Used for automounting.
`/etc/rc2.d/S80lp`	Used for printing.
`/etc/rc2.d/S88sendmail`	Used for listening for incoming mail. You can still send mail without this running.
`/etc/rc2.d/S71rpc`	RPC Portmapper is highly insecure, but required if CDE is running.
`/etc/rc2.d/S99dtlogin`	Starts CDE.
`/etc/rc3.d/S15nfs.server`	Used if you want to be an NFS server.
`/etc/rc3.d/S76snmpdx`	SNMP daemon, not usually necessary.

OS Logging and Tweaking

Once you have eliminated as many services as possible, you should enable some logging. Most system logging occurs in `/var/adm`. You should add two additional log files to that directory: `sulog` and `loginlog`. The file `/var/adm/sulog` logs all `su` attempts, both successful and failed. This allows you to monitor anyone who attempts to gain root access on your system. The file `/var/adm/loginlog` logs consecutive failed login attempts. When a user attempts to log in five times, and all five attempts fail, it is logged. To enable this, use the following commands:

```
# touch /var/adm/loginlog /var/adm/sulog
# chmod 640 /var/adm/loginlog /var/adm/sulog
```

Tweaking involves some file administration. You first want to create the file `/etc/issue`. This file is an ASCII text banner that appears for all Telnet logins. You also want to create the file `/etc/ftpusers`. This file simply contains names of accounts that cannot FTP to the system. Any account listed in this file cannot FTP to the system. It is meant to restrict root and other common system accounts from using FTP.

Ensure that root cannot Telnet to the system. This forces users to log in to the system as themselves, and then `su` to root. This is a system default, but always confirm this in the file `/etc/default/login`, where console is left uncommented.

In addition, eliminate the Telnet OS banner, and create a separate banner for FTP. The reason this is done is because it is usually not wise to advertise the operating system. For Telnet, this is easily done by creating the file `/etc/default/telnetd` and adding the statement:

```
BANNER=""     # Eliminates the "SunOS 5.x" banner for Telnet
```

For FTP, this is easily done by creating the file `/etc/default/ftpd` and adding the statement:

```
BANNER="WARNING:Authorized use only"     # Warning banner for ftp
```

To protect the OS itself when FireWall-1 is not running, it is recommended that you install and use TCP Wrappers. TCP Wrappers, although it does not encrypt, it does log and control who can access your system. It is a binary that wraps itself around inetd services, such as Telnet or FTP. With TCP Wrappers, the system launches the wrapper for inetd connections, logs all attempts, and then verifies the attempt against an access control list. If the connection is permitted, TCP Wrappers hands the connection to the proper binary, such as Telnet. If the connection is rejected by the access control list, the connection is dropped. For more information on TCP Wrappers, visit ftp://ftp.porcupine.org/pub/security/index.html.

Securing Windows NT

Windows NT, by default, runs many services that are potential security risks. The following sections contain some tips for setting up your Windows NT box to make it more secure. Note that the system should be physically disconnected from your network until you have made all of these changes. This minimizes the possibility that your firewall system will be compromised before you even get started.

Network Protocols

When setting up Windows NT for FireWall-1, only TCP/IP is needed. Use a static IP address.

Machine Name, Domain

Choose a machine name (*firewall* seems like a good choice, though do not choose *fw*), and choose a domain/workgroup that is unreachable. Disable Microsoft Networking services as well.

Services

By default, Windows NT installs the following services:

- Computer Browser
- NetBIOS Interface
- RPC Configuration

- Server
- Workstation

None of these services are actually needed by FireWall-1. Remove NetBIOS, RPC, and Server. The others will be disabled subsequently. You also need to install the SNMP service at this time (FireWall-1 uses this service). Install SNMP before installing FireWall-1 or any service packs.

Some may wonder why Workstation remains. The AT utility requires the Workstation service, which is useful. Computer Browser remains because Workstation has a dependency on it. It will be disabled.

IP Routing

In the Network Control Panel applet, click Protocols, and then double-click TCP/IP. Make sure that IP Routing is enabled in the TCP/IP Properties under the Routing tab. Also ensure that only your external interface has a default route defined (the other interfaces should not).

WINS TCP/IP

In the Network Control Panel applet, click Bindings. From the pull-down menu next to "Show bindings for," select "all protocols." Select "WINS TCP/IP," and click Disable.

WINS Client

If you are installing Windows NT from scratch, you will not be able to disable WINS Client on install. After a reboot, you will experience a hang of up to two minutes. This is perfectly normal and should not occur after disabling the WINS Client.

Go to Devices in Control Panel; scroll down, and find WINS Client (TCP/IP). Click Startup, and change startup to Manual.

Services to Disable after Installation

Go to Services in Control Panel. For each of the following services, select the service, click Startup and change startup to Manual. When you reboot, these services will be disabled:

- Computer Browser
- TCP/IP NetBIOS Helper
- Net Logon
- Workstation
- Server (if present)
- Network DDE
- Network DDE NSDM
- Messenger

Local Hosts File

Although not necessarily a security recommendation, it is highly recommended that you make sure that your hostname is resolvable to an IP address. In fact, FireWall-1 4.1 automatically adds an appropriate entry. Go to the local host file (`%SystemRoot%\System32\drivers\etc\hosts`), and make sure your firewall's hostname has an entry in the hosts file (it probably won't). Make it resolve to your external IP address.

Registry Hacks

Some Registry hacks help protect against people physically coming up to the machine and logging on to it.

To disable the display of the last userid in the logon window:

Set `DontDisplayLastUsername` to 1

`HKEY_LOCAL_MACHINE\SOFTWARE\Microsoft\Windows NT\Current Version\Winlogon` (REG_SZ)

To display a warning message when logging on to the server:

Set `LegalNoticeCaption` to Notice

`HKEY_LOCAL_MACHINE\SOFTWARE\Microsoft\Windows NT\Current Version\Winlogon` (REG_SZ)

Set `LegalNoticeText` to Authorized Users Only

`HKEY_LOCAL_MACHINE\SOFTWARE\Microsoft\Windows NT\Current Version\Wilogon` (REG_SZ)

To disable caching of logon credentials:

Set `CachedLogonsCount` to 0

`HKEY_LOCAL_MACHINE\SOFTWARE\Microsoft\Windows NT\Current Version\Winlogon` (REG_SZ)

To restrict anonymous connections to list account names:

Set `RestrictAnonymous` to 1

`HKEY_LOCAL_MACHINE\SYSTEM\CurrentControlSet\Control\Lsa` (REG_SZ)

To restrict network access to the Registry, create the following Registry key:

`HKEY_LOCAL_MACHINE\SYSTEM\CurrentcontrolSet\Control\SecurePip eServers\win reg`

Account Names Policies

It is important that you change the name of the Administrator account. Everyone knows that on a Windows NT platform, it is called Administrator. Changing this name to something else adds another level of security. Have all Admin users log on with their own respective accounts, and do not give them the password for the Admin account. This allows you to track who is doing what. Another idea is to create a new fictitious Administrator account that has no privileges, and track to see if anyone attempts to log on with that account.

Next, you want to control who has access to what on the system. No more than two groups should have access to the firewall: Administrators (for full access) and Power Users or Users (depending on what access they need). If access can be limited to only administrators, even better. Regardless, the actual number of people who have authorized access should be no more than two to four people. The next step is to focus on and modify the system policies, specifically the Account Policies:

- User Rights and Audit policies are found under User Manager and control how user passwords and logon accounts are used. Two changes are recommended to these policies:
  - Set Minimum Password Length to eight characters.
  - Set Account Lockout to lockout after three bad logon attempts, and reset the counter after 30 minutes.

- User Rights controls who can access what, such as Log On Locally and Manage Auditing and Security Log. Limiting access to the two Windows NT groups discussed earlier (Administrator and Power Users or Users) is recommended. Be sure to eliminate the group "everyone" from all access.

- Audit Policy determines which events are logged. As this is your firewall, you want to log a variety of events you may not normally care to log. You should log the following events:
  - Logon and logoff (both success and failure)
  - Security policy changes (both success and failure)
  - Restart, shutdown, and system (both success and failure)

Whenever users are done using the system for a particular session, they should *always* log out using Ctrl-Alt-Del. In case users forget to do this, ensure that you have a password-protected screen saver that kicks in within five minutes of inactivity.

Service Packs

Make sure the latest service pack and hot fixes are installed on your platform. Microsoft releases these regularly, and they can be downloaded from www.microsoft. com/NTServer/all/downloads.asp.

Securing Linux

This discussion of securing Linux assumes Red Hat 6.0, but the steps should be similar for most distributions of Linux.

Make sure you have the latest security fixes applied for your distribution. The following list contains the appropriate URLs for Red Hat and some of the other distributions reported to work with FireWall-1 on Linux:

- *Red Hat:* www.redhat.com/apps/support/updates.html
- *Mandrake Linux:* www.linux-mandrake.com/en/security/
- *SuSE:* www.suse.com/us/support/security/index.html
- *Debian:* www.debian.org/security/

Partitioning Your Hard Drive

A recommended partitioning scheme includes:

- / (root filesystem), everything else
- /var (for logging), 400MB
- swap, 256MB (or 2x physical RAM)
- /var/opt/CKPfw1-41/log (for FireWall-1 4.1, this should be a separate physical disk)

Eliminating Services

Comment out most of the services from /etc/inetd.conf by placing a pound sign/hash in front of all the lines. Telnet and FTP are possible exceptions, but if you install an SSH server, you don't even need those services.

Next, look at the .rc scripts, which determine what services the init process starts. For Red Hat, you will find these scripts in /etc/rc.d/rc3.d (or /etc/rc.d/rc5.d if you automatically boot to a GUI, such as Gnome or KDE). To stop a script from starting, rename the file by replacing the capital *S* with a small *s*. This will prevent the init process from starting the script. Or, if you prefer, Red Hat comes with a great utility, which you can use for turning off these services. Just type **/usr/sbin/setup** at the command prompt, and select System Services; you can then select which scripts are started during the boot process. Another option is to use the chkconfig command, which you will find on most distributions.

The startup scripts listed in Table A-2 may be installed by default but are not critical to system functioning. If you do not need them, turn these scripts off. The numbers in the names determine the sequence of initialization; they may vary based on your distribution and version. Scripts that start with a capital *K* instead of a capital *S* are used to kill services that are already running.

Table A-2 Services that can be disabled in Linux

Startup File	Description
S05apmd	Advanced power management daemon, only needed for laptops
S10xntpd	NTP daemon
S15sound	Sound card information
S15netfs	NFS client software
S20rusersd	Daemon to export who is logged on to the system to other hosts
S20rwhod	Daemon to export who is logged on to the system to other hosts
S20rwalld	Allows other systems to broadcast messages to all users
S20bootparamd	Used to allow diskless clients to boot
S25squid	A caching proxy server
S35dhcpd	DHCP server daemon
S40atd	Similar to cron, not necessary
S50snmpd	SNMP daemon, can give remote users information about your system
S55routed	RIP daemon, not necessary unless you must participate in a RIP-based routing network
S55named	DNS Server. Unless you need to run a DNS server on your firewall, disable this
S60lpd	Printing Services
S60mars-new	NetWare File and Printing Services
S60nfs	NFS server
S72amd	Automounter daemon
S75gated	Used to run routing protocols like OSPF and RIP
S80sendmail	Used to receive e-mail on the local system
S85httpd	Apache Web server
S87ypbind	Required if you are an NIS client, but can be disabled
S90xfs	X Font server. Only necessary if you run X applications
S95innd	News server
S99linuxconf	Used to remotely configure Linux boxes via HTTP

Logging and Tweaking

Once you have eliminated as many services as possible, you should enable logging. All system logging occurs in `/var/log`. By default, Linux has excellent logging except for FTP. You have two options for logging for FTP:

- Configure the `/etc/ftpaccess` file
- Edit `/etc/inetd.conf`

I recommend editing `/etc/inetd.conf`, as it is simpler (i.e., harder to make a mistake). Edit `/etc/inetd.conf` as follows to ensure full logging of all FTP sessions using the following options: `-l` logs each FTP session in syslog, `-L` logs all commands to syslog, `-i` logs all files received xferlog, and `-o` logs all files downloaded to xferlog.

```
ftp    stream   tcp   nowait    root   /usr/sbin/tcpd   in.ftpd -l -L -i -o
```

Tweaking involves some file administration. You should first secure your `/etc/passwd` file (this is the database file that holds your user accounts and passwords). Ensure that your system is using `/etc/shadow`, which securely stores everyone's password as hashes in a file that only root can access. This protects your passwords from being easily accessed and cracked (one of the first exploits a hacker looks for). The use of shadow passwords is the default as of RH 6.0; however, it never hurts to be sure. All you have to do is type **pwconv** as root. This automatically converts your passwords to the `/etc/shadow` file.

Next, remove most of the default system accounts in `/etc/passwd`. Linux provides these accounts for various system activities that you may not need. If you do not need the accounts, remove them. The more accounts you have, the easier it is to access your system. An example is the "news" account. If you are not running NNTP, a newsgroup server, you do not need the account (be sure to update `/etc/cron.hourly`, as this looks for the user "news"). Also, make sure you remove the "FTP" account, as this is the account used for anonymous FTP.

You also want to create the file `/etc/ftpusers`. This file simply contains names of accounts that cannot FTP to the system. Any account listed in this file cannot FTP to the system. It is meant to restrict root and other common system accounts from using FTP.

In addition, ensure that root cannot Telnet to the system. This forces users to log in to the system as themselves, and then `su` to root. The file `/etc/securetty` lists what ttys root can connect to. List only tty1, tty2, and so on in this file. This restricts root logins to local access only. ttyp1, ttyp2, and so on are pseudo terminals; they allow root to Telnet to the system remotely. For the ultra paranoid, you can remove all terminals from this file. This means that it will not be possible to log in as root at all.

Create the file /etc/issue. This file is an ASCII text banner that appears for all Telnet logins.

It is recommended that you use TCP Wrappers. TCP Wrappers, although it does not encrypt, does log and control who can access your system. It is a binary that wraps itself around inetd services, such as Telnet or FTP. With TCP Wrappers, the system launches the wrapper for inetd connections, logs all attempts, and then verifies the attempt against an access control list. If the connection is permitted, TCP Wrappers hands the connection to the proper binary, such as Telnet. If the connection is rejected by the access control list, the connection is dropped.

Fortunately for Linux users, TCP Wrappers is already installed; you only need to edit the /etc/hosts.allow and /etc/hosts.deny files. The syntax is relatively simple. Put the IP addresses or networks in the file /etc/hosts.allow that you want to permit connections from. Put IP addresses or networks in the file /etc/hosts.deny that you do not want to permit access from. By default, Linux allows connections from everyone, so you need to modify these files.

The following sample /etc/hosts.allow file allows a few services from specific hosts:

```
# Allow a few things
sshd:ALL
ALL:10.0.0.0/255.255.255.0
ALL:10.0.1.0/255.255.255.0
ALL:10.0.10.0/255.255.255.0
ALL:10.0.43.0/255.255.255.0
ALL:10.0.69.0/255.255.255.0
ALL:192.168.43.40/255.255.255.248
ALL:127.0.0.1/255.0.0.0
```

This /etc/hosts.deny file denies everything not allowed by /etc/hosts.allow:

```
ALL:ALL:DENY
```

firewall-1.conf File for Use with OpenLDAP v1

To use OpenLDAP v1 with FireWall-1, add the following line to your `slapd.conf`:

```
include              /etc/openldap/firewall-1.conf
```

The contents of `firewall-1.conf` follow:

```
attribute        fw1auth-method              ces
attribute        fw1auth-server              ces
attribute        fw1pwdlastmod               ces
attribute        fw1skey-number              ces
attribute        fw1skey-seed                ces
attribute        fw1skey-passwd              ces
attribute        fw1skey-mdm                 ces
attribute        fw1expiration-date          ces
attribute        fw1hour-range-from          ces
attribute        fw1hour-range-to            ces
attribute        fw1day                      ces
attribute        fw1allowed-src              ces
attribute        fw1allowed-dst              ces
attribute        fw1allowed-vlan             ces
attribute        fw1SR-keym                  ces
attribute        fw1SR-datam                 ces
attribute        fw1SR-mdm                   ces
attribute        fw1enc-fwz-expiration       ces
attribute        fw1sr-auth-track            ces
attribute        fw1grouptemplate            ces
attribute        fw1ISAKMP-EncMethod         ces
attribute        fw1ISAKMP-AuthMethods       ces
```

```
attribute        fw1ISAKMP-HashMethods                    ces
attribute        fw1ISAKMP-Transfork                      ces
attribute        fw1ISAKMP-DataIntegrityMethod            ces
attribute        fw1ISAKMP-SharedSecret                   ces
attribute        fw1ISAKMP-DataEncMethod                  ces
attribute        fw1enc-methods                           ces
objectclass fw1template
        requires
                objectClass,
                cn
        allows
                member,
                description,
                fw1auth-method,
                fw1auth-server,
                fw1pwdlastmod,
                fw1skey-number,
                fw1skey-seed,
                fw1skey-passwd,
                fw1skey-mdm,
                fw1expiration-date,
                fw1hour-range-from,
                fw1hour-range-to,
                fw1day,
                fw1allowed-src,
                fw1allowed-dst,
                fw1allowed-vlan,
                fw1SR-keym,
                fw1SR-datam,
                fw1SR-mdm,
                fw1enc-fwz-expiration,
                fw1sr-auth-track,
                fw1grouptemplate,
                fw1ISAKMP-EncMethod,
                fw1ISAKMP-AuthMethods,
                fw1ISAKMP-HashMethods,
                fw1ISAKMP-Transform,
                fw1ISAKMP-DataIntegrityMethod,
                fw1ISAKMP-SharedSecret,
```

```
                fw1ISAKMP-DataEncMethod,
                fw1enc-methods
objectclass fw1person
        requires
                objectClass,
                cn
        allows
                description,
                fw1auth-method,
                fw1auth-server,
                fw1pwdlastmod,
                fw1skey-number,
                fw1skey-seed,
                fw1skey-passwd,
                fw1skey-mdm,
                fw1expiration-date,
                fw1hour-range-from,
                fw1hour-range-to,
                fw1day,
                fw1allowed-src,
                fw1allowed-dst,
                fw1allowed-vlan,
                fw1SR-keym,
                fw1SR-datam,
                fw1SR-mdm,
                fw1enc-fwz-expiration,
                fw1sr-auth-track,
                fw1grouptemplate,
                fw1ISAKMP-EncMethod,
                fw1ISAKMP-AuthMethods,
                fw1ISAKMP-HashMethods,
                fw1ISAKMP-Transform,
                fw1ISAKMP-DataIntegrityMethod,
                fw1ISAKMP-SharedSecret,
                fw1ISAKMP-DataEncMethod,
                fw1enc-methods
```

`firewall1.schema` File for Use with OpenLDAP v2

To use the `firewall1.schema` file, add the following lines to your `slapd.conf` file. These lines assume the core, cosine, and inetorgperson schemas are stored in `/etc/openldap/schema`:

```
include      /etc/openldap/schema/core.schema
include      /etc/openldap/schema/cosine.schema
include      /etc/openldap/schema/inetorgperson.schema
include      /etc/openldap/schema/firewall1.schema
```

The `firewall1.schema` file looks like this:

```
attributeType ( 1.3.114.7.4.2.0.1
   NAME 'fw1auth-method'
   SYNTAX 1.3.6.1.4.1.1466.115.121.1.26 )
attributeType ( 1.3.114.7.4.2.0.2
   NAME 'fw1auth-server'
   SYNTAX 1.3.6.1.4.1.1466.115.121.1.26 )
attributeType ( 1.3.114.7.4.2.0.3
   NAME 'fw1pwdlastmod'
   SYNTAX 1.3.6.1.4.1.1466.115.121.1.26 )
attributeType ( 1.3.114.7.4.2.0.4
   NAME 'fw1skey-number'
   SYNTAX 1.3.6.1.4.1.1466.115.121.1.26 )
attributeType ( 1.3.114.7.4.2.0.5
   NAME 'fw1skey-seed'
   SYNTAX 1.3.6.1.4.1.1466.115.121.1.26 )
attributeType ( 1.3.114.7.4.2.0.6
   NAME 'fw1skey-passwd'
   SYNTAX 1.3.6.1.4.1.1466.115.121.1.26 )
attributeType ( 1.3.114.7.4.2.0.7
```

```
     NAME 'fw1skey-mdm'
     SYNTAX 1.3.6.1.4.1.1466.115.121.1.26 )
attributeType ( 1.3.114.7.4.2.0.8
     NAME 'fw1expiration-date'
     SYNTAX 1.3.6.1.4.1.1466.115.121.1.26 )
attributeType ( 1.3.114.7.4.2.0.9
     NAME 'fw1hour-range-from'
     SYNTAX 1.3.6.1.4.1.1466.115.121.1.26 )
attributeType ( 1.3.114.7.4.2.0.10
     NAME 'fw1hour-range-to'
     SYNTAX 1.3.6.1.4.1.1466.115.121.1.26 )
attributeType ( 1.3.114.7.4.2.0.11
     NAME 'fw1day'
     SYNTAX 1.3.6.1.4.1.1466.115.121.1.26 )
attributeType ( 1.3.114.7.4.2.0.12
     NAME 'fw1allowed-src'
     SYNTAX 1.3.6.1.4.1.1466.115.121.1.26 )
attributeType ( 1.3.114.7.4.2.0.13
     NAME 'fw1allowed-dst'
     SYNTAX 1.3.6.1.4.1.1466.115.121.1.26 )
attributeType ( 1.3.114.7.4.2.0.14
     NAME 'fw1allowed-vlan'
     SYNTAX 1.3.6.1.4.1.1466.115.121.1.26 )
attributeType ( 1.3.114.7.4.2.0.15
     NAME 'fw1SR-keym'
     SYNTAX 1.3.6.1.4.1.1466.115.121.1.26 )
attributeType ( 1.3.114.7.4.2.0.16
     NAME 'fw1SR-datam'
     SYNTAX 1.3.6.1.4.1.1466.115.121.1.26 )
attributeType ( 1.3.114.7.4.2.0.17
     NAME 'fw1SR-mdm'
     SYNTAX 1.3.6.1.4.1.1466.115.121.1.26 )
attributeType ( 1.3.114.7.4.2.0.18
     NAME 'fw1enc-fwz-expiration'
     SYNTAX 1.3.6.1.4.1.1466.115.121.1.26 )
attributeType ( 1.3.114.7.4.2.0.19
     NAME 'fw1sr-auth-track'
     SYNTAX 1.3.6.1.4.1.1466.115.121.1.26 )
attributeType ( 1.3.114.7.4.2.0.20
     NAME 'fw1grouptemplate'
     SYNTAX 1.3.6.1.4.1.1466.115.121.1.26 )
attributeType ( 1.3.114.7.4.2.0.21
     NAME 'fw1ISAKMP-EncMethod'
     SYNTAX 1.3.6.1.4.1.1466.115.121.1.26 )
attributeType ( 1.3.114.7.4.2.0.22
     NAME 'fw1ISAKMP-AuthMethods'
     SYNTAX 1.3.6.1.4.1.1466.115.121.1.26 )
attributeType ( 1.3.114.7.4.2.0.23
```

```
      NAME 'fw1ISAKMP-HashMethods'
      SYNTAX 1.3.6.1.4.1.1466.115.121.1.26 )
attributeType ( 1.3.114.7.4.2.0.24
      NAME 'fw1ISAKMP-Transform'
      SYNTAX 1.3.6.1.4.1.1466.115.121.1.26 )
attributeType ( 1.3.114.7.4.2.0.25
      NAME 'fw1ISAKMP-DataIntegrityMethod'
      SYNTAX 1.3.6.1.4.1.1466.115.121.1.26 )
attributeType ( 1.3.114.7.4.2.0.26
      NAME 'fw1ISAKMP-SharedSecret'
      SYNTAX 1.3.6.1.4.1.1466.115.121.1.26 )
attributeType ( 1.3.114.7.4.2.0.27
      NAME 'fw1ISAKMP-DataEncMethod'
      SYNTAX 1.3.6.1.4.1.1466.115.121.1.26 )
attributeType ( 1.3.114.7.4.2.0.28
      NAME 'fw1enc-methods'
      SYNTAX 1.3.6.1.4.1.1466.115.121.1.26 )
objectClass ( 1.3.114.7.3.2.0.1
      NAME 'fw1template'
      SUP 'top'
      MUST ( objectclass $ cn )
      MAY ( member $ description $ fw1auth-method $ fw1auth-server $
fw1pwdlastmod $ fw1skey-number $ fw1skey-seed $ fw1skey-passwd $
fw1skey-mdm $ fw1expiration-date $ fw1hour-range-from $ fw1hour-range-to
$ fw1day $ fw1allowed-src $ fw1allowed-dst $ fw1allowed-vlan $ fw1SR-
keym $ fw1SR-datam $ fw1SR-mdm $ fw1enc-fwz-expiration $ fw1sr-auth-
track $ fw1grouptemplate $ fw1ISAKMP-EncMethod $ fw1ISAKMP-AuthMethods $
fw1ISAKMP-HashMethods $ fw1ISAKMP-Transform $ fw1ISAKMP-
DataIntegrityMethod $ fw1ISAKMP-SharedSecret $ fw1ISAKMP-DataEncMethod $
fw1enc-methods )
      )
objectClass ( 1.3.114.7.3.2.0.2
      NAME 'fw1person'
      SUP 'top'
      MUST ( cn )
      MAY ( description $ fw1auth-method $ fw1auth-server $ fw1pwdlastmod $
fw1skey-number $ fw1skey-seed $ fw1skey-passwd $ fw1skey-mdm $
fw1expiration-date $ fw1hour-range-from $ fw1hour-range-to $ fw1day $
fw1allowed-src $ fw1allowed-dst $ fw1allowed-vlan $ fw1SR-keym $ fw1SR-
datam $ fw1SR-mdm $ fw1enc-fwz-expiration $ fw1sr-auth-track $
fw1grouptemplate $ fw1ISAKMP-EncMethod $ fw1ISAKMP-AuthMethods $
fw1ISAKMP-HashMethods $ fw1ISAKMP-Transform $ fw1ISAKMP-
DataIntegrityMethod $ fw1ISAKMP-SharedSecret $ fw1ISAKMP-DataEncMethod $
fw1enc-methods )
      )
```

Complete Program for Stateful Inspection of HTTP

```
// Stateful Inspection of HTTP Code
//
// Add all of this to $FWDIR/lib/user.def. Follow the directions
// in the comments.
//
// The logic is this:
//
// If the packet is tcp, has a destination port that is HTTP,
// and either:
//
// 1. Exists in http_table (i.e. a pre-verified HTTP session)
// 2. Matches an HTTP request
// 3. Contains no data
// 4. Is a FIN/RST packet (in this case, remove the entry from
// http_table)
//
// then accept the packet. Drop packets that are tcp and destined
// for an HTTP port (they should have been caught above). If the
// packet originates from the http server and is FIN/RST (most of
// them are), then we want to remove the entry from the
// http_table, too.
http_table = dynamic {} refresh expires 60;

#define HTTP_GET_MAGIC  0x47455420 /* "GET " */
#define HTTP_HEAD_MAGIC 0x48454144 /* "HEAD" */
#define HTTP_POST_MAGIC 0x504f5354 /* "POST" */

define http_match {
 [TCPDATA,b] = HTTP_GET_MAGIC or
 [TCPDATA,b] = HTTP_HEAD_MAGIC or
 [TCPDATA,b] = HTTP_POST_MAGIC
} ;

define http_prologue {
```

```
    accept (
     tcp, dport in http_port_tab, (
      ( <src,sport,dst> in http_table ) or
      ( established, ip_len = 40 ) or
      ( http_match,
        record <src,sport,dst> in http_table, log long ) or
      ( tcpdone,
        delete <dst,dport,src> from http_table )
     )
    ) or accept (
     tcp, sport in http_port_tab, <dst, dport, src> in http_table
    ) or reject (
     tcp, dport in http_port_tab, not http_match, log long
    ) or reject (
     tcp, not (sport in http_port_tab), ack, ip_len > 40, log long )
    ) or accept (
     tcp, sport in http_port_tab, syn, ack
    ) or accept (
     tcp, sport in http_port_tab, tcpdone,
       delete <dst,dport,src> from http_table
    )
    } ;

    //
    // Create a service of type other, the following fields need to be
       filled in:
    //
    // match: http_code
    // prologue: http_prologue
    //
    // Add the following line to fwui_head.def:
    //
    // http_port_tab = { 80, 8080, 81 } (or whatever ports you want)
    //
    // Or in FireWall-1 4.1 and later, you can add a tabledef entry
    // to the service definition manually in $FWDIR/conf/objects.C,
    // as in the following example:
    //
    //          : (http-pb
    //             :type (other)
    //             :tabledef ("http_port_tab = { 80, 8080, 81 } ;")
    //             :prolog ("http_prologue;")
    //             :exp (http_code)
    //             :inexp ()
    //             :outexp ()
    //             :comments ()
    //             :color (Blue)
    //          )
    //
    define http_code { tcp, dport in http_port_tab } ;
```

Complete Program for Stateful Inspection of Ping and Traceroute

To use this code:

- You can type this code into a file called `icmp13.def` or download it from http://people.netscape.com/shadow/work/inspect/index.html.
- Copy this file to `$FWDIR/lib` on your management console.
- Modify `$FWDIR/lib/user.def` on the management console, and add the following line after the "User Defined INSPECT" line: `#include "icmp13.def"`.
- Uncheck the "Allow ICMP" setting in Rulebase Properties.
- Create a service of type Other. In the Match field, enter "ping_request_accept or traceroute_request_accept." In the Prologue field, enter "ns_icmp_code."
- Define a new rule in the GUI that permits ping and traceroute to a destination that uses this new service.
- Reinstall the security policy.

The code follows with all of the legalese:

```
//
// Stateful icmp v1.3 William D. Burns (shadow@netscape.com)
// (c) Copyright 1997,1998,1999 Netscape Communications
// first released August 17, 1997.  Last updated: August 3, 1999
//
// ICMP INSPECT SCRIPT
//
//The initial version of this script was written at Netscape
// Communications Corporation.  Portions created by Netscape are
```

```
// Copyright (C) 1997-1999 Netscape Communications Corporation.
// All Rights Reserved.
//
// Short legal version:
//   Please use this code and make whatever modifications you
//   want to it. Please use this code as a springboard to make
//   other cool INSPECT modules.It works for us, but your mileage
//   may vary.  If this code breaks something at your site, we
//   aren't responsible. Test everything first.  Trust no one.
//
// Longer legal version: :)
//Use of this Script is subject to the terms below (the "Terms"):
//
// You may use, reproduce, modify, distribute, and sublicense
// this ICMP INSPECT scripting code (the "Script") and your
// derivative works thereof ("Derivative Works"), subject to the
// following terms:
//
//1. You may not charge a fee or royalty for the modified or
//   unmodified Script, but you may charge for products containing
//   the modified or unmodified Script so long as you also make
//   the included version of the Script (whether modified or
//   unmodified) publicly available without charge.
//
//2. Any product that contains the modified or unmodified
//   Script must be licensed solely under an agreement that
//   includes limitation of liability provisions and disclaimer
//   of warranty provisions at least as protective of Netscape as //
those in Sections 5 and 6 below.
//
//3. Any modified version of the Script must (A) retain the
//   copyright notice above and all of the Terms; and (B)
//   prominently state in the place indicated above that the
//   Script has been modified by you and include the date the
//   modifications were made and a brief description of the
//   modifications.
//
//4. Title, ownership rights, and intellectual property rights
//   in and to the original Script shall remain in Netscape and/
//   or its suppliers.  You may use the Script only as provided
//   herein. Netscape shall have no obligation to provide
//   maintenance, support, upgrades or new releases to you or any
//   person to whom you distribute any version of the Script or a
//   Derivative Work.  As between you and Netscape, you shall own
//   and be solely responsible for any Derivative Work that you
//   create (including without limitation any modified version of
//   the Script and any product containing the Script).
//
```

```
//5. Disclaimer of Warranty.   THE SCRIPT IS LICENSED "AS IS"
//   WITHOUT WARRANTY OF ANY KIND.   ALL EXPRESSED OR IMPLIED
//   WARRANTIES INCLUDING WITHOUT LIMITATION WARRANTIES OF
//   PERFORMANCE, MERCHANTABILITY, FITNESS FOR ANY PARTICULAR
//   PURPOSE AND NONINFRINGEMENT ARE HEREBY DISCLAIMED.   THE
//   ENTIRE RISK AS TO THE RESULTS AND PERFORMANCE OF THE SCRIPT
//   IS ASSUMED BY YOU. SHOULD THE SCRIPT PROVE DEFECTIVE, YOU
//   ASSUME THE ENTIRE COST OF ALL NECESSARY SERVICING, REPAIR, OR
//   CORRECTION.   THIS DISCLAIMER OF WARRANTY CONSTITUTES AN
//   ESSENTIAL PART OF THIS AGREEMENT. NO USE OF THE SCRIPT IS
//   AUTHORIZED EXCEPT UNDER THIS DISCLAIMER.
//
//6. Limitation of Liability. UNDER NO CIRCUMSTANCES AND UNDER
//   NO LEGAL THEORY, WHETHER TORT, CONTRACT, OR OTHERWISE, SHALL
//   NETSCAPE OR ITS SUPPLIERS OR RESELLERS BE LIABLE TO YOU OR
//   ANY OTHER PERSON FOR ANY INDIRECT, SPECIAL, INCIDENTAL, OR
//   CONSEQUENTIAL DAMAGES OF ANY CHARACTER INCLUDING, WITHOUT
//   LIMITATION, DAMAGES FOR LOSS OF GOODWILL, WORK STOPPAGE,
//   COMPUTER FAILURE OR MALFUNCTION, OR ANY AND ALL OTHER
//   COMMERCIAL DAMAGES OR LOSSES.   BECAUSE NETSCAPE HAS NOT
//   RECEIVED ANY PAYMENT FOR THE SCRIPT, IN NO EVENT WILL
//   NETSCAPE BE LIABLE FOR ANY DAMAGES, EVEN IF NETSCAPE SHALL
//   HAVE BEEN INFORMED OF THE POSSIBILITY OF SUCH DAMAGES, OR
//   FOR ANY CLAIM BY ANY THIRD PARTY.   THIS LIMITATION OF
//   LIABILITY SHALL NOT APPLY TO LIABILITY FOR DEATH OR PERSONAL
//   INJURY RESULTING FROM NETSCAPE'S NEGLIGENCE TO THE EXTENT
//   APPLICABLE LAW PROHIBITS SUCH LIMITATION.   SOME
//   JURISDICTIONS DO NOT ALLOW THE EXCLUSION OR LIMITATION OF
//   INCIDENTAL OR CONSEQUENTIAL DAMAGES, SO THIS EXCLUSION
//   AND LIMITATION MAY NOT APPLY TO YOU.
//
//7. Netscape may terminate this Agreement immediately in the
//   event of breach by you. You may terminate this Agreement at
//   any time by destroying the Script and all copies thereof.
//   Termination of your license will not terminate any
//   sublicenses previously granted by you so long as the
//   sublicensee complies with this Agreement.   Sections 4, 5 and
//   6 shall survive termination.
//
//8. Use, duplication, or disclosure by the United States
//   Government is subject to restrictions set forth in
//   subparagraphs (a) through (d) of the Commercial
//   Computer-Restricted Rights clause at FAR 52.227-19 when
//   applicable, or in subparagraph (c)(1)(ii) of the Rights in
//   Technical Data and Computer Program clause at DFARS
//   252.227-7013, and in similar clauses in the NASA FAR
//   Supplement. Contractor/manufacturer is Netscape
//   Communications Corporation, 501 East Middlefield Road,
```

```
//    Mountain View, CA 94043.
//
//9. This Agreement shall be governed by and construed under
//   California law as such law applies to agreements between
//   California residents entered into and to be performed
//   entirely within California, except as governed by United
//   States federal law.
//
//   internal testing builds:
//   - v1.1 added icmp_ip_seq and icmp_ip_id checking
//   - v1.2 first released version to check ping
//   - v1.2a removed ip_ttl < 30 check for ping
//   - v1.3 (internal) added tracert support
//   - v1.4 tracks unix traceroute, microsoft tracert, and ping
//   - v1.5 correctly delete spent records from tables
//
//   release builds:
//   - v1.1 name change from ns_ping15a.def to ns_icmp11.def
//   - v1.1 found a new bug in INSPECT
//       + noticed equality tests did not always work
//       + and Checkpoint always used a different syntax than I
//       + to use less ()s you should test tables as
//       + 'a_table[a,b] = value'   instead of
//       + 'value = a_table[a,b]'  because this doesnt work
//       + you have to say '(a_table[a,b] = value)'
//
//   - v1.2
//       + incorporated minor suggestions from Checkpoint
//       + implemented UNIX traceroute reply packet acceptance
//       + first release to public
//
//   - v1.3
//       + FW-1 v4.0 added a new icmp_sequence_number define which
//         caused my code to fail to compile.  No longer defining
//         it here
//       + fixed bug so a host can ping and traceroute to same target
//
// ================================================
//       Variable definition section
// redundant in FW-1 v4:
// #define icmp_icmp_seq [ 54 : 2, b ]
// ================================================
// where icmp sequence number is
#define icmp_ip_seq [ 24 : 2, b ]
#define Timeout 5
ping_table     = dynamic {} expires Timeout;
ms_trt_table   = dynamic {} expires Timeout;
unix_trt_table = dynamic {} expires Timeout;
```

```
// =============================================
//          Packet definition section
// =============================================
// =============================================
// What a ping request looks like
//
#define is_ping_request (                           \
  icmp, icmp_type=ICMP_ECHO                          \
)
// =============================================
// Per the ping of death and checkpoint web pages
// this will disallow fragmented packets from
// coming in
//
#define not_fragmented (                            \
  ((ip_off & 0x2000) = 0)                            \
)
// =============================================
// What a proper ping reply packet looks like
//
#define is_ping_reply (                             \
  icmp, icmp_type=ICMP_ECHOREPLY                     \
)
// =============================================
// What a proper ICMP Time exceeded (type 11)
//  looks like — will come from routers in path
//
#define is_timxceed_reply (                         \
  icmp, icmp_type=ICMP_TIMXCEED                      \
)
// =============================================
// What a unix traceroute request looks like
//
#define is_traceroute_request (                     \
  udp, uh_dport > 33000, ip_ttl < 30                \
)
// =============================================
// What a unix traceroute reply looks like
//
#define is_dstunreach_reply (                       \
  icmp, icmp_type = ICMP_UNREACH                     \
)
// =============================================
// Begin tracking and decision-making section
// =============================================
// =============================================
// ICMP echo request
//
```

```
// if it looks like an echo packet,
//    it is either a real ping packet
//      - record in ping_table
//      - replies will come from target
//    or it is a microsoft tracert packet
//      - record in ms_trt_table
//      - replies could come from target or
//        routers along the way
//
#define ping_request_accept (                        \
  is_ping_request, not_fragmented,                   \
  record <src,icmp_ip_id; icmp_ip_seq> in ms_trt_table, \
  record <src,dst,icmp_ip_id; icmp_ip_seq> in ping_table    \
)
// ================================================
// Got: ICMP echo reply
//
// accept the packet iff it corresponds to an
//    echo packet that we recorded
//
#define ping_reply_intercept (                       \
  is_ping_reply, not_fragmented,                     \
  accept (                                           \
    icmp_ip_seq = ping_table [dst,src,icmp_ip_id], \
    delete <dst,icmp_ip_id> from ms_trt_table,   \
    delete <dst,src,icmp_ip_id> from ping_table \
  or (log icmp_long, drop)                           \
  )                                                  \
)
// ================================================
// Got: ICMP time exceeded
//
// accept the packet iff it matches an echo packet
//   that we recorded
// Note that Ori wants us to use icmp_icmp_seq check for
//   ms_trt_table
//
#define timxceed_reply_intercept (                   \
  is_timxceed_reply, not_fragmented,                 \
  accept (                                           \
   (icmp_ip_seq = ms_trt_table [dst,icmp_ip_id] \
     or                                              \
    icmp_uh_dport = unix_trt_table [dst,icmp_uh_sport]), \
    delete <dst,icmp_ip_id> from ms_trt_table,   \
    delete <dst,icmp_uh_sport> from unix_trt_table \
  or (log icmp_long, drop)                           \
  )                                                  \
)
```

```
// ================================================
// Begin UNIX traceroute section
// ================================================
//
// Track any packets that look like "traceroute"
// packets and record them in the unix_trt_table.
//
// Responses will be similar to those for
// microsoft traceroute (icmp type 11) but will
// include icmp type 3
//
// ================================================
// Got: UNIX Traceroute Request packet
//
// Per the RFC, the udp source and destination
// ports MUST be in the reply packet.
// Replies will be tracked against this.
//
#define traceroute_request_accept (                 \
  is_traceroute_request,                            \
  record <src,uh_sport;uh_dport> in unix_trt_table      \
)
// ================================================
// Got: ICMP Destination Unreachable packet
//
// Accept the packet iff it matches a traceroute
// request that we recorded
//
#define dstunreach_reply_intercept (                \
  is_dstunreach_reply, not_fragmented,              \
  accept (                                          \
   icmp_uh_dport = unix_trt_table[dst,icmp_uh_sport],
    delete <dst,icmp_uh_sport> from unix_trt_table
  or (log icmp_long, drop)                          \
  )                                                 \
)
// ================================================
// ================================================
// Begin ICMP REPLY checking section
// ================================================
// ================================================
// only three ICMP packets we want
//    - echo reply or
//    - time exceeded reply or
//    - destination unreachable reply
//
#define ns_icmp_reply_intercept (                   \
  ping_reply_intercept or                           \
```

```
    timxceed_reply_intercept or                         \
    dstunreach_reply_intercept                          \
)

//This is what you put in the prologue section
//  and what gets executed on a match
//
#define ns_icmp_code {                                  \
        ns_icmp_reply_intercept;                        \
}
```

F

INSPECT Script for Different Policies on Different Interfaces

```
#include "tcpip.def"
//#include "fwui_head.def"

short = format {
    <"proto", proto, ip_p>,
    <"src", ipaddr, ip_src>,
    <"dst", ipaddr, ip_dst>,
    <"service", port, th_dport>
    } ;

private_domain1={10.10.40.76,10.10.10.10} ;
private_domain2={10.10.60.34,10.10.10.10} ;
public_domain={172.19.184.119, 172.19.184.68, 10.10.30.73,
172.19.183.73} ;

connections = dynamic refresh expires 180;

/* Accept pings */
<>    all@volvo
      accept (ip_p = 1);
/* Accept Return traffic */
<>    all@volvo
      accept <ip_dst, th_dport, ip_src, th_sport, ip_p> in connections
      or <ip_src, th_sport, ip_dst, th_dport, ip_p> in connections;
/* per -interface rules */
<=    eth-s1p1c0@volvo
      <ip_src> in private_domain1, (th_dport = 23),
      record <ip_src,th_sport,ip_dst,th_dport,ip_p> in connections,
      accept,
      log short;
=>    eth-s1p1c0@volvo
```

```
        <ip_src> in public_domain, (th_dport = 23) or (th_port=80),
        record <ip_src,th_sport,ip_dst,th_dport,ip_p> in connections,
        accept,
        log short;
<=  eth-s1p2c0@volvo
        <ip_src> in private_domain2, (th_dport=23),
        record <ip_src,th_sport,ip_dst,th_dport,ip_p> in connections,
        accept,
        log short;
=>  eth-s1p2c0@volvo
        <ip_src> in public_domain, (th_dport=23),
        record <ip_src,th_sport,ip_dst,th_dport,ip_p> in connections,
        accept,
        log short;
<=  eth-s1p3c0@volvo
        <ip_src> in private_domain1, (th_dport = 23),
        record <ip_src,th_sport,ip_dst,th_dport,ip_p> in connections,
        accept,
        log short;
=>  eth-s1p3c0@volvo
        <ip_src> in public_domain, (th_dport = 23),
        record <ip_src,th_sport,ip_dst,th_dport,ip_p> in connections,
        accept,
        log short;
<=  eth-s1p4c0@volvo
        <ip_src> in public_domain, (th_dport=23),
        record <ip_src,th_sport,ip_dst,th_dport,ip_p> in connections,
        accept,
        log short;
=>  eth-s1p4c0@volvo
        <ip_src> in private_domain2, (th_dport=23),
        record <ip_src,th_sport,ip_dst,th_dport,ip_p> in connections,
        accept,
        log short;
<> loop0c0@volvo

        accept;
```

Sample
`defaultfilter.pf` File

```
// IP source and destination
#define src [12,b]
#define dst [16,b]

// TCP or UDP source and destination ports
#define sport [20:2,b]
#define dport [22:2,b]

// IP protocol
#define ip_p [9:1]

// Table for recording outgoing sessions. Incoming packets are
// matched against this table.
connections = dynamic refresh expires 300;

// The following two rules deal with outgoing and incoming
// packets in which the IP source and destination are the same as
// well as connections originating from the firewall going to tcp
// port 256 (e.g. for fetching the security policy from the
// management console) or to tcp port 22 (for ssh access). The
// first rule accepts and records such outgoing packets. The
// second rule accepts such packet if a matching packet was
// previously] recorded.
<= all@all
      accept (
            (src = dst,
             record <0,src,ip_p,sport,dport> in connections)
                    or
            (ip_p = 6, dport = 256 or dport = 22,
             record <src,dst,ip_p,sport,dport> in connections)
      );

=> all@all
      accept (
```

```
                (src = dst,
                 <0,src,ip_p,sport,dport> in connections)
                      or
                 (ip_p = 6, sport = 256 or sport = 22,
                 <dst,src,ip_p,dport,sport> in connections)
        );

// The next rule just drops everything else.
drop;
```

Appendix

H
_____

Sample Internet Usage Policy

Company X Information Security Policy
Section 003 : Internet Access and Usage
SUMMARY

The wide array of new resources, new services, and interconnectivity available via the Internet all introduce new opportunities and new risks. In response to the risks, this document describes Company X's official policy regarding Internet security and access.

I. INTERNET DOWNLOADS

A. *Downloads:* All nontext files (databases, software object code, spreadsheets, formatted word processing package files, etc.) downloaded from non-Company X sources via the Internet must be screened with virus detection software prior to being used. Whenever an external provider of the software is not trusted, downloaded software should be tested on a stand-alone nonproduction machine that has been recently backed up. If this software contains a virus, worm, or Trojan horse, damage will be restricted to the involved machine only.

II. INFORMATION CONFIDENTIALITY

A. *Information Exchange:* Company X's software, documentation, and all other types of internal information must not be sold or otherwise transferred to any non-Company X party for any purposes other than business purposes expressly authorized by management. Exchanges of software and/or data between Company X and any third party may not proceed unless a written agreement has first been signed. Such an agreement must specify the terms of the exchange as well as the ways in which the software and/or data is to be handled and protected. Regular business practices, such as shipment of a product in response to a customer purchase order, need not involve such a specific agreement, because the terms are implied.

B. *Message Interception:* Wiretapping and other types of message interception are straightforward and frequently encountered on the Internet. Accordingly, Company X's secret, proprietary, or private information must not be sent over the Internet unless it has first been encrypted by approved methods authorized by the Chief Security Officer. Unless specifically known to be in the public domain, source code must always be encrypted before being sent over the Internet.

C. *Security Parameters:* Credit card numbers, telephone calling card numbers, fixed login passwords, and other security parameters that can be used to gain access to goods or services must not be sent over the Internet in readable form. The use of 128-bit or greater encryption is an acceptable Internet encryption standard for the protection of security parameters. Other encryption processes or standards are permissible if they are approved by the Chief Security Officer.

III. ACCESS CONTROL

A. *User Authentication:* All users wishing to establish a real-time connection with Company X's internal computers via the Internet must authenticate themselves at a firewall before gaining access to Company X's internal network. This authentication process must be achieved via a dynamic password system approved by the Chief Security Officer. Examples of approved technology include handheld smart cards with dynamic passwords and user-transparent challenge/response systems. These systems will prevent intruders from guessing fixed passwords or from replaying a fixed password captured via a "sniffer attack" (wiretap). Designated "public" systems (anonymous FTP, Web surfing, etc.) do not need user authentication processes, because anonymous interactions are expected.

B. *Internet Service Providers:* With the exception of telecommuters and mobile computer users, workers must not employ Internet Service Provider (ISP) accounts and dial-up lines to access the Internet with Company X's computers. Instead, all Internet activity must pass through Company X's firewalls so that access controls and related security mechanisms can be applied.

C. *Vendors, Partners, and Suppliers:* Any external party connecting to any part of Company X's information network must abide by Company X's security policies. No connection is permitted until approved in writing by the Chief Security Officer. The outside party must fully understand and agree to all security terms and conditions. Any and all such connections must be limited to only what the clients need, and no more. An example would include having an isolated, protected network for vendor or partner connections.

IV. PRIVACY EXPECTATIONS

A. *No Default Protection:* Workers using Company X's information systems and/or the Internet should realize that their communications are not automatically protected from being viewed by third parties. Unless encryption is used, workers should not send information over the Internet if they consider it to be confidential or private.

B. *Management Review:* At any time and without prior notice, Company X's management reserves the right to examine electronic mail messages, files on personal computers, Web browser cache files, Web browser bookmarks, and other information stored on or passing through Company X's computers. Such management access assures compliance with internal policies, assists with internal investigations, and assists with the management of Company X's information systems.

C. *Logging:* Company X routinely logs Web sites visited, files downloaded, time spent on the Internet, and related information. Department managers may receive reports of such information and use it to determine what types of Internet usage are appropriate for the business activities of their departments.

Appendix
I

Performance Tuning

This appendix discusses how to tune FireWall-1 and the OS of the three major platforms for FireWall-1: Solaris, Windows NT, and IPSO.

Memory Used for State Tables

When handling a large amount of connections with FireWall-1, you should first increase the amount of memory allocated by FireWall-1's Kernel Module at boot time. This is controlled by a parameter called fwhmem. The default value of this parameter varies with the version of FireWall-1 in question. The defaults are also different on the IPSO version. However, these guidelines apply to all platforms.

In FireWall-1 4.1 SP2 on IPSO 3.3, this parameter will be set based on the physical memory installed on the platform according to Table I-1. These settings provide a good base value to use on other platforms as well.

Table I-1 fwhmem settings for physical memory

Memory	fwhmem Setting
64MB	0xa00000 (10MB)
128MB	0xc00000 (12MB)
256MB	0x1000000 (16MB)
512MB	0x1b00000 (28MB)

In any case, this value can be changed based on your specific needs. For each connection, FireWall-1 requires a specific amount of memory per connection. See Table I-2.

Table I-2 Memory requirements for specific connections

Type	Number of Bytes
Normal	64 bytes
NAT	Additional 120 bytes
Client Auth	64 bytes per authenticated rule
User Auth	Additional 200 bytes
Session Auth	Additional 100 bytes
Encryption	Additional 200 bytes
Accounting	Additional 60 bytes

An additional 3MB of memory are needed (minimum) to manipulate the various tables used by FireWall-1. Based on this information, you can determine the appropriate size of fwhmem using the following formula:

fwhmem = working_space + connections*64 + nat_connections*120 + client_authed_rules*64 + user_auth_connections*200 + session_authed_connections*100 + encrypted_connections*200 + accounting_connections*60

For example, if you expect to handle 50,000 connections without NAT, authentication, or encryption, fwhmem should be 3MB + 50000*64 = 6,345,728 bytes (or 0x60D400). If NAT is involved for half of these connections, it should be 3MB + 50000*64 + 25000*120 = 9,345,728 bytes (or 0x8E9AC0).

Once you have determined the appropriate value for fwhmem, you need to change it. The following examples illustrate how to do this. Generally speaking, this process can be used to change other kernel variables as well by substituting the appropriate kernel variable for fwhmem in the following procedures. In the following example, fwhmem is changed to 10MB (0xa00000). On Solaris machines, add the following line to the bottom of the /etc/system file, and reboot:

```
set fw:fwhmem=0xa00000
```

On SunOS 4 machines, use the following commands:

```
# $FWDIR/bin/fwstop
# echo "fwhmem?Wa00000" | adb -w $FWDIR/modules/fwmod.4.1.3.o
# $FWDIR/bin/fwstart
```

On HP-UX 9 machines, use the following command, and reboot the gateway:

```
# echo "fwhmem?Wa00000" | adb -w /hp-ux
```

On HP-UX 10 machines, use the following command, and reboot the gateway:

```
# echo "fwhmem?Wa00000" | adb -w /stand/vmunix
```

On AIX machines, use the following commands:

```
# fwstop
# echo "fw_heap_size/W 800000" | adb -w $FWDIR/modules/fwmod.4.x.o
# echo "fwhmem/W a00000" | adb -w $FWDIR/modules/fwmod.4.x.o
# fwstart
```

NOTE! When using the preceding procedure to modify other kernel variables, you can skip the line referring to `fw_heap_size`. This change is specific to modifying fwhmem.

On Windows NT, do the following:

1. Run regedt32 (the Registry editor).
2. Go to `HKEY_LOCAL_MACHINE\SYSTEM\CurrentControlSet\ Services\ FW1\Parameters`.
3. Select Add Value from the Edit menu.
4. The value's name is Memory, and the data type is REG_DWORD.
5. Enter the new amount of kernel memory (in bytes, which is 10,485,760).
6. Reboot.

NOTE! On Windows NT, you cannot use the preceding procedure to modify other kernel variables. Check Point will either have to provide you with a specific procedure or a patched device driver that has the changes in place.

On an IPSO system (VPN-1 Appliance or Nokia IPxxx), you need to get the zap or modzap utility from Resolution 1261 in Nokia's Knowledge Base. You can then use the following command line to modify the fwhmem parameter and reboot the system:

```
# zap -s _fwhmem $FWDIR/modules/fwmod.o 0xa00000 (For FireWall-1 3.x)
# zap -s _fwhmem $FWDIR/boot/modules/fwmod.o 0xa00000 (For
FireWall-1 4.0)
# modzap _fwhmem $FWDIR/boot/modules/fwmod.o 0xa00000 (For
FireWall-1 4.1)
```

NOTE! On IPSO, all kernel variables begin with an underscore ("_").

On a Linux platform, you need to change the `fwinsmod` command located in *both* `/etc/rc.d/rc[35].d/S11fw1boot` and `$FWDIR/bin/fwstart`. It has the following format:

```
fwinsmod -f $smp_prefix $fwmod
```

To change fwhmem, change the command to read:

```
fwinsmod -f $smp_prefix $fwmod fwhmem=0xa00000
```

Note that if you want to change multiple kernel values, you list multiple name=value pairs. Also, make sure you update this in *both* scripts.

WARNING! Setting fwhmem higher than 10MB on a 64MB system is not recommended due to how IPSO restricts kernel modules from using more than a certain percentage of system resources. If you find that fwhmem needs to be set beyond this value, it is highly recommended you increase the amount of physical memory available on the platform.

Number of Entries Permitted in Tables

FireWall-1 keeps track of all connections in state tables that are maintained in the kernel. By default, most of the tables are limited to 25,000 entries. Two tables that often need to be increased in size are the connections table and the NAT connections table.

The connections table size is set on the management console in `$FWDIR/lib/table.def`. You should see a line similar to the following:

```
connections = dynamic refresh sync expires TCP_START_TIMEOUT
expcall KFUNC_CONN_EXPIRE kbuf 1 hashsize 8192;
```

Because there is no limit specified, the default limit is 25,000. The hashsize should be the next largest power of 2 from the limit you specify in this line. To handle 50,000 connections (hashsize of 65536, the next highest power of 2), you would change the line to read:

```
connections = dynamic refresh sync expires TCP_START_TIMEOUT
    expcall KFUNC_CONN_EXPIRE kbuf 1 hashsize 8192 limit 50000
    hashsize 65536;
```

Once you make this change, you need to reload the policy from your management console.

To change the number of NAT entries permitted in the tables, you need to make the following changes to `$FWDIR/conf/objects.C` on the management console. For guidelines on editing `objects.C`, see Chapter 4, FAQ 4.2. Add or modify these properties under the props section:

```
:nat_limit (any number - the default is 25000)
:nat_hashsize (next largest power of 2 from the nat_limit)
```

The preceding modifications will work on FireWall-1 4.0 SP3 or later.

OS-Specific Tweaks

The following sections discuss how to tweak Solaris, Windows NT, and IPSO's TCP/IP stack as well as provide some changes to help the Security Servers function better.

IPSO-Specific Changes

Each of the following changes should be added to `/var/etc/rc.local` so that they will be active across reboots. Most of these changes will increase the performance of the Security Servers, which will benefit from increased packet sizes, but will also help general TCP/IP traffic along.

```
ipsctl -w net:ip:tcp:sendspace 65535 # TCP/IP specific changes
ipsctl -w net:ip:tcp:recvspace 65535
ipsctl -w net:ip:tcp:default_mss 1460 # Should be MTU minus 40 bytes
```

Solaris-Specific Changes

All `ndd` commands listed in this section should be added to an rc startup script. My suggestion is to create a new one, such as `/etc/rc2.d/S99nddcmds`.

The following commands force 100MB full duplex on hme-type interfaces and will disable autonegotiation. You can also do this on qfe-type interfaces as well by replacing `/dev/hme` with `/dev/qfe` in the following commands:

```
ndd -set /dev/hme adv_autoneg_cap 0
ndd -set /dev/hme adv_100fdx_cap 1
```

The following commands tune the TCP stack with optimal settings:

```
ndd -set /dev/tcp tcp_xmit_hiwat 65535
ndd -set /dev/tcp tcp_recv_hiwat 65535
ndd -set /dev/tcp tcp_cwnd_max 65535
ndd -set /dev/tcp tcp_slow_start_initial 2
```

```
ndd -set /dev/tcp tcp_conn_req_max_q 1024
ndd -set /dev/tcp tcp_conn_req_max_q0 4096
ndd -set /dev/tcp tcp_close_wait_interval 60000
```

Additionally, you should add the following to /etc/system and reboot:

```
set tcp:tcp_conn_hash_size = 16384
```

Windows NT–Specific Changes

All of the following changes apply to Windows NT Server 4.0, not Windows 2000:

1. Set the Windows NT memory strategy to Maximize Throughput for Network Applications. By default it is set to Maximize Throughput for File Sharing, which allocates all available Windows NT memory to file cache. To change this setting, go to Control Panel, select Network, and then select Server.

2. Next, disable all unnecessary services and drivers. If you followed the suggestions for securing a Windows NT box in Appendix A, you have done most of this already.

3. If you are making use of the Security Servers, you should disable performance boost for foreground applications. Go to Control Panel, select System, and then select Performance. Move the Application Performance slider to None.

4. The Page file (i.e., swap) should be a fixed size at least twice the size of physical RAM and should exist on another (preferably dedicated) drive.

5. TCP/IP should be tuned for maximum performance. You need to employ regedt32 to make these changes:

```
HKEY_LOCAL_MACHINE\System\CurrentControlSet\Services\Tcpip\
            Parameters\ForwardBufferMemory = 296960
```

This REG_DWORD must be a multiple of 256 and be set to a default of 74240. This is the size of the buffer the IP stack allocates to store packet data in the router queue. The default value is enough for 50 1480-byte packets.

```
HKEY_LOCAL_MACHINE\System\CurrentControlSet\Services\Tcpip\
            Parameters\NumForwardPackets = 200
```

This REG_DWORD has a default of 50. This corresponds to the number of IP headers allocated for router queue. It should be at least as large as the Forward-BufferMemory/IP data size of the network. Increasing these two parameters can have a significant effect on throughput, especially with slow policies.

```
HKEY_LOCAL_MACHINE\System\CurrentControlSet\Services\Tcpip\
            Parameters\TcpWindowSize
```

This REG_DWORD has a default of 8760 for Ethernet. A larger TCP receive window size will improve performance over high-speed networks. For highest efficiency, it should be an even multiple of TCP Maximum Segment Size (MSS), which is usually 1460 for Ethernet.

```
HKEY_LOCAL_MACHINE\System\CurrentControlSet\Services\Tcpip\
              Parameters\MaxFreeTcbs = 4000
```

This REG_DWORD has a default of 2000 and corresponds to the TCP TIME_WAIT table size.

```
HKEY_LOCAL_MACHINE\system\CurrentControlSet\Services\Tcpip\
              Parameters\MaxHashTableSize = 65536
```

This REG_DWORD should be a power of 2 and correspond to the hash value for the TCP TIME_WAIT table size.

```
HKEY_LOCAL_MACHINE\System\CurrentControlSet\Services\Tcpip\
              Parameters\MaxUserPort = 65534
```

This REG_DWORD with a default value of 5000 increases the number of TCP user ports available to applications, which prevents the Security Servers from running out of ports to use.

6. Improve the CPU servicing of interrupts generated by network interface cards (NICs). Change the Processor Affinity Mask using regedt32:

```
HKEY_LOCAL_MACHINE\System\CurrentControlSet\Services\NDIS\
              Parameters\ProcessorAffinityMask = 0
```

7. Tune the specific vendor NIC's parameters for maximum performance. Note that not all vendors allow you to tune these variables, or the variables may have slightly different names. Go to Control Panel, select Network, select Adapter Properties, and then select Advanced. The actual performance gain will vary depending on the types of traffic. You may want to adjust these parameters for maximum performance gain; otherwise, use these suggestions:

Receive Buffers = 256
Transmit Control Blocks = 64
Coalesce Buffers = 16

8. If you are using encryption, make the following Registry changes with regedt32:

```
HKEY_LOCAL_MACHINE\System\CurrentControlSet\Services\FW1\ Parame-
            ters\PacketPoolSize = 3000 (default of 1000)
```

```
HKEY_LOCAL_MACHINE\System\Current\ControlSet\Services\FW1 \parame-
            ters\BufferPoolSize = 6000
```

```
            (default of 2000, should be 2xPacketPoolSize)
```

Other Resources

The URLs provided in this appendix were valid as of April 2001. The most up-to-date version of this list appears at www.phoneboy.com/links.html.

Internet Resources

Check Point FireWall-1 on AIX: A cookbook for stand-alone and High Availability SG24-5492-00 at www.redbooks.ibm.com/abstracts/sg245492.html

CERT Advisories: http://www.cert.org/advisories/

Check Point's Knowledge Base (some documents require a login and password): http://support.checkpoint.com/kb/

Check Point's News Server: news://nntp.checkpoint.com

Comprehensive List of Security Policies from UCDavis (good sample Security Policy texts): http://security.ucdavis.edu/policies/overall.html

DNS Resource Directory: www.dns.net/dnsrd/

Firewall's Mailing List (not specific to FireWall-1): http://lists.gnac.net/ firewalls/

Firewall Wizards' Mailing List (also not specific to FireWall-1): www.nfr.com/mail-man/listinfo/firewall-wizards

FireWall-1 FAQ Pages:

    Dreamwvr's FireWall-1 FAQ: www.dreamwvr.com/bastions/ FW1_faq.html

    Obiwankenobi: www.deathstar.ch/security/fw1/

    PhoneBoy's FireWall-1 FAQ: www.phoneboy.com/

    Secure-1: www.secure-1.com

fw-1-mailinglist (run by Check Point, but unofficial): www.checkpoint.com/services/mailing.html

    Searchable indexes:

    • http://msgs.SecurePoint.com/cgi-bin/get/fw1.html

    • http://www.shmoo.com/mail/fw1/

FireWall-1 Wizards' Mailing List (hosted on phoneboy.com): www.phoneboy.com/wizards/

Internet Firewalls FAQ: http://pubweb.nfr.net/~mjr/pubs/fwfaq/

ISS's X-Force Vulnerability Database: http://xforce.iss.net/

@stake Advisories (formerly L0pht Heavy Industries): www.atstake.com/research/advisories/index.html

Lance Spitzner's Publications: Contains various topics, including using snoop, configuring your NICs, hardening UNIX OSs (including a script to do most of the work for you on Solaris), and intrusion detection: www.enteract.com/~lspitz/pubs.html

ntbugtraq.com (Windows NT Security site): www.ntbugtraq.com/

ntsecurity.nu (Windows NT and 2000 Security site): www.ntsecurity.nu/

rootshell.com (a general networking security site): www.rootshell.com

SecuritySearch (a security-specific search engine): www.securitysearch.com

Securing Your HP/UX Bastion Host: http://people.hp.se/stevesk/bastion.html

Windows IT Security (another good Windows NT Security site): www.ntsecurity.net/

Software

Analyzer (or tcpdump; a public-domain protocol analyzer for Windows 95/98/NT): http://netgroup-serv.polito.it/analyzer/

Blat (a Windows NT command-line sendmail utility): http://gepasi.dbs.aber.ac.uk/softw/Blat.html

cron (a Windows port of the UNIX utility): www.kalab.com/freeware/cron/cron.htm

djgpp (a Windows version of GCC and various other GNU utilities): www.delorie.com/djgpp/

gated (a multipurpose routing daemon): www.gated.org

GNU Utilities for Win32 (ports of various GNU utilities for Win32 that run natively without an emulation layer; covers tar, gzip, and md5sum): www.weihenstephan.de/~syring/win32/UnxUtils.html

Some third-party log analysis programs for FireWall-1 include:

XaCCT (makes several products that can read information from FireWall-1): www.xacct.com

Logsurfer (a C program that does general log analysis): www.cert.dfn.de/eng/logsurf/home.html

Telemate Software's Product(s) (work with FireWall-1): www.telemate.net

Lance Spitzner's "Logger" Utility for Windows: www.enteract.com/~lspitz/logger.html

WebTrends (makes a product that works with FireWall-1): www.webtrends.com/products/firewall/

Report Summarizer (Peter Sundstrom wrote this for all versions of FireWall-1): www.ginini.com.au/tools/fw1/

fwlogstat (by Rajeev Kumar): www.geocities.com/SiliconValley/Bit/9363/

FWGold (a GPLed product): www.rotoni.com/FwGold/

Nessus (an open-source Security Scanner): www.nessus.org/

NetCat (the TCP/IP Swiss Army Knife): www.l0pht.com/~weld/netcat/

NetWorld and ConnectTo (a cool program to browse the Network Neighborhood when NetBIOS Name Resolution doesn't work): www.ocshoot.com/winutils.htm

NMAP (the Network Mapper): www.insecure.org/nmap/

Nomad Mobile Research Centre (lots of black-hat and white-hat programs for UNIX and Windows NT): www.nmrc.org/files/index.html

Osiris (a tripwire-like program for Windows NT): www.shmoo.com/osiris/

Perl for Win32 (Windows 95/NT): www.activestate.com/ASPN/Downloads/ActivePerl/index/

Phone Patch (a proxy for NetMeeting and other H.323-compliant software): www.equival.com/phonepatch/index.html

S/Key Generators:

  MD4 Generators (for various platforms): ftp://ftp.cs.sandia.gov/pub/firewall/skey/

  Opie (One-Time Passwords in Everything): www.inner.net/pub/opie/

  optgen (by Andy Bontoft): www.phoneboy.com/sw/otpgen.zip

  WinKey (an MD4 and MD5 S/Key Generator written by David Aylesworth): ftp://ftp.tlogic.com/pub/skey/

SniffIt (a packet sniffer for LINUX, SunOS, Solaris, FreeBSD and IRIX): http://reptile.rug.ac.be/~coder/sniffit/sniffit.html

net-snmp (an open source SNMP v3 implementation): http://reptile.rug.ac.be/~coder/sniffit/sniffit.html

The Laughing Bit (some useful FireWall-1 Scripts): www.tlb.ch/

Appendix
K
Further Reading

The following books are recommended for further reading.

Cheswick, William R., and Steven M. Bellovin. *Firewalls and Internet Security: Repelling the Wily Hacker.* Boston: Addison-Wesley Professional, 1994. ISBN: 0-201-63357-4.

Garfinkel, Simson, and Gene Spafford. *Practical UNIX and Internet Security.* Sebastopol, CA: O'Reilly & Associates, 1995. ISBN: 1-565-92148-8.

Norberg, Stefan. *Securing Windows NT/2000 Servers for the Internet.* Sebastopol, CA: O'Reilly & Associates, 2000. ISBN: 1-565-92768-0.

Schneier, Bruce. *Applied Cryptography : Protocols, Algorithms, and Source Code in C.* 2d ed. New York: Wiley, John & Sons, 1996. ISBN: 0-471-11709-9.

Sonnenreich, Wes, and Tom Yates. *Building Linux and OpenBSD Firewalls.* New York: Wiley, John & Sons, 1999. ISBN: 0-471-35366-3.

Steudler, Oliver. *Managing Cisco Network Security: Building Rock-Solid Networks.* Rockland, MA: Syngress Publishing, 2000. ISBN: 1-928-99417-2.

Stevens, W. Richard, and Gary R. Wright. *TCP/IP Illustrated.* Vols. 1, 2 and 3. Boston: Addison-Wesley Professional, 1993 (Volume 1), ISBN: 0-201-63346-9, (Volume 2) 1994, ISBN: 0-201-63354-X, (Volume 3) 1995, ISBN: 0-201-63495-3.

Zwicky, Elizabeth D., Simon Cooper, and Chapman, D. Brent. *Building Internet Firewalls.* 2d ed: Sebastopol, CA, 2000. ISBN: 1-565-92871-7.

Index

Register
Your Book
at www.aw.com/cseng/register

You may be eligible to receive:

- Advance notice of forthcoming editions of the book
- Related book recommendations
- Chapter excerpts and supplements of forthcoming titles
- Information about special contests and promotions throughout the year
- Notices and reminders about author appearances, tradeshows, and online chats with special guests

Contact us

If you are interested in writing a book or reviewing manuscripts prior to publication, please write to us at:

Editorial Department
Addison-Wesley Professional
75 Arlington Street, Suite 300
Boston, MA 02116 USA
Email: AWPro@aw.com

Addison-Wesley

Visit us on the Web: http://www.aw.com/cseng